Lecture Notes in Computer Science　　10067

Commenced Publication in 1973
Founding and Former Series Editors:
Gerhard Goos, Juris Hartmanis, and Jan van Leeuwen

More information about this series at http://www.springer.com/series/7410

Guojun Wang · Indrakshi Ray
Jose M. Alcaraz Calero · Sabu M. Thampi (Eds.)

Security, Privacy and Anonymity in Computation, Communication and Storage

SpaCCS 2016 International Workshops
TrustData, TSP, NOPE, DependSys, BigDataSPT, and WCSSC
Zhangjiajie, China, November 16–18, 2016
Proceedings

 Springer

Editors
Guojun Wang
Guangzhou University
Guangzhou
China

Jose M. Alcaraz Calero
University of the West of Scotland
Paisley
UK

Indrakshi Ray
Colorado State University
Fort Collins, CO
USA

Sabu M. Thampi
Indian Institute of Information Technology
   and Management Kerala (IIITM-K)
Trivandrum
India

ISSN 0302-9743   ISSN 1611-3349   (electronic)
Lecture Notes in Computer Science
ISBN 978-3-319-49144-8   ISBN 978-3-319-49145-5   (eBook)
DOI 10.1007/978-3-319-49145-5

Library of Congress Control Number: 2016956503

LNCS Sublibrary: SL4 – Security and Cryptology

Printed on acid-free paper

This Springer imprint is published by Springer Nature
The registered company is Springer International Publishing AG
The registered company address is: Gewerbestrasse 11, 6330 Cham, Switzerland

Preface

Welcome to the proceedings of the 9th International Conference on Security, Privacy and Anonymity in Computation, Communication and Storage (SpaCCS 2016), which was held in Zhangjiajie, China, during November 16–18, 2016. SpaCCS is jointly organized by Central South University, Guangzhou University, and Jishou University.

SpaCCS 2016 and the associated symposiums and workshops provided a forum for international and national scholars to gather and share their research findings, ideas, and emerging trends in information security research. Previous SpaCCS conferences were successfully held in Helsinki, Finland (2015), Beijing, China (2014), Melbourne, Australia (2013), Liverpool, UK (2012), and Changsha, China (2011).

The workshop program this year consisted of six symposiums and workshops covering a broad range of research topics on security, privacy, and anonymity in computation, communication, and storage:

(1) The 7th International Workshop on Trust, Security, and Privacy for Big Data (TrustData 2016)
(2) The 6th International Symposium on Trust, Security, and Privacy for Emerging Applications (TSP 2016)
(3) The 4th International Workshop on Network Optimization and Performance Evaluation (NOPE 2016)
(4) The Second International Symposium on Dependability in Sensor, Cloud, and Big Data Systems, and Applications (DependSys 2016)
(5) Annual Big Data Security, Privacy, and Trust Workshop (BigDataSPT 2016)
(6) The First International Workshop on Cloud Storage Service and Computing (WCSSC 2016)

The SpaCCS 2016 symposiums and workshops attracted 95 submissions from different countries and institutions. All submissions received at least three reviews from highly quality experts, resulting in 37 papers selected for oral presentation at the conference (i.e., acceptance rate of 38.9 %).

This event would not have been possible without the contributions of many experts who volunteered and devoted their time and expertise to make this happen. We would like to thank the symposium and workshop organizers for their hard work in soliciting high-quality submissions, assembling the Program Committee, managing the peer-review process, and planning the symposium and workshop agenda. We would also like to acknowledge the strong support of the Organizing Committee of SpaCCS 2016, and in particular the steering chairs, Guojun Wang and Prof. Gregorio Martinez, the general chairs, Jianbin Li, Prof. Felix Gomez Marmol, and Prof. Juan E. Tapiador, and the program chairs, Prof. Indrakshi Ray, Prof. Jose M. Alcaraz Calerovv, and

Prof. Sabu M. Thampi. Without their support and guidance, this event would not have been possible. We are also grateful to the experts who volunteered their time to act as reviewers and session chairs. Finally, we thank the contributing authors and attendees.

November 2016

Kim-Kwang Raymond Choo
Mianxiong Dong
Jin Li

Organization

TrustData 2016 Organizing and Program Committees

General Chairs

Konstantinos Lambrinoudakis	University of Piraeus, Greek
Qin Liu	Hunan University, China

Program Chairs

Isaac Agudo	University of Malaga, Spain
Jiankun Hu	University of New South Wales at the Australian, Australia

Publicity Chairs

Weirong Liu	Central South University, China
Shui Yu	Deakin University, Australia

Program Committee

Habtamu Abie	Norwegian Computing Center/Norsk Regnesentral, Norway
Yan Bai	University of Washington Tacoma, USA
Saad Bani-Mohammad	Al al-Bayt University, Jordan
Muneer Masadeh Bani Yassein	Jordan University of Science and Technology, Jordan
Salima Benbernou	Université Paris Descartes, France
Christian Callegari	The University of Pisa, Italy
Sudip Chakraborty	Valdosta State University, USA
Anupam Chattopadhyay	Nanyang Technological University, Singapore
John A. Clark	University of York, UK
Alfredo Cuzzocrea	University of Trieste and ICAR-CNR, Italy
Sabrina De Capitani di Vimercati	Università degli Studi di Milano, Italy
Roberto Di Pietro	Nokia Bell Labs, France
Zhihui Du	Tsinghua University, China
Yucong Duan	Hainan University, China
Luis Javier García Villalba	Universidad Complutense de Madrid, Spain

Saurabh Kumar Garg	University of Tasmania, Australia
Dieter Gollmann	Hamburg University of Technology, Germany
Sheikh M. Habib	Technical University of Darmstadt, Germany
Ching-Hsien Hsu	Chung Hua University, Taiwan
Xinyi Huang	Fujian Normal University, China
Young-Sik Jeong	Dongguk University, Korea
Hai Jiang	Arkansas State University, USA
Vana Kalogeraki	Athens University of Economics, Greece
Ryan Ko	University of Waikato, New Zealand
Ruggero Donida Labati	Università degli Studi di Milano, Italy
Yingjiu Li	Singapore Management University, Singapore
Xin Liao	Hunan University, China
Giovanni Livraga	Università degli Studi di Milano, Italy
Haibing Lu	Santa Clara University, USA
Rongxing Lu	Nanyang Technological University, Singapore
David Naccache	École Normale Supérieure, France
Joon S. Park	Syracuse University, USA
Günther Pernul	University of Regensburg, Germany
Vincenzo Piuri	Università degli Studi di Milano, Italy
Imed Romdhani	Edinburgh Napier University, UK
Bimal Roy	Indian Statistical Institute, India
Jun Shen	University of Wollongong, Australia
Dimitris E. Simos	SBA Research, Austria
Chao Song	University of Electronic Science and Technology of China, China
Chunhua Su	School of Information Science, Japan
Chang-ai Sun	University of Science and Technology Beijing, China
Baoliu Ye	Nanjing University, China
Hua Yu	Huazhong University of Science and Technology, China
Shucheng Yu	University of Arkansas at Little Rock, USA
Mingzhong Wang	University of the Sunshine Coast, Australia
Yunsheng Wang	Kettering University, USA
Hejun Wu	Sun Yat-Sen University, China
Yongdong Wu	Institute for Infocomm Research, Singapore
Sherali Zeadally	University of Kentucky, USA
Yun-Wei Zhao	Tilburg University, The Netherlands

Steering Committee

Jemal H. Abawajy	Deakin University, Australia
Isaac Agudo	University of Malaga, Spain
Jose M. Alcaraz Calero	University of the West of Scotland, UK
Jiannong Cao	Hong Kong Polytechnic University, Hong Kong, SAR China

Kim-Kwang Raymond Choo	University of Texas at San Antonio, USA
Minyi Guo	Shanghai Jiao Tong University, China
Jiankun Hu	University of New South Wales, Australia
Konstantinos Lambrinoudakis	University of Piraeus, Greece
Jianhua Ma	Hosei University, Japan
Peter Mueller	IBM Zurich Research Laboratory, Switzerland
Indrakshi Ray	Colorado State University, USA
Bhavani Thuraisingham	The University of Texas at Dallas, USA
Guojun Wang	Guangzhou University, China
Jie Wu	Temple University, USA
Yang Xiang	Deakin University, Australia
Laurence T. Yang	Francis Xavier University, Canada
Kun Yang	University of Essex, UK
Wanlei Zhou	Deakin University, Australia

TSP 2016 Organizing and Program Committees

Program Chairs

Imad Jawhar   United Arab Emirates University, UAE
Deqing Zou   Huazhong University of Science of Technology, China

Program Committee Members

Jameela Al-Jaroodi	Robert Morries University, USA
Toon De Pessemier	Ghent University, Belgium
Xiaofeng Ding	Huazhong University of Science and Technology, China
Ed Fernandez	Florida Atlantic University, USA
Xiaojun Hei	Huazhong University of Science and Technology, China
Enrique Herrera-Viedma	University of Granada, Spain
Bart Knijnenburg	Clemson University, USA
Haitao Lang	Beijing University of Chemical Technology, China
Xin Li	Nanjing University of Aeronautics and Astronautics, China
Chi Lin	Dalian University of Technology, China
Nader Mohamed	United Arab Emirates University, UAE
Filipa Peleja	Yahoo Research Barcelona, Spain
Ricky J. Sethi	Fitchburg State University, USA
Chao Song	University of Electronic Science and Technology of China, China
Guangzhong Sun	University of Science and Technology of China, China
Yunsheng Wang	Kettering University USA
Yanghua Xiao	Fudan University, China
Xuanxia Yao	University of Science and Technology Beijing, China
Lin Ye	Harbin Institute of Technology, China
Mingwu Zhang	Hubei University of Technology, China
Yaoxiong Zhao	Google Inc., USA
David Zheng	Frostburg State University, USA
Huan Zhou	China Three Gorges University, China
Youwen Zhu	Nanjing University of Aeronautics and Astronautics, China

Steering Committee

Minyi Guo	Shanghai Jiao Tong University, China
Wenjun Jiang	Hunan University, China (Chair)
Jie Li	University of Tsukuba, Japan
Jianhua Ma	Hosei University, Japan
Peter Mueller	IBM Zurich Research Laboratory, Switzerland
Indrakshi Ray	Colorado State University, USA
Kouichi Sakurai	Kyushu University, Japan
Bhavani Thuraisingham	The University of Texas at Dallas, USA
Guojun Wang	Guangzhou University, China
Jie Wu	Temple University, USA
Yang Xiang	Deakin University, Australia
Laurence T. Yang	St. Francis Xavier University, Canada
Kun Yang	University of Essex, UK
Wanlei Zhou	Deakin University, Australia

NOPE 2016 Organizing and Program Committees

Steering Committee Chairs

Wei Li   Texas Southern University, USA
Taoshen Li   Guangxi University, China

Program Chair

Gaocai Wang   Guangxi University, China

Program Committee Members

Dunqian Cao	Guangxi University for Nationalities, China
Hongbin Chen	Guilin University of Electronic Technology, China
Chengzhi Deng	Nanchang Institute of Technology, China
Xiaoheng Deng	Central South University, China
Yihui Deng	Jinan University, China
Dieter Fiems	Ghent University, Belgium
Shuqiang Huang	Jinan University, China
Daofeng Li	Guangxi University, China
Yan Li	Yunnan Minzu University, China
Junbin Liang	Hong Kong Polytechnic University, Hong Kong, SAR China
Xianfeng Liu	Hunan Normal University, China
Songfeng Lu	Huazhong University of Science & Technology, China
Mingxing Luo	Southwest Jiaotong University, China
Yitian Peng	Southeast University, China
Juan F. Perez	Imperial College London, UK
Zhefu Shi	University of Missouri, USA
Bin Sun	Beijing University of Posts and Telecommunications, China
Haoqian Wang	Tsinghua University, China
Zhiwei Wang	Nanjing University of Posts and Telecommunications, China
Chuyuan Wei	Beijing University of Civil Engineering and Architecture, China
Hongyun Xu	South China University of Technology, China
Jin Ye	Guangxi University, China
Hao Zhang	Central South University, China
Lei Zhang	Beijing University of Civil Engineering and Architecture, China
Yousheng Zhou	Chongqing University of Posts and Telecommunications, China

DependSys 2016 Organizing and Program Committees

General Chairs

Md. Zakirul Alam Bhuiyan	Fordham University, USA
Kim-Kwang Raymond Choo	University of Texas at San Antonio, USA
WenZhan Song	Georgia State University, USA

Program Chairs

Aniello Castiglione	University of Salerno, Italy
Guerroumi Mohamed	University of Sciences and Technology Houari Boumediene, Algeria
M. Thampi Sabu	Indian Institute of Information Technology and Management, India

Steering Committee Chairs

Guojun Wang	Guangzhou University, China
Jie Wu	Temple University, USA

Publicity Chairs

Sajal Bhatia	Fordham University, USA
Yuan-Fang Chen	University of Paris VI, France
Shahriar Hossain	Kennesaw State University, USA
Rossi Kamal	Kyung Hee University, South Korea
William Liu	Auckland University of Technology, New Zealand
Mahmuda Naznin	Bangladesh University of Engineering and Technology, Bangladesh
Risat Mahmud Pathan	Chalmers University of Technology, Sweden
Mubashir Husain Rehmani	COMSATS Institute of Information Technology, Pakistan
Tian Wang	Huaqiao University, China

Program Committee Members

Md. Abdur Razzaque	University of Dhaka, Bangladesh
Mamoun Alazab	Macquarie University, Australia
A.B.M. Alim Al Islam	Bangladesh University of Engineering and Technology, Bangladesh
Hamid Ali-Abed-Al-Asadi	Basra University, Iraq

Md. Arafatur Rahman	University of Naples Federico II, Italy
Mohammad Asad Rehman Chaudhry	University of Toronto, and Soptimizer, Canada
Saiful Azad	University Malaysia Pahang, Malaysia
Sajal Bhatia	Fordham University, USA
Tzung-Shi Chen	National University of Tainan, Taiwan
Yuan-Fang Chen	University of Paris VI, France
Phan Cong-Vinh	Nguyen Tat Thanh University, Vietnam
Salvatore Distefano	University of Messina, Italy
Yacine Djemaiel	University of Carthage, Tunisia
Subir Halder	B.C. Roy Engineering College, India
Mohammad Mehedi Hassan	King Saud University, KSA
Ragib Hasan	University of Alabama at Birmingham, USA
Raza Hasan	Middle East College, Oman
Shahriar Hossain	Kennesaw State University, USA
Jinkyu Jeong	Sungkyunkwan University, Korea
Rossi Kamal	Kyung Hee University, Korea
Joarder Kamruzzaman	Monash University, Australia
Gábor Kiss	University Obuda, Hungary
Ryan Ko	University of Waikato, New Zealand
Jianxin Li	Beihang University, China
Shan Lin	Stony Brook University, USA
Jialin Liu	Lawrence Berkeley National Lab, USA
William Liu	Auckland University of Technology, New Zealand
Xiangyong Liu	Central South University, China
Manuel Mazzara	Innopolis University, Russia
Subrota Kumar Mondol	Hong Kong University of Science and Technology, Hong Kong, SAR China
Felix Musau	Kenyatta University, Kenya
Mahmuda Naznin	Bangladesh University of Engineering and Technology, Bangladesh
Risat Mahmud Pathan	Chalmers University of Technology, Sweden
Sancheng Peng	Guangdong University of Foreign Studies, China
Mohammad Rahman	University of Asia Pacific, Bangladesh
Md. Obaidur Rahman	Dhaka University of Engineering & Technology, Bangladesh
Farzana Rahman	James Madison University, USA
M. Sohel Rahman	Bangladesh University of Engineering and Technology, Bangladesh
Shawon Rahman	University of Hawaii Hilo, USA
Mubashir Husain Rehmani	COMSATS Institute of Information Technology, Pakistan
Sajal Sarkar	IIT Kharagpur, India
Junggab Son	North Carolina Central University, USA
Mir Sajjad Hussain Talpur	Central South University, China
Bing Tang	Hunan University of Science and Technology, China

BigDataSPT 2016 Organizing and Program Committees

Workshop Chairs

Kim-Kwang Raymond Choo	University of Texas at San Antonio, USA
Zheng Xu	Tsinghua University and Shanghai University, China

Program Committee Members

Elias Athanasopoulos	Vrije Universiteit Amsterdam, The Netherlands
Abir Awad	Athlone Institute of Technology, Ireland
Reza Azarderakhsh	Rochester Institute of Technology, USA
Aniello Castiglione	University of Salerno, Italy
Kim-Kwang Raymond Choo	University of Texas at San Antonio, USA
Ali Dehghantanha	University of Salford, UK
Huan Du	Shanghai University, China
Virginia N.L. Franqueira	University of Derby, UK
Kun Gao	Zhejiang Wanli Institute, China
Jiankun Hu	University of New South Wales at the Australian Defence Force Academy, Australia
Joshua I. James	Digital Forensic Investigation Research Laboratory, Ireland
Thomas Kemmerich	Gjovik University College, Norway
Mehran Mozaffari Kermani	Rochester Institute of Technology, USA
Nhien An Le Khac	University College Dublin, Ireland
Tao Liao	Anhui University of Science and Technology, China
Lin Liu	University of South Australia, Australia
Yunhuai Liu	Hong Kong University of Science and Technology, Hong Kong, SAR China
Xiangfeng Luo	Shanghai University, China
Andrew Marrington	Zayed University, United Arab Emirates
Ben Martini	University of South Australia, Australia
Martin Mulazzani	SBA Research, Austria
Richard E. Overill	King's College London, UK
Carsten Rudolph	Monash University, Australia
Neetesh Saxena	Georgia Institute of Technology, USA
Mark Scanlon	University College Dublin, Ireland
Kathryn Seigfried-Spellar	Purdue University, USA
Matthew Simon	INTERPOL Global Complex for Innovation

WCSSC 2016 Organizing and Program Committees

Program Chairs

Yupeng Hu	Hunan University, China
Wenjia Li	New York Institute of Technology, USA

Program Committee

Habib Ammari	ETH Zürich, Switzerland
Victor Chen	Valdosta State University, USA
Daniel Grosu	Wayne State University, USA
Tahar Kechadi	University College Dublin, Ireland
Vimal Kumar	University of Waikato, New Zealand
Rui Li	Hunan University, China
Xiaolong Li	Guilin University of Electronic Technology, China
Fang Liu	National University of Defense Technology, China
Yonghe Liu	UT-Arlington, USA
Enzo Mingozzi	University of Pisa, Italy
Fei Peng	Hunan University, China
Zheng Qin	Hunan University, China
Danda Rawat	Georgia Southern University, USA
Xiaojun Ruan	West Chester University of Pennsylvania, USA
Kewei Sha	University of Houston Clear Lake, USA
Houbing Song	West Virginia University, USA
Nong Xiao	National University of Defense Technology, China
Quan Xu	City University London, UK
Shu Yin	Hunan University, China
Jianping Yu	Hunan Normal University, China
Sherali Zeadally	University of Kentucky, USA
Jiliang Zhang	Northeastern University, China
Siwang Zhou	Hunan University, China

Sponsors of SpaCCS 2016 Workshops

Contents

4th International Workshop on Network Optimization and Performance Evaluation (NOPE 2016)

Second International Symposium on Dependability in Sensor, Cloud, and Big Data Systems and Applications (DependSys 2016)

Annual Big Data Security, Privacy and Trust Workshop (BigDataSPT 2016)

**First International Workshop on Cloud Storage Service and Computing
(WCSSC 2016)**

7th International Workshop on Trust, Security and Privacy for Big Data (TrustData 2016)

Security and Privacy in Big Data Lifetime: A Review

Hanlu Chen[1] and Zheng Yan[1,2(✉)]

[1] The State Key Laboratory on Integrated Services Networks, School of Cyber Engineering,
Xidian University, Xi'an 710071, China
`1286187488@qq.com`
[2] Department of Communications and Networking, Aalto University, 02150 Espoo, Finland
`zyan@xidian.edu.cn`

Abstract. Due to the fast growth of emerging information technologies such as Internet of Things (IoT), cloud computing, Internet services, and social networking, an increasing interest in big data security and privacy is aroused. An entire lifetime of big data contains four phases: big data collection; transmission; processing and analytics; storage and management. However, the five salient features of big data: volume, variety, velocity, value, and veracity bring great challenges on protecting big data security and privacy during its whole lifetime. In this paper, we survey schemes and techniques that are applied to ensure big data security and privacy. Based on the literature review, we discuss open challenges and issues in this research area towards comprehensive protection on big data security and privacy in its lifetime.

Keywords: Big data · Big data security · Big data privacy · Cloud computing · Secure Multi-party computation (SMC) · Homomorphic encryption

1 Introduction

Due to the fast growth of emerging information technologies such as Internet of Things (IoT), cloud computing, Internet services, and social networking, we get into an era of big data, which is generated by sensors and mobile devices during social networking and Internet service consuming, as well as many other digital activities. In big data era, more and more data are residing in the cloud. This trend will continue to grow in the future. For example, the data in the United States that is replicated, created, and consumed each year was expected to grow from 898 exabytes to 6.6 zettabytes from 2012 to 2020, or more than 25 % a year [1]. It seems that the amounts of big data will double about every three years.

Big data has brought great chances for us to learn new and potential information through further processing and analytics. It is increasingly produced and used in different fields such as healthcare, education, finance and government. Based on big data analysis, corporations learn knowledge that can improve the correctness of business decision and realize the intelligence of business. Intelligent services can be offered to users based on big data mining. Big data brings not only convenience to people's daily life, but also opportunities to enterprises.

© Springer International Publishing AG 2016
G. Wang et al. (Eds.): SpaCCS 2016 Workshops, LNCS 10067, pp. 3–15, 2016.
DOI: 10.1007/978-3-319-49145-5_1

However, big data also introduces great challenges on security and privacy. Increasing interests in big data security and privacy are aroused due to growing demands on big data for various intelligent services. Big data normally contains valuable or sensitive information about user behaviors, preferences, interests, mobility, and so on. User privacy is easily leaked if the data cannot be protected well during its lifetime, which contains four stages: data collection, data transmission, data process and analytics, and data storage and management. Therefore, if we want to enjoy the convenience and benefits from big data, guarantee its security and privacy becomes an essential task.

Big data security and privacy has become a hot research topic in recent years. However, existing security schemes and technologies cannot adequately satisfy requirements and expectation in the practice of big data applications. Although many research activities have initiated in this field, we are still facing a number of challenges, which will definitely motive new innovations. It is essential to analyze the requirements of big data security and privacy with regard to its whole lifetime, review the current literature and discover open issues in order to direct future research and practice.

In this paper, we analyze the requirements of security and privacy of big data in its entire lifetime. We survey main schemes of big data security and privacy protection, which includes Secure Multi-party Computation (SMC), Homomorphic Encryption (HE), secure data storage and management, etc. Based on the review, we discuss the challenges in this research field. The rest paper is organized as follows. Section 2 overviews the basic concept of big data and its specific characteristics. Section 3 analyzes the requirements of big data security and privacy. Section 4 reviews the schemes of big data security and privacy. Section 5 discusses the challenges of big data security and privacy. A conclusion is provided in the last section.

2   Overview of Big Data

2.1   Definition and Features of Big Data

Definition of Big Data. Big data is used to describe any large number of structured and unstructured data. Researchers regard the linear data as structured data that can be stored in database and expressed by two-dimensional table. Structured data is traditional data when compared with unstructured data. Examples of unstructured data are office documents, text data, images data, web data, media data, etc. It is difficult to express unstructured data using dimensional database logic. Nowadays, big data has become a hot topic in many domains such as healthcare, education, finance, and business. With the fast development of IoT, cloud computing, Internet services, and social networking, the term "big data" appears almost everywhere in our social life. Though the importance of big data has been recognized extensively, different people have different opinions on its definitions. In [2], big data is a term that is used to describe large and complex data sets. Owing to this, it is awkward to deal with big data with standard statistical software. In [3], the authors thought that the definition of big data should refer to its nature of "information asset". Thus, the definition was based on the characteristics of big data such as high volume, velocity and variety to transform big data into values with some specific technologies and analytical methods. In this paper, we regard big data with five characteristics including volume, variety, velocity, value, and veracity (5 V).

2.2 Entire Lifetime of Big Data

In order to enjoy the benefits and convenience from big data, big data collection (CLC), transmission (TSM), processing and analytics (PA), and, big data storage and management (SM) are requisite. We may get wrong information from big data once some insecure events occur in the above four phases. Thus, security and privacy of big data in the above four phases are very important. Herein, we regard the four phases as big data lifetime.

Data Collection. Data can be also collected from huge number of sensors in Internet of Things. Enormous and chaotic data collection highly relates accurate data processing and analysis, which allows us to obtain worthy information from them. Many Internet companies have their own collection tools for massive data, such as Chukwa in Hadoop, Flume in Cloudera, and Scribe in Facebook. Regarding production and operation data in companies or research institutions with high confidentiality, a particular system interface can be applied for data collection.

Data Transmission. Data transmission plays an important role in data exchange and dissemination. The data collected by huge number of sensors in IoT and mobile devices used by human beings are normally needed to be transferred to a power server (e.g., in cloud) to store, process and manage, data transmission becomes essential. Data transmission helps data exchange among different parties, supports data aggregation and fusion, as well data mining and analytics.

Data Processing and Analytics. Big data processing and analytics refers to preprocessing and analyzing big data to get non-noise, valuable, and meaningful data and learn valuable information using specific techniques. During data processing, techniques such as data mining, machine learning, and language learning are mostly applied. In order to gain the Value of big data, processing and analytics phase becomes essential in big data lifetime. In this phase, users can get the valuable data that they expect rather than all data with useful and useless information mixed together.

Data Storage and Management. With the expanding of the Internet and cloud computing, traditional data storage and management system has collapsed. In big data era, the major technologies for big data storage and management are: distributed file system, distributed database, access interface and query language and so on.

2.3 Technologies of Big Data Process

In order to acquire worthy information from big data, various technologies are applied. Table 1 summarizes a number of traditional technologies for big data collection, processing, storage and management.

Table 1. Technology comparison

Technologies	CLC	TSM	PA	SM	Big data characteristics supported
DM			√		volume, value, veracity
CC			√	√	volume, variety
Hadoop	√		√	√	volume, variety, value, velocity
WEKA			√		volume, variety, velocity, value

Data Mining (DM). Data mining is one of the most important tools in Knowledge-Discovery in Databases, which refers to searching hiding information from a large big data set. Extracting information from a data set and transforming it into an understandable model for further research are the main targets if data mining. For example, a company always uses the data mining method to extract useful knowledge to make a correct business decision.

Cloud Computing (CC). Cloud computing is a key technology to provide cloud users a dependable and customized computation environment. Generally speaking, cloud computing is a service-oriented architecture (SOA) [4] that realizes user service in cloud anywhere and anytime. Users can access cloud services with a browser, through applications or mobile programs. Cloud supports reallocating IT resources to adapt to changing requirements of enterprises.

Cloud computing delivery schedule includes many types, e.g., Software as a Service (SaaS), Platform as a Service (Paas), Infrastructure as a Service (IaaS) and Monitoring as a Service (MaaS) [5]. IaaS is the foundation for all cloud services [6], upon which PaaS and SaaS are built. It is difficult to assurance that right security measures are in place and required applications are available in cloud computing. In Paas, some security issues like host and network intrusion still call for attention when developers intend to build their own applications. And in IaaS, the user need ensure reliability of the data stored in the cloud provider's hardware. Virtualization technology, data storage technology, resource management technology and power management technology are the prime technologies in cloud computing. The cloud data storage service is the most popular cloud service nowadays. Cloud can also be applied to offer such services as Data Mining as a Service, Data Processing as a Service, not only Data Storage as a Service. Thus cloud computing plays an important role in big data lifetime.

Hadoop. Simply speaking, Hadoop is a distributed system and parallel execution environment used to collect, store and process massive data. HParser is a data conversion environment presented by Informatica to optimize Hadoop for ensuring data integration. This software can support any document formats to process complex and various data source. The primary component of Hadoop is Hadoop Distributed File System (HDFS) and MapReduce. HDFS in Hadoop is the key to data storage and data management. It is designed to support big data set of PB level, provide sequence data access with highly reliable and high-throughput, and use cheap hardware to improve scalability. Nodes stored in HDFS also participate in MapReduce applications execution. MapReduce is a kind of programming model to realize massive data set parallel computation. It can be divided into two steps including Map and Reduce. Through specific actions on individual elements of the data set, Map generates intermediate results with the form of Key-Value; Reduce step is responsible for merging data into all "Value" among intermediate results in the same "Key" and obtain final results. With the widespread usage of Hadoop, security and privacy issues become more and more important in it. Company Cloudera presented an authorization system like Cloudera Sentry based on Role based Access Control [7]. In order to ensure security for a Hadoop cluster, company Hortonworks developed Apache Ranger. It can be used to provide data protection, audit, authorization and authentication for central security policy administration.

WEKA. The Waikato Environment for Knowledge Analysis (WEKA) big data processing software was accepted widely [8]. It has been more than twelve years since WEKA was used. The main point WEKA concerning is data mining and machine learning. Users can implement natural language processing, knowledge discovery, distributed and parallel data mining, open-source data mining, and so on based on WEKA. As studied in [9], the authors combine diverse ensemble Meta classifiers into one iterative hierarchical system called Large Iterative Multitier Ensemble (LIME) classifiers in order to improve classifications. The SimpleCLI in WEKA are used to generate and execute all classifiers that are combined into a four-tier system. It makes classification for a big data set more flexible. However, LIME classifiers need sufficient memory when it is used, its performance should be further improved.

Based on the above introduction, we can see that cloud computing and Hadoop can support data processing, analysis, storage and management. Hadoop is a big data processing platform, while cloud computing is a service architecture that supports data processing and storage. WEKA is a toolkit used for big data analysis and mining, which can apply machine learning, DM and natural language processing to perform data analytics with the concern on volume, value, and veracity. Hadoop and WEKA are specific big data toolkits, which concerns its main characteristics: volume, variety, value, and velocity. But current version cannot support veracity very well.

3 Requirements of Big Data Security and Privacy

Threats on big data motive us to investigate security and privacy solutions for big data. Considering its 5 V characteristics, big data security and privacy brings additional challenges on security and privacy studies. In order to resist these threats, we propose a number of requirements for ensuring security and privacy of big data by analyzing when and why the requirements are needed. Table 2 shows different security and privacy requirements in different phases of big data lifetime regarding a 5 V model.

Table 2. Security requirements

Security Requirements	CLC	TSM	PA	SM	Volume	Variety	Velocity	Value	Veracity
Confidentiality	√	√	√	√				√	√
Efficiency	√	√	√	√	√	√	√		
Authenticity	√	√	√	√				√	√
Availability	√	√	√	√	√	√	√	√	
Integrity	√	√	√	√				√	√

3.1 Confidentiality

Confidentiality is the cornerstone of big data security and privacy. We need to protect data from leakage in its whole lifetime. The hacker who wants to obtain useful information in big data will attack the storage system to steal sensitive data. The user may leak the data due to careless or improper operation. Confidentiality is concerned during data collection, data transmission, data processing and analytics, data storage and management. The requirement relates to the big data characteristic about value and veracity. Once data is leaked, its value will be lost. If hackers attack the data by changing the data or obtaining secret information, the value of the big data could be disappeared.

3.2 Efficiency

Different from traditional data, big data has its characteristics of variety and volume, velocity regarding the four phases of big data lifetime becomes essential. It requires efficient data collection, transmission, processing and analytic, storage and management. To meet these requirements, we need high network bandwidth. Many schemes such as homomorphic encryption, and secure multiparty computation are limited owing to the efficiency problem, which is a big challenging in the current literature. Efficiency is especially crucial in big data security and privacy, which relates to the 5 V characteristics of big data.

3.3 Authenticity

Big data has been used in many fields, such as a healthcare system to decide the disease of a patient with big data or a corporation to make a right business decision. Real-time data with veracity is needed to support wise decision-making. Thus, authenticity is necessary during the whole data lifetime to ensure trusted data sources, reputable data processers and eligible data requesters. Authenticity can avoid wrong analysis result and assist achieving high potential value from big data. This requirement corresponds to the value and veracity of 5 V.

3.4 Availability

It is indispensable to ensure availability of big data even the data was attacked in some ways such as DoS or DDoS attacks. Big data should be available anytime when we need it. Otherwise, it could lose its value. Corresponding applications or services based on big data cannot work well. Therefore, availability should be ensured during the whole lifetime of big data. The volume, variety, velocity and value of big data make availability more important.

3.5 Integrity

To get valuable and accurate data, ensuring its integrity becomes essential. Otherwise its veracity cannot be ensured. We can't analyze right result with incomplete data, especially, when the lost data is the most sensitive and useful. The integrity is required during the whole data lifetime. This requirement corresponds to the veracity and value of 5 V.

4 Security Schemes of Big Data

In this section, we review useful schemes and techniques for big data security and privacy protection, such as SMC, homomorphic encryption, and secure data storage and management schemes in cloud computing. We comment their pros and cons based on the requirements proposed in Sect. 3. Table 3 compares reviewed schemes with regard to different phases in big data lifetime.

Table 3. Schemes comparison

Schemes		CLC	TSM	PA	SM	Fulfilled security Requirements	Application fields
SMC	[11]		√			Veracity, confidentiality	Message exchange
	[12]				√	Efficiency	DFA execution and find shortest distance
	[14]	√	√			Veracity, volume, confidentiality, Integrity	Input of parties for distributed data mining
HE	[15]		√	√	√	Confidentiality	Query, search without key
	[16]				√	Value, confidentiality, integrity, authenticity	Multi-factor authentication
	[17]			√		Volume, confidentiality, efficiency, authenticity	data encryption
	[19]			√	√	Value, confidentiality, efficiency, integrity	Film companies rendering in a cloud environment
Anonymization	[20]			√		Confidentiality, integrity, efficiency	Big data clustering and mining
Auditing	[21] [22] [23]				√	Authenticity, availability, confidentiality, integrity	Verify outsourced data
ABE	[24] [25]				√	Volume, confidentiality, integrity	Big data access control

4.1 SMC Schemes

SMC concept was introduced firstly by Yao in 1982 [10]. He presented a story about two millionaire's problem to lead to SMC processing. The problem says that both two millionaires want to know who is the richest one, while they don't want to disclose individual wealth to another. In SMC, multiple participants calculate a function in a distributed computing environment with input provided by these participants and identity information of all participants keeping private. Once computation finished, each participants acquire correct calculations, but they can't learn additional input information except themselves.

In [11], Titze et al. described an extension of the SMC library SEPIA, which is a Java library to provide a number of SMC protocols for secure information exchange within an Information Sharing Network. Participating peers can input anonymous distribution of arbitrary binary data by using this scheme during data transmission phase to ensure data confidentiality. The mechanism can detect message collision and improve overall performance when comparing with the evaluation results of a standard. While each input vector has to be the same size, even though no data is sent. Thus, before data can be sent, peers have to know the vector size leading the scheme to be rigid. And the scheme is weak to prevent DoS attacks.

In [12], Laud used an extremely abstract SMC process called Arithmetic Black Box [13] that utilizes a private index to achieve fast lookup function from private tables. The techniques can implement sensitive data obliviously reading in a privacy preserving way during data storage and management phase. The private lookup protocol could consider three phases including offline, vector-only and online. In order to improve efficiency, the authors tried to speed up the offline phase and the vector-only phase. But the lookup function requires amounts of SMC operations, which may lead to a big cost. Thus, a dedicated high-bandwidth communication channel is needed.

In [14], Jahan et al. proposed a new secure sum protocol to provide more data security for multi-party computation and ensure zero data leakage among different participants. The novel protocol helps improve data security and privacy when data is collected from various sources. At the same time, the complexity of communication and computation was improved significantly owing to the protocol. However, this protocol restricts the number of parties as at least three.

4.2 Homomorphic Encryption Schemes

Homomorphic encryption is a famous encryption cryptographic technique. Some operations can be allowed on ciphered data without decrypting it. Generally, homomorphic encryption schemes are divided into two classes: partly homomorphic encryption (PHE) (support partly polynomial calculation for ciphered data) and fully homomorphic encryption (FHE) (support arbitrary polynomial calculation for ciphered data).

In partly homomorphic encryption the RSA is famous and wide spread. Gentry presented the fully homomorphic encryption scheme firstly in 2009 [15]. It was an important breakthrough in cryptography, which improves the efficiency of secure multi-party computation. It also enables private queries to a search engine, searching on encrypted data, and encrypted data transmission. While the scheme is so inefficient that it cannot be used in practice. Since 2009, some researches were committed to improve its efficient, and achieved great results. However, in many scenarios FHE cannot satisfy system requirements.

Liu et al. aimed to present a privacy-preserving multi-factor authentication system with user password as the first-factor and hybrid user profiles as the other authentication factor. They used FHE and fuzzy hashing to preserve user local profile privacy from servers and any trusted or distrusted third party [16]. Their work considered both usability and privacy issues. A server can determine distance between user profiles that are collected by information acquisition at user enrollment to decide authentication process. The privacy of users is not leaked to omnipresent cloud computing environment because of FHE and fuzzy hashing. However, the scheme performance needs to be improved in order to support more user enrollment features and achieve efficiency.

In [17], Rahmani et al. combined evolutionary cryptography with a new approach in order to improve the efficiency and the security level of a homomorphic cryptosystem known as TSZ [18]. Their system increases the size of encrypted text more than the original TSZ scheme [17]. It allows operations on encrypted data in processing and analytics phase. The security and privacy of datum will be strengthened if we repeat encryption several times. However, the scheme still needs more studies about its robustness against attacks.

Baharon et al. proposed a new fully homomorphic encryption scheme based on finite fields to solve efficiency in FHE schemes based on Lattices [19]. It supports n-multilinear maps that allow big animated film companies like Pixar to migrate their operations to a cloud environment securely. In this scheme, FHE can ensure the security and integrity of the outsourced and processed data in the cloud environments with no information leakage at any stage of the process. But before implementing this map in the scheme, they cannot prove the generator of n-multilinear maps existing.

4.3 Secure Data Storage and Management Schemes

Big Data Anonymization Scheme. Zhang et al. investigated local-recording for big data local-recoding anonymization [20]. They used clustering and MapReduce techniques to improve scalability and efficiency significantly for local-recording anonymization. In addition to record linkage attacks, this method is used to prevent users from sensitive attribute attacks. However, no experiment on big data mining or analytics was presented to prove privacy preservation.

Auditing for Data Storage and Computation. In order to improve authenticity and availability of big data, cloud service providers prefer to store multiple copies for data. Public data auditing is a common schemes allowing outsourced data verified by users without retrieving the entire dataset.

Wang et al. proposed a privacy-preserving third-party auditing system for security of data storing in the cloud computing environment [21]. During the efficient processing for auditing, the third party auditor wouldn't acquire any information from the data storing on the cloud server. And no new vulnerabilities of user data privacy are brought in. The proposed schemes are provably secure and highly efficient based on extensive analysis [21]. But performance of auditing should be improved with low computation complexity.

Wei et al. took account of the bridging between secure storage and secure computation to propose a privacy cheating discouragement and secure computation auditing protocol [22]. They defined two cloud computing security problems: Cloud Storage Security and Cloud Computation Security [22], where the former ensures the integrity of outsourced data and the latter ensures the correctness of outsourced data. Final validation results showed that their protocol is valid and very effective when implementing security in the cloud. However, the protocol increases the overall cost significantly, which should be greatly optimized for big data.

Liu et al. presented a new public auditing scheme called MuR-DPA [23]. The new scheme contains a new authenticated data structure based on a Merkle hash tree [23]. The scheme achieves a low cost during updating verification and integrity verification in cloud database with multiple replicas of data. It also provides a strong security mechanism to fight against dishonest cloud service providers. Fully dynamic data updating, block indices authentication and multiple replicas data updates verifying at the same time are all supported by this scheme. However, secure public auditing of dynamic data and data stream is still an open issue in the field of public data auditing.

Attribute-based Encryption. The attribute-based encryption technique is regarded as the most appropriate technologies used to control data access in the cloud environment. Traditional attribute-based encryption (ABE) techniques are classified into two major classes: ciphertext-policy ABE (CP-ABE) and key-policy ABE (KP-ABE). The CP-ABE is a scheme that binds the attributes of users and access policies with encrypted data. While in KP-ABE, attributes are always used to describe the access policies and encrypted data. And the user's secret keys generate using these attributes.

Yang et al. proposed an expressive, efficient and revocable multi-authority CP-ABE access control scheme to protect the data confidentiality from semi-trusted cloud [24]. They utilized previously encrypted data in the way of old access policies to avoid the transmission of ciphered data and reduce the calculation work of users. When the policy need to be updated, instead of updating the entire ciphered data, only the revoked attribute needs to be updated. Therefore, the scheme can minimize communication cost significantly when the policies are updating. At the same time, the scheme adapt to updating any types of access policies. However, when users use ABE to construct access control scheme, updating policies will be difficult for them because once data is outsourced to cloud by data owner, these data won't store in local systems. Thus, an efficient and effective method to ensure access control based on ABE to support policy revocation is still needed.

In [25], the same authors proposed a new outsourced policy method for ABE systems based on Lewko and Waters' scheme, and an attribute-based access control scheme for big data in the cloud. It can achieve access control with dynamic policy update more efficiently for big data in the cloud environment. In order to solve the problem in [24], the proposed scheme in [25] avoids cipher data transmission and reduces the computation load of data owners.

5 Challenges in Big Data Security and Privacy

In big data era, amounts of technologies emerge simultaneously, such as sensors, social network, IoT, cloud computing, and so on. Big data covers all fields of our daily life, which includes abundant records of governmental data, business data, health data, education data and customers' personal data about their various activities. However, the collection, transmission, processing, analytics, storage and management of big data inevitably increase the risk of information leakage. Although big data provides huge information value, it also increases the risk of privacy and security. If the data is abused, it will threaten the safety of individuals, firms and states [26].

Based on the above literature review, we summarize some challenges with regard to big data security and privacy.

First, more efficient FHE schemes are expected. Such schemes can be applied into SMC in order to improve its confidentiality and efficiency [15]. Although, many literatures have been made to improve computing efficiency of homomorphic encryption based SMC, new schemes for fully homomorphic encryption are still important for encryption and secure multiply computation. As a result, a good homomorphic encryption scheme can not only help encrypt data stored in the cloud, but also support various operations required in SMC.

Second, scalability and efficiency should be considered when we design big data security schemes. Referring to the above reviewed schemes, we found that scalability is not considered mostly except [14, 17, 25]. Considering the 5 V characteristics of big data, volume is an important characteristic, which highly requests scalability support.

Third, technologies for handling different data structure are required. Because of the variety of big data, the structure and unstructured data may be processed at the same time. Many literatures about big data security and privacy did not research the variety of big data. Obviously, handling different data structure is an interesting and significant challenge.

Forth, a balance between the security requirement and performance is an open issue in big data security and privacy. Security schemes normally impact system performance in big data processing and analytics phase. Cost is very high to ensure the security and privacy of data process in cloud, e.g., the work described in [22]. Thus, an effective and practical security and privacy scheme should balance between the security requirement and performance cost, which will greatly impact the success of a security and privacy scheme.

Finally, few studies explore security and privacy protection schemes at the stage of data collection according to our survey. How to achieve lightweight and usable security at this stage could be an interesting research topic worth our efforts.

6 Conclusions

In this paper, we performed a brief review on big data security and privacy based on the security requirements raised by its 5 V characteristics in the four-phase lifetime of big data. Our review mainly focused on three categories of technologies that enables big data security and privacy: SMC, homomorphic encryption, and Secure Data Storage and Management Schemes. Based on the literature study, we discussed a number of challenges and open issues that motivate our future research.

Acknowledgments. This work is sponsored by the National Key Research and Development Program of China (grant 2016YFB0800704), the NSFC (grants 61672410 and U1536202), the 111 project (grants B08038 and B16037), the Ph.D. Programs Foundation of Ministry of Education of China (grant JY0300130104), the Project Supported by Natural Science Basic Research Plan in Shaanxi Province of China (Program No. 2016ZDJC-06), and Aalto University.

References

1. Gantz, J., John, Reinsel, D.: The digital universe in 2020: big data, bigger digital shadows, and biggest growth in the far east. In: IDC iView: IDC Analyze the Future, pp. 1–16 (2007)
2. Snijders, C., Matzat, U., Reips, U.D.: "Big data": Big gaps of knowledge in the field of internet science. Int. J. Internet Sci. **7**, 1–5 (2012)
3. De Mauro, A., Greco, M., Grimaldi, M.: A formal definition of Big Data based on its essential features. Libr. Rev. **65**, 122–135 (2016)
4. Tan, Z., Nagar, U.T., He, X., Nanda, P., Liu, R.P., Wang, S., Hu, J.: Enhancing big data security with collaborative intrusion detection. IEEE Cloud Computing **1**, 27–33 (2014). IEEE
5. Sung, S., Youn, C., Kong, E., and Ryou, J.: A distributed mobile cloud computing model for secure big data. In: 2016 International Conference on Information Networking (ICOIN), pp. 312–316. IEEE (2016)
6. Subashini, S., Kavitha, V.: A survey issues in service delivery models of cloud computing. J. Netw. Comput. Appl. **34**, 1–11 (2011)
7. Srinivas, S., Nair, A.: Security maturity in NoSQL database-are they secure enough to haul the modern IT applications? In: Advances in Computing, Communications and Informatics (ICACCI), pp. 739–744. IEEE (2015)
8. Hall, M., Frank, E., Holmes, G., Pfahringer, B., Reutemann, P., Witten, I.H.: The WEKA data mining software: An update. SIGKDD Explor. **11**, 10–18 (2009)
9. Abawajy, J.H., Kelarev, A., Chowdhury, M.: Large iterative multitier ensemble classifiers for security of big data. IEEE Trans. Emerg. **2**, 352–363 (2014). IEEE
10. Yao, A.C.: Protocol for secure computations. In: Proceedings of the 23rd Annual IEEE Symposium on Foundation of Computer Science, pp. 160–164. IEEE (1982)
11. Titze, D., Hofinger, H., and Schoo, P.: Using secure multiparty computation for collaborative information exchange. In: 2013 12th IEEE International Conference on Trust, Security and Privacy in Computing and Communications, pp. 1717–1722. IEEE (2013)
12. Laud, P.: A private lookup protocol with low online complexity for secure multiparty computation. In: Hui, L.C.K., Qing, S.H., Shi, E., Yiu, S.M. (eds.) ICICS 2014. LNCS, vol. 8958, pp. 143–157. Springer, Heidelberg (2015). doi:10.1007/978-3-319-21966-0_11
13. Damgård, I., Nielsen, J.B.: Universally composable efficient multiparty computation from threshold homomorphic encryption. In: Boneh, D. (ed.) CRYPTO 2003. LNCS, vol. 2729, pp. 247–264. Springer, Heidelberg (2003). doi:10.1007/978-3-540-45146-4_15
14. Jahan, I. Sharmy, N. N., Jahan, S., Ebha, F. A., and Lisa, N. J.: Design of a secure sum protocol using trusted third party system for secure multi-party computations. In: Information and Communication Systems (ICICS), 2015 6th International Conference on IEEE, pp. 136–141. IEEE (2015)

15. Gentry C.: A fully homomorphic encryption scheme. In: Dissertation Stanford University (2009)
16. Liu, W., Uluagac, A. S., Beyah, R.: MACA: a privacy-preserving multi-factor cloud authentication system utilizing big data. In: 2014 IEEE Conference on Computer Communications Workshops (INFOCOM WKSHPS), pp. 518–523. IEEE (2014)
17. Rahmani, A., Amine, A., and Mohamed, R.H.: A multilayer evolutionary homomorphic encryption approach for privacy preserving over big data. In: Cyber-Enable Distributed Computing and Knowledge Discovery (CyberC), pp. 19–26. IEEE (2014)
18. Chabanne, H., Phan, D.H., Pointcheval, D.: Public traceability in traitor tracing schemes. In: Cramer, R. (ed.) EUROCRYPT 2005. LNCS, vol. 3494, pp. 542–558. Springer, Heidelberg (2005). doi:10.1007/11426639_32
19. Baharon, M. R., Shi, Q., Llewellyn-Jones, D., and Merabti,M.: Secure rendering process in cloud computing. In: Eleventh Annual International Conference on Privacy, pp. 82–87. Security and Trust (PST) (2013)
20. Zhang, X., Dou, W., Pei, J., Nepal, S., Yang, C., Liu, C., Chen, J.: Proximity-Aware Local-Recoding anonymization with MapReduce for scalable big data privacy preservation in cloud. IEEE Trans. Comput. **64**, 2293–2306 (2015). IEEE
21. Wang, C., Wang, Q., Ren, K., Lou, W.: Privacy-Preserving public auditing for data storage security in cloud computing. In: 2010 Proceedings IEEE INFOCOM, pp. 1–9, 14–19. IEEE (2010)
22. Wei, L., Zhu, H., Cao, Z., Dong, X., Jia, W., Chen, Y., Vasilakos, A.V.: Security and privacy for storage and computation in cloud computing. Inf. Sci. **258**, 371–386 (2014). ACM
23. Liu, C., Ranjan, R., Yang, C., Zhang, X., Wang, L., Chen, J.: MuR-DPA: Top-Down levelled Multi-Replica Merkle hash tree based secure public auditing for dynamic big data storage on cloud. IEEE Trans. Comput. **64**, 2609–2622 (2015). IEEE
24. Yang, K., Jia, X.: Expressive, efficient, and revocable data access control for multi-authority cloud storage. IEEE Trans. Parallel Distrib. Syst. **25**, 1735–1744 (2014). IEEE
25. Yang, K., Jia, X., Ren, K.: Secure and verifiable policy update outsourcing for big data access control in the cloud. IEEE Trans. Parall. Distrib. Syst. **26**, 3461–3470 (2014). IEEE
26. Shrivastva, K.M.P., Rizvi, M.A., Singh, S.: Big data privacy based on differential privacy a hope for big data. In: 2014 International Conference on Computation Intelligence and Communication Networks (CICN), pp. 776–781. IEEE (2014)

Community-Based Adaptive Buffer Management Strategy in Opportunistic Network

Junhai Zhou, Yapin Lin[✉], Siwang Zhou, and Qin Liu

College of Computer Science and Electronic Engineering, Hunan University,
Changsha 410082, China
lucky2001ok@163.com

Abstract. Networks composed of devices, which having short-range wireless communications capabilities and carried by people, is a major application scenarios in opportunistic network, whose nodes movement has the characteristics of community. In this paper, we combine nodes meeting frequency with nodes separation duration time to assign nodes to communities, and present a community-based self-adaptive buffer management strategy in opportunistic network. The strategy makes decisions of buffered messages discarding and message transmission scheduling based on nodes' community attribute. At the same time, it generates message feedback adaptively according to the message delivery status, to remove unnecessary redundancy copies of messages in nodes buffer timely, then to reduce buffer overflow and avoid many unnecessary messages transmission. Simulation results show that the strategy can effectively improve the message delivery ratio and has significant lower network overhead.

Keywords: Opportunistic network · Community · Buffer management · Transmission scheduling

1 Introduction

Since the node mobility, the time of interruption is always longer than the time of connection in opportunistic networks, which makes it difficult to establish a live communication link between nodes [1, 2]. Messages forwarding between nodes take the pattern of storage-carrying- forwarding [3, 4]. For improving the success rate of messages transmission, it often needs to make many copies of a message. In the situation of limited space in node buffer and limited communication opportunity between nodes, messages always can't reach destination node timely and have to stay in nodes buffer for a long time, which always leads to overflow of nodes buffer. So it is a very meaningful to take effective buffer management strategy for improving routing protocol performance in opportunistic networks.

© Springer International Publishing AG 2016
G. Wang et al. (Eds.): SpaCCS 2016 Workshops, LNCS 10067, pp. 16–25, 2016.
DOI: 10.1007/978-3-319-49145-5_2

2   Related Work

Many buffer management strategies only consider the state of the node itself to make buffer replacement decisions, such as DF (Drop Front) [5], which makes a FIFO(First In First Out) messages queue and always drops the forefront messages in buffer queue; DO (Drop the Oldest) [5], which discard the oldest messages, namely the messages having the least remaining lifetime, in nodes buffer; DRA (Drop-random) [6], which discard messages in the node buffer randomly. These strategies don't consider the case of network, and all have larger limitations.

Some buffer management strategies, which use the network information among nodes in opportunistic networks, have more excellent transmission performance. Literature [7] proposes a HBD(History Based Drop) strategy which drops messages based on nodes meeting history. It proposes a distributed algorithm based on message meeting dispatcher theory, and uses statistical learning method to approach global knowledge to optimize specific performance indicators. Literature [8] manages messages in node buffer using the ACK confirmation information issued in the network, and discards buffered messages timely according to the received ACK information to avoid buffer overflow.

Most existing buffer management strategies focus on priority problems of message discarding when buffer overflowed, and pay less attention on avoiding buffer overflow and transmission scheduling problem of buffered messages. And most of them don't consider the characteristics of node mobility when deciding buffer management strategy. There is a great relation between messages forwarding efficiency and node mobility model in opportunistic networks. The network composed of devices, which carried by people and having the ability of short-range wireless communications, is a very important application scenario in opportunistic networks [9–11]. Its nodes movement has the phenomenon of gathering, reflecting the characteristics of community. According to meeting history information of nodes and delivery status of messages in such network, we propose a CABMS (Community based Adaptive Buffer Management Strategy) strategy. Then we analyze and contrast CABMS strategy with three other buffer management strategies, which are Drop Front(DF), Drop the Oldest(DO) and Drop Based on History(HBD).

3   Community-Based Mobility Model in Opportunistic Networks

3.1   Community-Based Node Mobility Model

The opportunistic network composed of devices, which carried by people and having the ability of short-range wireless communications (Bluetooth /Wi-Fi, etc.), has the characteristics of the community. Its nodes movement always has the phenomenon of gathering due to relatively stable social relationships among people and certain dependence each other, and it always forms some more stable communities. We name such network as community opportunistic network. Within the community, the node density is relatively high, and the meeting frequency is higher. On the other hand, nodes in different community have lower meeting frequency, and some nodes are relatively active, often travel among several communities and enhance the contact among communities.

3.2   Community Detection Method

CABMS strategy improves the efficiency of buffer management in opportunistic network by detecting and using the characteristics of the human community. It assigns nodes to different communities according to closeness degree of node contacts. The detail method is listed as follows:

Shaded block in Fig. 1 represents that node i and node j are in the communication range of each other in the time interval of [0, T].

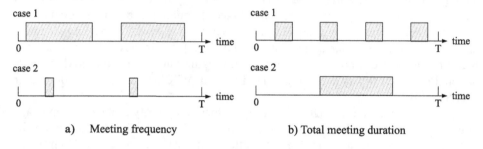

a)   Meeting frequency   b) Total meeting duration

Fig. 1. The comparison of node encounter

In sub graph (a) of Fig. 1, both cases have only two blocks, that is, two nodes only meet twice in the time interval T. But the width of the box in the first case is much larger than that of the second case. Although the encounter frequency are the same in both cases, but the length of contact time between the nodes in the first case is much longer than that of the second case, so the communicate opportunity of first case is much better than that of the second case. In sub graph (b) of Fig. 1, even though the total contact time between nodes are the same in both cases, in the first case nodes can contact more other nodes to exchange relevant information for periodically separation, and nodes can exchange data better for cycle of connection, which makes data dissemination more effective.

Consider these encounter cases in Fig. 1, we propose a new measure rule to reflect the encounter frequency and encounter duration time.

$$AVG(S_{i,j}) = \frac{\int_0^T \rho_{i,j}(t)dt}{n_{i,j}} \tag{1}$$

Where $S_{i,j}$ denotes the length of separation time between node i and node j. T is the total time elapsed. $n_{i,j}$ represents disconnection times of two nodes, $\rho_{i,j}(t)$ indicates whether two nodes are in the state of separation.

$$\begin{cases} \rho_{i,j}(t) = 1 \text{ When node i and j are not in communication range of each other} \\ \rho_{i,j}(t) = 0 \text{ When node i and j are in communication range of each other} \end{cases}$$

The smaller the value of $AVG(S_{i,j})$, the lower is the communication delay between node i and j. We take Gaussian similarity function to normalize the value of $AVG(S_{i,j})$, as shown in Formula 2, to denote the association closeness degree between the nodes.

$$R_{i,j} = e^{-\frac{(AVG(S_{i,j}))^2}{2\sigma^2}} \tag{2}$$

Where σ is a scaling parameter of the separation time interval between nodes [9].

The fluctuation of the separation periods between nodes will result in a negligible impact on the communication between nodes. If two cases have the same average separation periods, one fluctuates greatly, and the other fluctuates less, then in the situation of less fluctuation, nodes have good predictability for separation between nodes, so it is more suitable for communication between nodes. We use irregular scale $I_{i,j}$ to measure the fluctuation of such separation period.

$$I_{i,j} = VAR(S_{i,j}) = \frac{\sum_l (D_l - AVG(S_{i,j}))^2}{n_{i,j}} \tag{3}$$

Where D_l represents the length of each separation period.

We model the neighbor graph of node in opportunistic network as $G = (V, E)$, where V is the set of nodes, E is the set of edges which connects nodes in the network. Every edge $< i, j >$ in E represents the closeness degree between node i and node j, we use a weight value $W_{i,j}$ to denote it. Because $(R_{i,j}, I_{i,j})$ may represent the closeness degree between nodes, so we let

$$W_{i,j} = R_{i,j} - \alpha I_{i,j} \tag{4}$$

Where α is irregular fluctuations impact factor, its value should be small enough. The bigger the fluctuation of nodes separation periods, the greater is the negative impact on the closeness between nodes. We use Newman's weightiness network analysis algorithm [10] to make community division, and let relationship matrix composed with $W_{i,j}$ be the input of the algorithm, then divide all nodes in opportunistic network into different community.

Definition 1: Destination Community: the community which destination node of message belongs to is called the destination community of the message.

4   Community-Based Adaptive Buffer Management Strategy in Opportunistic Network

CAMBS strategy consists of two parts: the discard strategy and transmitting scheduling strategy of buffered messages. We discuss them respectively as following:

4.1 Community-Based Message Discarding Strategy

To reduce message transmission delay and optimize network performance, CABMS strategy discards messages based on the community property of nodes: When the node buffer overflowing, it drops messages which have not yet entered the destination community firstly. Then for same type messages, they are sorted by the value of $W_{i,j}$ which represents the closeness degree of the node i and destination node j. The message which has smaller $W_{i,j}$ value will be discarded from node i preferentially.

4.2 Adaptive Lightweight Clearance Mechanism for Redundant Copy

In order to improve the successful rate of message delivery in opportunistic network, it always produces multiple copies of message when delivering message. So when messages have successfully reached their destination nodes, a large number of copies of these messages still exist in the networks, which occupy much network buffer space. And these copies will still be spread in the network, which leads to a serious drain on network resources and affect the performance of network seriously. Therefore, we present an adaptive lightweight clearance mechanism for these unnecessary redundant copies. According to the message delivery status, the mechanism can generate delivery status beacon for the message adaptively. By exchanging these beacons among nodes, it can clear these unnecessary redundant copies in distributed way. The detailed method is described as follows:

When a message enters its destination community or reaches its destination node, the mechanism will both generate a delivery status beacon for the message, which specific format is shown in Table 1:

Table 1. Message delivery status beacon

32bit	1bit	7bit
Message ID	Reaching Flag	TTL

Where the reaching flag is used to distinguish delivery status of message: If a message has reached its destination node, the value is set to 1, if the message has just entered its destination community; the value is set to 0. TTL is the maximum number of hops that the delivery status beacon may be spread. According to the small-world theory, it is not more than six intervals for any two people to get connection in social network, so we set the TTL value to be 6 jumps.

When a message enters its destination community, the first receiving node will generate a status beacon for the message. All the nodes, which receive the status beacon and don't belong to such destination community, will clear the copy of the message in their buffer. Then it can reduce buffer occupancy and avoid the message to spread unnecessarily outside the destination community again.

When a message has been successfully delivered to its destination node, the destination node will generate a delivery status beacon for the message again. All other nodes which receive the beacon, will remove the redundant copies of the message to reduce the buffer occupancy and avoid the message to spread unnecessarily throughout the network again, thereby reduce network resource consumption, and it's helpful to improve the transmission performance.

When two nodes meet in opportunistic network, they'll exchange summary vector of buffered messages, and the message delivery status beacons are packed with summary vector and exchanged together. Nodes will handle the delivery status beacon firstly to remove unnecessary copy of messages.

Compared with a normal message, the size of its delivery status beacon is very small, and beacons lifetime has been restricted by their TTL value. Every time beacons are transmitted, their TTL value are decrease by one, when the value is 0, the beacon is cleared. So the spreading of message delivery status beacon list in the network consumes very little network resources. And simulation result shows that its negative affecting to network performance can be negligible.

4.3 Adaptive Message Transmission Scheduling Strategy

In order to let messages be delivered to their destination community and then to their destination node as soon as possible, we propose an adaptive buffer message transmission scheduling strategy based on the community that nodes belong to.

When node i meets node j and wants to send messages to it, node i will sort the sending messages adaptively based on relevant community information, and then make a schedule to decide messages sending sequence which described as follows:

1. Node i sends messages which destination node is node j firstly;
2. If a message has not yet entered its destination community, and node j belongs to the destination community, such message is send secondly;
3. Then, node i sends messages, which have entered their destination community, preferentially to ensure that these messages reach their destination nodes as soon as possible;
4. Furthermore, node i transmissions messages which have not entered their destination community;
5. Same type messages are sorted and scheduled as follows: For messages which are same type, they are sorted by their closeness degree value $W_{i,d}$, where node i is the receiving node and node d is the destination node of messages. Messages which have bigger value of $W_{i,d}$, will be send priority.

5 Simulation and Analysis

5.1 Simulation Environment

This paper selects a datasets collected in real environment to study the buffer management strategy in community-based opportunistic network. This dataset comes from the Infocom 2006 conference project which is a subproject of Cambridge Haggle project [11]. The project has 98 Imote nodes, which use Bluetooth technology to communicate with each other. 20 of which are fixed nodes deployed in different parts of the venue and act as access points, 78 nodes are distributed to volunteers participating in the conference. Such experiment carries out total time of three days; the Bluetooth devices make a scan every 120 s to discovery neighbors.

5.2 Simulation Result and Analysis

In this paper, we use the ONE platform which is an opportunistic network simulation environment, to verify the performance of the CABMS strategy, and compare it with some other typical buffer management strategies such as Drop Front strategy, Drop Oldest strategy, and HBD strategy. We import the real dataset of Infocom 2006 into the ONE platform and make the following experimental model validation based on epidemic forwarding mechanism, where the first 20 % experimental time is the warm-up time of the network, so that nodes can collect some meeting historical data to make community division. After the warm-up time, we assume that each node has known the communities that all other nodes belong to.

1. Comparative analysis of delivery ratio with different buffer sizes. As shown in Fig. 2, with the increase of node buffer size, the possibility of message discarded due to buffer overflow degreases, and delivery ratios are all improved in all four kinds of buffer management strategies. Since CABMS strategy takes advantage of the characteristics of community of nodes movement, and it generates message delivery status beacon to clear redundant messages, when message enters its destination community and reaches its destination node, so the possibility of node buffer overflow is greatly reduced, and the utilization rate of buffer is increased conspicuously. Thereby it can greatly reduce the possibility of useful message discarded. At the same time, CABMS strategy optimizes the schedule of messages sending based on community property of nodes, so the message delivery ratio is improved significantly compared with other three buffer strategies. The delivery ratio of HBD strategy is better than that of DO and DF strategy for it makes message replacement according to the number of message copies in the network. DF strategy only drops messages in the front of the queue, which may result in the loss of some messages in their distribution phase, so DF strategy has the lowest delivery ratio.

   As we can know from the statistical analysis result, the delivery ratio of CABMS strategy can outperforms the second-best HBD strategy by approximately 18.9 % averagely.

2. Comparative analysis of average network overhead with different buffer sizes. As shown in Fig. 3, with the increase of buffer space, the message delivery success rate increases, and the number of messages being successfully delivered to the destination node also increases, which makes the average network overhead all decrease for all four strategy. When message enters its destination community and reaches its destination node, the CABMS strategy generates delivery status beacon for message to clear its redundant copies, and avoids a lot of unnecessary message forwarding, so the messages forwarding times of CABMS strategy is far less than that of other three strategies, and its average network overhead is average only 48.6 %, 40.5 % and 37.9 % compared to that of HBD, DO and DF strategy respectively.

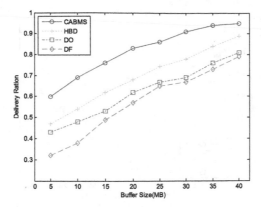

Fig. 2. Delivery ratio against buffer size

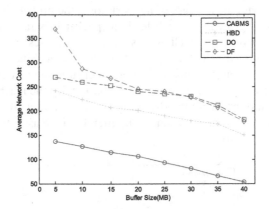

Fig. 3. Average network cost against buffer size

3. Comparative analysis of delivery ratio with different network load. As shown in Fig. 4, with the increase of message generation rate, network load increases gradually, and the probability of node buffer overflow increases either, which leads to packet loss rate increases and message delivery ratio decrease correspondingly. Especially, the delivery ratio decrease relatively larger in HBD, DO and DF strategy than that of CABMS strategy. For CABMS strategy takes a lightweight clearance mechanism for redundant messages copies, it drops unnecessary copies of messages timely and reduces the pressure on the node buffer greatly. Furthermore, CABMS strategy takes community-based optimal scheduling when sending messages, it is helpful to improve message delivery ratio, and thereby the decrease of its delivery ratio is much slower than that of other three strategies when message generation rate increases. The delivery ratio of CABMS strategy can outperforms the second-best HBD strategy by approximately 21.9 % averagely.

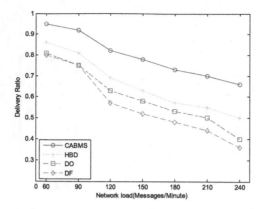

Fig. 4. Delivery ratio against network load

4. Comparative analysis of average network overhead with different network load. As shown in Fig. 5, with the increase of network load, the probability of nodes buffer overflow increases gradually, which leads to packet loss rate increasing. So the average network overhead of all four strategies increases gradually, while the increase of that of CABMS strategy is relatively slower. Since CABMS strategy generates delivery status beacon for message to clear redundant copies of message twice when the message enters its destination community and reaches its destination node, which greatly reduces the probability of nodes buffer overflow and avoids many unnecessary message transmission, thereby increases the probability of successful message delivery.

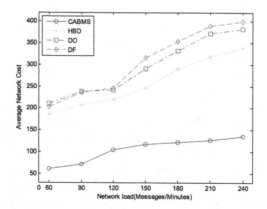

Fig. 5. Average network cost against network load

As we can know from the statistical analysis result, the average network overhead of CABMS strategy is averagely only 40.6 %, 35.6 % and 34.4 % of that of HBD, DO and DF strategy respectively.

6   Conclusion

Networks composed of devices, which are carried by people and have short-range wireless communications capabilities, is a major application scenarios in opportunistic network, whose nodes movement has the characteristics of community. In this paper, we present a community-based adaptive buffer management strategy for such network. When message enters its destination community or reaches its destination node, the CABMS strategy will generate delivery status beacon adaptively for the message to clear its unnecessary copies, which decreases the possibility of nodes buffer overflow greatly and avoid much unnecessary transmission of redundant copies. At the same time, the CABMS strategy optimizes the dropping strategy and the sending sequence of buffered messages adaptively according to the community attribute of nodes, which reduces messages delivery latency and helps to improve the success rate of message delivery. The simulation based on dataset from real environment shows that the CABMS strategy can improve message delivery ratio, reduce average delivery delay and network overhead effectively in community-based opportunistic networks.

Acknowledgments. We acknowledge the support of the National Natural Science Foundation of China under Grant No. 61472125, 61272546.

References

1. Li, Y., Jin, D.P., Pan, H., et al.: Contact-aware data replication in roadside unit aided vehicular opportunistic networks. IEEE Trans. Mobile Comput. **15**(2), 306–321 (2016)
2. Zhao, D., Ma, H., Tang, S.J., et al.: COUPON: a cooperative framework for building sensing maps in mobile opportunistic networks. IEEE Trans. Parall. Distrib. Syst. **26**(2), 392–402 (2015)
3. Hyytiä, E., Bayhan, S., Ott, J., et al.: On search and content availability in opportunistic networks. Comput. Commun. **73**, 118–131 (2016)
4. Xiao, M.J., Wu, J., Huang, L.S.: Community-aware opportunistic routing in mobile social networks. IEEE Trans. Comput. **63**(7), 1682–1695 (2014)
5. Lindgren, A., Phanse, K.S.: Evaluation of queuing policies and forwarding strategies for routing in intermittently connected networks. In: Proceedings of IEEE COMSWARE, pp. 1–10 (2006)
6. Davis, J.A., Fagg, A.H., Levine, B.N.: Wearable computers as packet transport mechanisms in highly partitioned Ad Hoc networks. IEEE ISWC, pp. 141–148 (2001)
7. Krifa, A., Barakat, C., Spyropoulos, T.: Optimal buffer management policies for delay tolerant networks. In: Proceedings of IEEE SECON, San Francisco, pp. 260–268 (2008)
8. Kaveevivitchai, S., Ochiai, H., Esaki, H.: Message deletion and mobility patterns for efficient message delivery in DTNs. In: Pervasive Computing & Communications Workshops IEEE International Conference, pp. 760–763 (2010)
9. Luxburg, U.: A tutorial on spectral clustering. Stat. Comput. **17**(4), 395–416 (2007)
10. Newman, M.E.J.: Analysis of weighted networks. Phys. Rev. E Stat. Nonlinear Soft Matter Phys. **70**, 1–9 (2004)
11. Chaintreau, A., Pan, H., Scott, J., et al.: Impact of human mobility on opportunistic forwarding algorithms. IEEE Trans. Mobile Comput. **6**(6), 606–620 (2007)

Energy-Aware Location Privacy Routing for Wireless Sensor Networks

Jingjing Zhang$^{(\boxtimes)}$ and Zhengping Jin

Institute of Network Technology, Beijing University of Posts
and Telecommunications, Beijing 100876, China
zjj_bupt@163.com, 75410062@qq.com

Abstract. Source location privacy (SLP) in wireless sensor networks (WSN) intends to protect the location privacy of monitoring objects, as the resources of WSN are limited, the essence of the SLP is to balance the security and energy-cost. Among the existing solutions, the scheme based on random walk (DROW) is most attractive. However, DROW didn't consider the balance of each node's energy consumption and the safety period is unstable. What's more, it didn't change the data flow either. To solve these problems, in this paper, we put forward an energy-aware location privacy routing protocol which consists of two parts: non-repeat polling routing protocol and strategy of fake messages based on energy-aware. On the premise of not influence the network lifetime seriously, we make full use of the high-energy nodes, strength the security of the network and change the data flow. Simulation results verify that we can provide higher stability as the variance of our protocol is only about one over forty of that based on random-walk. Meanwhile, more nodes participate in packets transmission so the energy consumption is balanced and safety period is extended by 20 % to 30 %.

Keywords: WSN · Source location privacy · Random walk · Energy-aware

1 Introduction

Wireless sensor networks (WSN) is a new network technology which is consisted of amount of micro sensor nodes. It has broad respects in application. However, source location privacy (SLP) is a seriously factor restricting the actual application. In 2004, Ozturk et al. [1] put forward the model named hunter panda game, which first described the SLP issue in WSN formally. They made it distinct from content-privacy and identity-privacy but define it as context-privacy, which pays attention to hide the context information in WSN [2]. Normally, attackers analyze the wireless signal, and then according to the strength of wireless signal and transmission of data flow, they finally determine where the monitoring object is. From the attack mode, we can see that the essence of SLP is to against the network flow analysis. Researchers have proposed a variety of routing solutions to solve this problem [3]. The existing schemas can be divided into two categories.

The first one is that the network flow direction is not been changed. The represented schemas is phantom routing schema [4] (PRS), Routing through a Randomly Selected Intermediary Node [5] RRSIN), Directed Random Walk [5, 6] (DROW) and so on.

© Springer International Publishing AG 2016
G. Wang et al. (Eds.): SpaCCS 2016 Workshops, LNCS 10067, pp. 26–32, 2016.
DOI: 10.1007/978-3-319-49145-5_3

PSR need to find a fake source node and then deliver the packets through the way of flooding or single path [2]. However, flooding costs too much overhead and ingle path doesn't provide efficient measures to hide the real source node when select the fake one. Based on phantom routing, Li et al. [5] put forward RRSIN which doesn't give away any location information of the real source node when it finds the fake one. But, it needs to know the whole network topology well which is hard to do. So the above schemas we mentioned are limited.

Yao et al. [6] proposed DROW. In this protocol, according to the distance or the hops between the source and sink node, the neighbor nodes of each node will be divided into two groups, near group N and far group F. When a node starts to send messages, if N has nodes, it will choose a node in N randomly and then send message to it. If not, it will send the message to the node in F randomly. Hop by hop, the message can be sent from source to sink. DROW has smaller transmission delay. Compared to the PSR and RRSIN, it consumes less energy. Also, it provides longer safety period than the PSR.

However, in DROW, although it disperses the intermediate nodes energy consumption, it still should be formed hot spots of energy consumption and message exchange around source and sink node which easily attracts the attacker's attention. Meanwhile, as we select the next hop randomly, it leads to the unstable safety period, and the minimum is just as short as the product of the number of the nodes between source and sink and transmission interval. In order to settle this issue, researchers proposed the thought of polling which means to select the node in N in turn as the next node. But we cannot ignore such situation as the Fig. 1 shows.

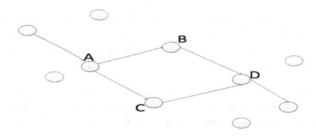

Fig. 1. Nodes deployment

The WSN contains two path A->B->D and A->C->D, when attacker stays in D waiting for a new message, no matter node A select node B or node C, attacker always can arrive at a node (B or C) more closer to source A. So with only simple thought of polling cannot address this problem.

The second category is changing the direction of data flow. The represented scenarios are based on Cyclic Entrapment Method [7] and Dynamic Bidirectional Tree [8, 9] and so on. However, it is difficult to design appropriate generation algorithm and in meantime, fake packets can seriously affect the whole network lifetime as they consume large amount of resources when they transmit in WSN. Also, because of the unbalanced use of nodes, there are lots of unused nodes with high residual energy.

Of course there are existing schemas [10] referring to the energy. However it doesn't consider the safety.

From the analysis from the above, we can see that the existing problem of the traditional DROW can be divided into two aspects. First one is the thought of pure polling cannot assure the stability of the safety period. And the second one is the generation algorithm of is difficult, at the same time, many nodes with high residual energy are not used.

In our paper, we put forward an energy-aware location privacy routing containing two parts: non-repeat polling routing protocol and strategy of fake messages based on energy-aware. In the first part, we provide non-repeat polling protocol to solve the problem about instability. First, when the node sends packets, it will attach its ID to the next node, and then we can build a polling list for each node according to the same ID. Second, after the polling list are finished, each nodes in polling list are used for only once in one round. Through it, we not only make the safety period more stable but also improve it by 20 % to 30 %. In the second part, we add a strategy of fake messages based on energy-aware to our routing. We put forward a conception of average residual energy. If the residual energy of a node is greater than the average residual energy, the node will be likely to generate fake message to balancing the resource consumption in WSN. In the case of not influence the lifetime of WSN too much, we make more node participate in packets delivery and extend the network consumption by 45 % to 65 %.

2   Energy-Aware Location Privacy Routing

2.1   Attacked Model and Network Assumption

In our protocol, we assume that there only one source node and one sink node in WSN as most literatures do [3]. At first, the attacker stays at the sink node. During the transmission, node can exchange information with neighbor nodes including residual energy and location. The attacker also has following characters:

- Passive attacker who cannot affect the direction of data transmission.
- Don't know the whole network topology and the contents of packets.
- The radius of the attacker's detection and the sensor communication is equal.
- Move one step when it detect a new packet.

2.2   Non-repeat Polling Routing Protocol

Assume $P_{i,j}$ is the probability of node i selects node j in its near group as the next hop, and then

$$P_{i,j} = \begin{cases} 1, & x_i \bmod t_i = j \\ 0, & T_i \neq \emptyset \mid j \notin T_i \\ 1/n_i, & T_i = \emptyset, \end{cases} \tag{1}$$

T_i is node i polling list and t_i is the number of nodes in T_i, x_i is the number of transfer of node i, n_i is the number of nodes in node i near group.

Lemma 1. Non-repeat polling routing

---

1. The sink node floods message to the whole network and every node obtain hops or distance L between sink and itself. Then according to L, neighbor nodes are divided into near group and far group respectively.

2. In begin, all nodes are not marked. Source node starts to send packets to sink node with the ways of polling, and the node will attack its ID to the packets.

3. When the intermediate node receives the packets, it will tag itself with the ID of the pre-hop node, then mark the packet with its ID and send it.

4. If the node sends packets to a node NEXT which is not marked with its ID, the node will remove NEXT from the polling list and send the packets to another node in near group

5. Repeat the step 2, 3, 4, until all nodes are marked and finally each node has its polling list. In the list, all nodes are marked with its ID. Polling list as the first priority and other node in near group as the second priority. Only when the polling list is null, we select the node in the second priority group to transfer the packets

---

2.3   Strategy of Fake Messages Based on Energy-Aware

We make full use of the high residual nodes and put forward a new conception average residual energy which decides the frequency of fake packet generation.

Lemma 2. Strategy of fake messages based on energy-aware

---

1. Each node has certain initial energy E, after a period time of simulation, node check its left energy and exchange with the neighbor node periodically.

2. Calculate the average residual energy $\overline{E}_{left}$, according to $P = f(\overline{E}_{left}, \overline{E}_{self}, \beta) = \overline{E}_{self} - \beta\overline{E}_{left}$. we can get the probability of the node generating fake packets. When $P \geq 0$, generating, $P < 0$, not generating.

3. To avoid to excessive energy consumption, we add a parameter TTL to fake packets as the maximum hop

---

3   Protocol Analysis

From formula (1), we can easily derive the safety period of the non-repeat polling routing. We assume Δt as the source node sending packets interval and s_l as the number of all nodes which are i hop away from sink node, then a node in such layer receive the packets again need to wait for $s_l \times \Delta t$ so the total safety period of the WSN as T is:

$$T = \sum_{l=1}^{l=m} s_l * \Delta t = S_0 * \Delta t \tag{2}$$

m is the hops between sink node and source node, S_0 is the total number of node participate in transmission.

Compared to DROW, our routing improves the network average safety period and makes it more stable. Also, we use as many as possible nodes to send packets so the area of energy consumption is spread and the whole network consumption is balanced.

From Algorithm 2, we can see that the smaller the β is, the more fake packets we generate. Respectively, the fake packets need to cost some energy and the network lifetime is decreased. So it depends on the actual demand to define the β. If we want to get higher safety and are not sensitive to the energy consumption, we can make the β smaller. On the contrary, we can make β the bigger. It depends on our demands to define β, we cannot get better performance in terms of both safety and energy consumption because if we want to get higher safety, we need to consume more energy to generate more fake packets.

4   Simulation Results

We take the OMNET++ as the simulate tool. We use the grid network which contains nodes 200*200. The distance between sink and source node is 1000,1100,1200, 1300,1400,1500 respectively. In different distance, we compare our protocol EALPR to the DROW.

In literature [3], safety period is a main measure of the SLP which is the number of messages a source node sends out before the adversary locates the subject. The stability of the safety period concerns whether it is suitable to apply in actual environment. Obviously, we should extend the safety period as bigger as possible and make it stable.

In our simulation, we define the safety period as the time period from the start to the adversary locating the source node. Figure 2 shows the safety period in our simulation. We can see from the Fig. 2 obviously that the EALPR has more stable and higher safety period. After computation, the variance of EALPR is only about one over forty of that based on random-walk and safety period is extended by 20 % to 30 %.

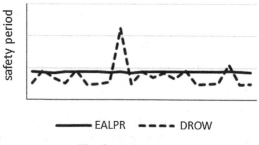

Fig. 2. Safety period

Table 1 records some simulate result. The more nodes participate process of the packets transmission, the network energy consumption is more balanced and that avoids forming the hot energy consumption spaces, too. We can see that in ELAPR, more node participate in packets transmission. The sum total of real and fake packets are almost equal and that is to say we change the data flow successfully.

Table 1. Nodes and packets

	DROW	ELAPR
Participating node	84,104,116,121,131,128	90,106,129,151,143,150
Fake packets	None	150,161,160,171,165,180
Real packets	229,227,183,233,241,250	170, 183, 183, 182,185, 202

Now that network lifetime records the time how long a WSN can work normally, we had better extend the network lifetime as longer as possible. However, when we consider the SLP, the situation is changed. If the source node is located, it is meaningless even if the network can alive for quite long time. So, we need to compare the network lifetime and safety comprehensively. Energy consumption records how much energy we consume when the WSN died. And this indicator can represent the safety to some extent as more nodes participating in the transmission, more packets are transmitted and so on.

Because we add the strategy of fake packets, so the whole network lifetime is reduced as Fig. 3 left shows. The lifetime is reduced by 20 % to 30 %. However, we can see that the whole network energy consumption in Fig. 3 right is abviously increased, that is about 45 % to 65 %.

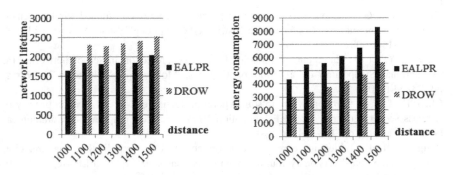

Fig. 3. Network lifetime and energy consumption

5 Conclusions and Future Directions

In this paper, we presented an Energy-Aware Location Privacy Routing (EALPR) for Wireless Sensor Networks to balance the energy consumption and safety period. In traditional DROW, the network lifetime is unstable and the minimum value is quite low, and we not only address them but also add strategy of fake packets based on high residual node. Through the fake packets strategy, we balanced the whole network consumption and avoided to form consumption hot space around the sink and source node, as well as change the data flow. On the premise of not affect the network lifetime seriously, we improved the network safety period conspicuously. In future work, we need to consider how to improve EALPR under the condition of multiple sources or source and sink mobility.

Acknowledgments. This work is supported by NSFC (Grant Nos. 61300181, 61502044), the Fundamental Research Funds for the Central Universities (Grant No. 2015RC23).

References

1. Ozturk, C., Zhang, Y., Trappe, W.: Source-location privacy in energy-constrained sensor network routing. In: ACM Workshop on Security of Ad Hoc and Sensor Networks, SASN 2004, Washington, DC, USA, October 2004, pp. 88–93 (2004)
2. Kamat, P., Zhang, Y., Trappe, W., Ozturk, C.: Enhancing source-location privacy in sensor network routing. In: 25th IEEE International Conference on Distributed Computing Systems (ICDCS 2005), Columbus, OH, pp. 599–608 (2005)
3. Conti, M., Willemsen, J., Crispo, B.: Providing source location privacy in wireless sensor networks: a survey. IEEE Commun. Surv. Tutor. 15(3), 1238–1280 (2013)
4. Ozturk, C., et al.: Source-location privacy for networks of energy-constrained sensors. In: Proceedings. Second IEEE Workshop on Software Technologies for Future Embedded and Ubiquitous Systems, pp. 68–68 (2004)
5. Li, Y., Lightfoot, L., Ren, J.: Routing-based source-location privacy protection in wireless sensor networks. In: IEEE International Conference on Electro/Information Technology, pp. 29–34 (2009)
6. Yao, J., Wen, G.: Preserving source-location privacy in energy-constrained wireless sensor networks. In: International Conference on Distributed Computing Systems Workshops IEEE, pp. 412–416 (2008)
7. Ouyang, Y., et al.: Entrapping adversaries for source protection in sensor networks. In: International Symposium on a World of Wireless, Mobile and Multimedia Networks, pp. 23–34 (2006)
8. Chen, H., Lou, W.: From nowhere to somewhere: protecting end-to-end location privacy in wireless sensor networks. In: IEEE International Performance Computing & Communications Conference, pp. 1–8 (2010)
9. Long, J., et al.: Achieving source location privacy and network lifetime maximization through tree-based diversionary routing in wireless sensor networks. IEEE Access 2(10), 633–651 (2014)
10. Chang, H.Y., Huang, S.C.: Contention-free station communication matching algorithm in multi-hop power management for wireless ad-hoc networks. Int. J. Grid High Perform. Comput. 7(1), 52–66 (2015)

ChainMR Crawler: A Distributed Vertical Crawler Based on MapReduce

Xixia Liu[✉] and Zhengping Jin

State Key Laboratory of Networking and Switching Technology,
Beijing University of Posts and Telecommunications, Beijing 100876, China
hy3321351@126.com, zhpjin@bupt.edu.cn

Abstract. With the explosive growth of data in the Internet, the single vertical crawler cannot meet the requirements of the high performance of the crawler. The existing distributed vertical crawlers also have the problem of weak capability of customization. In order to solve the above problem, this paper proposes a distributed vertical crawler named ChainMR Crawler. We adopt ChainMapper/ChainReducer model to design each module of the crawler, use Redis to manage URLs and choose the distributed database Hbase to store the key content of web pages. Experimental results demonstrate that the efficiency of ChainMR Crawler is 6 % higher than Nutch in the field of vertical crawler, which achieves the expected effect.

Keywords: Vertical Crawler · Distributed Crawler · MapReduce · ChainMaper/ChainReducer · Redis

1 Introduction

Web crawler can automatically crawl all kinds of information which people need from the Internet. It is one of the most indispensable modules for the search engines or the collectors of special information [1]. The information of Google search statistics shows that the number of indexed pages is more than 30 trillion [2], and the number of pages in china has reached 189.9 billion [3]. How to get the information people need from the Internet fast and accurately has become people's urgent demand. Studies point out that around 85 % of Internet users use search engines to find information from the WWW [4]. We believe that different crawling methods should be developed to fit for different types of Web sites [5]. The traditional information retrieval service provided by the search engine has been unable to meet the growing demand for personalized service in a specific area [6]. So in order to get to the information of specific area quickly, the application of retrieval based on vertical crawler has become more and more popular.

With the explosive growth of information, the traditional single-thread crawler is unable to meet our demand for information both in quantity and quality [7–9]. Distributed crawlers can use a number of stand-alone crawlers to work in parallel and highly improve the efficiency. MapReduce [10] emerges as the model of choice for processing massive data. There are also some distributed crawlers in wide use, for instance Nutch

© Springer International Publishing AG 2016
G. Wang et al. (Eds.): SpaCCS 2016 Workshops, LNCS 10067, pp. 33–39, 2016.
DOI: 10.1007/978-3-319-49145-5_4

[11] and its optimization schemes. Hengfei Zhan [12] has optimized Nutch by limiting the latency time of crawling and monitoring invalid links. Wei Yuan [13] improved the efficiency and accuracy of Nutch by optimizing relevant parameters and models of Nutch. Although the crawling efficiency is improved in such ways, however its custom ability is weak, and is not suitable for secondary development according to the needs of the users.

In order to improve the efficiency and scalability of vertical crawler, we design a distributed vertical crawler based on ChainMaper/ChainReducer chain structure [14]. The computing tasks are divided into: DownloadMapper, ProcessMapper, ProcessReducer, HBaseMapper. ProcessReducer are responsible for the extraction of the key information from the target sites. We use a combination of CSS Selector, XPath and regular expression to parse web-page contents. We can easily implement different websites by changing the module, which makes the crawler have a good scalability and users can customize the development according to their own needs. We use Redis to store and manage URLs. At the same time, the BloomFilter algorithm is used to filter reduplicate URLs. We compare ChainMR Crawler with signal vertical crawler and Nutch in the experiments and the experimental results show that the efficiency of ChainMR Crawler on three nodes is 3.43 times as high as that of single vertical crawler and on average the efficiency of ChainMR Crawler is 6 % higher than Nutch, which demonstrates that ChainMR Crawler has a better performance.

2   ChainMR Crawler Structure

The distributed vertical crawler system, ChainMR Crawler, consists of four function modules, which are download module, URL management module, parse module and storage module. The architecture of the system is shown in Fig. 1.

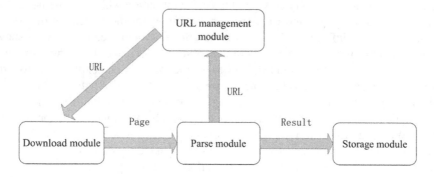

Fig. 1 The Architecture of ChainMR Crawler

2.1   Download Module

Downloading page is the beginning of a crawler. Downloading starts from a set of seed URLs, which receives the response from the web pages by simulating Http requests to the seed URLs. Apache HttpClient is used in this paper. It supports custom HTTP header, containing User-agent and cookie which are useful for downloading. Further, it also has many powerful functions such as automatic redirect, connection reuse, cookie reservation, setting agent and so on. The implementation of this module is encapsulated in the class DownloadMapper.

2.2 URL Management Module

In order to avoid crawling over the same URL, it is necessary to manage the URLs. In this paper, we use Redis to store the URL queue A in which URLs have been crawled and the URL queue B in which URLs are to be crawled. When extracting a new URL, BloomFilter algorithm is first used to determine whether it is in A. If it is not in A, add it to B. As B is stored in the form of set, if the new URL is the same with any URL in B, just save one. This can effectively avoid crawling over a certain URL repeatedly, resulting in wasting resources.

2.3 Parse Module

This module is mainly to parse the HTML pages which are crawled by download module. The parse module is divided into two parts: One part is responsible for the extraction of new web links. The implementation of this part is encapsulated in the class Process-Mapper. The other part is mainly responsible for the extraction of web contents which users need. The implementation of this part is encapsulated in the class ProcessReducer. Parsing Pages is a complex task. In a detailed analysis of the structure of web pages, we use CSS Selector, XPath and regular expressions to extract the contents of the pages in this paper.

2.4 Storage Module

This module is mainly to store data which is from parse module. The database used in this paper is HBase, which is a sub project of the Hadoop project. It is a kind of high reliability, high performance, column oriented, and scalable distributed database. It takes HDFS [15] as its file storage system in Hadoop, which is suitable for applications having big data. At the same time, Hbase is also relying on the MapReduce massive data processing capacity. A high performance and large scale structured storage cluster can be built on a number of inexpensive PC machines. The implementation of this module is encapsulated in the class HBaseMapper.

3 ChainMR Crawler Design Based on ChainMapper/ ChainReducer

ChainMaper/ChainReducer is a chain structure of MapReduce. MapReduce is one part of Hadoop [16], which is an open source framework for distributed applications. MapReduce is a data processing model and it can process massive data over multiple computing nodes efficiently. In this structure, there are more than one Mapper in the

Map or Reduce phase. These Mappers like Linux pipes, the output of the former Mapper redirect to the input of the next Mapper directly, forming a pipeline, avoiding the process of the intermediate output data written to the disk. Designed in this way, Mapper function is focused and the time of the input and output of disks is saved, which makes the crawler system have a higher efficiency of crawling.

According to the principle of ChainMaper/ChainReducer, the process of crawling can be divided into DownloadMapper, ProcessMapper, ProcessReducer and HBase-Mapper, which makes up Mapper+Mapper+Reducer+Mapper chain tasks. Figure 2 shows the chain structure of ChainMR Crawler which is based on ChainMapper/Chain-Reducer.

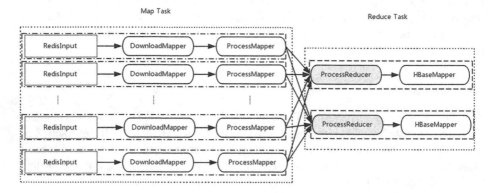

Fig. 2 Chain structure of ChainMR Crawler

Redis here is used as an input source for Mapper. As now existing Hadoop input-Format cannot satisfy our demand, this paper customizes the implementation of Redis-InputFormat. The seeds URLs are split according to their number as the input of Down-loadMapper. Web pages are downloaded in DownloadMapper. Then the downloaded HTML contents are redirected to ProcessMapper by stream. And in ProcessMapper, HTML contents are parsed and extracted features page links. In ProcessMapper the URL management module is also called to filter reduplicate URLs. Next entering the Reducer phase, web contents are shuffled and sorted according to the domain names and then feature content data is extracted. Finally, redirect the feature content information to HBaseMapper and call HBase interface for information persistence.

4 Experimental Results

All of our experiments are completed on virtual machines which are configured as Hat Enterprise Linux Red 6, 1 core, 2G memory, built on 4 core, 8G, windows64 machines. For verifying the efficiency of the distributed crawling system, we select http://www.qidian.com/Default.aspx Web as the test site. Take the crawled website quantity of stand-alone crawler system-webmagic and ChainMR Crawler system within 30 min respectively for contrast. Cluster system set up 3 and 6 virtual machines for performance test.

Next we take three nodes in the distributed cluster. In the same test environment, compare the performance of ChainMR Crawler and Nutch for crawling over the same website http://www.qidian.com/Default.aspx.

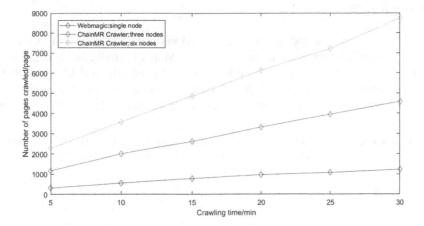

Fig. 3 Performance comparison between single and distributed vertical crawler

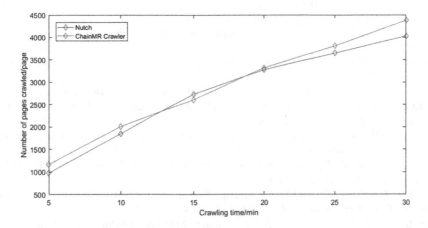

Fig. 4 Performance comparison between ChainMR Crawler and Nutch

From Fig. 3, we can see the numbers of pages crawled by signal crawler Webmagic and ChainMR Crawlerin different crawling time, through which we can get that the efficiency of ChainMR Crawler on three nodes is 3.43 times as high as that of single vertical crawler on average and the crawler performance can be improved by properly increasing the number of cluster nodes, which makes ChainMR Crawler have a good scalability. From Fig. 4, we can see the numbers of pages crawled by Nutch and ChainMR Crawler in different crawling time, through which we can see that the performance of ChainMR Crawler is higher than Nutch on the whole and on average the efficiency of ChainMR

Crawler is 6 % higher than Nutch. From the experimental data we can know that ChainMR Crawler has good crawling efficiency and good scalability.

5 Conclusion

In this paper, we propose and design a distributed vertical crawler system - ChainMR Crawler. We design each module based on ChainMaper/ChainReducer, using Redis memory database to manage URL, adopting BloomFilter algorithm to filter reduplicate URLs. And Hbase are put to use to store crawled content information. The efficiency of ChainMR Crawler is proved more efficient and it can be extended to a variety of needs.

Acknowledgments. This work is supported by NSFC (Grant Nos. 61300181, 61502044), the Fundamental Research Funds for the Central Universities (Grant Nos. 2015RC23).

References

1. Zhou, B., Xiao, B., Lin, Z., et al.: A distributed vertical crawler using crawling-period based strategy. In: 2010 2nd International Conference on Future Computer and Communication (ICFCC), pp. 306–311. IEEE (2010)
2. Google search statistics, http://www.internetlivestats.com (2012)
3. The 35th China Internet network development state statistical report (2015). http://www.cnnic.cn
4. Kobayashi, M., Takeda, K.: Information retrieval on the web. ACM Comput. Surv. (CSUR) **32**, 144–173 (2000)
5. Guo, Y., Li, K., Zhang, K., et al.: Board forum crawling: a Web crawling method for Web forum. In: Proceedings of the 2006 IEEE/WIC/ACM International Conference on Web Intelligence, pp. 745–748. IEEE Computer Society (2006)
6. Trivedi, H.P., Daxini, G.N., Oswal, J.A., et al.: An approach to design personalized focused crawler. Int. J. Comput. Sci. Eng. (2014)
7. Zhang, X., Xian, M.: Optimization of distributed crawler under Hadoop. In: MATEC Web of Conferences. EDP Sciences (2015)
8. Li, X.Z., Cheng, G., Zhao, Q.J., et al.: Design and implementation of the distributed crawler system. China Sci. Technol. Inf. **15**, 116–117 (2014)
9. Boldi, A., Marino, M., Santini, S.V.: Bubing: Massive crawling for the masses. In: Proceedings of the Companion Publication of the 23rd International Conference on World Wide Web Companion, pp. 227–228 (2014)
10. Dean, J., Ghemawat, S.: MapReduce: simplified data processing on large clusters. Commun. ACM **51**(1), 107–113 (2008)
11. Nutch Apache. http://nutch.apache.Org
12. Zhan, H.F., Yang, Y.X., Fang, H., et al.: A study on distributed network crawler and its applications. J. Front. Comput. Sci. Technol. **5**, 68–74 (2011)
13. Yuan, W., Xue, A.R., Zhou, X.M., et al.: A study on the optimization of distributed crawler based on Nutch. Wirel. Commun. Tech. **23**(3), 44–47 (2014)
14. Zhu, X.L., Wang, B.: Community mining in complex network based on parallel genetic algorithm. In: 2010 Fourth International Conference on Genetic and Evolutionary Computing (ICGEC), pp. 325–328. IEEE (2010)

15. Shvachko, K., Kuang, H., Radia, S., et al.: The hadoop distributed file system. In: 2010 IEEE 26th Symposium on Mass Storage Systems and Technologies (MSST), pp. 1–10. IEEE (2010)
16. Junsheng, W., Yunmei, S., Yangsen, Z.: Key technologies of distributed search engine based on Hadoop. J. Beijing Inf. Univ. Sci. Technol. **26**(4), 4–7 (2011)

An Improved Ring-Based Model for Big Data Storage and Retrieval in Wireless Sensor Networks

Hongling Chen[1(✉)], Quangang Wen[2], and Xiaoyang Fu[2]

[1] Department of Computer Science and Technology, Zhuhai College of Jilin University,
Zhuhai 519041, China
17066415@qq.com

[2] Zhuhai Laboratory of Key Laboratory of Symbolic Computation and Knowledge Engineering
of Ministry of Education, Zhuhai 519041, China
7633629@qq.com, 93964281@qq.com

Abstract. In wireless sensor network, sensor nodes generate continuous data, such as the variety of ambient temperature and humidity data. Because of the sensor node energy is limited, frequently transmiting data will lead to the sensor node energy consume too fast. In addition, there are usually active nodes that produce data or query data more frequently in sensor network, if using traditional data centric storage method will produce the hotspot problem. In this paper, we proposed an improved ring-based data storage and retrieval model named IRSR. IRSR divides the nodes into some rings and chooses an optimal ring according to the frequencies of event and query, and uses adjacency ring rotation working to ensure the network load balance. We show by simulation that IRSR achieves more balanced traffic load on sensor nodes and prolongs the lifetime of the senor networks even under the extreme circumstance.

Keywords: Wireless sensor networks · Data storage and retrieval · Big data · Hotspot problem · Network load balance

1 Introduction

A wireless sensor network [1] consists of a large number of sensor nodes which can acquire useful information (e.g. environmental monitoring, biological detection, smart spaces, and battlefield surveillance data) from the physical environment around. With the development and wide spread application of wireless sensor networks, the amount of sensory data grows sharply and the volumes of some sensory datasets are larger than terabytes or petabytes. Therefore, how to store and retrieve the big data more efficiently has become a widespread and important research subject in wireless sensor network.

The wireless sensor network can be regarded as a "distributed database" and the sensor nodes in that store the sensing data in a distributed way. Users can access the "database" at any point of the sensor network. E.g., in an intelligent building, the sensor nodes collect and store temperature and humidity data of each room. If any user wants to look for a meeting room which temperature is close to 25°C and humidity is close to

G. Wang et al. (Eds.): SpaCCS 2016 Workshops, LNCS 10067, pp. 40–47, 2016.
DOI: 10.1007/978-3-319-49145-5_5

35 %, he can send a query on any sensor node of the sensor network at any place in the building, then the sensor network will process the query and send a query result back to the user.

In those applications, each sensor node will produce data and also will query other's data or answer other's query. Due to the sensor network has a number of distinctive feature, so there is a series of challenging problems to the researchers [2, 3]:

Firstly, the energy, the storage space and the computation capacity of each sensor node is limited, how to reduce the message transmission and save the energy in the working network is a challenge to sensor network study; Secondly, the communication radius of each sensor node is short, how to perform the observed information's transmission under the condition of limited communication ability is another challenge. Thirdly, it is difficult to find an optimal storage strategy when the data generating rates of the sensor nodes and the query frequencies of the users are considered. Fourthly, when some individual nodes in the sensor network produce data frequently or are queried frequently, its energy will quickly exhaust, how to avoid the emergence of the hotspot problem is also a challenge.

To solve these problems, we present an improved ring-based model for the storage and retrieval of big data (IRSR) in this paper. IRSR divides the whole sensor network field into virtual rings, and chooses the least energy cost ring as the rendezvous ring which can store data and process queries efficiently. In order to avoid the hotspot problem on the rendezvous ring, IRSR designs a data migration algorithm between adjacent rings to prolong network lifetime. The simulation uses the modified GPSR routing as the data transmission protocol.

The rest of this paper is organized as follows. Section 2 discusses the related work. Section 3 presents the scheme IRSR in detail. Section 4 shows the simulation result. Section 5 gives the conclusion.

2 Related Work

The data storage and retrieval in wireless sensor networks research the storage strategy of the perception data on the sensor nodes, including how to store the data on suitable position in sensor network and how to route the query to the storage position and get the data. According to the different storage strategy of sensory data, data storage can be divided into centralized storage, local storage, and distributed storage [4]. The distributed storage strategy is better than the formers on network scale, data transmission cost, query efficiency, network lifetime, and so on [5, 6]. Therefore the distributed storage strategy has widespread use.

Distributed storage is a data-centric storage strategy, its core idea is that the data of sensory node may not store locally, instead of using distributed technology to store the data in other nodes, and uses effective information brokerage mechanisms to coordinate the relationship between the data storage and retrieval, which make sure the data access request can be met. These mechanisms include hash mapping, create index, routing data and query based on certain rules [7].

In [8], the authors proposed a data-centric storage (DCS) concept firstly, then they divided sensor network into multiple child area in [9, 10], each child area includes a storage node, to ease global event storage node load. The geographical hash tables (GHT) [8] is a classic work that uses the data-centric approach. In GHT, one sensor node is chosen as the storage node which not only stores all the data generated but also processes all the queries, so one of the shortcomings in GHT is that it brings a hotspot problem. DBAS [11] and DCAAR [12] hash an event type or an attribute of an event type to a grid region, instead of a point. Rumor routing [13] also uses the data-centric routing approach, events agent and queries all transmit in random direction, if them visit, the data on the event can be retrieved. Comb [14] is an extended algorithm on the rumor routing. Literature [15] proposes using multiple rings working in turn in different time slice to solve the hotspot problem.

All the research mentioned above does not consider the frequencies of event and query when choosing the data storage nodes. Although ODS [16] and SRVR [17] take those factors into consideration, but ODS does not present a load balance scheme and SRVR does not solve the hotspot problem on the rendezvous ring.

3   Improved Ring-Based Model for Big Data Storage and Retrieval

In this section, we present our scheme IRSR, and the main idea of IRSR is as follows.

Firstly, IRSR divides the whole sensor network field into virtual rings and the width of each ring is the communication radius of the sensor nodes. Then, IRSR regards each ring as the rendezvous ring, and calculates the total energy cost of the sensor network one by one ring, respectively. When calculating the total cost, the frequencies of event and query are considered. Finally, the least energy cost ring will be chosen as the final rendezvous ring, and all the nodes on the rendezvous ring will be taken as the storage nodes. In the following, we will show how to choose the rendezvous ring and how store and retrieve data with the rendezvous ring. In addition, when the nodes on the rendezvous ring generate data and query data frequently, we show a data migration algorithm to avoid energy deplete of sensor nodes on the rendezvous ring.

3.1   Choosing the Rendezvous Ring

To store and retrieve the data, each sensor node should know which ring is the rendezvous ring. In order to easy analysis, we give each virtual ring a unique ID. For each node, it first computes the straight-line distance from itself to Sink, and then it can decide which virtual ring it belongs to by simple calculation.

After the sensor nodes were deployed, each sensor node finds their neighbors and stores their locations using some localization techniques. At the beginning, each sensor node stores their data and the queries they received locally for a short time epoch. At the end of this epoch, each sensor node calculates their data generating rates and the query frequencies, and sends them to the Sink node. Then the Sink node calculates the rendezvous ring according to the information received from all the sensor nodes. The main idea of calculating the rendezvous ring is as follows.

1. Calculating the energy consumption sum of generating data and receiving queries and transmitting results of each node;
2. On the basis of the above, calculating the total energy consumption of each ring;
3. Choosing the least energy cost ring as the rendezvous ring.

Finally, the Sink node broadcasts the ID of the rendezvous ring to all the sensor nodes in the sensor network.

3.2 Data Storage

In IRSR, the sensor node that produced data may be or not be in the rendezvous ring. If the node is in the rendezvous ring, it just needs to store its data locally. But if the node is not in the rendezvous ring, the case is more complex. Because at least one copy of each event data should be stored by the nodes in the rendezvous ring, so the node outside the rendezvous ring should route its data to the rendezvous ring first and then stores the data on the rendezvous ring.

How to route the data to the nodes on the rendezvous ring for the sensor nodes outside the rendezvous ring is not too hard to solve. The sensor nodes that are outside the rendezvous ring just need to route their data toward the central point of the network field or any point outside the network field using GPSR routing protocol, and try to make the routing tracks cross the rendezvous ring. When the data cross the rendezvous ring, they must be received by the nodes on the rendezvous ring. Then the data stop being routed and are stored by the nodes on the rendezvous ring.

3.3 Data Retrieval

During the data storage stage, each event data produced by sensor node will have at least one copy stored on the rendezvous ring. In this paper, we pay attention to region-based queries. That is, the consumers are interested in the event data that are generated in special regions.

There are two case existed when executing the query procedure. One case is that the query node is in the rendezvous ring, while the other case is that the query node is outside the rendezvous ring. Because the solution of the latter can also solves the former case, so we only present the query procedure in the latter case. The procedure of data retrieval in IRSR is as follows.

When a sensor node outside the rendezvous ring puts forward a query, this query will be transmitted to its nearest neighbor node close to the direction of rendezvous ring. If the neighbor node has the desired data, it sends the event data back to the consumer. On the contrary, if the node hasn't the data, it will send the query to the next neighbor node. Along this direction, if no one node outside the rendezvous ring has the desired data, the query will be sent to the rendezvous ring at last. After that, the query will be broadcasted on the rendezvous ring. If any sensor node on the rendezvous ring receives the query, it checks its own storage space to see whether it has the data. If the node has the data, it will send the data to the consumer using GPSR routing protocol.

3.4   Data Migration

Data storage strategy showed in Sect. 3.2 distributes the data to store on the multiple nodes of the rendezvous ring, it can balance network load in a certain degree. But in extreme circumstances, the nodes on the rendezvous ring possibly generate data and query frequently in most of the network lifetime. For example, in an observing animal application, many sensors have been deployed in a vast prairie to observe the animals' migration. The animals tend to stay in the area which has rich aquatic plants in a period of time. Until the region's food is not rich, they will migrate to other areas. So in this time of animals stay, the sensors deployed in the region will find that event frequently. That is to say, in the network lifetime, the active ring will be selected to be the rendezvous ring at most of the time, so the nodes' energy in the ring will be easy to exhaust.

SRVR does not consider these extreme circumstances. To solve this problem, the paper improved the data storage mechanism and designed a data migration algorithm. The main idea of data migration algorithm is that, when the node's energy consumption reaches the risk value on the rendezvous ring, data will be migrated to adjacency ring of the rendezvous ring toward the Sink node and the adjacency ring will become new rendezvous ring. Due to the randomness of the event production, when the node energy will exhaust is unpredictable. So IRSR lets the low-energy nodes send an alarm to the Sink node, when the Sink node receives the alarm, it will broadcast this information to all nodes on the rendezvous ring. These nodes begin migrate the newest collected data to its nearest node in the adjacency ring. The procedure is shown in Fig. 1. The replacement of rings will make the data migrate to the Sink node gradually. At last, the data will store on the Sink node. One of the best possible is that, the outermost ring is the most active ring, and which will become the first rendezvous ring. In this case, the rendezvous ring will perform its migration from the outermost ring to the Sink node gradually, which can fully balance the load of all nodes in the network.

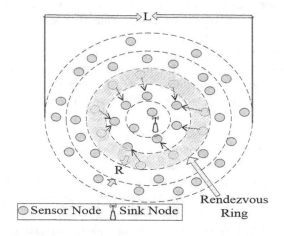

Fig. 1. Example of data migration in IRSR.

In this paper, we are interested in real-time event information in wireless sensor networks. In each migration period, just the newest data will be migrated to the new rendezvous ring, so the amount of the migration data is relatively small and the energy cost is less.

4 Simulation Results and Analysis

In this section, we mainly compare IRSR with ODS and SRVR. ODS and SRVR also take the frequencies of event and query into consideration, but there are some different from IRSR. In ODS, data are stored and retrieved on the optimal storage node rather than the optimal ring. In SRVR, data are stored and retrieved on the optimal ring but the data migration between rings don't mentioned.

Due to limited space, the paper mainly use network lifetime as the metric. We design two groups of experiments and use OMNET ++ [18] as the simulation platform.

In the two groups of experiments, we simulate IRSR, ODS and SRVR for a sensor network with 100,120,140,160,180 and 200 nodes respectively in a 300 m * 300 m square field. All the sensor nodes are deployed in the square field randomly and their caches store their neighbor nodes' location information. Other parameters of the simulation are listed in Table 1.

Table 1. The simulation parameter settings

Parameter	Value
Data generating rate	0 ~ 10 packets/100 s
Query frequency	0 ~ 10 packets/100 s
Size of an event data package	30 bytes
Size of a query package	10 bytes
Energy cost of sending one byte data	0.0144 mJ/byte
Energy cost of receiving one byte data	0.00864 mJ/byte
Radio transmission range	37 m
Initial energy of sensor node	100 mJ
Event data compression ratio	0.5

In the first group of experiment, each node chooses two numbers from range (0, 10) randomly as its event frequency and query frequency, respectively. The simulation results are shown in Fig. 2.

In the second group of experiment, we simulate the condition that data and query generate in one fixed area frequently. In this paper, we set a quarter of the sector of the outermost ring is the high frequency region, the nodes in this region continually choose random numbers as its data production rates and query frequencies in each period of time. The simulation results are shown in Fig. 3.

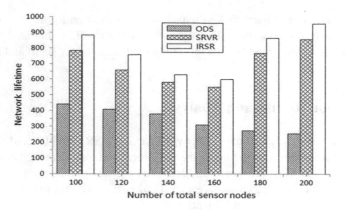

Fig. 2. Simulation results of network lifetime in random

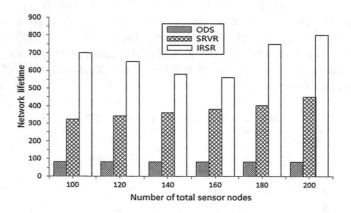

Fig. 3. Simulation results of network lifetime in extreme

From the Fig. 2 we can see that IRSR and SRVR have much longer lifetime than ODS. Figure 2 also shows that the lifetime of the sensor network in IRSR and SRVR does not change in a regular way as the number of sensor nodes increases. This is because IRSR and SRVR store and retrieve data on the optimal ring which can balance the load of the sensor nodes much better than ODS. In addition, the two figures show that IRSR performs much better than SRVR, especially in extreme condition. It is mainly because that IRSR considered the hotspot problem of the rendezvous ring and used data migration to realize the balance of the whole network.

5   Conclusions

In this paper, we propose an improved ring-based model which is named IRSR to realize the big data storage and retrieval in wireless sensor networks. In IRSR, two important factors are considered when choosing the storage nodes. One is the frequencies of event and query; other is the hotspot problem of the rendezvous ring. To reduce transmission cost, IRSR divides the network into some rings and uses the optimal ring as the rendez-vous ring. Meanwhile, IRSR uses a data migration algorithm to balance the load of nodes in the wireless network. Simulation results show that IRSR can more efficiently prolong the lifetime of the sensor network not only in random condition but also in extreme condition.

References

1. Jennifer, Y., Biswanath, M., Dipak, G.: Wireless sensor network survey. Int. J. Comput. Telecommun. Networking **52**(12), 2292–2330 (2008)
2. Chong, C.Y., Kumar, S.P.: Sensor networks: evolution, opportunities and challenges. In: Proceeding of the IEEE, pp. 1247–1256 (2003)
3. Elson, J., Estrin, D.: Wireless sensor networks: an bridge to the physical world. In: Raghavendra, C.S., Sivalingam, K.M., Znati, T. (eds.) Wireless Sensor Networks, pp. 3–20. Springer, Heidelberg (2004)
4. Yu, Z., Zhou, S., Guan, J.: Data storage and access in wireless sensor networks: a survey. Acta Electronica Sin. **36**(10), 2001–2010 (2008)
5. Intanagonwiwat, C., Govindan, R., Estrin, D., Heidemann, J.S., Silva, F.: Directed diffusion for wireless sensor networking. IEEE/ACM Trans. Networking **11**(1), 2–16 (2003)
6. Ganesan, D., Greenstein, B., Estrin, D., Heidemann, J., Govindan, R.: Multi-resolution storage and search in sensor networks. ACM Trans. Storage **1**(3), 277–315 (2005)
7. Shenker, S., Ratnasamy, S., Karp, B., Govindan, R., Estrin, D.: Data-centric storage in sensor nets. ACM SIGCOMM Comput. Commun. Rev. **33**(1), 137–142 (2003)
8. Sylvia, R., Brad, K., Scott, S., et al.: Data-centric storage in sensornets with GHT, a geographic hash table. Mobile Netw. Appl. **8**(4), 427–442 (2003)
9. Scott, S., Sylvia, R., Brad, K., et al.: Data-centric storage in sensornets. ACM SIGCOMM Comput. Commun. Rev. **33**(1), 137–142 (2003)
10. Abhishek, G., Jens, G., Resilient, C.J.: Data-centric storage in wireless ad-hoc sensor networks. In: Proceedings of the 4th International Conference on Mobile Data Management, London, pp. 45–62 (2003)
11. Yongxuan, L., Hong, C., Yufeng, W.: Dynamic balanced storage in wireless sensor networks. In: Proceedings of the 4th Workshop on Data Management for Sensor Networks (2007)
12. Ratnabali, B., Kaushik, C., Agrawa, P.: Attribute allocation and retrieval scheme for large-scale sensor networks. Int. J. Wirel. Inf. Netw. **13**(4), 303–315 (2006)
13. Braginsky, D., Estrin, D.: Rumor routing algorithm for sensor networks. In: Proceedings of the 1st Workshop on Sensor Networks and Applications (2002)
14. Liu, X., Huang, Q., Zhang, Y.: Combs, needles, haystacks: balancing push and pull for discovery in large scale sensor networks. In: Proceeding of the 2nd ACM Conference on Embedded Networked Sensor Systems, pp. 122–133 (2004)
15. Li, G.L., Gao, H.: A load balance data storage method based on ring for sensor networks. J. Softw. **18**(5), 1173–1185 (2007)
16. Zhaochun, Y., Bin, X., Shuigeng, Z.: Achieving optimal data storage position in wireless sensor networks. Comput. Commun. **33**(1), 92–102 (2009)
17. Chen, H.L., Ma, X.P.: Adaptive information brokerage in wireless sensor networks with virtual rings. Appl. Mech. Mater. **687–691**, 3044–3047 (2014)
18. Objective Modular Network Testbed in C ++. https://omnetpp.org/

Detection of Malicious Executables Using Static and Dynamic Features of Portable Executable (PE) File

Saba Awan[✉] and Nazar Abbas Saqib

College of Electrical and Mechanical Engineering, National University
of Sciences and Technology (NUST), Islamabad 44000, Pakistan
sabaawan90@gmail.com, nazar.abbas@ceme.nust.edu.pk

Abstract. Malware continues to evolve despite intense use of antimalware techniques. Detecting malware becomes a tough task as malware attackers adapt different counter detection methods. The long forgotten signature method used by many antimalware companies has become inefficient due to different new and unknown malwares. This paper presents an effective classification method that integrates static and dynamic features of a binary executable and classifies data using machine learning algorithms. The method initially gathers static features by exploring binary code of an executable which includes PE header Information and Printable Strings. After executing binary file in a sandbox environment, it gathers dynamic features i.e. API call logs. The integrated feature vector is then analyzed and classified using classification algorithms. In this work, we also present a comparison of the performance of four classifiers i.e. SVM, Naïve Bayes, J48 and Random Forest. Based on the classification results, we deduce that Random Forest performs best with an accuracy of 97.2 %.

Keywords: Malware detection · Static features · Dynamic features · Machine learning · Portable executable

1 Introduction

Malware, a short term used for Malicious Software, is a sequence of instructions intended to perform harmful activities on a system. Growth in malware production becomes a major challenge for the security companies to detect them. Traditionally, security companies and Antivirus vendors rely on antivirus tools to differentiate between malware and clean files [1]. Majority of these tools used signature based approach to detect malicious programs by comparing them with the known malware signatures stored in a database. Signature is a particular identification of an executable file. Static, Dynamic and Hybrid techniques can be used to create a signature and store in the signature databases. These signatures need a frequent update due to an increase in the production of new malware samples every day. Therefore it becomes ineffective in detecting new malware samples, which is a drawback of this technique. In static analysis approach, features are extracted by exploring binary code of the programs and creating models from it which describes them. These models are used to differentiate between malware and benign files. Although static analysis approach gives very

© Springer International Publishing AG 2016
G. Wang et al. (Eds.): SpaCCS 2016 Workshops, LNCS 10067, pp. 48–58, 2016.
DOI: 10.1007/978-3-319-49145-5_6

valuable information about the behavior of programs, functions and parameters used in it but this method can be evaded easily, as malware writers use various code obfuscation techniques, metamorphic and polymorphic methods [2]. To overcome these techniques, malware researchers introduced a second method, which is dynamic analysis that executes the program in a secure environment in order to depict its behavior [3]. Code obfuscation techniques used by the malware writers fail during dynamic analysis. But this analysis needs to be done in a safe environment to prevent any damage to the system. This process is time consuming but it is effective in case of packed files. Although virtual (safe) environment is quite different from the actual environment, possibility is that malware can behave differently which leads to inaccurate log of the behavior [4].

Both methods (static and dynamic) have their own benefits and drawbacks. A combination of these methods can prove to be more robust and reliable approach in malware detection. Therefore in this work we proposed an integrated approach to use both the static and dynamic features of a PE file to perform malware detection.

Rest of the paper is organized as follows: Sect. 2 gives the literature review of the work, Sect. 3 presents the proposed methodology, Sect. 4 presents the integrated feature approach, Sect. 5 gives the experimental results and Sect. 6 concludes the paper and describes the future work.

2 Literature Review

This section presents an overview of the techniques proposed so far. Traditionally, there are two major techniques used i.e. Static Analysis and Dynamic Analysis.

Schultz et al. [5] proposed a method to detect new malicious executables by using machine learning techniques. They extracted three unique static features: Portable Executable, byte sequences and printable strings to classify the malware. They used a collection of 4266 files. Naive Bayes algorithm was used as the classification and taking string as an input data, it showed an accuracy of 97.11 %. Usukhbayar et al. [6] presented a framework, combining three static features: PE header information, DLLs and API function calls within DLLs and used data mining techniques such as information gain to select the subset of features. They used three classification algorithms i.e. SVM, Naïve Bayes and J48. As a result, J48 performed better giving highest accuracy of 98 %. In Tzu-Yen Wang et al. [7] made use of the information present in the PE headers. They collected a total of 9771 programs. Their dataset comprised of viruses, Trojans, email worms and backdoors. An accuracy of 97.19 %, 93.96 %, 84.11 % and 89.54 % were achieved for viruses, email worms, Trojans and backdoors. It clearly shows that the detection rates of viruses and email worms were quite high.

After the static feature extraction technique, malware researchers moved towards the dynamic malware analysis. In [8] Tian et al. extracted dynamic features (API call sequences) of an executable file while running it in a virtual environment. Weka classifiers were used to distinguish between clean and malware as well as assigning malware family to which it belongs, once it is detected. The dataset consisted of 1824 executables and they gained 97 % accuracy. Wangener et al. [9] also proposed a dynamic analysis method to detect malware. They used a small set of almost 104 files and used the similarity matrices of dynamic extraction technologies. As a result, they were able to achieve an accuracy of 93 %, which means 7 % files were wrongly classified. Santos et al. [10] proposed a hybrid approach in which they used both the static and dynamic features of an executable file. Their methodology was based on semi supervise learning approach, which means half of the training data was labelled and half was unlabeled and they achieved 88 % accuracy.

In light of this background, we propose a novel hybrid approach (integration of static and dynamic features) for malware detection. Three features are used: Printable Strings and PE Header information as static features and API call sequences (functions and its parameters) as dynamic features. Each feature integrated in our work performed better in the previous works separately. Accuracy achieved by these features individually, revealed that they can be combined to form a single classification method to improve the detection rate.

Introduction of the Selected Classification Algorithms. Many classification algorithms have been introduced with the aid of learning algorithms such as SVM, Decision Tree, KNN, Naïve Bayes (NB) and Random Forest. These classifiers are learning methods and follow certain set of rules. Support Vector Machine (SVM) is a powerful, state-of-the-art algorithm with strong theoretical foundations based on Vapnik's theory [15]. SVM is widely used due to its accuracy in various applications such as image classification, hand written characters.

Random Forest is a classifier, consists of a group of decision trees which predicts an output value. The decision trees are created using random sub samples of the training dataset [17]. Every decision tree acts as a classifier and input vector is passed through each tree in the forest. Each decision tree votes for the class. Final output is generated on the basis of the higher votes given by a tree above all the other trees in the forest.

Naïve Bayesian classifier is based on the Bayesian probabilistic rule. It does not use any iterative methods to reach the final output, which makes it more suitable on large datasets. In this, each class is associated with a probability and all the class attributes are considered independent that means presence or absence of an attribute does not affect any other attribute [16].

Basically J48 classifier implements C4.5 algorithm, it builds decision trees from the provided training data using the idea of information gain. It is based on the concept that each feature in the class is used to make a decision by dividing the data into smaller subsets. It calculates the information gain of each attribute and attribute with the highest information gain is selected for the splitting of data.

These four classification algorithms are chosen due to the above literature review. As in the past, these classifiers have performed better in malware analysis.

3 Proposed Methodology

This section describes the proposed methodology in detail. Figure 1 gives an architecture overview of the proposed methodology. The system initially disassembles executables and performs the static analysis by extracting static features from the executables (PE). These features i.e. PE header information and Printable Strings are then analyzed and classified using four different classifiers.

The executables are then executed in a virtual environment to analyze the behavior of file and API call logs of each file are stored. After extraction of both the static and dynamic features, these features are integrated. The integrated feature set serve as an input to the machine learning classifiers in order to detect files as malware or benign.

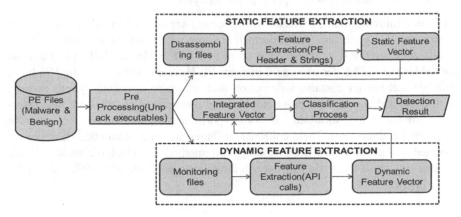

Fig. 1. Architecture of our proposed methodology

3.1 Dataset

Portable Executable (PE) is a general file format for all variants of Windows Operation System. In present years Researchers have reported that PE files are most vulnerable to malware attacks. A collection of 1600 random malware samples are taken from Virus Share community (www.VirusShare.com) [12]. This website contains millions of malware dataset for malware analysts. Our dataset ranges from a period of 9 years (2007–2016) and consists of virus, trojans and worms. Table 1 presents executables used in the experiment. Clean files are collected from System32 directories of Windows XP and Windows 7 (600 samples).

Table 1. Malicious executables used in the experiment

Family		# of Samples
Virus	Emerleox	210
	Agobot	156
	Looked	131
Trojans	Banker	269
	Bancos	331
	Alureon	256
Worms	Frethog	132
	Autorun	115
Clean files		**600**
Total		**2200**

3.2 Static Feature Extraction and Static Analysis

After disassembling the files using IDA Pro (Interactive Disassembler) the required static features are extracted and thus the gathered data was passed onto the classification method as explained in Fig. 1. The sections below describe how these features are represented and integrated to perform the analysis.

PE Header Information. PE Header is the second segment of PE file format. It is a data structure that gives important information about a PE (portable executable) file. It contains three sections: a magic code (4 bytes), COFF Header (20 bytes) and an Optional Header (224 bytes). Figure 2 presents PE Header structure. The first 96 bytes of the optional header contains information such as major operating system version, size of code, address of entry point etc., and the remaining 128 bytes are data directories, providing the locations of the export, import, resource, and alternate import-binding directories. These collected attributes are great in number, therefore we performed feature selection (information gain) method to select the most relevant attributes and avoid the irrelevant ones. Information gain method is described in the section below.

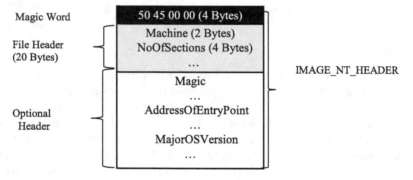

Fig. 2. Structure of PE header

Information Gain Method. Information Gain method is the most common and popular feature selection methods used in machine learning [14]. The Information Gain of feature t_k over the class c_i is the reduction in uncertainty about value of c_i when the value of t_k is known. The Information Gain of the feature t_k over the class c_i can be calculated as:

$$\text{IG} \left(t_k, c_i\right) = \sum_{cE\{c_i, \bar{c}i\}} \sum_{tE\{t_i, \bar{t}i\}} P(t, c) \log \frac{P(t, c)}{P(t)P(c)}$$

Where

$P(c)$ is the fraction of the documents in category c over the total number of documents

$P(t, c)$ is the fraction of documents in the category c that contain the word t over the total number of documents. $P(t)$ is the fraction of the documents containing term t over total number of documents.

Higher the Information Gain (IG) of an attribute, the more useful feature it is in the discrimination of the classes and the attributes with lower information gain was removed. List of PE attributes are given in Table 2, selected through information gain method.

Table 2. Top PE header features selected through feature selection algorithm

	PE Header Attributes		
1	Magic	16	CheckSum
2	SizeOfInitializedData	17	Subsystem
3	SizeOfUninitializedData	18	NumberOfRvaAndSizes
4	NumberOfSections	19	SizeOfRawData
5	NumberOfSymbols	20	FileAlignment
6	DLLCharacteristics	21	MajorOperatingSystemVersion
7	SizeOfOptionalHeader	22	MinorOperatingSystemVersion
8	ImportAdressTableSize	23	MajorImageVersion
9	MajorLinkerVersion	24	MinorImageVersion
10	SizeOfCode	25	SizeOfStackReserve
11	AddressOfEntryPoint	26	LoaderFlags
12	ImageBase	27	NumberOfRelocations
13	SectionAlignment	28	DataDirectory
14	SizeOfImage	29	BaseOfCode
15	SizeOfHeaders	30	BaseOfData

Printable Strings. Printable strings are the un-ciphered strings inside the executable files code and can be extracted by doing the static analysis. These strings contain Comments, URLs, API references and more [5]. Strings prove to be a valuable feature in distinguishing malware and benign files in the past. Malware writers can insert many garbage strings to evade the detection techniques. Therefore every string is not meaningful and used in the classification process. In order to prevent such strings we set the frequency threshold value of the extracted strings. The strings below the frequency threshold are eliminated. After preprocessing of the extracted strings, a global list is created known as global feature list.

Suppose that the global feature list **G** contains n number of strings such that:-

$$G = \{s_1, s_2, s_3 \ldots \ldots \ldots \ldots , s_n\} \qquad (1)$$

$\{s_1, s_2, s_3 \ldots \ldots \ldots \ldots , s_n\}$ is the ordered set of strings present in the executables of training set. Then any executable E_j is monitored to search for string s_j.

$$s_j = \begin{cases} 1, & s_j \text{ is present} \\ 0, & \text{otherwise} \end{cases} \qquad (2)$$

To better understand the process, look at the following example. The global list G contains these 6 strings {*QueryPerformanceCounter, GetTickCount, GetCurrentProcessId, TerminateProcess, GetCurrentProcess, Get OEMCP*} then the binary feature vector of an executable $e_j = \{1, 1, 0, 0, 1, 1\}$ means that the strings *QueryPerformanceCounter, GetTickCount, GetCurrentProcess, Get OEMCP* are present while *GetCurrentProcessId, Terminate Process* are not. Table 3 gives a list of printable strings in a PE file as an example to explain Printable String feature vector.

3.3 Dynamic Feature Extraction and Dynamic Analysis

Dynamic analysis is done by executing the program in a virtual environment to notify its behavior. For dynamic analysis, we have extracted API call sequences.

Application Programing Interface (API) provided by the Operating System to approach low level hardware by system calls for application programs. These APIs are also used by malware authors to perform malicious interruptions [10]. Therefore, in our approach, after running files and recording log files of Windows API, we then extract the API features which include API functions and API parameters. Both of them are treated as unique entities because they can affect separately in malware detection. We also created a global list **G** of API features such that:-

$$G = \{p_1, p_2, p_3 \ldots \ldots \ldots \ldots , p_n\} \qquad (3)$$

Where

$\{p_1, p_2, p_3 \ldots \ldots \ldots \ldots , p_n\}$ is the set of API features present in the executables of training set. Then any executable e_j is monitored to search for API feature p_j.

$$p_j = \begin{cases} 1, & p_j \text{ is present} \\ 0, & \text{otherwise} \end{cases} \qquad (4)$$

To better understand the process, look at the following example. The global list **G** contains these 6 API functions {*NtOpenfile, NtQueryInformationFile, LdrGet DllHandle, RegEnumValueW, NtReadVirtualMemory, RegQueryValueExW*} then the binary feature vector of an executable $e_j = \{1, 1, 0, 2, 0, 1\}$ means that the API features *NtOpenfile, NtQueryInformationFile, RegEnumValueW, RegQueryValueExW* are present while *LdrGetDllHandle, NtReadVirtualMemory* are not.

Table 4 shows a list of API calls (API functions and parameters) in a PE file as an example to explain the dynamic feature vector. We used Cuckoo malware analyzer [11] as a virtual environment which is a very well accepted tool in analyzing malicious files.

Table 3. Example of a string feature vector

Printable strings	
Total Strings	**5**
QueryPerformanceCounter	1
GetTickCount	1
GetCurrentProcessId	0
Terminate Process	0
GetCurrentProcess	1
GetOEMCP	1

Table 4. Example of API feature vector

API List	Frequency
NtOpenfile	1
NtQueryInformationFile	1
LdrGetDllHandle	0
RegEnumValueW	2
NtReadVirtualMemory	0
RegQueryValueExW	1

4   Integrated Feature Approach

In this section, the static and dynamic features extracted separately are now integrated. Table 4 displays representation of integrated feature vector. The reason behind integrating both the features (static and dynamic) is to avoid malware authors to evade antivirus techniques by making it more powerful and effective. Antivirus techniques detecting a malware through change in the PE Header attributes, a malware writer can prevent it by adding real values to the attributes in PE Header Information. Antivirus technique analyzing an executable through Printable Strings feature can easily be avoided by adding irrelevant strings thus making it difficult to get detected. In a similar way, a malware detection based on API call feature can be prevented by inserting unusable functionalities. But changes in these three features is impractical and results in an outlier thus making file easy to detect. Table 5 displays representation of an integrated feature vector.

Table 5. Integrated feature vector representation

Integrated Feature Vector		
SizeOfInitializedData	491	PE Header
SizeOfUninitializedData	0	
.		
.		
Total Strings	5	Printable Strings
QueryPerformanceCounter	1	
GetTickCount	1	
.		
.		
NtOpenfile	1	API Calls
NtQueryInformationFile	1	

5   Results and Discussion

In this work, we examine the malware detection rate on the basis of four classifiers from the Weka [13] i.e. SVM, Random Forest, J48 and Naïve Bayes. Our feature vectors serve as an input to the classifiers. We have used K (K = 10) fold cross validation method to test the accuracy of our system, which is a well-known and quite popular method in a number of fields including malware analysis. According to K (K = 10) fold cross validation method, it divides the complete dataset into 10 smaller subsets, where 9 subsets are used for the training of classifier and 1 subset used for testing purpose. Table 6 presents an accuracy of the three features and the integrated feature approach. As we can see in Table 6, the integrated feature approach has better accuracy as compared to the individual static and dynamic analysis. Figure 3 shows a comparison of these features.

Table 6. Classification results of three features and the integrated method

Features	Naïve Bayes (NB)	SVM	J48	Random Forest (RF)
PE header	84.5	83.4	78.7	86.8
Strings	85.3	86.5	84.38	87.9
API calls	88.9	88.5	89.7	91.3
Integrated method	94.6	95.3	92.1	**97.2**

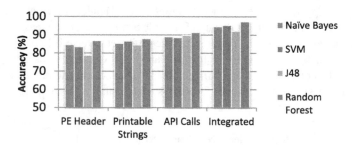

Fig. 3. Accuracy comparison of the features with every classifier

5.1   Performance Comparison with the Existing Research

In this section, we have done a performance comparison of our proposed methodology with some research work carried out in the recent years and attaining an accuracy of more than 85 % as one of our major target was to achieve higher accuracy. Table 7 displays the comparison.

In Tian et al. [8] proposed a static method by using Printable Strings information as a feature for detecting malicious executables. They performed the experiment on a total of 1367 samples and attained an accuracy of 97 %. Schultz et al. [5] presented a static analysis method to discriminate malware and benign files and they were the first one to use data mining techniques for the classification of dataset. The researches carried out in future are an extension of it. Kasama et al. [20] detected malware using dynamic analysis with a target to achieve very low False Positive (FP) rate. There system was able to detect 67 % malware with a 1 % False Positive Rate (FPR). They used 5697 malware and 819 clean files to carry out the research. Islam et al. [18] proposed a hybrid approach to detect malware. They used Function Length Frequency and Printable Strings as static features and API calls as dynamic features of an executable. In their work, they integrated both types of analysis and used 2939 total executable to perform the experiment.

While some of the research works mentioned in the Table 6, achieve nearly equal accuracy as our methodology, we argue that our dataset is taken from a lengthy time period (10 years) and includes malware, which has the ability to obfuscate and evade detection. The proposed methodology also use a hybrid approach to deal with the evolving malware whereas in the past, researchers used only a single feature of an executable for malware detection. If, in case, malware authors obfuscate that single feature, the malware will evade detection. In this way, our current method is robust towards zero day malware attacks.

Table 7. Performance comparison with the existing techniquea

Authors	Samples	Accuracy	Features extracted
Tian et al. (2009) [8]	1367	97 %	Printable strings
Schultz et al. (2001) [5]	4266	97.1 %	Strings
Kasama et al. (2012) [20]	6516	67 %	Behavioral patterns
Islam et al. (2013) [18]	2939	97.05 %	Hybrid (FLF, PSI, API)
Santos et al. (2011) [10]	2000	88 %	Integrated (n-grams, opcodes)
Our proposed method	2200	97.2 %	Hybrid (PE header, PSI and API calls)

6 Conclusion and Future Works

This paper presents a technique to deal with the zero day malware attacks. The proposed methodology combines three different PE file features i.e. PE Header attributes, Printable Strings and API call logs to detect and classify executable into malware and benign. These features are then classified using machine learning algorithms. Results in Sect. 4 with Table 5 shows that Random Forest performs best on our data. From the results we can also deduce that J48 performed worst. Integration of static and dynamic features is a novel approach and improves the accuracy along with the decrease in false positive rate. Feature selection algorithms can be performed to minimize features without affecting the performance.

As a future work, we consider to extract many other valuable static and dynamic features and decrease the number of irrelevant features to enhance the classification accuracy and minimize the time. In addition, we would also like to extend our methodology to perform clustering of malware families.

References

1. Stallings, W.: Cryptography and Network Security Principles and Practices, 4th edn. Prentice Hall, Upper Saddle River (2005)
2. Moser, A., Kruegel, C., Kirda, E.: Limits of static analysis for malware detection. In: Computer Security Applications Conference, ACSAC 2007, pp. 421–430, December 2007
3. Gurrutxaga, I., Arbelaitz, O., Ma Perez, J., Muguerza, J., Martin, J.I., Perona, I.: Evaluation of malware clustering based on its dynamic behavior. In: Roddick, J.F., Li, J., Christen, P., Kennedy, P.J. (eds.) Seventh Australasian data mining conference (AusDM 2008), Glenelg, South Australia, ACS 2008, pp. 163–70 (2008)
4. Egele, M., Scholte, T., Kirda, E., Kruegel, C.: A survey on automated dynamic malware-analysis techniques and tools. ACM Comput. Surv. **44**, 6:1–6:42 (2008)
5. Schultz, M., Eskin, E., Zadok, F., Stolfo, S.: Data mining methods for detection of new malicious executables. In: Proceedings of 2001 IEEE Symposium on Security and Privacy, Oakland, 14–16 May 2001, pp. 38–49 (2001)
6. Baldangombo, U., Jambaljav, N., Horng, S.-J.: A static malware detection system using data mining methods. Int. J. Artif. Intell. Appl. (IJAIA) **4**(4), 113–126 (2013)
7. Wang, T.-Y., Wu, C.-H., Hsieh, C.-C.: Detecting unknown malicious executables using portable executable headers. In: NCM, Fifth International Joint Conference on INC, IMS and IDC, pp. 278–284 (2009)
8. Tian, R., Islam, R., Batten, L., Versteeg, S.: Differentiating malware from cleanware using behavioural analysis. In: Proceedings of the 5th International Conference on Malicious and Unwanted Software: MALWARE 2010, pp. 23–30 (2010). Wagener, G., State, R., Dulaunoy, A.: Malware behaviour analysis. J. Comput. Virol. **4**(4), 279–287 (2008)
9. Wang, C., Pang, J., Zhao, R., Liu, X.: Using API sequence and Bayes algorithm to detect suspicious behavior. In: International Conference on Communication Software and Networks, pp. 544–548 (2009)
10. Santos, I., Nieves, J., Bringas, P.G.: Semi-supervised learning for unknown malware detection. In: Abraham, A., Corchado, J.M., González, S.R., De Paz Santana, J.F. (eds.) International Symposium on DCAI. AISC, vol. 91, pp. 415–422. Springer, Heidelberg (2011)
11. The Cuckoo sandbox. http://www.cuckoosandbox.org/
12. VirusShare Malware dataset. http://virusshare.com/
13. Weka 3: Data Mining open source Software. www.cs.waikato.ac.nz/ml/weka/
14. Han, J., Kamber, M.: Data Mining: Concepts and Techniques. The Morgan Kaufmann, San Francisco (2006)
15. Vapnik, V.N.: An overview of statistical learning theory. IEEE Trans. Neural Netw. **10**(5), 988–999 (1999)
16. Langley, P., Iba, W., Thompson, K.: An analysis of Bayesian classifiers. In: Proceedings of the Tenth National Conference on Artificial Intelligence, pp. 223–228. MIT Press (1992)
17. Breiman, L.: Random forests. Mach. Learn. **45**(1), 5–32 (2001)
18. Islam, R., Tian, R., Batten, L.M., Versteeg, S.: Classification of malware based on integrated static and dynamic features. J. Netw. Comput. Appl. **36**(2013), 646–656 (2013)
19. Zhao, H., Xu, M., Zheng, N., Yao, J., Ho, Q.: Malicious executables classification based on behavioral factor analysis. In: International Conference on e- Education, e-Business, e-Management and e-Learning, pp. 502–506 (2010)
20. Kasama, T., Yoshioka, K., Inoue, D., Matsumoto, T.: Malware detection method by catching their random behavior in multiple executions. In: 2012 IEEE/IPSJ 12th International Symposium on Applications and the Internet (SAINT), pp. 262–266 (2012)

Entropy Feature Based on 2D Gabor Wavelets for JPEG Steganalysis

Xiaofeng Song[✉], Zhiyuan Li, Liju Chen, and Jiong Liu

Xi'an Communication Institute, Xi'an 710106, China
xiaofengsong@sina.com

Abstract. To improve the detection accuracy for adaptive JPEG steganography which constrains embedding changes to image texture regions difficult to model, a new steganalysis feature based on the Shannon entropy of 2-dimensional (2D) Gabor wavelets is proposed. For the proposed feature extraction method, the 2D Gabor wavelets which have certain optimal joint localization properties in spatial domain and in the spatial frequency are employed to capture the image texture characteristics, and then the Shannon entropy values of image filtering coefficients are used as steganalysis feature. First, the decompressed JPEG image is filtered by 2D Gabor wavelets with different scale and orientation parameters. Second, the entropy features are extracted from all the filtered images and then they are merged according to symmetry. Last, the ensemble classifier trained by entropy features is used as the final steganalyzer. The experimental results show that the proposed feature can achieve a competitive performance by comparing with the state-of-the-art steganalysis features for the latest adaptive JPEG steganography algorithms.

Keywords: Gabor wavelets · Entropy · JPEG steganography · Steganalysis

1 Introduction

Wavelet entropy is widely used for the analysis of transient features of non-stationary signals. For image processing such as image segmentation, image classification and so on, the wavelet entropy is often utilized to characterize the image texture feature. In this paper, the attentions are paid to the application of wavelet entropy for image steganography and steganalysis. Image Steganography is an art of hiding communication by embedding secret messages into innocuous-looking cover image [1]. Compared with the typical encrypted communications which convert the messages to obscure ciphertext, image steganography conceals the ongoing communications. Therefore, it is rather deceptive and enables people to exchange their important information conveniently. The countermeasure against steganography technology is steganalysis [2] which focuses on detecting the presence of the secret messages according to the statistical image features and can even realize the extraction of the embedded messages. Currently, JPEG is one of the most popular image formats on the Internet, so the steganography and steganalysis technology about JPEG image are attracting more and more attentions. Here, we mainly focus on the steganalysis of the latest adaptive JPEG steganography based on the Shannon entropy [2] of JPEG image decomposition coefficients.

© Springer International Publishing AG 2016
G. Wang et al. (Eds.): SpaCCS 2016 Workshops, LNCS 10067, pp. 59–72, 2016.
DOI: 10.1007/978-3-319-49145-5_7

As we know, the steganography algorithms for JPEG image can be divided into non-adaptive steganography and adaptive steganography. The latter include PQt (texture-adaptive PQ), PQe (energy-adaptive PQ), MOD (Model Optimized Distortion) [3], EBS (Entropy Block Steganography) [4], UED (Uniform Embedding Distortion) [5], J-UNIWARD (JPEG UNIversal WAvelet Relative Distortion) [6], SI-UNIWARD (Side-informed UNIWARD) [6] and so on. For the above adaptive JPEG steganography algorithms, the steganographic schemes are similar. They all define an embedding distortion function related with the statistical undetectability firstly and then the messages are embedded by special encoding methods. For example, as to PQt and PQe, the embedding distortion function is defined according to the texture and energy measure of 8×8 DCT block respectively and then the given messages are embedded by wet paper code [7]; as to MOD, UED, EBS, J-UNIWARD and SI-UNIWARD, the different embedding distortion functions are defined respectively and then the messages are embedded while the embedding distortion function is minimized by Syndrome-Trellis Codes (STCs) [8]. For adaptive JPEG steganography algorithms constrain the embedding changes to the complex image regions, they can achieve better statistical undetectability and the traditional steganalysis methods [9, 10] can not achieve good detection performances.

With the continuous emergence of the adaptive JPEG steganography algorithms, the corresponding steganalysis methods are also being proposed in recent years. For most of these steganalysis methods, the detection performance of steganalysis is realized by statistical image feature and classifier. In literature [11], the interblock co-occurrences feature beyond the optimized model is proposed for MOD steganography whose distortion function optimized to maximize security is overtrained to an incomplete cover model. In literature [12], the enhanced histogram feature extracted from the possible embedding changes positions is proposed to improve the detection performance for PQt and PQe. In literature [13], the JRM (JPEG Rich Model) feature is proposed to capture the embedding changes to DCT coefficients more comprehensively. In literature [14], the PSRM (Projection Spatial Rich Model) feature is proposed by projecting neighboring residual samples onto a set of random vectors, The PSRM feature takes the histogram of the projections as the feature instead of forming the co-occurrence matrix to reduce the feature dimensionality and improve the detection accuracy. In literature [15], the DCTR (Discrete Cosine Transform Residual) feature which utilizes 64 kernels of the discrete cosine transform is proposed by extracting the first-order statistics of quantized noise residuals obtained through convoluting the decompressed JPEG image with DCT kernels. The DCTR feature can achieve better detection performance while preserve relatively low feature dimensionality. In literature [16], the PHARM (Phase-Aware Projection Model) feature is proposed by utilizing the JPEG image pixel residuals and their phase w.r.t. the 8×8 grid. The PHARM feature can get better detection accuracy than DCTR for adaptive JPEG steganography. In addition, in literature [12–16], the final detection accuracies are all obtained by ensemble classifier [17] after feature extraction.

From the above steganalysis methods, it can be seen that these methods mainly depend on more effective feature to improve the detection performance for adaptive

JPEG steganography. However, as we know, the current JPEG steganalysis methods do not consider capturing the changes of image texture feature caused by steganography embedding when the steganalysis feature is extracted. In fact, adaptive JPEG steganography often constrains the embedding changes to the complex texture regions. Therefore, for the steganalyzer, if the image texture can be represented more accurately, then the statistical features extracted from the rich image representations can capture the embedding changes more effectively and the detection performance may be improved. So, in this paper, a new steganalysis feature is proposed based on the entropy value of image filtering coefficients obtained by 2D Gabor wavelets decomposition [18]. In contrast to DCTR feature [15] which utilizes 64 DCT kernels for image filtering, the 2D Gabor wavelets can capture the embedding changes from more scales and orientations. In addition, the entropy value of image filtering coefficients obtained by 2D Gabor wavelets is a common statistical feature for image texture [19], so the steganalysis feature extracted using the entropy of 2D Gabor wavelets may be more effective for the detection performance of adaptive JPEG steganography.

2   Principle of Adaptive JPEG Steganography

The minimal distortion adaptive JPEG steganography [20] embeds the given messages while minimizing a heuristically defined embedding distortion function which must be related to statistical undetectability. The embedding process can be realized using syndrome-coding algorithms, such as the STCs. The latest JPEG steganography algorithms such as UED, EBS and J-UNIWARD all follow the minimal distortion embedding framework.

Let $\mathbf{x} = (x_1, x_2, \cdots, x_n)$ be a cover image and x_i specifies the i th cover element (DCT coefficient). The message is binary bit stream and the corresponding stego image is denoted as $\mathbf{y} = (y_1, y_2, \cdots, y_n)$. According to the embedding operation for cover elements, the adaptive JPEG steganography includes binary embedding, ternary embedding and so on. Furthermore, the embedding distortion of stego image $\mathbf{y}$ is denoted as $D(\mathbf{y})$ and $\pi(\mathbf{y})$ specifies the probability of $\mathbf{x}$ be modified into $\mathbf{y}$. Then, the expected distortion can be expressed as:

$$E_\pi[D] = \sum_{\mathbf{y} \in \mathbf{Y}} \pi(\mathbf{y})D(\mathbf{y}) \tag{1}$$

where $\mathbf{Y}$ denotes the set of all stego images into which $\mathbf{x}$ can be modified.

The minimal distortion adaptive steganography expects to embed a given payload of m bits with minimal possible distortion. The problem is to determine a distribution π that communicates a required payload while minimizing the distortion [20]:

$$\underset{\pi}{\text{minimize}} \quad E_\pi[D] = \sum_{\mathbf{y} \in \Upsilon} \pi(\mathbf{y})D(\mathbf{y}) \tag{2}$$

$$\text{subject to } H(\pi) = m \tag{3}$$

where $H(\pi) = - \sum_{y \in \Upsilon} \pi(\mathbf{y}) \log \pi(\mathbf{y})$ specifies the entropy of the distribution $\pi(\mathbf{y})$.

When the embedding distortion function $D(y)$ is additive over the cover elements, the distortion caused by embedding changes can be expressed as:

$$D(y) = \sum_{i=1}^{n} \rho_i(y_i) \qquad (4)$$

where $0 \leq \rho_i(y_i) \leq \infty$ specifies the distortion caused by modifying cover element x_i into stego element y_i. In this case, the embedding changes do not interact and the probability π can be factorized into a product of marginal probabilities of changing the individual cover element.

$$\pi_\lambda(\mathbf{y}) = \prod_{i=1}^{n} \pi_\lambda(y_i) = \prod_{i=1}^{n} \frac{\exp(-\lambda \rho_i(y_i))}{\sum_{y_i \in I_i} \exp(-\lambda \rho_i(y_i))} \qquad (5)$$

where $\pi_\lambda(y_i)$ specifies the probability of x_i be modified into y_i.

In Eq. (5), $I_i = \{x_i, \bar{x}_i\}$ for binary embedding and the bar denotes the operation of flipping the LSB (Least Significant Bit) of cover element, $I_i = \{x_i - 1, x, x_i + 1\}$ for ternary embedding.

From all above, it can be seen that the adaptive JPEG steganography by minimizing embedding distortion should includes embedding distortion function definition and coding methods. The former mainly pay attention to measure the distortion caused by embedding changes while the latter should embed the given messages while minimizing the distortion.

3 Feature Extraction Based on Entropy Value of 2D Gabor Wavelets

3.1 Decomposing Image Using 2D Gabor Wavelets

When the 2D Gabor wavelets are used for image processing and analysis, the image should be filtered by 2D Gabor wavelets firstly, and then the feature extraction, edge detection and other processing or analysis can be performed. The 2D Gabor filtering for image is that an input image $I(x, y)$ is convolved with a 2-D Gabor function $g(x, y)$ to obtain a Gabor feature image $u(x, y)$ as follows:

$$u(x, y) = \iint_\Omega I(\xi, \eta) g(x - \xi, y - \eta) d\xi d\eta \qquad (6)$$

where, $(x, y) \in \Omega$, Ω denotes the set of image points.

In this paper, the 2D Gabor function $g(x, y)$ in Eq. (6) uses the following family of Gabor functions [21, 22], it is a product of a Gaussian and a cosine function.

$$g_{\lambda,\theta,\varphi}(x,y) = e^{-\left((x'^2 + \gamma^2 y'^2)/2\sigma^2\right)} \cos\left(2\pi\frac{x'}{\lambda} + \varphi\right) \tag{7}$$

where, $x' = x\cos\theta + y\sin\theta$, $y' = -x\sin\theta + y\cos\theta$, $\sigma = 0.56\lambda$, $\gamma = 0.5$.

In Eq. (7), σ represents the scale parameter. The small σ means high spatial resolution and the image filtering coefficients reflect local properties in fine scale. On the contrary, the large σ means low spatial resolution and the image filtering coefficients reflect local properties in coarse scale. The other parameters in Eq. (7) can be explained as follows: θ specifies the orientations of 2D Gabor wavelets; λ denotes the wavelength of the cosine factor; γ denotes the spatial aspect ratio and specifies the ellipticity of Gaussian factor; φ specifies the phase offset of the cosine factor ($\varphi = 0$, π correspond to symmetric 'centre-on' functions while $\varphi = -\pi/2$, $\pi/2$ correspond to anti-symmetric functions). In addition, in order to capture the embedding changes, all the 2D Gabor wavelets are made zero mean by subtracting the kernel mean from all its elements to form the high-pass filters.

Adaptive JPEG steganography constrains the embedding changes to the complex image texture regions while the 2D Gabor wavelets can capture the image texture and edge properties from different scales and orientations effectively. Therefore, the 2D Gabor wavelets are suitable for the steganalysis feature extraction of adaptive JPEG steganography. In addition, for the generation of 2D Gabor wavelets with different scale and orientation parameters, we suppose the scale number is S (the scale parameter σ has S different values), the orientation number is L, the parameter φ is set to 0 and $\pi/\pi2.2$, then the number of the 2D Gabor wavelets is $2 \cdot S \cdot L$. For example, if $S = 6$ and $L = 48$, then the number of the 2D Gabor wavelets is 576. For steganalysis feature extraction, the scale parameter S and orientation parameter L can be determined according to the experiments.

3.2   Feature Extraction

3.2.1   Analyzing Embedding Changes of Image Filtering Coefficients

Before the JPEG image is filtered by 2D Gabor wavelets, the JPEG file should be decompressed to the spatial domain. In order to avoid any loss of information, the JPEG image should be decompressed without quantizing the pixel values to {0, 1, ..., 255}. Let us suppose the decompressed JPEG image is denoted as $\mathbf{I}'$, then the filtered image $\mathbf{U}^{s,l} = \mathbf{I}' \star \mathbf{G}^{s,l}$, $\mathbf{G}^{s,l}$ specifies the 8×8 2D Gabor filter in s scale and l orientation, '$\star$' denotes a convolution without padding. Furthermore, suppose $\mathbf{B}^{(i,j)}$ denotes a 8×8 DCT basis pattern, $\mathbf{B}^{(i,j)} = \left(B_{mn}^{(i,j)}\right)$, $0 \leq m, n \leq 7$, $0 \leq i, j \leq 7$,

$$B_{mn}^{(i,j)} = \frac{w_i w_j}{4} \cos\frac{\pi i(2m+1)}{16} \cos\frac{\pi j(2n+1)}{16} \tag{8}$$

where, $w_0 = 1/\sqrt{2}$, $w_i = 1$ ($i > 0$).

Then, the modification of DCT coefficient in mode (i, j) of 8×8 DCT block will affect all the 8×8 pixels in the corresponding block, and an entire 15×15

neighborhood of values in $\mathbf{U}^{s,l}$. The values will be modified by "unit response" [15] expressed in Eq. (9).

$$\mathbf{R}^{(i,j)\,(s,l)} = \mathbf{B}^{(i,j)} \otimes \mathbf{G}^{s,l} \tag{9}$$

where, $\otimes$ denotes the full cross-correlation.

3.2.2   Analyzing Embedding Change of Entropy Value

The entropy value of image filtering coefficients is a randomness measure that is often used to characterize the image texture. Suppose the vector $\mathbf{p} = (p_1, p_2, \cdots)$ denotes the histogram distribution of image filtering coefficients, the entropy value of image filtering coefficients can be computed as the following:

$$Entropy = -\sum_i p_i \log_2(p_i) \tag{10}$$

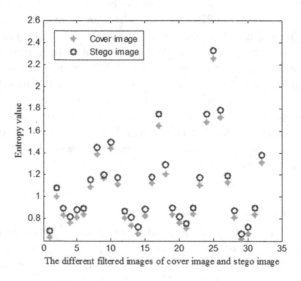

Fig. 1. Entropy values of different filtered images of cover and the corresponding stego images.

After adaptive JPEG steganography, the correlations of image pixels will be disturbed and the disorder of image filtering coefficients will be increased. In other words, the entropy value of image filtering coefficients will become large after steganography embedding. In Fig. 1, the entropy values of the 32 filtered images are given for cover image (Lena image) and stego image generated by J-UNIWARD steganography with 1.0bpac. From Fig. 1, it can be seen that the entropy values obtained from stego image are all larger than the entropy values obtained from cover image. Therefore, the entropy values of image filtering coefficients have discriminant ability for cover and stego image and can be used as steganalysis feature.

3.2.3   Extraction Algorithm

For steganalysis feature extraction, the decompressed JPEG image is convolved with 2D Gabor wavelets with different scales and orientations parameters to get the filtered images firstly. Then, as we known, the JPEG image can be divided into 8×8 DCT blocks and each DCT block has 64 different DCT modes, therefore the each filtered image can be subsampled by step 8 to form 64 subimages and then the entropy feature of each subimage can be extracted and merged [15]. Lastly, all the features of the filtered image are merged according to the symmetric orientation to obtain the steganalysis feature.

The detailed extraction procedures are summarized in the following Algorithm.

Algorithm.

Input:

Training image set;

The number of scale and orientation of 2D Gabor wavelets, S, L ;

Quantization step, q ;

Feature extraction function.

Output: Entropy feature

Step1: The JPEG image is decompressed to spatial domain without quantizing the pixel values to $\{0, 1, \ldots , 255\}$ to avoid any loss of information.

Step2: The 2D Gabor wavelets with different scale and orientation parameters are generated.

Step3: The decompressed JPEG image is convolved with each 2D Gabor wavelet $\mathbf{G}^{s,l}$ and the filtered image $\mathbf{U}^{s,l}$ is operated as the following:

1) According to the 64 DCT modes $(a,b)(0 \le a \le 7, 0 \le b \le 7)$ in 8×8 DCT block, the filtered image $\mathbf{U}^{s,l}$ is subsampled by step 8 to get 64 subimages $\mathbf{U}_{a,b}^{s,l}$ (as shown in Fig.2);

2) For each subimage $\mathbf{U}_{a,b}^{s,l}$, the entropy feature is extracted by equation (11), (12),

$$E = -\sum_{x=-T}^{T} P_{a,b}^{s,l}(x) \log_2 P_{a,b}^{s,l}(x) \tag{11}$$

$$P_{a,b}^{s,l}(x) = \frac{1}{\left|\mathbf{U}_{a,b}^{s,l}\right|} \sum_{u \in \mathbf{U}_{a,b}^{s,l}} \left[Q_T \left(|u|/q \right) = x \right] \tag{12}$$

where, Q_T is a quantizer with integer centroids $\{0,1,\cdots,T\}$, q denotes the quantization step and $[P]$ is the Iverson bracket equal to 0 when the statement P is false and 1 when P is true.

3) According to literature [15], all the entropy features of 64 subimages $\mathbf{U}_{a,b}^{s,l}$ are merged to obtain the entropy feature $\mathbf{E}^{s,l}$ of the filtered image $\mathbf{U}^{s,l}$.

Step4: For the filtered image generated by 2D Gabor wavelet with the same scale parameter σ , the corresponding entropy features can be merged according to the symmetric orientation. For example, suppose the orientation parameter $\theta = \{0, \pi/8, 2\pi/8, \ldots, 6\pi/8, 7\pi/8\}$, then the entropy features of the filtered image with $\theta = \pi/8, 7\pi/8$, $\theta = 2\pi/8, 6\pi/8$ and so on should be merged by averaging.

Step5: All the merged entropy features are joined to form the final steganalysis feature.

Next, the further illustrations are given for feature merging.

(1) Feature merging according to DCT modes

For the entropy feature extraction, the decompressed JPEG image is convolved with each 2D Gabor wavelet, and then the filtered image is subsampled and the entropy feature is extracted. The feature extraction by subsampling the filtered image into 64 subimages according to the 64 DCT modes in 8×8 DCT block. Morover, the entropy features extracted from the 64 subimages can be merged to reduce the feature dimensionality further according to the spatial affects caused by modifying the DCT coefficients in different DCT modes [15]. Therefore, for each filtered image, the 64 entropy features can be obtained and merged to one feature with 25 dimensions. Furthermore, the entropy features with $2 \cdot S \cdot L \cdot 25$ dimensions can be obtained by all the $2 \cdot S \cdot L$ 2D Gabor wavelets.

(2) Feature merging according to symmetrical orientations

When the entropy features of the decompressed JPEG image are obtained, the feature dimensionality can be reduced further by merging the features got by 2D Gabor wavelets with symmetrical orientations and same scale parameter. For example, the entropy features of the filtered image with $\theta = \pi/\pi 8$, .8, $7\pi/\pi 8.8$, $\theta = 2\pi/2\pi 8$, .8, $6\pi/\pi 8.8$ and so on should be merged by averaging. After the entropy features are merged by symmetrical orientations, the dimensionality of the final feature is $2 \cdot S \cdot (L/2 + 1) \cdot 25$.

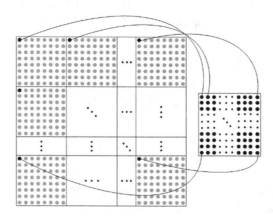

Fig. 2. The procedure of the filtered image subsampling.

4   Experimental Results and Analysis

4.1   Parameter Setting

For the proposed feature extraction method, all the parameters θ, σ, q should be determined according to the experiments. In the following, the detection performances of different parameter settings are discussed. In the experiments, 10000 grayscale images from BossBase1.01[1] are converted into JPEG image with QF (Quality Factor) 75, and then stego images are generated by J-UNIWARD steganography which is a state-of-the-art hiding method in JPEG domain. The detectors are trained as binary classifiers implemented using ensemble classifier proposed in literature [17].The E_{OOB} (out-of-bag estimate of the testing error) is used to evaluate the detection performance of the proposed steganalysis feature. The E_{OOB} is used widely for the evaluation of the detection performances of steganalysis features [12–16].

(1) Orientation parameter θ

Based on the 2D Gabor wavelets with different orientations, the changes of the statistical features of JPEG image can be captured more effectively after steganography embedding. In Fig. 3, the detection performances are presented for QF 75 and 95 when the number of orientations is 4, 8, 16, 32, 48, 64, 96. The other parameters for the detection performance are set as $\sigma = 1$, $q = 6$. In addition, in Fig. 3(a) and (b), the payloads of J-UNIWARD steganography are both 0.4bpac.

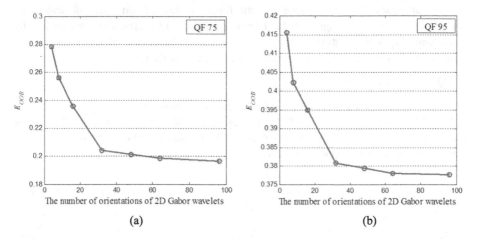

(a)   (b)

Fig. 3. Effect of the number of the orientations on detection accuracy. (a) QF 75; (b) QF 95.

From Fig. 3, it can be seen that the detection accuracy of the proposed steganalysis feature will be better when more 2D Gabor wavelets with different orientations are employed. At the same time, it should be noticed that the feature dimensionality will increase with the number of orientations. The increase in feature dimensionality will lead to more time and space consumptions.

(2) Scale parameter σ

In Table 1, the detection performances are given for J-UNIWARD with QF 75 when the scale parameter σ of 2D Gabor wavelet is set as 0.25, 0.5, 0.75, 1, 1.25, 1.5

---

[1] BossBase-1.01[EB/OL]. http://exile.felk.cvut.cz/boss/BOSSFinal/.2013.

Table 1. E_{OOB} for J-UNIWARD by 2D Gabor wavelets with different scale parameter

Payload (bpac)	Scale paramter σ						
	0.25	0.5	0.75	1	1.25	1.5	Combinatorial
0.1	0.4510	0.4420	0.4357	0.4323	0.4432	0.4567	**0.4166**
0.2	0.3842	0.3627	0.3509	0.3592	0.3711	0.4023	**0.2890**
0.3	0.3205	0.2876	0.2732	0.2789	0.2979	0.3357	**0.1886**
0.4	0.2343	0.2044	0.1763	0.1979	0.2210	0.2823	**0.1016**
0.5	0.1171	0.0954	0.0812	0.0876	0.0974	0.1233	**0.0598**

respectively and the number of orientations of 2D Gabor wavelets is 48. So, the feature dimensionality for each scale parameter is 1250. The detection performances of combinatorial feature which is formed by joining the entropy features obtained in different scales are also presented.

From Table 1, it can be seen that the detection errors of the features obtained in different scales are also different and the combinatorial feature can achieve better detection accuracy. This is because that the features obtain from different scales can capture the changes of image statistical feature in different scales after steganography embedding. The combination of these features can enhance the effectiveness of the steganalysis feature and then the detection accuracy is improved.

(3) Quantization step q

In Fig. 4, the effects of the quantization step q on detection accuracy are shown for J-UNIWARD steganography at 0.4bpac payload with QF 75 and 95. The other parameters of 2D Gabor wavelets are set as $\sigma = 1$, the number of orientations is 48, and then the feature dimensionality is 1250.

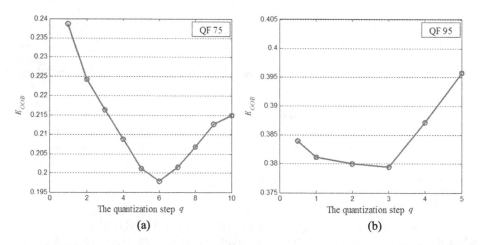

(a)   (b)

Fig. 4. Effect of the quantization step q on detection accuracy. (a) QF = 75; (b) QF = 95.

From Fig. 4, it can be seen that the detection accuracy is changeable with different quantization step q and it can be improved by selecting the appropriate value of q. In addition, for the same quality factor, we should notice that the quantization step q for optimal detection accuracy is larger when the scale parameter σ is relatively large. This is because that the corresponding image filtering coefficient values are large.

4.2   Comparisons to Prior Art

In this subsection, the proposed steganalysis feature is compared with CC-JRM, DCTR and PHARM. In the experiments, the image database is also BossBase-1.01 with 10000 grayscale images. For UED and J-UNIWARD steganography, all the grayscale images are converted into JPEG images with QF 75 and 95 respectively, and then the corresponding stego images are generated with payload 0.05, 0.1, 0.15, 0.2, 0.3, 0.4, 0.5bpac. For SI-UNIWARD steganography, the original grayscale images are used as precover images and then the corresponding stego images are generated with payloads from 0.05 to 0.5bpac when the grayscale images are compressed to JPEG image with QF 75 and 95. So, for each steganography algorithm and quality factor, we have one group of cover images and seven groups of stego images.

For the steganalysis feature extraction, the parameters are set as: scale parameter $\sigma = 0.25, 0.5, 0.75, 1, 1.25, 1.5$ respectively, the number of orientations of 2D Gabor wavelets is 48 for each scale parameter, the quantization step q is set to 1, 2, 4, 6, 8, 10 for different scales with σ in ascending order when QF is 75, the q is set to 0.5, 1, 2, 3, 4, 5 for QF 95. Lastly, the feature dimensionality is 7500. In all the experiments, ensemble classifier [17] is used for the training and testing.

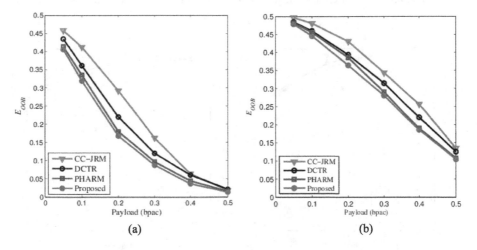

(a)   (b)

Fig. 5. Detection error E_{OOB} for UED. (a) QF = 75; (b) QF = 95.

In Fig. 5, the detection errors E_{OOB} of the four different steganalysis features are presented for UED with seven payloads and two quality factors. From Fig. 5, it can be seen that the proposed steganalysis feature based on 2D Gabor wavelets can achieve the competitive detection performances by comparing with the other steganalysis features. For example, in contrast to CC-JRM, the testing error E_{OOB} can be improved by 11.86 % when payload is 0.2bpac and QF is 75, the improvement is 4.87 % and 1.21 % respectively by comparison with DCTR and PHARM. When QF is 95, the improvement is 6.88 %, 3.16 % and 0.97 % respectively when payload is 0.2bpac. The reason is that 2D Gabor wavelets with different scale and orientation parameters can capture the embedding changes in image texture regions more effectively, therefore the detection performances can be improved.

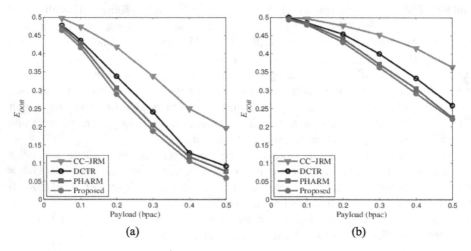

(a)   (b)

Fig. 6. Detection error E_{OOB} for J-UNIWARD. (a) QF = 75; (b) QF = 95.

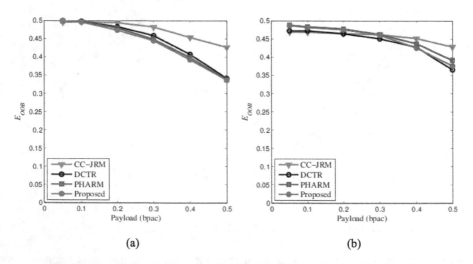

(a)   (b)

Fig. 7. Detection error E_{OOB} for SI-UNIWARD. (a) QF = 75; (b) QF = 95.

In Fig. 6, the detection errors E_{OOB} of the four steganalysis features are presented for J-UNIWARD with different payloads. From Fig. 6, it can be seen that the proposed steganalysis feature can achieve the best detection performance for J-UNIWARD with different payloads and quality factors. For example, when QF is 75, in contrast to CC-JRM, the testing error E_{OOB} can be improved by 11.75 % when payload is 0.2bpac, the improvement is 3.70 % and 1.34 % respectively by comparison with CC-JRM and PHARM; when QF is 95, the improvements are 4.43 %, 2.13 % and 1.42 % respectively when payload is 0.2bpac.

In Fig. 7, the detection errors E_{OOB} of the steganalysis features are given for SI-UNIWARD with different payloads. From Fig. 7, it can be seen that the proposed steganalysis feature can achieve the best detection performance when QF is 75. For example, when payload is 0.2bpac and QF is 75, in contrast to CC-JRM, the detection error E_{OOB} can be improved by 2.04 %, the improvement is 1.12 % and 0.54 % respectively by comparison with DCTR and PHARM. However, the detection performance of DCTR is more accurate when QF is 95.

5   Conclusions

In this paper, one steganalysis feature based on the entropy value of 2D Gabor wavelets is proposed for adaptive JPEG steganography which often constrains the embedding changes to complex texture and edge regions. The proposed feature extraction method is described in details.The parameter setting for feature extraction is also discussed and the detection performances of the proposed steganalysis feature are evaluated by comparing with the latest steganalysis features. From the experimental results, it can be seen that the detection performances can be improved by the proposed steganalysis feature. In the future, the relations between the proposed steganalysis feature with the other steganalysis features will be studied and the feature selection and fusion method will be employed to improve the detection accuracy further.

Acknowledgments. This work was supported by the National Natural Science Foundation of China (No. 61272489, 61379151 and 61302159) and the Natural Science Basic Research Plan in Shaanxi Province of China (No. 2014JM2-6103).

References

1. Fridrich, J.: Steganography in Digital Media: Principles, Algorithms, and Applications. Cambridge University Press, Cambridge (2009)
2. Shannon, C.E.: A mathematical theory of communication. Bell Syst. Tech. J. **27**(3), 379–423 (1948)
3. Filler, T., Fridrich, J: Design of adaptive steganographic schemes for digital images. In: Proceedings of SPIE, Electronic Imaging, Security and Forensics of Multimedia XIII, vol. 7880, pp. OF 1–14. SPIE (2011)
4. Wang, C., Ni, J.Q: An efficient JPEG steganographic scheme based on the block–entropy of DCT coefficients. In: Proceedings of IEEE ICASSP, pp. 1785–1788 (2012)

5. Guo, L.J., Ni, J.Q., Shi, Y.Q: An efficient JPEG steganographic scheme using uniform embedding. In: Proceedings of 4th IEEE International Workshop on Information Forensics and Security, pp. 169–174 (2012)
6. Holub, V., Fridrich, J: Digital image steganography using universal distortion. In: Proceedings of 1st ACM Information Hiding and Multimedia Security Workshop, pp. 59–68. ACM (2013)
7. Fridrich, J., Goljan, M., Soukal, D.: Wet paper codes with improved embedding efficiency. IEEE Trans. Inf. Forensics Secur. 1(1), 102–110 (2006)
8. Filler, T., Judas, J., Fridrich, J.: Minimizing additive distortion in steganography using syndrome-trellis codes. IEEE Trans. Inf. Forensics Secur. 6(1), 920–935 (2011)
9. Pevný, T., Fridrich, J: Merging markov and DCT features for multi-class JPEG steganalysis. In: Proceedings SPIE, Electronic Imaging, Security, Steganography, and Watermarking of Multimedia Contents IX, vol. 65053, pp. 1–14 (2007)
10. Chen, C., Shi, Y.Q.: JPEG image steganalysis utilizing both intrablock and interblock correlations. In: Proceedings of IEEE International Symposium on Circuits and Systems, pp. 3029–3032 (2008)
11. Kodovský, J., Fridrich, J., Holub, V.: On dangers of overtraining steganography to incomplete cover model. In: Proceedings of the 13th ACM Multimedia & Security Workshop, pp. 69–76. ACM (2011)
12. Song, X.F., Liu, F.L., Luo, X.Y., et al.: Steganalysis of perturbed quantization steganography based on the enhanced histogram features. Multimedia Tools Appl. 74(24), 11045–11071 (2015)
13. Kodovský, J., Fridrich, J: Steganalysis of JPEG images using rich models. In: Proceedings of SPIE, Electronic Imaging, Media Watermarking, Security, and Forensics of Multimedia XIV, vol. 8303, pp. 0A 1–13. SPIE (2012)
14. Holub, V., Fridrich, J.: Random projections of residuals for digital image steganalysis. IEEE Trans. Inf. Forensics Secur. 8(12), 1996–2006 (2013)
15. Holub, V., Fridrich, J.: Low complexity features for JPEG steganalysis using undecimated DCT. IEEE Trans. Inf. Forensics Secur. 10(2), 219–228 (2015)
16. Holub, V., Fridrich, J.: Phase-aware projection model for steganalysis of JPEG images. In: Proceedings of SPIE, Electronic Imaging, Media Watermarking, Security, and Forensics of Multimedia XIV, vol. 9409, pp. 94090T–94090T-11 (2015)
17. Kodovský, J., Fridrich, J., Holub, V.: Ensemble classifiers for steganalysis of digital media. IEEE Trans. Inf. Forensics Secur. 7(2), 432–444 (2012)
18. Daugman, J.G.: Uncertainty relation for resolution in space, spatial frequency, and orientation optimized by two-dimensional visual cortical filters. J. Opt. Soc. Am. A: 2(7), 1160–1169 (1985)
19. Pharwaha, A.P.S., Singh, B.: Shannon and non-Shannon measures of entropy for statistical texture feature extraction in digitized mammograms. In: Proceedings of the World Congress on Engineering and Computer Science, vol. 2, pp. 20–22 (2009)
20. Filler, T., Fridrich, J.: Gibbs construction in steganography. IEEE Trans. Inf. Forensics Secur. 5(4), 705–720 (2010)
21. Denemark, T., Sedighi, V., Holub, V., et al.: Selection-channel-aware rich model for steganalysis of digital images. In: Proceedings of IEEE International Workshop on Information Forensics and Security, pp. 1–5 (2014)
22. Grigorescu, S.E., Petkov, N., Kruizinga, P.: Comparison of texture features based on Gabor filters. IEEE Trans. Image Process. 11(10), 1160–1167 (2012)

A Caching-Based Privacy-Preserving Scheme for Continuous Location-Based Services

Shaobo Zhang[1,4], Qin Liu[2], and Guojun Wang[3(✉)]

[1] School of Information Science and Engineering, Central South University,
Changsha 410083, China
csgjwang@gmail.com
[2] College of Computer Science and Electronic Engineering, Hunan University,
Changsha 410082, China
[3] School of Computer Science and Educational Software, Guangzhou University,
Guangzhou 510006, China
[4] School of Computer Science and Engineering,
Hunan University of Science and Technology, Xiangtan 411201, China

Abstract. With the rapid pervasion of location-based services (LBSs), location privacy protection has become a critical issue. In most previous solutions, the users get the query result data from the LBS server and discard it immediately. However, the data can be cached and reused to answer future queries. In this paper, we propose a caching-based solution to protect location privacy in continuous LBSs. Our scheme adopts a two-level caching mechanism to cache the users' result data at both the client and the anonymizer sides. Therefore, the continuous query user can directly obtain the query result data from the cache, which can reduce the interaction between the user and the LBS server to reduce the risk of user's information being exposed to the LBS server. At the same time, we propose the cloaking region mechanism based on the move direction of the user to improve the cache hit ratio. Security analysis shows that our proposal can effectively protect the user's location privacy.

Keywords: Location-Based Services (LBSs) · Location privacy · Caching · Cloaking region · Anonymizer

1 Introduction

With the rapid development of wireless communication technologies and personal mobile devices with global positioning functionality (e.g., GPS), Location-Based Services (LBSs) have been obtaining extensive concerns and becoming the fastest-growing activities in recent years [1–3]. In LBSs, a mobile user sends a query with his location to LBS server, and he can find Point Of Interests (POIs) nearby, such as finding the nearest cinema, hospital and restaurant. However, when users enjoy the great convenience from LBSs, they may confront privacy risks of sensitive information leakage. By collecting the queries submitted, the LBS server can infer some sensitive information about a particular user, such as

© Springer International Publishing AG 2016
G. Wang et al. (Eds.): SpaCCS 2016 Workshops, LNCS 10067, pp. 73–82, 2016.
DOI: 10.1007/978-3-319-49145-5_8

his location, health condition and even behavior pattern [4]. What's worse, the LBS servers may disclose users' private information to third parties for pecuniary advantage, which may become the serious threat. Therefore, much attention should be paid to protect user privacy.

To reduce the risk of privacy disclosure in continuous LBSs, many approaches have been proposed to protect users' location privacy over recent years. Generally, these approaches can be classified into two categories: mobile device-based approaches [5,6] and Trusted Third Party (TTP) based on approaches [7–9]. In TTP based on approaches, the TTP, called anonymizer, is introduced into the system, which acts as an intermediate tier between the users and the Location Service Provider (LSP) [10]. When a service user sends a query, the query is sent to the anonymizer to form a cloaked region that including k users, which is sent to LSP for query. Then the query result data is returned to the anonymizer for refinement, which will accurate results to the service user. In this process, when the user gets the query result data, the user and the anonymizer discard the query data immediately. However, the query data can be used to answer future queries. A natural solution is to use caching to reduce the number of queries sent to the LSP, which can improve the user's privacy.

In recent years, the caching technique has been used in a few previous works on the user's privacy protection [11–14]. Niu et al. [15] proposed a collaborative scheme, which combined a privacy-preserving spatial cloaking algorithm and the collaborative caching to protect user's privacy. In the follow-up work, they also proposed an entropy-based privacy metric to show the quantitative relation between caching and privacy, and designed two caching-aware dummy selection algorithms to enhance the location privacy [16]. However, these methods are only suitable for the snapshot query, and they cannot be used for continuous queries in LBSs.

In this paper, we propose a Caching-based Privacy-Preserving (CPP) scheme for continuous LBSs. Our scheme adopts a two-level caching mechanism to cache the users' result data at both the client and the anonymizer sides in continuous LBSs. When a service user sends a query request, he firstly searches the query result in the cache of the client and anonymizer, and uses the cached result data to answer future queries to reduce the queries sent to the LBS server, which can reduce the risk of user's information being exposed to the LBS server. The main contributions of this paper are shown as follows.

(1) We propose a two-level caching mechanism to cache the users' result data at both the client and the anonymizer sides in continuous LBSs, so that the query result can be obtained by the cache of the client and anonymizer. Therefore, it can decrease the amount of private information exposed to the LBS server and improve the users' location privacy.

(2) We utilize the k-anonymity principle to improve the users' location privacy on the LBS server. According to the grid cells that the service user needs to query, the anonymizer looks for other grid cells and forms the cloaking region, which can confuse the real user's location to improve the user's location privacy on the LBS server.

(3) We propose the cloaking region mechanism based on the move direction of the service user to improve the cache hit ratio. In the process of forming the cloaking region, the anonymizer selects the grid cells according to the move direction and velocity to improve the cache hit ratio of the future query point in continuous LBSs.

(4) We thoroughly analyze the security of our scheme, which can resist the eavesdropping attacks and protect users' location privacy effectively in continuous LBSs.

2 The System Model and Definition

2.1 System Architecture

In this paper, we propose a CPP scheme to enhance privacy in continuous LBSs. The scheme is to cache the query result data in the client and anonymizer and use the cached result data to answer future queries to reduce the risk of user information being exposed to the LBS server. The architecture of CPP is made up of three main entities: service user, anonymizer and LBS server, which is shown in Fig. 1 and works as follows: (1) When a service user sends the query request, he firstly specifies the query spatial region on the grid structure and gets the grid cell identifiers on it. Then he searches each grid cell identifier in the client cache. If the client cache has the grid cell identifiers, the query result data is returned, or the grid cell identifiers that need to be queried are sent to anonymizer. (2) When the anonymizer receives the grid cell identifiers, he searches in the anonymizer cache. If he can obtain all the grid cell identifiers, the query result data is returned, or it will form cloaking region based on the k-anonymity and send to the LBS server. (3) The LBS service searches the POIs of the service user within the cloaking region, which gets the grid cell identifiers of this candidate POIs and returns to anonymizer. (4) The anonymizer updates each grid cell identifiers along with the POIs to the cache. Then he matches the grid cell identifiers that the service user needs. If matched, he will return it to the service user. (5) The service user receives the matched grid cell identifiers and updates it, then filters the candidate POIs and gets the accurate result data.

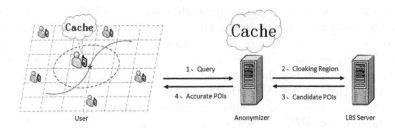

Fig. 1. The architecture of CPP

Table 1. The meaning of entropy

Random events	Probability of success	Probability of failure	The entropy
A	0.9	0.1	0.325
B	0.1	0.9	0.325
C	0.5	0.5	0.693

2.2 Problem Statement

We consider the following scenario: a service user needs to issue a continuous range query to find the same POIs to the LBS server for a certain time period, such as continuously query the traffic condition around five kilometres every five minutes. If the service user only moves one kilometre within five minutes and issues a range query again, there will be a certain intersecting region. However, the intersecting region is needed to be repeated query in the next query point, and it will increase the query overhead of the LBS server. More seriously, because the submitted queries include the location of the service user, he will frequently submits queries to the LBS server, which will increase the risk that his locations are exposed in continuous LBSs. To address the above problems, our basic idea is to integrate caching and k-anonymity to improve the user's location privacy.

2.3 Privacy Metrics

Definition 1 (Entropy). The probability distribution of discrete random variables is assumed as:

$$\begin{pmatrix} x \\ p(x) \end{pmatrix} = \begin{bmatrix} x_1, & x_2 & \dots & x_n \\ p(x_1), & p(x_2) \dots p(x_n) \end{bmatrix} \tag{1}$$

where $p(x_i) \in [0,1]$, $\sum_{i=1}^{n} p(x_i) = 1$. The entropy of x is defined as the weighted average information:

$$H(X) = -\sum_{i=1}^{n} p(x_i) \log p(x_i) \tag{2}$$

The intuitive meaning of the entropy is shown in Table 1. From the Table 1 we can see, the greater the uncertainty of the variables is, the higher the entropy is, so we can describe the location privacy metrics by the entropy. The $p(x_i)$ denote the probability that the ith location is the user's real location, and the entropy denotes that it can identify the user's real location in anonymity. The greater the uncertainty of the user's real location is, the higher the location privacy degree is. If all the k possible locations have the same probability in anonymity, it has the maximum entropy $H_{\max} = \log_2 k$ and the highest privacy degree [12].

Definition 2 (The cache privacy metric). Let us consider the impact of caching on the user's location privacy. If a query request is answered by cache, the LBS server can't get any information about the user's real location [17]. Every grid cell may be the user's real location in the query, and they have the same query probability and the entropy is $\log_2 m^2$ [16]. So the privacy metrics based on cache can be represented as:

$$\varphi = \frac{\sum_{g \in G_{server}} H(g) + \log_2 m^2 \times |G_{cache}|}{|G_{server}| + |G_{cache}|} \tag{3}$$

where $H(g)$ is the uncertainty of the real grid cell in the query g calculated using Eq. (2), $|G_{cache}|$ denotes the number of grid cells that can be found in cache, $|G_{server}|$ denotes the number of grid cells that need to be queried in the LBS server, and m denotes the number of grid cells in the query area.

In the process of querying, the cache hit ratio of the grid cells can be expressed as:

$$\delta = \frac{|G_{cache}|}{|G_{server}| + |G_{cache}|} \tag{4}$$

the formula (3) can be rewritten as:

$$\varphi = \frac{\sum_{g \in G_{server}} H(g)}{|G_{server}| + |G_{cache}|} + \delta \log_2 m^2 \tag{5}$$

From the Eq. (5) we can see, the privacy based on cache can be improved by increasing the cache hit ratio.

3   The caching-based privacy-preserving scheme

In this section, we will depict the caching-based privacy-preserving scheme in continuous LBSs. In general, the scheme has five main steps.

3.1   The Client Cache Query and Service Request

Before the service user requests a query to LBS server, he firstly specifies a query area according to his move direction and velocity, which is represented by the coordinates of its bottom-left vertex (x_1, y_1) and top-right vertex (x_2, y_2), and the entire query area is divided into $m \times m$ grids of equal size. Then the grid structure can be expressed as:

$$Grid\_structure \leftarrow ((x_1,\ y_1),(x_2,\ y_2),\ m) \tag{6}$$

In the grid structure, there is a unique identifier for each grid cell, which is identified by (c_i, r_j), where c_i is the column index from left to right and r_j is the row index from bottom to top respectively [18]. For example, you choose a point (x_i, y_i) in the query area, and the grid cell identifier (c_i, r_j) can be computed by the formula (7).

$$(c_i,\ r_i) = \left(\left\lceil \frac{x_i - x_1}{(x_2 - x_1)/m} \right\rceil,\ \left\lceil \frac{y_i - y_1}{(y_2 - y_1)/m} \right\rceil \right) \tag{7}$$

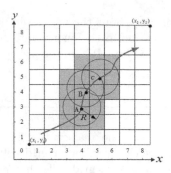

Fig. 2. The intersecting region formed by continuous query

The service user specifies the query range with the radius R on the grid structure and gets the query spatial region that is the spatial region of grid cells that intersect the query range. Then we can obtain the grid cell identifiers in query spatial region. As shown in Fig. 2, there are three continuous range query points A, B and C. When a service user sends a request at the point A, the query spatial region includes 9 grid cells, and he moves to the point B and sends a request again, the query spatial region also includes 9 grid cells. However, this query spatial regions in the points A and B have intersecting grid cells, whose identifiers are $(3,3), (4,3), (5,3), (3,4), (4,4)$ and $(5,4)$. Similarly, this query spatial regions in the points B and C also have intersecting grid cells. It can be seen that there is always a certain intersecting query spatial region in two continuous range query points, so the next range query point can obtain the part or all the result data from the previous query point.

After the service user obtains all grid cell identifiers in the query spatial region, he searches them in the client cache. If the client cache has all or part of this grid cell identifiers, the service user refines them and gets all or part of accurate result. Otherwise, the grid cell identifiers that are not found in the client cache will form a grid cell identifier set I_z.

$$I_z \leftarrow \{(c_i, \; r_j)\}, \; 1 \leq i, \; j \leq m, \; 1 \leq z \leq n \tag{8}$$

where m is a user-specified grid parameter and n denotes the number of the query point. Then the service user forms a request message that includes the query point location L_z, the move direction D_z and velocity V_z, the grid cell identifier set I_z that need to be queried, the randomly generated key k_u, the query range radius R, the grid structure $Grid\_structure$ and the query content Q, which is encrypted by asymmetric encryption E with the public key PK_A of anonymizer, and gets the MSG_{U2A} that sends to anonymizer.

$$MSG_{U2A} = E_{PK_A}\{L_z, D_z, V_z, I_z, k_u, R, Grid\_structure, Q\} \tag{9}$$

3.2   The anonymizer cache query and location anonymity

When anonymizer receives the request message MSG_{U2A}, he firstly decrypts it with his private key SK_A, which can get the grid cell identifier set. Then he searches each grid cell identifier in anonymizer cache. If anonymizer can obtain all grid cell identifiers along with the POIs, he encrypts them with the key k_u and returns to the client. Otherwise, it will form cloaking region based on k-anonymity. Suppose there is at least one user in each grid cell, we form the cloaking region according to the move direction and velocity to improve the cache hit ratio. The process of anonymity is shown in Algorithm 1. Finally, anonymizer forms a new request message that includes the cloaking region $Region$, the grid structure $Grid\_structure$ and the query content Q, which is encrypted by asymmetric encryption E with the public key PK_S of the LBS server, and the anonymizer sends the MSG_{A2S} to the LBS server.

$$MSG_{A2S} = E_{PK_S}\{Region, \ Grid\_structure, Q\} \tag{10}$$

Algorithm 1. The Process of Anonymity

Input:
The $Grid\_structure, k, L_z, D_z, V_z, I_z, R, 1 \leq z \leq n$.
Output:
The cloaking region $Region$.

1: Restore the grid structure according to the parameters (x_1, y_1), (x_2, y_2) and m from $Grid\_structure$;
2: Get the grid cell identifier set $I_z \leftarrow \{(c_i, \ r_j)\}, 1 \leq i, \ j \leq m, 1 \leq z \leq n$ and $Region = I_z$;
3: Determine the location L_{z+1} of the next query point according to the $L_z, D_z, V_z,$ and compute the $(c_{z+1}, r_{z+1}) = \left(\left\lceil \frac{x_{z+1}-x_1}{(x_2-x_1)/m} \right\rceil, \left\lceil \frac{y_{z+1}-y_1}{(y_2-y_1)/m} \right\rceil \right)$;
4: $I_t = 0$;
5: **if** The I_z are not adjacent **then**
6:      Select the grid cell identifiers I_t between them, $Region = Region + I_t$;
7: **end if**
8: Select the $k - Number(I_z + I_t)$ grid cell identifiers (c_i, r_j) in the range radius R of the (c_{z+1}, r_{z+1}), $Region = Region + (c_i, r_j)$;
9: **return** $Region$

3.3   The Server Data Query and Candidate Results Return

When the LBS server obtains the request message MSG_{A2S}, he decrypts it with his private key SK_S. He firstly restores the grid structure to determine the cloaking region from the $Region$ on the grid structure. According to the cloaking region, he can get f grid cells that need to be queried. Then the LBS server searches the POIs according to the query content Q and gets g POIs. If the location of the jth POI is $(x_j, y_j)(1 \leq i, j \leq g)$, the grid cell identifier can be computed by the formula (7), and we can get the grid cell identifier set φ_r. Finally, the LBS server encrypts the grid cell identifier set φ_r by asymmetric encryption E with the public key PK_A of the anonymizer and forms the query result message MSG_{S2A}, which returns it to anonymizer.

$$(c_s, r_t) = \{(x_i, y_j)\} \quad (1 \leq i, j \leq g) \tag{11}$$

$$\varphi_r = \{(c_s, r_t)\} \quad (1 \leq r \leq f) \tag{12}$$

$$MSG_{S2A} = E_{PK_A}\{\varphi_r\} \quad (1 \leq r \leq f) \tag{13}$$

3.4   The anonymizer cache update and identifier matching

The anonymizer receives the query result message MSG_{S2A} and decrypts it, which can get each grid cell identifier along with the POIs. He updates it to the anonymizer cache and then matches the grid cell identifiers by comparing the grid cell identifiers φ_r $(1 \leq r \leq f)$ of the received POI with the grid cell identifier set I_z previously received from the service user. Finally, the anonymizer encrypts the grid cell identifier set I_z along with the POIs by symmetric encryption En with the key k_u. The message MSG_{A2U} that anonymizer forwards to the service user.

$$MSG_{A2U} = En_{k_u}\{I_z, (x_i, y_j)\} \quad (1 \leq z \leq n) \tag{14}$$

3.5   The Client Cache Update and Refinement Results

The service user firstly decrypts the MSG_{A2U} with the key k_u and gets the exact location of each POI for each grid cell identifier in the I_z. Then he updates the grid cell identifiers along with the POIs to the client cache. Finally, the service user calculates the POIs that is included in the query range and gets the accurate result.

4   Security Analysis

The security of the proposed scheme against dishonest LSP and eavesdropping attacks will be analyzed in the following respectively.

Privacy Against LSP. When the service user sends a query to the LSP, and the cache of client and anonymizer has all result data, the service user extracts the POIs directly from cache. In this process, the service user does not interact with the LSP, who can't get any information from the service user.

If the service user can't obtain all result data in cache, the anonymizer will form the cloaking region and forward to the LSP, who receives the request message MSG_{A2S} that includes the cloaking region $Region$, the grid structure $Grid\_structure$ and the encrypted query content Q. From the MSG_{A2S} the LSP only recognizes the query spatial region and the query content Q, without associating with a specific user and getting the exact location. Even if the LSP recognizes all users in the cloaking region, but each grid cell has at least one user, so it can guess the probability of a specified user up to only $1/k$.

Resistance to Eavesdropping Attacks. When a service user sends the query request message MSG_{U2A} to anonymizer and the query results message MSG_{S2A} returns to anonymizer, this two messages are encrypted by asymmetrical algorithm E with the public key PK_A of the anonymizer. In this process, the attackers can't get the private key SK_A of the anonymizer, which can't get useful information.

When anonymizer forwards query message MSG_{A2S} to LBS server, the transmitting message will be encrypted by asymmetrical algorithm E with the public key PK_S of the LBS server. At the same time, the query results that anonymizer forwards to the service user is encrypted by symmetric encryption En with the key k_u. Similarly, the attackers can't get the private key SK_S and the key k_u in this process, so they can't get useful information.

5 Conclusion

In this paper, we propose a caching-based solution to protect location privacy in continuous LBSs. Our scheme adopts a two-level caching mechanism and the k-anonymity principle to improve the users' location privacy on the LBS server. In the process of forming the cloaking region, we propose the cloaking region mechanism based on the move direction of the user to improve the cache hit ratio. Security analysis shows that the CPP scheme can resist the LSP and eavesdropping attacks and protect the user's location privacy.

Acknowledgments. This work is supported in part by the National Natural Science Foundation of China under Grant Numbers 61632009, 61272151, 61472451 and 61402161, the High Level Talents Program of Higher Education in Guangdong Province under Grant Number 2016ZJ01, the Hunan Provincial Education Department of China under Grant Number 2015C0589, the Hunan Provincial Natural Science Foundation of China under Grant Number 2015JJ3046, the Fundamental Research Funds for the Central Universities of Central South University under Grant Number 2016zzts058.

References

1. Wang, X., Pande, A., Zhu, J., Mohapatra, P.: STAMP: enabling privacy-preserving location proofs for mobile users. IEEE Trans. Netw., 1–14 (2016). doi:10.1109/TNET.2016.2515119
2. Zhang, S., Liu, Q., Wang, G.: Deviation-based location switching protocol for trajectory privacy protection. In: Wang, G., Zomaya, A., Perez, G.M., Li, K. (eds.) ICA3PP 2015. LNCS, vol. 9530, pp. 417–428. Springer, Heidelberg (2015). doi:10.1007/978-3-319-27137-8_31
3. Peng, T., Liu, Q., Wang, G.: Enhanced location privacy preserving scheme in location-based services. IEEE Syst. J., 1–12 (2014). doi:10.1109/JSYST.2014.2354235
4. Shin, K.G., Ju, X., Chen, Z., Hu, X.: Privacy protection for users of location-based services. IEEE Wirel. Commun. **19**(1), 30–39 (2012)
5. Sweeney, L.: k-anonymity: a model for protecting privacy. Int. J. Uncertain. Fuzziness Knowl. Based Syst. **10**(05), 557–570 (2002)

6. Xu, T., Cai, Y.: Feeling-based location privacy protection for location-based services. In: Proceedings of the 16th ACM Conference on Computer and Communications Security, pp. 348–357. ACM (2009)

7. Gedik, B., Liu, L.: Protecting location privacy with personalized k-anonymous: architecture and algorithms. IEEE Trans. Mob. Comput. **7**(1), 1–18 (2008)

8. Pan, X., Xu, J., Meng, X.: Protecting location privacy against locationdependent attacks in mobile services. Trans. Knowl. Data Eng. **24**(8), 1506–1519 (2012)

9. Hwang, R.H., Hsueh, Y.L., Chung, H.W.: A novel time-obfuscated algorithm for trajectory privacy protection. IEEE Trans. Serv. Comput. **7**(2), 126–139 (2014)

10. Zhang, S., Liu, Q., Wang, G.: Enhancing location privacy through user-defined grid in location-based services. In: Proceedings of the 15th International Conference on Trust, Security and Privacy in Computing and Communication (TrustCom 2016), pp. 730–736. IEEE (2016)

11. Amini, S., Lindqvist, J., Hong, J., Lin, J., Toch, E., Sadeh, N.: Cache: caching location-enhanced content to improve user privacy. In: Proceedings of the 9th International Conference on Mobile Systems, Applications, and Services, pp. 197–210. ACM (2011)

12. Shokri, R., Theodorakopoulos, G., Papadimitratos, P., Kazemi, E., Hubaux, J.P.: Hiding in the mobile crowd: locationprivacy through collaboration. IEEE Trans. Dependable Secur. Comput. **11**(3), 266–279 (2014)

13. Park, K., Jeong, Y.S.: A caching strategy for spatial queries in mobile networks. J. Inf. Sci. Eng. **30**(4), 1187–1207 (2014)

14. Jung, K., Jo, S., Park, S.: A game theoretic approach for collaborative caching techniques in privacy preserving location-based services. In: Proceedings of 2015 International Conference on Big Data and Smart Computing (BIGCOMP), pp. 59–62. IEEE (2015)

15. Niu, B., Zhu, X., Li, W., Li, H.: EPcloak: an efficient and privacy-preserving spatial cloaking scheme for LBSs. In: Proceedings of the 11th International Conference on Mobile Ad Hoc and Sensor Systems, pp. 398–406. IEEE (2014)

16. Niu, B., Li, Q., Zhu, X., Cao, G., Li, H.: Enhancing privacy through caching in location-based services. In: Proceedings of the Conference on Computer Communications(INFOCOM 2015), pp. 1017–1025. IEEE (2015)

17. Xiao, C., Chen, Z., Wang, X., Zhao, J., Chen, C.: DeCache: a decentralized two-level cache for mobile location privacy protection. In: Proceedings of the Sixth International Conference on Ubiquitous and Future Networks (ICUFN 2014), pp. 81–86. IEEE (2014)

18. Schlegel, R., Chow, C., Huang, Q., Wong, D.: User-defined privacy grid system for continuous location-based services. Trans. Mob. Comput. **14**(10), 2158–2172 (2015)

6th International Symposium on Trust, Security and Privacy for Emerging Applications (TSP-16)

AppWalker: Efficient and Accurate Dynamic Analysis of Apps via Concolic Walking Along the Event-Dependency Graph

Tianjun Wu$^{(\boxtimes)}$ and Yuexiang Yang

College of Computer, National University of Defense Technology,
Changsha 410073, China
{wutianjun08,yyx}@nudt.edu.cn

Abstract. Dynamic analyzing techniques play an important and unique role in detecting Android malware and vulnerabilities, as they can provide higher precision than static methods. However, they are inherently incomplete and inefficiency. We attack this problem by proposing a novel method, i.e., concolic walking along the event-dependency graph. We implement AppWalker based on it. Evaluation over a real-life app set shows that better efficiency and accuracy than state-of-the-art concolic analysis tools are achieved.

Keywords: Dynamic analysis · Android application · Concolic execution · Efficiency · Accuracy

1 Introduction

Android is by far the most widespread mobile operating system, and there has been a surge in the development and adoption of mobile applications, or *apps*. In 2014, 2000 mobile malware instances per day are reported by Sophos [11]. The severe situation is the same for app vulnerabilities. According to a report from AliBaba [12], 97% of top 10 apps of 18 areas in the third app markets are found to be vulnerable. The need is growing for analyzing Android apps, aimed at discovering such safety issues as malware behavior and application vulnerabilities.

Static app analysis tools, such as the static taint analysis tool FlowDroid [1], successfully solve the problems of determining app entry points and connecting isolated and asymmetric life-cycle callbacks. They usually can efficiently analyze all the code in the application, but they are inherently imprecise, as there may be behavior misses or falsely behavior report. Dynamic analysis tools, such as Acteve [3], avoid those shortcoming of static tools. However, they are relatively slow as they have to run the code, and are inherently incomplete as they can only tell the behavior that they execute. Thus they incur relatively poor efficiency and low code coverage.

In this paper, we combined static and dynamic approaches to improve the efficiency and accuracy of dynamic analysis for Android apps. To improve efficiency, we apply static call graph analysis to extract static model which is used for guiding concolic execution [2] (which we call as *concolic walk*). To improve accuracy, we performed

G. Wang et al. (Eds.): SpaCCS 2016 Workshops, LNCS 10067, pp. 85–94, 2016.
DOI: 10.1007/978-3-319-49145-5_9

concolic walking along the *event-dependency graph* built on static models, accurately capturing the control-flow dependent relations between events.

The contribution of this paper is three fold. First, we propose the concept of event-dependency graph which extends that of *event space* [5] by considering the control-flow dependency between events. We accurately model those dependencies such as *self-dependency* or *multi-dependency*. Second, we extend the traditional technique of *concolic walk* [6] from walking within the path constraint's continuous solution space to the discrete space of possible input events to the target app. This approach efficiently guides concolic execution of Android apps. Third, we implement our approach as a dynamic analyzer called AppWalker for analyzing Android malware and vulnerabilities.

2 Related Work

TaintDroid [12] is probably the most prominent tool for dynamic analysis of Android apps. It dynamically traces data leaks occurred during the execution of apps by applying dynamic taint analysis. Such tools are not suited for fully automated analysis since they require user interaction to drive execution of the apps.

Concolic execution [2] successfully tackles the problem of automate input generation. It traces symbolic registers at each conditional statement in order to build path conditions for specific execution traces. After collecting path constraints, a constraint solver is used for solving them and the result is the desired program input.

Constraint solving is non-trial task. Among various approaches trying to tackle that, concolic walk [5] is one of the most comprehensive and efficient solutions. It splits path constraints into linear and none-linear parts, and then heuristically walking within the polytopes formed by the linear part to find solution for the other part.

One of the first and still among the state-of-the-art tools that apply concolic execution for analyzing mobile apps is Acteve [3]. It blindly searches all paths which results in heavy performance load. AppIntent [4] identifies information-leaking paths and performs concolic execution only for them. The proposed concept of event space is incomplete, as it only considers method-call like control flow. ConDroid [6] is a directed concolic analyzer built on Acteve, similar to AppIntent. Instead of focusing on taint paths, it targets at dynamic class loading instructions. IntelliDroid [7] further extract event dependency according to path conditions to generate event chains. However, the dependency it considers is not general.

3 Approach Overview

To illustrate our approach, consider a simple bank app that simulates ATM operations. The code snippet is given in Fig. 1.

Android apps implement various callbacks defined by Android SDK API and do not contain a main method. When launched, the SDK creates an instance of the apps'

```
public class MainActivity extends Activity {            oclDeposit = new View.OnClickListener() {
    ...                                                     @Override
    @Override                                               public void onClick(View v) {
    protected void onResume(){                                  balance = balance + 100;
        ...                                                 }
        monitorBatteryChange(){                         };
            // fetch battery info between 10 min          ...
            ...
            bm = new BroadcastReceiver(){                oclWithdraw = new View.OnClickListener() {
                @Override                                    @Override
                public void onReceive(Context ctx, Intent i){    public void onClick(View v) {
                    int batlevel = i.getIntExtra("level",-1);    if (balance < 100) {
                }                                               return;
            }                                                }
        }                                                   if (numberOfWithdrawals >= 3) {
    }                                                           // BUG
    ...                                                         return;
                                                            }
                                                            balance = balance - 100;
                                                            nWithdrawals = nWithdrawals + 1;
                                                        }
                                                    };
}
```

Fig. 1. Source code snippet of the illustrative app.

Fig. 2. (Partial) user interface of the illustrative app.

main activity MainActivity, and calls its onCreate(). This displays the main screen. Just take our app for example, the user interface is given in Fig. 2, which contains two buttons, "Deposit $100" and "Withdraw $100". User can either deposit or withdraw $100 by clicking the respecting button. Button-click listeners register themselves to Activities so that user click events can be passed from view hierarchy of the screen to the target button event listener. When any button is clicked, the SDK calls the main activity's onClick() method. Besides GUI events like button click event, apps may require various events, including life-cycle callbacks (such as onResume()), and system events (such as volume +/− button clicks, GPS, and SMS).

Our approach first locates possible target instructions of interest. Presumptively, we arbitrarily bury the erroneous code in our example as marked "//BUG".

We then determine the main entry point of the main Activity, and from which call paths to the target instruction are extracted. The paths are further extended for dependent event handlers, thus resulting the event-dependency graph in Fig. 3 (read edges indicate control-flow induced event dependencies). Note that the execution of the target code requires the withdraw button be clicked more than 3 times, and what is more, several times of click of deposit is further required as we cannot withdraw from account when there is no money left. This strict constraint cannot be easily determined by any current concolic tools.

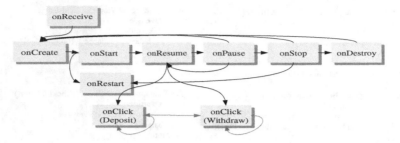

Fig. 3. Illustration of event-dependency graph.

Afterwards, we perform concolic walking along the graph to generate inputs for driving the app to the target instruction. Once we cannot promote from certain nodes in the graph, for example we cannot trigger the bug as the withdraw button is clicked only once, we just walk along the self-closed directed edge onClick(Withdraw) → onClick (Withdraw) to generate the self-dependent events. The explored whole path is: onReceive → onCreate → onStart → onResume → onClick(Deposit) → onClick (Deposit) → onClick(Deposit) → onClick(Withdraw) → onClick(Withdraw) → onClick(Withdraw). For inputs involved in branch conditions along the path, concolic execution just dumps path constraints and feeds to a solver for solution.

4   Design and Implementation

Figure 4 shows the overall dataflow diagram of our system, AppWalker. We will describe the approach in following sub-sections.

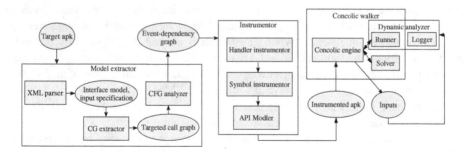

Fig. 4. System overview.

4.1   Static App Model Extraction

We apply FlowDroid [1] to extract three kinds of static models from the decompiled Java bytecode of the target apk.

The interface model provides information about all input fields, as well as information about the Android IPC message (i.e., Intent) handled by Activities. All Android components contained in the app and Intent information can be decided by parsing the Manifest file. Input fields can be obtained from the layout XML files.

Targeted call graph model is extracted by firstly locating the target instructions. Blindly execution all possible program paths is boring, and instructions such as sensitive-information source/sink APIs, reflection and dynamic loading are better places which deserve our focus. Secondly, we determine the main entry point of the app, such as onResume() of the main Activity. Thirdly, as apps rely on various Android callbacks implemented by Android SDK rather than by the app itself, we directly inserting edges from Activity's default entry to callback methods such as life-cycle callbacks, UI and system event handlers, and Intents. Extracting paths from the default entry to target instructions and we get the targeted call graph model.

The event-dependency graph is constructed according to Algorithm 1. We examine control-flow dependency between events, for which we here only consider channels of static fields. Other channels such as file system and network should be future works. Static field, or global variable, represents the state of apps, which are set by incoming events depending on the previous state. We say two events are dependent when the field read by one event is previous written by the other. For each dependency relationship, we added a directed edge. Unlike IntelliDroid, we also consider complex situations where one event depends on itself or on multiple other events, as it is easy to coding these relations into the graph.

Algorithm 1. Event-dependency graph extraction

```
  Input: T:target app
  Output: G:event-dependency graph
1 IM ← extractInterfaceModel()
2 G ← extractTargetedCallGraph(T)
3 foreach entry in IM.getEntries() do
4   foreach handler in IM.getHandlers do
5     if registered(entry.getComponent(),handler) then
6       if G.contains(handler) then
7         G.add(handler,entry)
8   end
9 end
10foreach meth in paths do
11  foreach branchCondition in meth do
12    foreach field in branchCondition do
13      G.add(findfieldWriterHandlers(field),meth)
14    end
15  end
16end
17return G
```

4.2   Java Bytecode Instrumentation

After static analysis, we need further instrument the bytecode so that concolic execution can be guided by our extracted event-dependency graph. Instrumentation includes: instrumenting Android life-cycle entry point, instrumenting symbolic registers, assignments and path conditions along event-dependency graph, and modeling user-specified external APIs.

It is necessary to instrument Activity's default entry point, onCreate()/onResume(), for allowing direct calling event handlers. Although it is more general to inject raw events in the Android framework boundary, tracing the extra injection path require heavy instrumentation of Android system. Therefore, we just directly invoke those events at the end of default entry point.

To allow for symbolic tracing, dumping path conditions for solving, and over-writing registers with solutions at runtime, instrumenting is just crucial. We need instrument registers, assignments and path conditions with their symbolic counterparts. However, we do not instrument all of their occurrences in the app, rather than limit to those on the event-dependency graph. We borrow Acteve's instrumentation utilities, which in fact are transplanted from SPF, to achieve this.

4.3   Concolic Walking

Traditional static symbolic execution traces symbolic registers at each conditional statement in order to build path conditions for specific execution traces. Dynamic symbolic execution, or concolic execution, however, aims to address the state explosion problem of static symbolic execution by executing the program with concrete values and tracing symbolic counterparts of only certain registers in parallel.

We run and symbolically trace the instrumented app in Android emulators. We use Android 4.4.2 as emulators' default operation system.

Concolic execution iteratively does following procedures until hits the target statement: dumping path conditions, negating the last condition and fed the resulted path constraint to the solver, and injecting the solution to symbolic registers in the instrumented app. This is performed by the concolic execution engine. We used Acteve [3], one of the state of art concolic app tester, as our concolic execution engine. In order to perform target-instruction originated execution and String constraint solving, we also referred to the code of ConDroid [6] which, though cannot be launched as the authors only provide partial code, shed light on our work.

The process of concolic walk is depicted in Algorithm 2. During concolic walk, concolic execution is enforced only along the event-dependency graph in a step-by-step manner. By default, we do not walk along self-closed circles. However, when the coverage stops increase and the target is still not hit, we try to walk along those circles. This is similar to the tabu search in [5].

```
Algorithm 2. Concolic walk
   Input: G:event-dependency graph
   Output: In:data inputs,Ev:event inputs
 1 In ← {},Ev ← {}
 2 path ← G.getFirstPath()
 3 if G.contains(path) then
 4    Ev.add(path.getHandlers())
 5    In.add(ConcolicExe(path))
 6 if !isTargetHit() then
 7    do
 8       handler ← target.getPreHandler()
 9       // returns upper-bounded self-dependent event
10       //    handler, muti-dependent event handlers, or
11       //    other simple-dependent Handler
12    while !path.addCircle()
13    goto line 2
14 if isTargetHit() then
15    if path.hasNextPath() then
16       path ← path.getNextPath()
17       goto line 2
18 return In,Ev
```

5 Empirical Evaluation

We first explain why we choose Acteve[1] as the comparing reference. Acteve is one of the state-of-the-art concolic testing tools closing to AppWalker. Although there have emerged several projects recently, such as AppIntent, ConDroid, and IntelliDroid, none are capable for our evaluation as they are either totally or partially publicly unavailable by far. When necessary, however, we also try to make comparisons with the other works conceptually to make the evaluation more comprehensive.

Subject Apps. We choose the benchmark used by Acteve, which consists of 5 real life apps which are open-sourced in F-Droid. Random Music Player (RMP) plays music from local filesystem. Sprite is used for speed comparison of various 2D drawing methods. Translate translates texts using Google's translation web API. Timer provides a countdown timer that ultimately plays an alarm when time is out. Ringdroid is intended for recording and editing ring tones.

5.1 Efficiency

First, we aim at measuring the efficiency of both Acteve and AppWalker. For each app, we choose five paths for each app covered with (and at least with) 15 events by Acteve. We then re-run Acteve and run AppWalker to generate inputs to drive execution to

---

[1] Acteve, benchmark, and corresponding coverage measurement tools are all taken from the AndroidTest [13] project.

cover all those paths. We choose the number of events as 15 to make sure the length of events is long enough while not exceeds the maximal event number of each app.

The result is shown in Table 1. AppWalker obtains orders of magnitude of acceleration comparing to Acteve. The reason behind is that Acteve blindly explores program paths and often run into redundant paths to finally reach those targets. App-Walker only walks along exactly the path from the app entry to the target, thus the saving is exponential.

Table 1. Running time of Acteve and AppWalker.

App Case	Acteve (h)	AppWalker (min)
RMP	3.7	8
Translate	2.8	7
Sprite	2.2	5
Timer	1.9	3
Ringdroid	1.5	3

5.2   Accuracy

We now evaluate the accuracy of AppWalker in terms of line coverage. We use Emma to measure code coverage. To make AppWalker comparable of such coverage goal, we just configure AppWalker to perform coverage-style depth-first path search instead of only searching for target statements. We measure the coverages of both Acteve and AppWalker when they stop increase.

Figure 5 gives the result. We can see that AppWalker reaches a higher coverage rate than Acteve on most application. The increase is app dependent. For example, RMP and Ringdroid each enjoy the highest increase of 4% and 5%, while Sprite enjoys no bonus. We give an inspection to describe the reason.

RMP switches its state based on its previous state and the current incoming event. It uses a global variable to save its state. For example, it will only become PLAYING when the previous state is STOPPED and the incoming event is a click on the "Play" button; and it will only become SKIPPING when previous state of STOPPED and "Skip" button click event are both satisfied. Button click events are the trigger of app state transfer, and therefore, multiple button click events are indeed correlated. Acteve (and ConDroid, likely,) can hardly figure out those dependencies and therefore usually the searching is confined locally. AppWalker, on the other hand, once run into a statement that is conditionally dependent on the global variable, it one step ahead to generate premise events that sets the variable (i.e., state).

The feature of event dependency extraction is similar to IntelliDroid. However, our approach is more general. InteliDroid only traces the dependency of one event on the other event, while AppWalker also traces that on the event itself (self-dependency) or on multiple other events (multi-dependency). Many apps often contain a user license view which consists of a button to be clicked to show further few lines of the license text, and therefore repeated click events of the same button is required to reach the bottom line of the license text so as to jump to the main view. In another more concrete

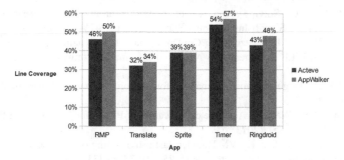

Fig. 5. Line coverage of Acteve and AppWalker.

case with Ringdroid, when we are editing the ring tune, volume +/− buttons are used to decide the start and end bound of the region to be cut out from the music file. The region should not be empty, so the events volume +/− can be inter-dependent.

6 Conclusion

In this paper, we combined static and dynamic approaches for testing android apps. We proposed a novel approach of concolic walking along the event-dependency graph, to increase efficiency and accuracy. We have implemented it as the AppWalker tool.

There still exist several limitations for us to further work on. Embedded circles may reduce our efficiency, but this situation is rare and we can just set the upper bound of walks within each circle to ease the problem. AppWalker currently only support android components such as Activity and BroadcastReceiver. Channels of event-dependency such as file system and network should be taken into account.

Acknowledgments. The authors would like to thank the reviewers for their detailed reviews and constructive comments, which have helped to improve the quality of this paper. This work was supported by the National Natural Science Foundation of China under Grants Nos. 61170286, 61202486.

References

1. Arzt, S., Rasthofer, S., Fritz, C.: FlowDroid. ACM Sigplan Not. **49**(6), 259–269 (2014)
2. Schwartz, E.J., Avgerinos, T., Brumley, D.: All you ever wanted to know about dynamic taint analysis and forward symbolic execution (but might have been afraid to ask). IEEE Symp. Secur. Priv. **7**, 317–331 (2010)
3. Anand, S., Naik, M., Harrold, M.J.: Automated concolic testing of smartphone apps. In: International Symposium on the Foundations of Software Engineering, pp. 1–11 (2012)
4. Yang, Z., Yang, M., Zhang, Y.: AppIntent: analyzing sensitive data transmission in android for privacy leakage detection. In: ACM Sigsac Conference on Computer & Communications Security, pp. 1043–1054 (2013)

5. Dinges, P., Agha, G.: Solving complex path conditions through heuristic search on induced polytopes. In: ACM Sigsoft International Symposium, pp. 425–436 (2014)
6. Schutte, J., Fedler, R., Titze, D.: ConDroid: targeted dynamic analysis of android applications. In: IEEE Conference on Advanced Information Networking and Applications, pp. 571–578 (2015)
7. Wong, M.Y.Y.: Targeted dynamic analysis for android malware. Dissertations & Theses Gradworks (2015)
8. He, J., Yang, Y.X., Qiao, Y.: Accurate classification of P2P traffic by clustering flows. China Commun. **10**(11), 42–51 (2013)
9. Zhang, Z.N., Li, D.S., Wu, K.: VMThunder: fast provisioning of large-scale virtual machine clusters. IEEE Trans. Parallel Distrib. Syst. **25**(12), 3328–3338 (2014)
10. Zhang, Z.N., Li, D.S., Wu, K.: Large-scale virtual machines provisioning in clouds: challenges and approaches. Front. Comput. Sci. **10**(1), 2–18 (2016)
11. Svajcer, V.: Sophos mobile security threat report. http://www.sophos.com/en-us/medialibrary/PDFs/other/sophos-mobile-security-threat-report.pdf
12. Ali: mobile vulnerability annual report (2015). http://jaq.alibaba.com/community/index
13. Enck, W., Gilbert, P., Chun, B.G., Cox, L.P., Jung, J., McDaniel, P., Sheth, A.N.: Taintdroid: an information-flow tracking system for realtime privacy monitoring on smartphones. In: USENIX Conference on Operating Systems Design and Implementation, pp. 1–6 (2010)
14. Shauvik, R.C., Alessandra, G., Alessandro, O.: Automated test input generation for android: are we there yet? In: International Conference on Automated Software Engineering, pp. 44–52 (2015)

CapaDroid: Detecting Capability Leak for Android Applications

Tianjun Wu[✉] and Yuexiang Yang

College of Computer, National University of Defense Technology,
Changsha 410073, China
{wutianjun08,yyx}@nudt.edu.cn

Abstract. Android app capabilities are restricted by the Android sand-boxing security enforcement. However, an app may leak its capabilities to other applications so that the latter can act beyond the permission they are granted originally. We demonstrate CapaDroid, a tool implementing our approach that applies accurate static analysis of capability leak of apps, which is based on inter-procedure vulnerable call-graph (*IVCG*, for short) that accurately models the capability-leak vulnerability, and which is conducted on Jimple code rather than relying on decompilers. Furthermore, it enables dynamic confirmation of the reported leakage, thus pruning false positive.

Keywords: Capability leak · Privilege escalation · Android application · Static control-flow analysis · Dynamic analysis

1 Introduction

Mobile applications, for example Android apps, are receiving an increase attention by the market, with their flexibility, usability, and rich functionality. The situation for app security is severe. In the year of 2015, apps from more than 10 famous vendors are reported by WooYun to contain various vulnerabilities and potentially leak 10 million user data [5]. It is worse on third-party market. For example, according to the 2015 annual security report of Google, the amount of capability leak vulnerabilities grows by 10 times than one year ago [7].

Although Android implements various safety-strengthen mechanisms, they can be easily broken down, when an app with less privileges manages to access an unintentionally exposed component and achieves more privileges which are granted to the latter. This vulnerability is called *capability leak*, and the exploitation of the vulnerability is often referred to as *privilege escalation attack*. An illustrative example is given in Fig. 1.

Despite recent year's efforts by various researchers, the detection and analysis of this type of vulnerability is far from satisfying. Among those state-of-the-art methods, they either require decompilation of Java bytecodes to java or smali files which inevitably loses lots of bytecode information and often comes into crash [8], or mainly focus on implicit intent checking and often cannot accurately detect capability leak [15, 19]. What is more, all of those tools are pure static analysis and incur high false positive and false negative as there may be behavior misses or falsely behavior report. As far as we are

© Springer International Publishing AG 2016
G. Wang et al. (Eds.): SpaCCS 2016 Workshops, LNCS 10067, pp. 95–104, 2016.
DOI: 10.1007/978-3-319-49145-5_10

```
public class edu.nudt.privEscal2.MainActivity extends Activity {

    @Override
    protected void onCreate(Bundle savedInstanceState) {
        super.onCreate(savedInstanceState);
        setContentView(R.layout.activity_main);

        // check emul
        if (!android.os.Build.BOARD.contains("goldfish")) {
            Intent i = new Intent(this, PhoneActivity.class);
            i.setAction("PHONE_CALL");
            startActivity(i);
        }
    }
}
```

```
public class edu.nudt.privEscal2.PhoneActivity extends Activity {
    @Override
    protected void onCreate(Bundle savedInstanceState) {
        super.onCreate(savedInstanceState);
        setContentView(R.layout.activity_second);

        Intent i = getIntent();
        String number = i.getStringExtra("PHONE_NUM");
        makePhoneCall(number);
    }

    void makePhoneCall(String number) {
        Intent callIntent = new Intent(Intent.ACTION_CALL);
        callIntent.setData(Uri.parse("tel:" + number));
        startActivity(callIntent); // privEscal vul
    }
}
```

Fig. 1. Code snippets of capability leak.

concerned, there are none dynamic analysis tools specifically targeted for capability leak analysis [16–18].

Thus, in this paper, we propose the first tool named "CapaDroid" that enforces analysis on a more accurate intermediate representation of bytecode, i.e., Jimple, and hybrids static analysis and dynamic analysis. It applies accurate static analysis of capability leak of apps based on Jimple code rather than relying on decompilers. It then uses concolic execution to generate inputs to trigger the capability leak behavior and dynamically confirm the reported leakage.

The contribution of this paper is three fold. First, we propose a static analysis method for capability leak which is based on inter-procedure vulnerable call-graph (*IVCG*, for short) thus accurately modeling the capability-leak vulnerability, and which is directly conducted on Jimple code thus overcoming the problem of information lose and occasional crashes experienced by decompliation adopted by tools such as [8]. Second, to our knowledge, we are the first to apply hybridized static and dynamic analysis of this type of vulnerability, which achieves higher precision and recall than state-of-the-art tools. Third, we developed CapaDroid, an open-source tool and evaluated it on 105 real-world apps from Google Play [21].

2 Background

Android Basis. Android defines four types of app component, i.e., *Activity* (defining user interface), *Service* (performing background processing), *ContentProvider* (managing database), and *BroadcastReceiver* (receiving Inter-App broadcast messages). Android provides specific methods, for triggering Inter-Component communications (*ICC*). These methods are called with *Intent*, which specifies the *action*, *category*, *mimetype*, *data*, etc. Intent can be either *explicit* or *implicit* by define the receiver component or not. Components determine which Intent to receive by specifying an *Intent Filter*.

Capability Leak. The capability leak and introduced privilege escalation attack was first proposed by Lucas Davi et al. In [20], which can be stated as follows: An application with less permissions (a non-privileged caller) is not restricted to access components of a more privileged application (a privileged callee).

Static Analysis. Static analysis comes in various forms. Static taint analysis starts at a sensitive source and then tracks the sensitive data through the app until it reaches a sensitive sink [3]. Call-graph analysis begins with a specified method and backtracks along the Control-flow graph to extract a method chain that lead to the calling of the target method. Model checking extracts models for apps and Android framework and then checks whether a specified vulnerable pattern exists.

Dynamic Analysis. Dynamic taint analysis propagates and tracks tainted data dynamically. It not suited for fully automated analysis since they require user interaction to drive execution of the apps. *Concolic* (concrete+symbolic) *execution* (or dynamic symbolic execution) uses a combination of concrete and symbolic execution to analyze how input values flow through a program as it executes, and uses this analysis to identify other inputs that can result in alternative execution behaviors [9].

3   Analysis Method and Implementation

The workflow of CapaDroid can be depicted as Fig. 2, which will be detailed in following subsections.

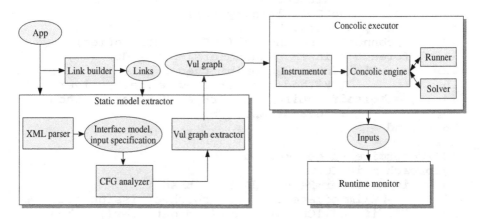

Fig. 2. Overview of CapaDroid.

3.1   IVCG Extraction

This phase produces following models, which is argumented to IccTA [1].

(1) *ICC link extraction:*

An ICC link [1] is a link in which the source component contains an ICC method *m* that holds explicit/implicit Intent information to access the target component *C*. We identifies ICC methods, Intent information, target components by parsing the Intent Filters statically declared in manifest file or dynamically defined in Java bytecode, and finally matches ICC methods with target components according to [4].

(2) *The interface model:*

It provides information about all input fields, as well as information about the Android IPC message (i.e., Intent) handled by Activities. All Android components contained in the app and Intent informations can be decided by parsing the manifest file. Input fields can be obtained from the layout XML files.

(3) *Inter-procedure vulnerable call-graph (IVCG):*

This procedure is given in Algorithm 1.

```
Algorithm 1. IVCG extraction
   Input: IM:interface model, APK:target apk
   Output: IVCG:inter-procedure vulnerable call-graph
1 ExposedCmp,tgt,dEntry,ICVG ← {}
2 ICFG ← getCFGs()
3 foreach cmp in IM.getComponents() do
4      //identify exposed component
5      if isExposedOrFilterDeclared(cmp) then
6           ExposedCmp ← ExposedCmp U cmp
7      //get default entry
8      entry ← getDefaultEntry(cmp)
9      dEntry ← dEntry U entry
10     //connect disconnecty (ICFG construcntion)
11     foreach h in IM.getHandlers(entry) do
12          if isIntentSender(h) then
13               ICFG.add(handler,handler.getReceiver())
14          elseif isLifeCircleOrEventHandler(h) then
15               ICFG.add(dEntry,h)
16     end
17end
18//determine target method
19foreach m in ICFG
20     if callsPermRequiredAPI(m) then
21          //immediate/indirect checkPermission call
22          if !callCheckPermAPI(m,m.getCaler()) then
23               tgt ← tgt U m
24end
25//construct IVCG
26ICVG ← findTransitiveMethods(dEntry,tgt,ICFG)
27return ICVG
```

For each component we parsed from interface model, we check whether it is exposed to other apps. One component can be exposed either by statically labeling it with "exported" or defining an intent filter (can be either statically or dynamically). Either will enable the component to receive intent from app beyond its local sandbox.

Components are required to overwrite one entry method by the Android Documentation [4], so that Android framework can implicitly start or resume the component when the app is launched. There are two kinds of default entry method we consider for Activities, i.e., onCreate() and onResume(). For other types of components, relative entries can be defined similarly.

We firstly extract control-flow graphs (CFG) for each basic block. Then we perform several connections to get inter-procedure CFG (ICFG). There are various other types of dis-connectivity, besides those entry points, which are also triggered at run-time by Android events. (*a*) For intra-procedure intents, an edge is inserted from the sender method to the receiver method into the call graph.(*b*) We will extend the call graph by edges from the default Activity's onResume methods to methods of all other components implementing the ActivityLifecycleCallbacks interface. (*c*) Extension of edges to UI event handlers will be performed, even without user interaction.

Embedded in the ICFG, we now construct IVCG which models the capability leak vulnerability of the entire app. This is the key point of our static analysis. For each node in ICFG that call sensitive APIs requiring specific permissions, we just pick out those without properly check of caller component's original capability. Control-flow analysis is performed so that any immediate or indirect calls to check permission APIs can be located. If none is found, the node is vulnerable to leak capability and thus marked as one of our targets.

After collecting all targets, we perform reachability analysis from entry points to targets along ICFG, resulting in the IVCG we desire.

3.2 Instrumentation and Concolic Execution

The app is mostly executed normally, while only some variables have to be traced symbolically. To achieve this, instrumentation is needed, which does following works. *(1) Inserting calls to event handlers:* It is an optional heuristic to instrument component's default entry point, such as *onCreate()/onResume()* of Activity, to allowing for direct calls to event handlers thus simulating the injection of raw events. *(2) Symbolizing registers, assignments and path conditions:* This prepares for symbolic tracing, dumping path conditions, and overwriting registers with solutions at runtime. We need instrument registers, assignments and path conditions with their symbolic counterparts. *(3) Modeling user-specified external APIs or fields:* We specify user inputs such as UI text field according to the interface model we get in the static model extraction phase, to enable symbolic tracing of them. We model user-specified APIs or fields by replacing the actual API methods with stub methods which return certain concrete values or even symbolic variable. *(4) Injecting solutions:* After constraint solver find a solution, we replace each symbolic register or model w.r.t. the r-value of the original assignment with its corresponding solution. We implement all above on ConDroid's [7] instrumentation utility.

After instrumentation, we run and symbolically trace the target app in Android emulators. Our IVCG guided concolic execution iteratively does following procedures. For each path, we first generate symbolic model/input configuration according to interface model which specifies user inputs. Secondly, the emulator's environment is cleaned and the instrumented apk is installed. Thirdly, we determine the default entry component according our IVCG analysis. And then we start the component via am-start command. Fourthly, the solutions to inputs and modeled APIs will be injected into symbolic registers in the instrumented app*. When execution deviates from the intended path by branching to the wrong basic block, we dump conditions over symbolic registers in a path condition*, negate the last clause of the path condition*[1], and then feed the resulted path constraint to a SMT solver for a new solution of concrete register values leading to execution of the intended basic block. Iterate above steps until we hit the target methods of IVCG. Acteve [7] is used as our concolic execution engine.

3.3 Runtime Monitoring

We inject events and inputs through Android Debug Bridge (adb) [10], step by step along each path of IVCG, without any repacking of the original app. According to the triggering order of events and inputs along the path, we generate a script for each path which contains directly injectable events. For instance, it can be a Monkey script [11] for UI events according to their location on the screen, or may be a list of the Activity Manager tool (am) [12] commands for system events according to their concrete types and the solutions to event parameters.

For those modeled environment-dependent APIs or fields which cannot be directly injected, such as emulator checkers or timing bombs, we set them with the solution we get from the SMT solver facilitated by Android InstrumentationTestRunner [13].

Finally, by observing the triggered behavior for each path, we can confirm the existence of capability leak in our original app. To do this, we need to instrument the method *checkPermission* to record what UID of Android app is checked, and what permission is checked.

4   Experimental Evaluation

In the following subsections, we evaluate how CapaDroid compares with existing tools, and what capabilities CapaDroid has to analyze real-world apps.

4.1   Experimental Design

We choose 105 real-world free apps from Google Play [21], covering different most popular app categories. For better comparison and confirmation, we only select those open-sourced apps. This facilitates us to inspect analyzer's warnings for these apps to evaluate how many warnings correspond to real exploitable vulnerabilities.

---

[1] These steps marked with the superscript "*" will be done by the instrumented app itself, rather than by the concolic engine.

Following tools are chosen for comparison. *(a)* DroidChecker [8] is the closest work to CapaDroid, while the author neither open-sourced it nor provided any executable binary of the tool. For evaluation, we add a optional module to CapaDroid so that it can also perform static analysis on java sources decompiled with dex2jar [22] and without any dynamic confirmation, which mimics the functionality of Droid-Checker. *(b)* JAADAS [19] is proposed to statically detect various vulnerabilities also using the Soot framework [14], including capability leak. We do not consider COV-ERT [2], as the executable provided by the author does not provide capability leak detection as described in their paper at all.

Back-end analysis is conducted on an Intel Xeon machine with 2 eight-core 2.60 Ghz CPUs and 128 GB physical memory, which runs Ubuntu 14.04 with kernel version 3.19.0. Dynamic analyzer resides in emulators of Android 4.4.2.

4.2   Results

CapaDroid takes 320 min for static analysis of all 105 apps. Suspicious apps which might contain capability leak are found and sent to concolic executor to generate inputs, which cost 8 min on average. Finally, the dynamic monitor drives the execution of those apps with those inputs to confirm vulnerabilities.

The capabilities leaked in the apps are listed in Table 1. We can see that many apps leak capability through more than one component. The analysis result is given in Table 2. Overall, 6 apps are true positives of capablity leaks, i.e., *com.madgag.agit (v238), com.matburt.mobileorg (v30), com.robert.maps (v308), com.jadn.cc (v26), com.cradle.iitc.mobile.IITC (v446), com.voidcode.diasporawebclient (v20)*.

Table 1. Permission leaked in subject apps.

Permission	# Packages	# Components
USE_CREDENTIALS	2	4
INTERNET	5	8
ACCESS_NETWORK_STATE	2	5
ACCESS_COARSE_LOCATION	3	4
ACCESS_FINE_LOCATION	3	4
AUTHENTICATE_ACCOUNTS	5	5
WAKE_LOCK	1	1
WRITE_SYNC_SETTINGS	1	1
GET_ACCOUNTS	4	8

(1)   DroidChecker relies on dex2jar to decompile bytecode to perform static analysis. However, decompiles often run into crash or fail to decompile the entire or partial app. Therefore, DroidChecker fails much more than the other tools. As its control-flow analysis is based on decompiled java code, lots of useful information is lost, incurring higher false positive.

(2) JAADAS analyzes apps using Soot framework and is more robust. But it reports a potential capability leak whenever it finds a component exposed to receive implicit intents. This is coarse grained, as the component might check the permission gained by the caller and the capability won't be leaked, thus resulting in many false warnings.

(3) CapaDroid also uses Soot to generate Jimple code to facilitate static analysis. Therefore, the number of failures is low. CapaDroid performs accurate modeling of capability leaks via IVCG, thus its static module achieves the lowest false positive among all the three tools. The false positive is further lowered as the reported leaks are confirmed by the dynamic module. Among the 6 false-positive cases reported by static analysis, five are benign and intended by the end user, and the other one is dynamically unreachable as one extra key is built with complicated string operations.

Table 2. Analysis results of three different tools.

Permission	DroidChecker	JAADAS	CapaDroid
Failed	27	3	3
False alarms	18	38	12(static) → 6(dynamic)
True alarms	6	6	6

4.3 Case Study

We here describe one of our findings. *MobileOrg*, a FREE (open-source) mobile application for storing, searching, viewing and editing user's Org-mode files, is reported to be vulnerable to privilege escalation. In that case, if another app installed along with it and without the INTERNET permission, sends an Intent with SEND action and text/plain payload data to the EditActivity component of *MobileOrg* which has INTERNET permission to send out information via Internet.

On statically capturing this potential vulnerability, CapaDroid dynamically checks it by acting as a privilege-less malicious application that sends elaborated intent to the victim application. As the monitor logs permission-required actions are taken, it immediately confirms that the victim app does contain any capability leak vulnerability.

5 Discussion and Limitations

Here are some sources of unsoundness and imprecision of CapaDroid. *(1) Complex object symbolization.* Objects which require complex initialization are difficult to statically analyze and symbolically trace. *(2) Native code, reflection and dynamic loading.* This is a common difficulty for all existing static and dynamic analysis tools. *(3) Remote procedure calls (RPC).* Besides Intent-based ICC/IAC, apps also can communicate through remote procedure calls. The latter induces method-invocation interaction using stubs which is much harder for analysis.

6 Related Work

DroidChecker [8] is by far the most frequently cited work on detecting capability leak. It performs static control-flow analysis similar to our work, while it merely bases on decompliation by means of dex2jar. The latter procedure is full of bugs, easy to crash, and the AST extracted from decomplied java source code is far from enough.

FlowDroid [3] is the Android implementation of Soot [14]. When performing analysis on Jimple code produced by Soot, following benefits are achieved: only 15 instruction types are needed, constant propagation is done on the fly, handful APIs are provided, direct transformation is done via dexpler, and CG/CFG analysis is boosted. IccTA [1] statically detects Android ICC leaks. It extracts the ICC links and then modifies the Jimple code of apps to directly connect the components to enable data-flow analysis between components.

Other tools, such as JAADAS [19] and AndroBugs [15], aimed to detect various vulnerabilities, claims to be able to detect capability leak. However, their rule-based analysis only roughly find out all implicit intent receivers, and are not able to further accurately determine whether the receivers can leak capability. COVERT [2] detects Inter-App vulnerabilities with static model checking. It performs call graph analysis for privilege escalation vulnerability.

AppIntent [5], ConDroid [6] and IntelliDroid [8] use concolic execution for dynamic analysis of apps. None of these dynamic tools are capable of capability analysis.

7 Conclusion

We proposed a tool for detecting capability leaks of Android apps. It statically extracts inter-procedure vulnerable call-graph (IVCG) from the target app and then uses concolic execution to dynamically observe whether the paths in IVCG execute at runtime, thus conforming real capability leaks. Future works include conducting tests on more real-world apps, and analyzing other types of vulnerabilities by applying model checking.

Acknowledgments. The authors would like to thank the reviewers for their detailed reviews and constructive comments, which have helped to improve the quality of this paper. This work was supported by the National Natural Science Foundation of China under Grants Nos. 61170286, 61202486.

References

1. Li, L., Bartel, A., Bissyandé, T.F., Klein, J., Traon, Y.L., Arzt, S.: IccTA: detecting inter-component privacy leaks in android apps. In: International Conference on Software Engineering, pp. 280–291 (2015)
2. Bagheri, H., Sadeghi, A., Garcia, J., Malek, S.: Covert: compositional analysis of android inter-app permission leakage. IEEE Trans. Softw. Eng. **41**(6), 6–37 (2015)
3. Arzt, S., Rasthofer, S., Fritz, C.: FlowDroid. ACM Sigplan Not. **49**(6), 259–269 (2014)

4. Android   documention.   http://developer.android.com/guide/components/intents-filters.html#Resolution
5. WooYun. http://wooyun.org
6. Schutte, J., Fedler, R., Titze, D.: ConDroid: targeted dynamic analysis of android applications. In: IEEE Conference on Advanced Information Networking and Applications, pp. 571–578 (2015)
7. Android security annual. http://security.googleblog.com/2016/04/android
8. Chan, P.P.F., Hui, L.C.K., and Yiu, S.M.: DroidChecker: analyzing android applications for capability leak. In: ACM Conference on Security & Privacy in Wireless & Mobile Networks, pp. 125–136 (2012)
9. Schwartz, E.J., Avgerinos, T., Brumley, D.: All you ever wanted to know about dynamic taint analysis and forward symbolic execution (but might have been afraid to ask). IEEE Symp. Secur. Priv. **7**, 317–331 (2010)
10. Android debug bridge. http://developer.android.com/tools/help/adb.html
11. UI/Application exerciser monkey. http://developer.android.com/tools/help/monkey.html
12. Android activity manager. http://developer.android.com/android/app/ActivityManager.html
13. Android   InstrumentationTestRunner.   http://developer.android.com/reference/android/test/InstrumentationTestRunner.html
14. Soot analysis framework. http://www.sable.mcgill.ca/soot/
15. AndroBugs. http://www.androbugs.com/
16. He, J., Yang, Y.X., Qiao, Y.: Accurate classification of P2P traffic by clustering flows. China Commun. **10**(11), 42–51 (2013)
17. Zhang, Z.N., Li, D.S., Wu, K.: VMThunder: fast provisioning of large-scale virtual machine clusters. IEEE Trans. Parallel Distrib. Syst. **25**(12), 3328–3338 (2014)
18. Zhang, Z.N., Li, D.S., Wu, K.: Large-scale virtual machines provisioning in clouds: challenges and approaches. Front. Comput. Sci. **10**(1), 2–18 (2016)
19. JAADAS. https://github.com/flankerhqd/JAADAS
20. Davi, L., Dmitrienko, A., Sadeghi, A.R., Winandy, M.: Privilege escalation attacks on android. In: International Conference on Information Security, pp. 346–360 (2010)
21. Google play market. http://play.google.com/store/apps/
22. dex2jar. http://code.google.com/p/dex2jar/

Research and Implementation Key Technology of Security Mobile Office

Feng Qiu[1(✉)] and Xiaoqian Li[2]

[1] Institute of Information Engineering, Chinese Academy of Sciences, Beijing 10093, China
qiufeng@iie.ac.cn
[2] National Computer Network Emergency Response Technical Team/
Coordination Center of China, Beijing 10029, China

Abstract. To address the information leakage problems existed in the smartphone mobility office of enterprises and institutions, we propose security mobile office architecture and design application security authentication mechanism, software and hardware resource control mechanism, security storage isolation mechanism, which provide safe protection for sensitive data. To evaluate the propose schemes, we implement them in the android system and cloud service platform. The evaluation results verify the feasibility and effectiveness of the security mobile office technology.

Keywords: Security · Mobile office · Smartphones · Sensitive data

1 Introduction

With the increasing popularity of intelligent terminals, more and more employees carry personal mobile devices (including mobile phones, tablets, etc.) into the office areas. Mobile office has becoming the future trend. While the mobile office brings convenience, information security is undoubtedly also new challenges. Smart terminals to save more and more enterprises need to protect data and information, such as e-mail messages, the personal accounts, contacts, etc. The disclosure of sensitive information will be a serious threat to corporate security.

Although security threats of mobile office mainly presents in smart terminals, the threat from all the aspects of the mobile Internet field, such as application services, terminal software or hardware resources management and data storage.

In the aspect of application services, application security audit lacks. There are malicious applications on no matter official or third-party electronic markets [1]. Users could use smartphones to download and install various software applications anytime and anywhere, it provides the opportunity for malicious applications to grab enterprises sensitive information. Thus, it is necessary to establish secure mobile office application authentication and authorization platform, in order to achieve apps management.

In the aspect of terminal software or hardware resources management, there is not fine-grained software or hardware resources control mechanisms and unified device management platform in smart terminal operation systems, so it is unable to protect

© Springer International Publishing AG 2016
G. Wang et al. (Eds.): SpaCCS 2016 Workshops, LNCS 10067, pp. 105–114, 2016.
DOI: 10.1007/978-3-319-49145-5_11

sensitive internal information from being leaked. Currently Android operation system only could provide coarse-grained access control. When apps install, Android forbids the app obtaining permission to further access to sensitive information. However, there is not a deep analysis of the use of sensitive information. Users not only know whether the application to send corporate sensitive information to advertisers, application developers or other network entities, but also do not know intelligent terminal whether obtains video, audio, pictures and other acts in the corporate office environment. Therefore, the control mechanisms of hardware and software resources need to be designed in order to achieve the monitor and management of intelligent terminals.

In the aspect of data storage, Android applications could obtain the permission of reading SD memory card, and it has the ability of reading and uploading the databases of other applications. Due to this reason and a security vulnerability of WhatsApp, it causes other applications can access and read all of the users chat record. From here we see that Android operating system lacks secure storage mechanisms to protecting sensitive data. Therefore, an effective security storage mechanism is necessary to enterprise.

To resolve the disclosure of sensitive corporate information on mobile intelligent terminals during the process of mobile office, this paper presents the security architecture of mobile office. It could solve the data problem of in aspect of application service, smartphone hardware and software resources management and sensitive data storage.

For the issue of malicious applications lacking of supervision and auditing, this paper propose application security authentication mechanism. Through the security evaluation and certification of application platform, apps could be installed in mobile intelligent terminal to ensure the application of safe and reliable.

For the disclosure of enterprise sensitive data in mobile office environment, this paper proposes an intelligent terminal hardware and software resources management and control mechanisms. Utilizing the security policy of cloud platform, smartphones prohibit cameras, sound recordings, photographs and other acts in the office environment.

Due to the lack of a security isolate in Android operating system, this paper proposes a data security storage mechanism by the use of security hardware TF card isolation to protect the user's data.

The reset of this paper is organized as follows. Section 2 gives the overview of intelligent terminal safety in the aspect of mobile office. Section 3 gives mobile office security architecture, and designs appropriate security mechanisms. Section 4 provides the performance results. Section 5 is the conclusion.

2   Background

To ensure the security of mobile intelligent terminal in mobile office, this paper proposes security schemes in application services, terminal resource management and data storage. Correspondingly application service security, authority control and data security storage of these three areas has been research jobs.

2.1   Research on Application Security Services

In the security of applications, it needs apps security analysis and distribution. Security analysis mainly uses the detection of static and dynamic analysis. Application distribution mainly uses Mobile Application Management (MAM) implementation.

Static analysis tools of application are developed to analyze applications malicious privacy disclosure behavior. SCANDAL [2] directly uses Android application bytecode to analyze. DED [3] decompiles application bytecode into Java code using a decompilation tool, but the process of the decompilation presents information loss problem. Android [4] designs a static malware analysis architecture that integrates the static taint flow analysis and the least privilege analysis, and provides a rich user interface to allow users to detect man-made. Literature [2–4] could analyze the privacy leak of application software effectively with static bytecodes or source codes.

Dynamic analysis uses the common method that inserting a probe module into Android operation system, in order to monitor privacy behavior of application dynamicly. Scandroid [5] implements an automatic analysis tool to check the data flow through the application process whether consistent with the security specification or not. To provide users with application security proof, the disadvantage of this method is dependent on obtaining the application of Java source code. TaintDroid [6] proposes a dynamic taint tracking technology. When private data leaves Android through a network interface, TaintDroid will warn the user. However, it is just private data stream monitoring tool does not provide a mechanism to prevent loss of privacy effectively. Meanwhile it requires the user to anthropogenic manual trigger, which is difficult to implement all the paths of the application to detect the privacy disclosure. On the basis of Taint-Droid, AppFence [7] protects privacy data using shading data and flight simulator mode. The two ways resolve the program crashes of application caused by accessing private data being prevented.

For the secure distribution of applications, MAM method pushes apps to smartphones in the enterprise, which realizes automated configuration and increases the security and license control of applications. MAM established app store and enterprise management platform. Through internal safety audits or custom development, IT administrators can quickly deploy mobile office applications to various types of mobile devices.

In the aspects of the installation restrictions, Kirin [8] analyzes the apps configuration file and imports static rights policy. If configuration file does not meet the permission policy, Kirin refuses the installation of apps. But it needs to consider all the possible rights policy. [5] restricts the installation of apps according to the static permissions policy. However, there is no mechanism to provide visual reference assessment and unified security authentication mechanism for users.

2.2   Research on Permission Control

Permission Control is the aspect of terminal granting user permission. Apex et al. [9] allowed users to grant permission to applications selectively in the installation process, and limit the time or the number of times of applications to access resources through the configuration policy files. However, they can only restrict part of applications and lack of fine-grained control mechanism. Jeon [10] proposed to replace the control system by fine-grained permission. They first inferred whether the application calls the sensitive permission and then use fine-grained permission to substitute sensitive permissions of the applications to restrict the access to resources. CRePE et al. [11] allowed users to make the control policy according the context (such as location, power, time), and then insert the policy into the relevant policy permission check. The calls in line with the policy can be performed. TISSA [12] realized the privacy mode and users grant the application dynamic in a flexible manner to access personal data privacy.

The above researches are mainly about terminals. In this paper, we intercept the instruction in terminal framework layer and manage device resources and distribute security policy in the cloud. The collaboration of terminal and cloud manages the application permission calls in mobile office process.

2.3 Research on Data Secure Storage

Data secure storage in the terminal side realizes the secure isolation through virtualization technology and mandatory access control. L4Android [13] proposed a general framework for the operation system, and ran the original smartphone operating system in the virtual machine. Then it isolates the virtual machine and the application by advanced micro-kernel technology. But the technology based on virtualization costs too many resources of the mobile devices. TrustDroid [14] colors the applications and data, the applications and data with the same colour enter the same logical region. The constraint access control policy prevents the application communication and data exchange. This strong isolation mechanism is strictly prohibited Android inter-process communication, data sharing, and to some extent undermines the effectiveness of the system. Data secure storage ensures users access to encrypted data safely and effectively. In [15], author use the key derivation method to solve cloud data storage update issues.

In summary, although the mobile intelligent terminal based on the Android platform security office has been considerable research, but most of them more or less there are some flaws and shortcomings. They solve the problem only from a single aspect, and do not accomplish complete system. This paper proposes a mobile office security architecture to protect sensitive data within the enterprise and support secure mobile office.

3 Mobile Office Security Architecture

Mobile office secure architecture is shown in Fig. 1. A mobile office security cloud platform is established including a key management center, a security apps market, a resource management server, a security evaluation system, a cloud storage server and a security gateway, which provides a security privacy service for smartphone.

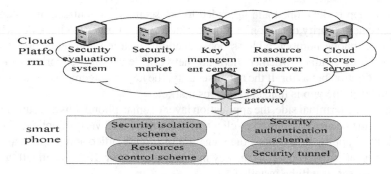

Fig. 1. Mobile office security architecture

In the respect of smartphone, we implement application security authentication, terminal resources control and secure storage isolation to protect sensitive data. Cloud platform implements the distribution of security policy and the management of apps, and establishes secure VPN tunnel with smartphone.

3.1 Application Security Authentication Scheme

App security authentication scheme is shown in Fig. 2. In Cloud platform, we established mobile office security authentication system, including a security evaluation system, a key management center and a security apps market.

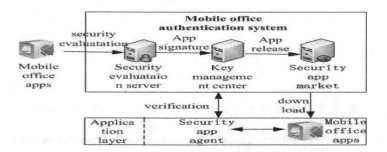

Fig. 2. App security authentication scheme

The security evaluation system detects and evaluates apps behavior. The key management center achieves the signature and verification of apps. The security apps market provides a download platform for smartphones. Security authentication mechanism make sure without authority signing, forgery signing or destruction of the apps integrity could not be installed and run on smartphones.

As shown in Fig. 2. Cloud platform establishes mobile office app security checking scheme through the security authentication system. First, the security authentication system formulates development specifications of mobile office app, and third-party apps developers design apps based on the security requirement.

After an app is developed and uploaded to the security authentication system, the system executes security detection of mobile office apps, in order to check out whether the app leaks phone number, address book, account, location and other private data. Meanwhile it determines whether there are network detection, network attacks and privilege escalation behavior. If the app is security, the key management center will sign the app and then the app is uploaded to apps market.

In the mobile terminal side, the application layer of smartphone runs a secure desktop program as the security app market client to implement and verify applications. The secure desktop application obtains the signature of mobile office applications and then sends an authentication request to the key management center. If the verification of the application passes, it will be installed.

3.2   Hardware and Software Resources Control Scheme

Figure 3 illustrates smartphone hardware and software resources control scheme. In the cloud platform, the application access control module and policy management module execute security management policies and deliver to smartphones. In this way, the cloud platform controls the camera, Bluetooth, WiFi and microphone of smartphone.

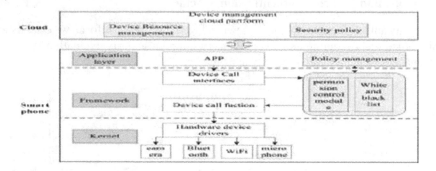

Fig. 3.   Smartphone hardware and software resources control scheme

In the user layer of smartphone, the policy management module receives and resolves security management policies, which provides interfaces for permission control module in framework layer. To achieve fine-grained permission control scheme, the permission control module establishes a white list and manages each permission of apps deeply.

When an app wants to use permission, it invokes the security policies of permission control module. If the security policy of the cloud platform prohibits this privilege, the request will be refused and the permission could not allowed. If the cloud platform strategy at this time allows this permission to be opened, the application query whether the application is in the white list and has the permission to allow access to the corresponding hardware resources.

For security apps in mobile office domain, they pass the security assessment, which are included in the white list. For the policy management module in operating system application layer, it processes software and hardware resource management policy from the cloud platform, and controls the white and black list in the frame layer. Depending on security threats, the cloud platform develops control strategies. For malicious applications which steal enterprises sensitive information, the cloud platform adds them into black list.

3.3   Data Security Storage Isolation Scheme

Based on a security SD card, this paper performs a data security storage isolation scheme so as to encrypt and isolate data mobile office data in smartphones.

As shown in Fig. 4, in the system and the frame layer, a data access control module is added which performs permission access commands interception mechanism. In the system layer, through the kernel black and white list access control protocol, the module monitors apps invoke data, to achieve the access control of user data. When an app stores files, it calls SD card encryption interface, and encrypts files. In this way, user data is isolated and stored in SD card.

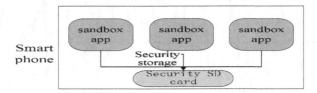

Fig. 4.   Data security storage isolation scheme

4   Performance Analysis

4.1   App Security Authentication Scheme

Application security authentication scheme introduces additional verification time. To evaluate verification delay we establish a delay analytical model. t_{cs} represent the transmission delay between the key management server and smartphone. t_c represents the signature time of the key management server. t_s represents the processing signature time in smartphones. For the common apps installation, the total delay is the processing signature time t_s in smartphones. For the app security authentication scheme, the total delay is $t_a = t_s + 2t_{cs} + t_c$. The added delay is $t_a - t_s = 2t_{cs} + t_c$. We analaze the added delay as follows.

To calculate the transmission delay t_{cs}, we use PING command to obtain round trip time (RTT) between the key management and smartphones. The scene in this paper is secure mobile office. Smartphones and the key management server in the same work area and smartphones connect server via WiFi. As shown in Table 1, the average time (RTT) is 0.856 ms.

Table 1. The RTT between the server and smartphone

Round Trip Time (ms)		
Minimum	Maximum	Average
0.489	1.568	0.856

To calculate the processing delay in the server, we use Wireshark software to capture the authentication request message and the reply message. When the smartphone installs apps, it send an authentication request message to the key management server. The server processes the message and replies a response message. The interval of two messages is the processing delay t_c.

As shown in Fig. 5, the smartphone installs 100 apps and we obtain the minimum processing time is 1.71 ms, the maximum processing time is 3.21 ms and the average time is 2.407 ms.

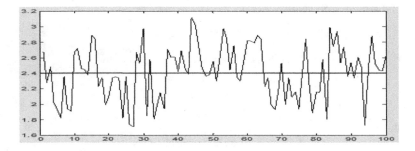

Fig. 5. The processing delay in the key management server

We obtain that the added delay is $2t_{cs} + t_c = 0.856 + 1.407 = 3.263$ ms. The introduced delay is only milliseconds, so application security authentication scheme is feasible and effective.

4.2 Software and Hardware Resource Control Scheme

In the system implementation, we modify the framework layer of Android and add hardware access control module for privacy-related permissing control. In addition, we monitor equipment call interface using the hook function to intercept the call instruction from hardware devices. We modify the checkUidPermission() function in PackageMa-nagerService class and add a hook function to deliver app UID and permission to access control module. The access control module calls application white list, and based on UID and permission mapping relationship table it decides to authorize or reject app permission request.

4.3 Data Security Storage Isolation Scheme

To evaluate data security storage isolation scheme, we calculate the average time of data encryption and decryption. The data of mobile office storages in the SD card. The app calls storeencrypt() function and executes ciphertext = storeencrypt (plaintext) to encrypt data. And the app calls storedecrypt() function and executes plaintext = store-decrypt (ciphertext) to decrypt data.

As shown in Table 2, we encrypt and decrypt the doc formate document and the JPG format picture to calculate the average time. The Java tools have the class of encryption and decryption. This paper security storage scheme compare to the Java, the results show that the security hardware SD card storage mechanism is superior to Java-based encryption and decryption methods in storage speed.

Table 2. Average time of data encryption and decryption

	Average time (Java)	Average time (Data security storage isolation scheme)
791 K doc encryption	320 ms	130 ms
791 K doc decryption	284 ms	112 ms
2.4 M JPG encryption	958 ms	387 ms
2.4 M JPG decryption	896 ms	371 ms

5 Conclusions

This paper proposes security mobile office architecture and designs app security authentication scheme, software and hardware resource control scheme, data security storage isolation scheme, which provide safe protection for sensitive data. To evaluate the propose schemes, we implement them in the android system and cloud service platform. The evaluation results verify the feasibility and effectiveness of the security mobile office technology.

Acknowledgments. Supported by the "Strategic Priority Research Program" of the Chinese Academy of Sciences, Grant No. XDA06010703.

References

1. Zhou, Y., Wang, Z., Zhou, W., Jiang, X.: Hey, you, get off of my market: detecting malicious apps in official and alternative android markets. In: Proceedings of the 19th Annual Symposium on Network and Distributed System Security (NDSS 2012), San Diego, USA, February 2012
2. Kim, J., Yoon, Y., Yi, K., Shin, J.: SCANDAL: static analyzer for detecting privacy leaks in android applications. In: Proceedings of the Mobile Security Technologies (MoST 2012), San Francisco, USA, May 2012
3. Enck, W., Octeau, D., McDaniel, P., Chaudhuri, S.: A study of Android application security. In: Proceedings of the 20th USENIX Conference on Security (SEC 2011), San Francisco, USA, August 2011
4. Liang, S., Keep, A.W., Might, M., Lyde, S., Gilray, T., Aldous, P., Horn, D.V.: Sound and precise malware analysis for android via pushdown reachability and entry-point saturation. In: Proceedings of the 3rd ACM CCS Workshop on Security and Privacy in Smartphones and Mobile Devices (SPSM 2013), Berlin, Germany, November 2013

5. Fuchs, A., Chaudhuri, A., Foster, J.: Scandroid: automated security certification of android applications (2009). http://www.cs.umd.edu/~avik/papers/scandroidascaa.pdf
6. Enck, W., Gilbert, P., Chun, B.: TaintDroid: an information-flow tracking system for realtime privacy monitoring on smartphones. In: Proceedings of the 7th USENIX Conference on Operating Systems Design and Implementation (OSDI 2010), Canada, October 2010
7. Hornyack, P., Han, S., Jung, J., Schechter, S., Wetherall, D.: These aren't the droids you're looking for: retrofitting Android to protect data from imperious applications. In: Proceedings of the 18th ACM Conference on Computer and Communications Security (CCS 2011), Chicago, Illinois, USA, October 2011
8. Enck, W., Ongtang, M., McDaniel, P.: On lightweight mobile phone application certification. In: Proceedings of the 16th ACM Conference on Computer and Communications Security (CCS 2009), Chicago, USA, November 2009
9. Nauman, M., Khan, S., Zhang, X.: Apex: extending Android permission model and enforcement with user-defined runtime constraints. In: Proceedings of the 5th ACM Symposium on Information, Computer and Communication Security (ASIACCS 2010), Beijing, China, April 2010
10. Jeon, J., Micinski, K., Vaughan, J., Fogel, A., Reddy, N., Foster, J., Millstein, T.: Dr. Android and Mr. Hide: fine-grained permissions in Android applications. In: Proceedings of the Second ACM Workshop on Security and Privacy in Smartphones and Mobile Devices (SPSM 2012), North Carolina, USA, October 2012
11. Conti, M., Crispo, B., Pernandes, E., Zhauniarovich, Y.: CRePE: a system for enforcing fine-grained context-related policy on Android. IEEE Trans. Inf. Forensics Secur. 7(5), 1426–1438 (2012)
12. Zhou, Y., Zhang, X., Jiang, X., Freeh, V.W.: Taming information-stealing smartphone applications (on Android). In: McCune, J.M., Balacheff, B., Perrig, A., Sadeghi, A.-R., Sasse, A., Beres, Y. (eds.) Trust 2011. LNCS, vol. 6740, pp. 93–107. Springer, Heidelberg (2011). doi:10.1007/978-3-642-21599-5_7
13. Lange, M., Liebergeld, S., Lackorzynski, A., Warg, A., Peter, M.: L4Android: a generic operating system framework for secure smartphones. In: Proceedings of the 1st ACM Workshop on Security and Privacy in Smartphones and Mobile devices (SPSM 2011), Chicago, USA, October 2011
14. Sven, B., Lucas, D., Alexandra, D., Stephan, H., Ahmad-reza, S., Bhargava, S.: Practical and lightweight domain isolation on Android. In: Proceedings of the 1st ACM Workshop on Security and Privacy in Smartphones and Mobile devices (SPSM 2011), Chicago, USA, October 2011
15. Wang, W., Li, Z., Owens, R., Bhargava, B.: Secure and efficient access to outsourced data. In: Proceedings of CCSW 2009, Chicago, USA, November 2009

Makespan Minimization for Batch Tasks in Data Centers

Xin Li[1,2,3]([envelope]) and Cui Tang[1]

[1] College of Computer Science and Technology,
Nanjing University of Aeronautics and Astronautics, Nanjing 211106, China
lics@nuaa.edu.cn
[2] State Key Laboratory for Novel Software Technology,
Nanjing University, Nanjing 210023, China
[3] Collaborative Innovation Center of Novel Software Technology
and Industrialization, Nanjing 210093, China

Abstract. Makespan is one for crucial factors to determine the performance of job scheduling in cloud data center, short makespan could lead to more job throughput and less energy consumption. In this paper, we study the joint task and data assignment problem to realized makespan minimization. We propose the data migration method to overcome the memory space limitation of servers, and realize better data locality for task execution. We conduct extensive simulations, and the simulation results show that our algorithm has significant improvement on makespan reduction.

Keywords: Big data analysis · Data assignment · Data center · Job scheduling · Makespan minimization

1 Introduction

Big data analysis is showing significant importance for many applications. For example, big data analysis help companies to make better predictions and decisions. This motivates firms employing cloud computing for powerful computational performance to carry out data analysis. Efficient task/job scheduling policy has critical influence on data analysis performance. Because of the importance of data locality for task execution, data assignment also affect the data analysis performance significantly.

In this paper, we jointly investigate the job and data deployment problem. We aim to find an effective job assignment and data deployment approach to achieve optimized makespan, which means the time consumed to execute given jobs. We should be aware that data block is the necessary condition for the data-intensive jobs, i.e. big data analysis job. Hence, there would be two cases for job execution: *data-locality* and *remote-access*. Some job will be called *data-locality job* when the job and its input data are assigned to the same server. Otherwise, the job will be named as *remote-access job*. Obviously, the remote-access mode will consume more time and energy than the data-locality mode,

© Springer International Publishing AG 2016
G. Wang et al. (Eds.): SpaCCS 2016 Workshops, LNCS 10067, pp. 115–123, 2016.
DOI: 10.1007/978-3-319-49145-5_12

since the remote-access job needs to read and load data from another server in the network. It is time consuming and energy consuming for data transferring. Hence, the problem is to find a proper data deployment policy such as most of the jobs could be executed locally, and propose a job assignment policy to schedule the jobs so as to reduce makespan.

Intuitively, we should assign the job and its input data block to the same server as much as possible. However, there is limited resource slots and memory space to host job execution and data blocks for each server. There are two methods to reduce the time for remote accessing data. One is to let the job wait for enough time until some resource slot is available on the server that hosts its input data block. But, the waiting time is always longer than the time for remote accessing data. The other one is conduct data migration which refers to migrate the wanted data block to the server contains unoccupied resource slot to realize data-locality. In this case, the migration time must be carefully treated, since the total migration time will be determined by various complex factors.

Our contribution are summarized as:

- We formalize a joint task and data assignment problem for makespan minimization, which takes into account the data migration operation and its cost.
- We propose an algorithm to measure the appropriateness to conduct data migration, and the approach to reduce makespan.
- We conduct extensive simulations, and the simulation results demonstrate that our algorithm has significant performance improvement on makespan reduction.

The rest of this paper is organized as follows. We review the related work in Sect. 2. The problem and algorithm are presented in Sect. 3. Simulation results are shown in Sect. 4. Finally, we conclude our paper in Sect. 5.

2   Related Work

As the traditional issue, scheduling problem has significant importance for various computing systems [9]. The job/task scheduling policy affects the performance of the MapReduce system [5], one of the most popular data analysis paradigms. Though the FIFO algorithm is very simple, the performance is unsatisfactory. Hence, various scheduling policies are proposed to handle all kinds of applications.

The Hadoop is the most popular implementation of MapReduce-like computing systems. Hadoop uses a local optimization polity, i.e., the scheduler greedily picks the job with data closest to the node that has a slot to launch the job, which cannot always lead to data locality. Many modified works have been carried out to optimize the scheduler [10,11,14]. Also, three replicas of each data block are stored in Hadoop implementation, which cannot reflect the popularity of each data block.

Data locality is one of the most important concerns that determine the task execution time [13]. To guarantee better data locality, delay scheduling [15] policy is proposed to make a tradeoff between locality and fairness. The basic idea is that, when the job should be scheduled, according to fairness, it cannot achieve data locality: it waits for a small amount of time, and lets the other jobs be scheduled first. This is the representative work to realize data locality by scheduling jobs/tasks unilaterally, similar work includes ShuffleWatcher [2] and Tetris [7]. However, the schedulers do not jointly optimize over data and compute location [8], since the dynamics for online jobs.

From the aspect of data placement, CoHadoop [6], PACMan [4], and Scarlett [3] are the representative works to conduct data replication placement. However, the method of data migration to optimize data locality is still not investigated. In this paper, other than the regular data and task assignment method, we introduce the data migration operation to achieve better data locality and less makespan.

3   Problem Statement and Algorithm

3.1   Scenario and Notations

For a given data centers with homogeneous server, jobs share the data blocks and resources. For each server, the resources can be regarded as many resource slots. For each job execution, some resource slot and its input data block are necessary. Otherwise, we should be aware that there are limited memory space to host data blocks for each server. Hence, there would be at least one replica for each data block, but it could not own too many replicas due to the limitation of memory space.

As mentioned above, there are two job execution modes: *data-locality* and *remote-access*. We assume the jobs have the same execution time when the jobs execute in data-locality mode. It is an acceptable assumption since the map tasks or reduce tasks of one job in MapReduce have similar execution time [12]. For the jobs execute in remote-access mode, the job execution time will be longer since the remote data transferring. Here, we let T_{loc} represent the job execution time when the job is carried out in data-locality mode. Meanwhile, T_{rmt} stands for the job execution time for the jobs execute in remote-access manner. Furthermore, since the time consumption of data transferring is also affected by the network condition, we let $T_{rmt} = T_{loc} + \lambda \cdot r$, where λ is a constant determined by the data center architecture and networking situation, r is the number of jobs that will be executed in remote-access mode.

The network condition will be worse when many jobs need to read their input data blocks remotely, and it will lead to longer data transfer time. A potential method is to migrate some data block from the busy servers and reduce the number of jobs that need to remote access data. However, there are two major concerns during data migration. The first one is the memory space is limited for each server. The data migration would reduce replica of some data block. The other one is the migration cost, which means the time consumption of data migration. We use T_{mgt} to represent the data migration time.

Table 1. Notation table

Symbol	Description
T_{loc}	task execution time in data-locality mode
T_{rmt}	task execution time in remote-access mode
T_{mig}	data migration time
m	number of task in the system
n	number of servers in the data center
b	number of data blocks
θ	memory capacity to host data block for each server
$S_i \; (i \in [1, n])$	the ith server
$J_k \; (k \in [1, m])$	the kth task
$D_j \; (j \in [1, b])$	the jth data block
$D(J_k) \; (k \in [1, m])$	the input data block of task J_k
$\varsigma(J_k)$	the server that contains job J_k
$\varsigma(D_j)$	the server that contains data block D_j
L_i^{ini}	the normalized initial load for server S_i
$[]D_j$	the task set of tasks want D_j as their input data

In this paper, we take the makespan as the optimization object. Intuitively, the best job assignment is guaranteeing all of the jobs will be executed in data-locality mode. However, the ideal best assignment hardly can be realized due to the limited resource slots and memory space. Hence, there will be a tradeoff between remote execution and data migration.

Generally, we introduce the following notations so as to describe the problem properly (Table 1).

3.2 Problem Formulation

Joint Assignment Problem. Given a data center with n uniform servers, which can host θ data blocks. We let that each server can support one job execution once. To complete some data analysis job, there are m tasks need to be executed and the tasks share b data blocks. For each task, there is one data block as its input data. The task need to access the data block remotely if the task and its wanted data block are not hosted on the same server. Or, we can migration the data block to realize data locality. The problem is to give a proper strategy of joint task and data deployment, such that the makespan is minimized. It could be formalized as follows:

$$min. \; \max_{1 \leq i \leq n} \left\{ L_i^{ini} + \sum_{J_k : \varsigma(J_k) = S_i} T_{exe}(J_k) + T_{mig} \right\}$$

where
$$T_{exe}(J_k) = \begin{cases} T_{loc}(J_k), \ if \ \varsigma(J_k) = \varsigma(D(J_k)); \\ T_{rmt}(J_k) = T_{loc}(J_k) + \lambda \cdot r, \ otherwise. \end{cases}$$

3.3 Problem Analysis and Algorithm

To describe the problem and our algorithm more clearly, we give a toy example to explain the notations. Assuming there are two servers (S_1 and S_2) in the system, and the data placement is shown in Fig. 1. The server S_1 contains data block D_1, D_3, D_4 and D_6. Data block D_2 and D_5 are placed on server S_2. Currently, server S_1 is idle now, and there are 30 tasks that want data block D_5 as their input data, i.e. $|[]D_5| = 30$. Now, we should determine placing all of the tasks in to server S_2, or move some of them to server S_1. From the figure, we know that there is no memory space for server S_1 though it is idle. However, we can replace some data block, say D_1, with the data block D_5, if all of the tasks wanted data block D_1 have completed. Obviously, the makespan will be reduced if we migrate data block D_5 from S_2 to S_1. Hence, the key is be aware that which data block on each server is unwanted, and judge the data migration cost is valuable or not.

Based on the above analysis, we present an algorithm to carry out the job and data deployment. The basic idea of the algorithm can be summarized as:

- **Grouping.** Group the tasks according to their input data block, which means that the tasks that share the common data block will be regarded as the same. Then, we can focus on the data deployment problem. Assigning one data block on some server means that the tasks wanting the data block will also be assigned to the same server.
- **Greedy Assignment.** Assign the data block and its associated tasks in greedy manner. This means we will select some data block to be deployed on the server that has least workload.
- **Migration.** For the data blocks that have no associated tasks, we can conduct data migration to replace it with others to reduce the makespan.

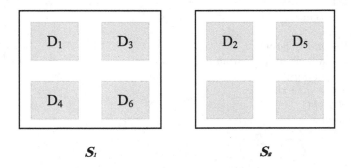

Fig. 1. Toy example

Algorithm 1. Joint Assignment Algorithm: $DMigrate$

Input:

> The set of tasks, $\bigcup J_k$;
> The set of servers, $\bigcup S_i$;
> The set of data blocks, $\bigcup D_j$.

1: **for** $j = 1 \rightarrow b$ **do**
2:     $s \leftarrow minLoadServer(\bigcup S_i)$
3:     $assign(D_j, []D_j, s)$
4:     $updateLoad(s)$
5: **end for**
6: $flag \leftarrow true$
7: **while** $flag$ **do**
8:     $flag \leftarrow false$
9:     $s_{min} \leftarrow minLoadServer(\bigcup S_i)$
10:     $s_{max} \leftarrow maxLoadServer(\bigcup S_i)$
11:     $D^m \leftarrow maxDegreeData(s_{max})$
12:     **if** $\pi(D^m, s_{min}) == 1$ **then**
13:         **repeat**
14:             $ms1 \leftarrow makespan()$
15:             move one task of $[]D^m$ from s_{max} to s_{min}
16:             $ms2 \leftarrow makespan()$
17:             **if** $ms1 < ms2$ **then**
18:                 $rollback()$
19:                 break
20:             **end if**
21:             $flag \leftarrow true$
22:         **until** $(makespan(s_{min}) = makespan(s_{max}))||([]D^m = 0)$
23:     **else if** $load(s_{max}) - load(s_{min}) \geq T_{mig}$ **then**
24:         $ms1 \leftarrow makespan()$
25:         migrate D^m to s_{min} and replace some unnecessary data block
26:         $ms2 \leftarrow makespan()$
27:         **if** $ms1 < ms2$ **then**
28:             $rollback()$
29:             continue
30:         **end if**
31:         $flag \leftarrow true$
32:     **else**
33:         $ms1 \leftarrow makespan()$
34:         move one task of $[]D^m$ from s_{max} to s_{min}
35:         $ms2 \leftarrow makespan()$
36:         **if** $ms1 < ms2$ **then**
37:             $rollback()$
38:             continue
39:         **end if**
40:         $flag \leftarrow true$
41:     **end if**
42: **end while**

The proposed algorithm is shown in Algorithm 1. The input of the algorithm is the sets of task, servers and data blocks. At the beginning, the data blocks and their associated tasks are assigned in greedy manner, i.e. assign the tasks to the server with least workload and have usable memory space, as shown in line 1 to line 4. The function $minLoadServer(\bigcup S_i)$ returns the usable server with least workload. After this first round, all of the data blocks and tasks should be assigned. Then, we start to optimize the assignment by splitting the tasks share the common data block.

To realize minimized makespan, the basic idea is to move some tasks in high workload server to the servers with lower workload, so as to realize load balance, which leads to minimized makespan. In the algorithm, the variable $flag$ indicates whether some movement is conducted or not. The assignment will finish if none of movement is conducted any more. The function $minLoadServer(\bigcup S_i)$ returns the server with minimum workload, while the function $maxLoadServer(\bigcup S_i)$ returns the server with maximum workload, currently. For given server S_i, we can get the data block with most associated tasks by the function $maxDegreeData(S_i)$. We use the function $\pi(D_j, S_i)$ to indicate the data block D_k is deployed on server S_i or not, it could be formalized as:

$$\pi(D_j, S_i) = \begin{cases} 0, \text{ there is no replica of } D_j \text{ on } S_i; \\ 1, \text{ otherwise.} \end{cases}$$

There are three methods to carry out task shift.

1. We can move some tasks to the server that contains their input data block, and this movement can guarantee the tasks be executed in data-locality manner. The method is shown in line 11 to line 19 in Algorithm 1. The function $makespan()$ returns the current makespan for the system. If the movement leads worse result, the movement will be rollback by the function $rollback()$. The movement continues until all of the tasks have been moved or the makespan becomes worse.
2. Data block is migrated from S_{max} to s_{min}. Though the data migration will introduce some cost, the tasks moved to the server s_{min} will realize data locality, which can reduce task execution time. However, if the data migration leads to worse makespan, this operation will be canceled. This method is shown from line 23 to line 31.
3. The last method is to just move some tasks to server with lower workload, and the task will be executed in remote-access mode. This method will not introduce data migration cost, and has no demand on memory space. It also may lead less makespan.

4 Simulation

We conduct a small-scale simulation to evaluate the performance of our algorithm. We take the traditional FIFO algorithm as the baseline, which is also one of the basic scheduling algorithms in Hadoop System [1]. In the simulation, we

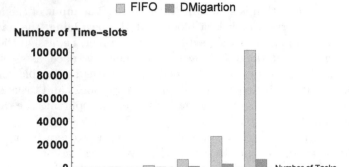

Fig. 2. Simulation results

assume there are 10 servers, and each server can host 6 data blocks. There are 40 data blocks totally, and each task will choose one data block as its input data randomly. Let the task execution time in data-locality mode and data migration time is 20 time-slots, i.e. $T_{loc} = T_{mig} = 20$. The parameter λ equals to 0.2 for the task execution in remote-access mode, i.e. $\lambda = 0.2$. We conducted extensive simulations based on the above settings. The simulation results are shown in Fig. 2. In the figure, the $DMigrate$ is our algorithm.

In this figure, the x-axis indicates the number of tasks, which varies from 100 to 3200. The consumed time-slots are shown in the y-axis. Learn from the results, we know that the performance of our algorithm becomes better along with the rising of number of tasks. The time consumed, i.e. makespan, by our algorithm is less than FIFO algorithm significantly when $m \geq 800$. Another fact should be noticed is that the makespan determined by the $DMigration$ algorithm increase slowly when the number of tasks rising significantly. This indicates our algorithm has very stable performance.

5   Conclusion

In this paper, we investigate the joint job and data assignment problem for makespan minimization. Different from the previous work, we introduce the data migration method as an important approach to reduce task execution time. analysis on the task execution mode, we make a tradeoff between the data locality and data migration. Then we propose the $DMigrate$ algorithm, and introduce the data migration operation in proper opportunity. We conduct extensive simulations on small-scale data center. The simulation results show that our algorithm has significant performance improvement compared to the traditional FIFO algorithm, and has very stable performance.

Acknowledgments. This work is supported in part by the Jiangsu Natural Science Foundation under Grant No. BK20160813, National High Technology Research and Development Program of China under Grant No. 2015AA015303, Project Funded by China Postdoctoral Science Foundation, Fundamental Research Funds for the Central Universities under Grant NO. NS2016097.

References

1. Apach Hadoop. http://hadoop.apache.org
2. Ahmad, F., Chakradhar, S., Raghunathan, A., Vijaykumar, T.: Shufflewatcher: shuffle-aware scheduling in multi-tenant mapreduce clusters. In: USENIX ATC (2014)
3. Ananthanarayanan, G., Agarwal, S., Kandula, S., Greenberg, A., Stoica, I., Harlan, D., Harris, E.: Scarlett: coping with skewed content popularity in mapreduce clusters. In: EuroSys (2011)
4. Ananthanarayanan, G., Ghodsi, G., Wang, A., Borthakur, D., Kandula, S., Shenker, S., Stoica, I.: Pacman: coordinated memory caching for parallel jobs. In: USENIX NSDI (2012)
5. Dean, J., Ghemawat, S.: Mapreduce: simplified data processing on large clusters. Commun. ACM **51**(1), 107–113 (2008)
6. Eltabakh, M., Tian, Y., Ozcan, F., Gemulla, R., Krettek, A., McPherson, J.: Cohadoop: flexible data placement and its exploitation in hadoop. In: VLDB Endow (2011)
7. Grandl, R., Ananthanarayanan, G., Kandula, S., Rao, S., Akella, A.: Multi-resource packing for cluster schedulers. In: ACM SIGCOMM (2014)
8. Jalaparti, V., Bodik, P., Menache, I., Rao, S., Makarychev, K., Caesar, M.: Network-aware scheduling for data-parallel jobs: plan when you can. In: ACM SIGCOMM (2015)
9. Leung, J., Kelly, L., Anderson, J.H.: Handbook of Scheduling: Algorithms, Models, and Performance Analysis. CRC Press, Boca Raton (2004)
10. Maguluri, S.T., Srikant, R.: Scheduling jobs with unknown duration in clouds. In: IEEE INFOCOM (2013)
11. Tan, J., Meng, X., Zhang, L.: Coupling task progress for mapreduce resource-aware scheduling. In: IEEE INFOCOM (2013)
12. Verma, A., Cherkasova, L., Campbell, R.H.: Two sides of a coin: Optimizing the schedule of mapreduce jobs to minimize their makespan and improve cluster performance. In: IEEE MASCOTS (2012)
13. Wang, W., Zhu, K., Ying, L., Tan, J., Zhang, L.: Map task scheduling in mapreduce with data locality: throughput and heavy-traffic optimality. In: IEEE INFOCOM (2013)
14. Wolf, J., Rajan, D., Hildrum, K., Khandekar, R., Kumar, V., Parekh, S., Wu, K.L., Balmin, A.: Flex: a slot allocation scheduling optimizer for mapredcue workloads. In: ACM/IFIP/USENIX Middleware (2010)
15. Zaharia, M., Borthakur, D., Sarma, J.S., Elmeleegy, K., Shenker, S., Stoica, I.: Delay scheduling: a simple technique for achieving locality and fairness in cluster scheduling. In: EuroSys (2010)

Opportunistic Resource Sharing Based Elastic Resource Allocation in a Data Center

Guoquan Yuan[1], Songyun Wang[2,3]($\boxtimes$), Mingming Zhang[1], Yefei Li[2], Xin Li[3], Tiantian Wang[4], and Zhuzhong Qian[4]

[1] State Grid Jiang Su Electric Power Company Information and Telecommunication Branch, Nanjing 210000, China
[2] Jiang Su Frontier Electric Technology Co., Ltd., Nanjing 210000, China
wsy_hi@163.com
[3] Nanjing University of Aeronautics and Astronautics, Nanjing 211106, China
[4] State Key Laboratory for Novel Software Technology,
Nanjing University, Nanjing 210023, China

Abstract. Resource allocation is the primary issue for multi-tenant cloud data centers. Opportunistic resource sharing is an efficient way to optimize resource utilization for data centers. However, the resource collision makes it challenging. In this paper, we introduce a Markov-chain based model (MST) to characterize the dynamical resource requirements for application, instead of the traditional static virtual network. To deal with the resource collision problem, we introduce a waiting time indicator (WTE) to describe the resource usage, and achieve a tradeoff between utilization and performance. Based on the MST model and WTE indicator, we propose a TRRA algorithm. The basic idea is to select the PM with reasonable WTE value for any extra resource requirement from applications. The experimental results show that our algorithm can realize better resource utilization while guaranteeing acceptable application performance.

Keywords: Data center · Elastic resource allocation · Markov chain · Opportunistic resource sharing · Utilization optimization

1 Introduction

Cloud computing platform allows pay-on-demand applications to specify resources they need to serve a specified amount of end users. Each application that running in a cloud is considered as a tenant and the resource requirement is generally defined as a group of virtual machines (VMs) with typical computing capacity. How to allocate VMs to physical machines (PMs) in a cloud so that the active number of PMs is minimum, is a challenge problem, which is proved to be NP-hardness. This VM consolidation problem is widely investigated in recent years [3,12] and researchers propose several effective VM allocation mechanisms [10,17]. However, since the workload of many applications are dynamic, it is difficult to give a fixed resource requirement. Thus, dynamic resource scheduling is

G. Wang et al. (Eds.): SpaCCS 2016 Workshops, LNCS 10067, pp. 124–133, 2016.
DOI: 10.1007/978-3-319-49145-5_13

proposed to adjust resource allocation based on the real time resource monitor during the run time. Although these mechanisms could improve the resource utilization, the resource re-allocation is just based on the current workload, which may lead to over-frequent resource adjustment. Since we do not have the knowledge of real resource requirement, system only could guess how much resource should re-allocate to the application.

Actually, as we observed a large amount of applications, most of them offer several sub-functions that require different resources. For example, an OA system offers message/email delivering, video conference and documents transfer, these functions requires different resource patterns. Thus, when the running application switches from one function to another, it may result in a big change of resource requirement. This is also why there may be some significant workload fluctuation during the running time of most applications.

In this paper, we present a Markov-chain based model to characterize the dynamic resource requirement for applications. The proposed model is different from the static virtual network model, and can describe the real workload with better precision. For each state of the model, a two-state Markov chain is introduced to investigate the resource dynamics more clearly. In addition, a waiting time based indicator (WTE) is proposed to overcome resource collision and realize performance guarantee, when multi-tenant apply for resource simultaneously.

We present a TRRA algorithm to copy with the resource allocation and resource collision problem. The basic idea is to select a proper PM to offer the required resource while guaranteing total performance. Simulation results show that TRRA algorithm can achieve better resource utilization, i.e. less number of PMs, compared with the strategy that provisions for peak resource demand, and achieves a better trade-off between application performance and utilization of data centers. The contributions of our paper are summarized as follows.

1. We propose a novel multiple state transition model MST to describe the application resource requirement, and use the two-state Markov chain to analyze the resource quantitatively.
   Capture the adoption of AR while figure out the unequivocal map from function patterns in MST to nature resource demand.
2. We develop an allocation algorithm, TRRA, for resource requirement model MST, based on resource evaluation method using WTE as the judge threshold.
3. Simulations are conducted to validate the effectiveness and advantage of TRRA.

The remainder of this paper is organized as follows. We introduce the related work in Sect. 2. The problem formulation and algorithm are proposed in Sects. 3 and 4. We evaluate our algorithm in Sect. 5. Finally we conclude our paper in Sect. 6.

2   Related Work

Resource allocation, also known as the virtual network embedding problem in the existing literature, with constraints on nodes and links, can be reduced to the NP-hard multi-way separator problem [4] even when all virtual network requests are known in advance [6]. It has been shown in previous work [3] that the arrival and departure of requests may occur at any time, an application may also desire more resources as time progresses. To handle the above usage scenarios, resources available in the different data centers are monitored under the continually updated view of resource allocation such as their capabilities, and their current and future allocations. Thus, resource allocation have a very high impact on the ability of the data center to accommodate the maximal number of user requests such that the substrate resources are adopted fully and efficiently. There are some advisable indicators to measure the degree of and efficiently resource usage in data center taken up in the existing research, which are defined as VN requests acceptance ratio, physical resource utilization and the long-term average revenue of infrastructure [5,11,15,18].

In recent years, the cloud-datacenters-oriented dynamic resource allocation techniques are highly applied. Embedding virtual network in cloud data center require taking the peculiarity of datacenter into account such as regular topology structure, network and service controllability. Public cloud platforms such as Amazon EC2 supply the determined requirements to applications deployed on it without providing scalable resource demand pattern. Google App Engine support the on-demand use of infrastructure but do not offer specific QoS guarantee to end-host [1,2]. For cloud users, unpredictable performance increase the cost paid for the reserved virtual machines (VMs) for the entire duration of their jobs while for cloud providers, underutilized underlying resource impede the cloud adoption and market occupancy [4].

Whereby, to provide performance guarantees, several works [4,8,14] have proposed scalable virtual network models, which allow cloud users to explicitly specify computing and networking requirements to achieve predictable performance. On virtual machine deployment, prior studies [9,12] concentrated more on minimizing the number of active PMs from the perspective of bin packing. Network-aware virtual machine placement was considered in [3]. Stable resource allocation in geographically-distributed clouds was considered in [16]. Source routing is applied to implement the virtual network embedding in datacenter [8]. Synthetically considering fluctuate of resource usage quantity in datacenter and time-delay tolerance of partial application, it designed incentive mechanism to prompt cloud user to specify the resource demand curve for his application [7].

Some of the models above [3,4,8,12], however, only allow fixed bandwidth guarantees. They fundamentally assume the applications have the same bandwidth requirement throughout the entire execution, which is rarely true in practice. Although some work [13,14,17] have noticed the dynamics nature even raise some deterministic model, the resource change obtained by prediction bear uncertainty and the core idea is to optimize resource deployment to match the demand of applications without consideration of providing info from application layer.

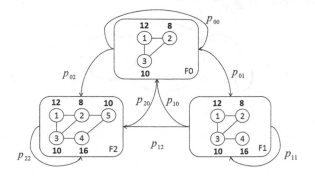

Fig. 1. An example of multiple state transition model

3   Problem Statement

3.1   Resource Requirement Model

A virtual network is a useful model to characterize the application resource requirement [13,17]. However, it has been well recognized in previous studies [4, 14,17] that the resource requirement of many cloud applications varies over time, the signal virtual network cannot reflect the dynamics of resource requirement. Hence, we present a Multiple States Transition (MST) model to reveal the time-varying resource requirement for applications.

The Multiple State Transition model is formulated by the multi-state Markov chain. Figure 1 shows an example of the MST model. In this figure, there are 3 states, which are represented by rectangles (F_0, F_1, and F_2). For each rectangle (also known as state), the graph in the rectangle indicates an virtual network that describes the application resource requirement under this state. For the MST model, $o(t)$ denotes the application state or function patterns at t^{th} time-slot. Therefore, $o(t) = x$ refers that the application is in state F_x at t^{th} time-slot. Assuming the initial state of the application is F_0. For any state F_x, the resource requirement contains two parts: essential resource and extra resource. Here, the essential resource equals to the resource requirement under state F_0. For example, the essential resource requirement for the application in Fig. 1 contains 3 VMs with 12, 8, and 10 resource slots. It should be aware that the states for the application can be transformed probabilistically. The probability of state transformation is represented as P_{ij}, which indicates the probability of transforming from state F_i to F_j.

3.2   On-Off Model for Extra Resource Requirement

To investigate the states of MST model more clearly, we introduce a *ON-OFF* model to characterize the usage of extra resource for each state. Since all states have the same essential resource part, we only focus on the extra resource requirement in the *ON-OFF* model. The model is shown as in Fig. 2.

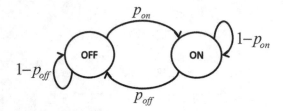

Fig. 2. *ON-OFF* model for extra resource requirement

The state *ON* in the model means the busy phase, i.e. the extra resource requirement of this application state is activated. The state *OFF* indicates that the mount of extra resource requirement differs from this application state. We use P_{on} and P_{off} to represent the state switch probabilities. Hence, the *ON-OFF* model can be presented by a three-tuple,

$$AR_i = (c^i, p^i_{on}, p^i_{off}), \forall 1 \le i \le m$$

where m is the number of application stated mention in MST model, c is the value of the extra resource requirement.

Let $U_i(t)$ be the usage of AR_i at time t. Based on the Markov chain model, we have

$$U_i(t) = \begin{cases} 0, & \text{if } AR_i \text{ is in the OFF state at time } t \\ 1, & \text{if } AR_i \text{ is in the ON state at time } t \end{cases}$$

Let σ_i denote the state set that employ AR_i, while $\overline{\sigma}_i$ is the complementary set of σ_i. We have

$$p^i_{on} = Pr\{U_i(t) = 1 \mid U_i(t-1) = 0\}$$
$$= \sum_{x \in \sigma_i, y \in \overline{\sigma}_i} Pr\{o(t) = x \mid o(t-1) = y\} = \sum_{x \in \sigma_i, y \in \overline{\sigma}_i} p_{xy}$$

$$p^i_{off} = Pr\{U_i(t) = 0 \mid U_i(t-1) = 1\}$$
$$= \sum_{x \in \sigma_i, y \in \overline{\sigma}_i} Pr\{o(t) = y \mid o(t-1) = x\} = \sum_{x \in \sigma_i, y \in \overline{\sigma}_i} p_{yx}$$

3.3   Problem Formulation

Considering there are K applications applying for resources in the data center, and can be described by $R_k(1 \le k \le K)$. We assume that there are m states in the MST model, which also means that there are m different *ON-OFF* model instances. There are h physical machines (PMs) in the data center to offer the resources. We use a binary matrix $\boldsymbol{X} = [x_{ij}]_{m \times h}$ to represent the mapping from resource requirement to resource allocation. Here, x_{ij} equals to 1 if AR_i is placed on PM H_j, and 0 otherwise.

Due to the resource limitation for each PM, collision exists when multiple application compete for limited resource. To strike a tradeoff between utilization and performance, we propose the metric *Waiting Time Expectation* (WTE). WTE is defined as the waiting time from some application apply resource to the resource is really allocated to the application. Our problem can be formalized as follows.

Definition 1 (Elastic Resource Allocation Problem, ERA). *Given a set of application and PMs, find the mapping $\boldsymbol{X}$ from AR to PM, such as the number of PMs is minimized.*

$$\min \quad |\{j \mid \sum_{i=1}^{m} x_{ij} > 0, 1 \leq j \leq h\}|$$

$$s.t. \quad WTE_k^j \leq \rho, k \in A_j, \forall 1 \leq j \leq h \tag{1}$$

$$\sum_{i \in I_k^j} c^i \leq C_j, \forall 1 \leq j \leq h, \forall 1 \leq k \leq K$$

where A_j is the set of applications sharing the PM j, ρ is a pre-defined threshold, I_k^j represents the set of arguments which belongs to application k while allocate to PM j, C_j is the resource capacity for PM.

4   Elastic Resource Allocation Algorithm

In this section, we present our TRRA algorithm, as shown in Algorithm 1. The key idea of TRRA algorithm is to satisfy the extra resource by polling the PMs in turn. If the WTE of some PM is less than the threshold when the extra resource is allocated, the PM is selected to deploy the extra resource.

In the algorithm, the function $CalWTE(AR_i, H_j)$ returns the WTE value for satisfying the extra resource requirement AR_i, it can be defined as

$$WTE_v = \sum_{n=0}^{\infty} n \times P_{choose_v} \times (1 - P_{choose_v})^n$$

$$= (1 - P_{choose_v})/P_{choose_v} \tag{2}$$

where $P_{choose_v} = 1/n$ when there are totally n applications applying for extra resource at the current time-slot.

5   Performance Evaluation

5.1   Simulation Settings

Since the essential resource requirement is common for all application states, we only consider the extra resource requirement in the simulations. The resource

---

Algorithm 1. Time-Restrained Resource Allocation(TRRA)

Input:

$\{R_1, R_2, R_3, \ldots, R_K\}$,the set of applications; $\{H_1, H_2, H_3, \ldots, H_h\}$,the set of PMs;

Output:

An AR-to-PM placement matrix, X;

1: initialize $r_j = 0$ for all PMs to ensure no AR deploying on it.

2: $Index^{AR} = 0$;

3: **for** each $k \in [1, K]$ **do**

4:     $preid = Index^{AR}$

5:     extract the argument resources from R_k and number these ARs in order with the $Index^A R$ ascending;

6:     $complete = Index^{AR} - preid$;

7:     **for** $i \leftarrow (prein + 1)$ to $index^{AR}$ **do**

8:         $flag_{assign} = 0$

9:         **for all** $j \in [1, h]$ **do**

10:            **if** $r_j > \rho_{r_j}$ **then**

11:                go to the next j;

12:            **else** $\{r_j = 0\}$

13:                deploy the AR_i to H_j, $x_{ij} = 1$;

14:                $r_j \leftarrow r_j + 1$, $flag_{assign} = 0$, $complete - -$;

15:            **else**

16:                $WTE \leftarrow CalWTE(AR_i, H_j)$

17:                judge whether $WTE_v \leq \rho_{wte}$

18:            **if** YES **then**

19:                deploy the AR_i to H_j, $x_{ij} = 1$;

20:                $r_j \leftarrow r_j + 1$, $flag_{assign} \leftarrow 0$, $complete - -$;

21:        **if** $flag_{assign} = 1$ **then**

22:            deploy the next AR_i;

23:        **if** $complete! = 0$ **then**

24:            refuse the application;

25: **return** X;

---

capacity of PM is generated randomly within a certain range. The parameters in application resource requirement model MST are generated randomly within rational limits. The arrivals of application requests are modeled as a Poisson process with an average rate of α requests per time unit. The lifetime of each virtual network is assumed to be exponentially distributed with an average of β time units. We observe that with a continuous application requests sequence relayed on α and β, the number of applications deployed on datacenter will reach a relatively stable value θ after a period of time, which means that the new coming applications and leaving applications tend to stable within a small range. The stable value θ refer to the number of peak-phase requests.

It should be aware that the ARs from the same application can be deployed on different PMs. However, when the cloud allocate resource to one AR of application, other ARs should be taken into consideration that whether other ARs can obtain the required resources. Similarly, when an AR do not obtained the needed resource, the cloud should ignore all the AR request for physical resource from the same application.

We compared our TRRA resource allocation algorithm with the max-resource allocation strategy. The latter uses the FFD heuristic strategy in its algorithm. Some algorithm performance indicators are proposed to measure the two allocation strategy, such as utilization ratio (the reduced proportion of number of used physical machines), average waiting time ratio (the fraction of the realistic application lifetime within which the application is in idle due to resource collision), the time cost of applying one allocation algorithm with different scale of applications deployed on data center.

5.2   Simulation Result

To measure the utilization of underlying resources in different-scale data center under three threshold value, we conduct the simulations as follows. The relevant parameters are randomly generated from corresponding ranges and under every group of configuration parameters, we repeat the simulation many times so as to obtain the more general results used for analysis.

Number of peak-phase requests θ embodies loaded-scale in datacenter. To investigate the performance of our algorithm in various θ, three kinds of threshold values are used for each experiment. Observe the number of used PMs under the

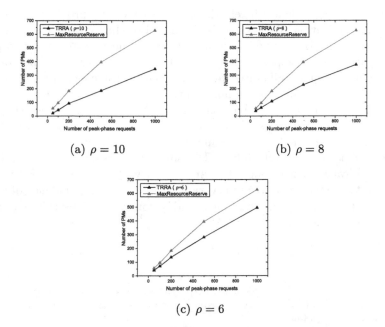

Fig. 3. Deployment results in comparison with MaxResource strategy under different scale of θ value. (a) TRRA with $\rho_{wte} = 10$, (b) TRRA with $\rho_{wte} = 8$, (c) TRRA with $\rho_{wte} = 6$

different loaded-scale. Figure 3(a), (b) and (c) manifest that, compared with the max-resource allocation algorithm (MR), TRRA significantly reduce the number of used PMs. Specifically, when $\rho_{wte} = 6$, the average number of used PMs decreases by about 13 %; when $\rho_{wte} = 8$, the average number decreases by about 38 % and up to about 49 % when $\rho_{wte} = 10$. As the trend shows that TRRA effectively improve the utilization of data center. Focused on one of the three figures, as the loaded-scale enlarge, the reduction rate emerge the same trend, which indicates that our algorithm can admirably adapt to large scale data centers.

Threshold ρ_{wte} is designed to restrain the waiting time during the process of application execution. In experiment, we observe that whether the setting of ρ_{wte} influence the fraction of waiting time in the practical implementation. As showed in Fig. 3, with different threshold, the average waiting ratios are conditioned to a small specific range as well as show the control of the utilization degree in data centers. Further analyzing, in practical deployment, applications from a wide diverse types serve its users with different requirement in response time, which realize a tradeoff between the execution performance and utilization by selecting one appropriate threshold. In conclusion, the proposed TRRA can commendably reduce the overall resource usage and provide better performance to applications.

6   Conclusion

In this paper, we investigate the elastic resource allocation problem for resource utilization optimization. We present MST model to characterize the dynamical resource requirements for applications, and divide the resource into two parts: essential part and extra part. The essential part is regarded as the common resource requirement for all states, and extra part is the concern we focus. The opportunistic resource sharing method is introduced to improve the resource utilization. To overcome the resource collision by sharing, we introduce the WTE variable to restrict the collision deterioration. Finally, we present a resource allocation algorithm TRRA for dynamic resource requirements in data centers to realize elastic resource scheduling. The simulation results show that, TRRA reduces the physical machines used by up to 49 % with a proper WTE threshold as compare to the max-resource reservation strategy. A better balance of performance and datacenter utilization is achieved according to the service characteristic provided by the application.

References

1. Amazon ec2 service level agreement. http://aws.amazon.com/ec2-sla/
2. Windows azure platform service level agreements. http://www.microsoft.com/windowsazure/pricing/
3. Alicherry, M., Lakshman, T.V.: Network aware resource allocation in distributed clouds. In: IEEE Infocom, pp. 963–971 (2012)
4. Ballani, H., Costa, P., Karagiannis, T., Rowstron, A.: Towards predictable data-center networks. ACM SIGCOMM Comput. Commun. Rev. **41**(4), 242–253 (2011)

5. Chowdhury, M., Rahman, M.R., Boutaba, R.: Vineyard: virtual network embedding algorithms with coordinated node and link mapping. IEEE/ACM Trans. Netw. **20**(1), 206–219 (2012)
6. Chowdhury, N., Boutaba, R.: A survey of network virtualization. Comput. Netw. **54**(5), 862–876 (2010)
7. Ghazar, T., Samaan, N.: Pricing utility-based virtual networks. IEEE Trans. Netw. Serv. Manag. **10**(2), 119–132 (2013)
8. Guo, C., Lu, G., Wang, H.J., Yang, S., Kong, C., Sun, P., Wu, W., Zhang, Y.: Secondnet: a data center network virtualization architecture with bandwidth guarantees. In: ACM CONEXT 2010, Philadelphia, PA, USA, 30 November-December, pp. 620–622 (2010)
9. Jayasinghe, D., Pu, C., Eilam, T., Steinder, M., Whally, I., Snible, E.: Improving performance and availability of services hosted on iaas clouds with structural constraint-aware virtual machine placement. In: IEEE International Conference on Services Computing, pp. 72–79 (2011)
10. Li, X., Qian, Z., Lu, S., Wu, J.: Energy efficient virtual machine placement algorithm with balanced and improved resource utilization in a data center. Math. Comput. Model. **58**(5), 1222–1235 (2013)
11. Lischka, J., Karl, H.: A virtual network mapping algorithm based on subgraph isomorphism detection. In: ACM Workshop on Virtualized Infrastructure Systems and Architectures, pp. 81–88 (2009)
12. Meng, X., Pappas, V., Zhang, L.: Improving the scalability of data center networks with traffic-aware virtual machine placement. In: Proceedings-IEEE INFOCOM, vol. 54(1), pp. 1–9 (2010)
13. Wang, M., Meng, X., Zhang, L.: Consolidating virtual machines with dynamic bandwidth demand in data centers. In: Proceedings-IEEE INFOCOM, vol. 34(17), pp. 71–75 (2011)
14. Xie, D., Ding, N., Hu, Y.C., Kompella, R.: The only constant is change: incorporating time-varying network reservations in data centers. In: Proceedings of ACM SIGCOMM 2012, pp. 199–210 (2012)
15. Yu, M., Yi, Y., Rexford, J., Chiang, M.: Rethinking virtual network embedding: substrate support for path splitting and migration. ACM SIGCOMM Comput. Commun. Rev. **38**(2), 17–29 (2008)
16. Zhang, S., Qian, Z., Wu, J., Lu, S.: Sea: stable resource allocation in geographically distributed clouds. In: ICC 2014, IEEE International Conference on Communications, pp. 2932–2937 (2014)
17. Zhang, S., Qian, Z., Wu, J., Lu, S., Epstein, L.: Virtual network embedding with opportunistic resource sharing. IEEE Trans. Parallel Distrib. Syst. **25**(3), 816–827 (2014)
18. Zhu, Y., Ammar, M.: Algorithms for assigning substrate network resources to virtual network components. In: Infocom IEEE International Conference on Computer Communications, pp. 1–12 (2006)

A Software Detection Mechanism Based on SMM in Network Computing

Lei Zhou[1], Yang Shu[1], and Guojun Wang[2(✉)]

[1] School of Information Science and Engineering, Central South University,
Changsha 410083, China
[2] School of Computer Science and Educational Software, Guangzhou University,
Guangzhou 510006, China
csgjwang@gmail.com

Abstract. To guarantee the network computing system security, the effective method is illegal or malicious software detection. Most of the former researches implement it on OS kernel or hypervisor level. However, if the system is attacked by the ring 0 or ring 1 level risks, the OS kernel or hypervisor is unable to provide the trusted base, which may cause an incorrect result. To solve the shortcomings, we choose the System Management Mode (SMM) to build a trusted execution environment. The SMM is a special cpu mode in the x86 architecture, which could create a security and isolated area on firmware level for malicious attacks detection.

In this paper, we remotely interrupt the local system, and design a secure module in SMM to obtain messages from registers and physical memory space. Those messages are used to back analyze the software executing code segment for further information comparing. Beside the local detection, we use remote attestation approach for verifying the secure module. Our approach resists the attack surface under the OS level, and advances state-of-the-art detecting transparently. Furthermore, the analysis process could implement in the server to reduce the overheads on the client platform.

Keywords: Software detection · Memory forensics · SMM · Semantic gap · Security agent

1 Introduction

Network computing security has long been the basic requirement for computing services. In recent years, as with the fast development of network services, the security of network operating system faces more challenges which should pay more attention by administrations and firms. Many former researches implement security policies on OS to build a safe computing environment, like anti-virus technology, access control policy, isolation executing environment mechanism, etc.

G. Wang et al. (Eds.): SpaCCS 2016 Workshops, LNCS 10067, pp. 134–143, 2016.
DOI: 10.1007/978-3-319-49145-5_14

Anti-virus software are a normally choose for the user. Generally, it has two operation modes, host-based and network-based [1,2]. Both of those two modes have the same problem that the anti-virus could be broken by higher level attacks. Access control is to limit the actions or operations for a legitimate user who intend to access the computer resource. Different access control approaches and application are developed as will as the developing of computer technology [3,4].

Meanwhile, the attractive security guarantees provided by virtual machine monitors (VMMs) or Trusted Third Party (TTP), etc. [5–7], are proposed while the cloud service development. More recently, researchers have been proposed a hardware-centric approach, like HIEE [8], TrustZone [9], to provide a isolate execution environment. Such isolation [10] is central to the architecture of system integrity monitors that inspect the code and data of a potentially compromised target.

However, the CSP is able to access the hypervisor or other software platform by its higher privilege [11–13], further research on remote secure network computing environment should be given. In the paper [14], it propose a new mechanism to solve the problem on OS kernel-level. In this paper, we choose the SMM [15] as a method to create a cleanroom computing platform on firmware-level. Thus, the primary task is to create a protocol, to assure the user that only the cleanroom protocol-based software can be run. Another key technology is how to guarantee the SMM-based security module running in valid state through remote attestation and memory forensics approaches, same researches has been done to protect it [16–18].

In order to address the above challenges, in this paper, we propose a software detection mechanism based on SMM which supports a hardware-level trusted base. The contributions of this paper are summarized as follows:

(1) We utilize the SMM-based approach to construct a unipolar isolated computing environment, which set as firmware-level trust base and outside of the OS, it will products minimal user services environmental impact.
(3) We design special functions to acquire register data and physical memory in SMM space, and a semantic gap reconstruction scheme for process detection. The SMM-based computing environment make those operations transparent to the user and the OS.
(3) We analyze the security and effectiveness about our proposed SMM-based secure system.

The rest of the paper is organized as follows. Section 1 summarizes the features of related work. Section 2 presents introduces the system model, definition of SMM-based secure system, semantic gap reconstruction and preliminaries. Following in Sect. 3, we describe the details of our proposed SMM-based secure system and presents security analysis. Finally, Sect. 4 concludes our paper.

2   System Architecture

2.1   Assumptions and Attacks

Our mechanism is intended to transparently protect the user computing environment from any invasion of illegal software. We consider such a network computing service mode that the operating system was provided by the cloud server and user terminal. However, the operating system is a compromised service platform. The user space or kernel-level security mechanism can not provides correct detecting result, and the malware or rootkits running in OS will not be found by the user, while the operating system was broken by those high-privilege attacks.

Before we describe the security mode, we need to analyze the basic technology and conditions. As the functions for memory forensics are store in SMM handler, which is part of the BIOS/UEFI, we assume the BIOS/UEFI will not be compromised. Now, although we use SMM for a trusted base to check the software information, the SMM may be attacked by some other hardware-assisted risks, like side-channel attacks. To simplify the mode, we assume it is security with STM technology. Furthermore, we consider that an attacker with less control permissions to physical access the computer resources.

2.2   System Model

In this paper, we propose the software detection model for network computing mode which considered three entities: Secure Server (SS), Client, User.

In this model, the secure server is the most important role for software detection. First, it contains all software that a client needed for computing services; Second, it signs a access control policy with the user, named cleanroom security protocol, which is used to protect the software running in the client from outside or inside attacking. The client device may be a public terminal which use to provide user network service with untrusted system. Thus, in this paper, the basic goal for this model is to limit running software in the cleanroom policy.

2.3   Security Function Based on SMM

System Management Mode is a special-purpose operating mode in Intel x86 platforms, which is execution similar to Real and Protected modes available. SMM was designed to provide for handling system-wide functions like power management, system hardware control, or proprietary OEM-designed code. It is intended for use only by system firmware from the manufacturer and not intended to be 3rd party extensible [8,19].

In this section, we design a Security Agent (SA) in OS kernel firstly. The main functions for the SA is to catch the process event and read the virtual address of the first field of programs code segment. SA runs as a daemon in the background when the OS started. Once a new process running in OS intent to call a system operating instruction. The module will hook this action, and find the process identity, file path, then the virtual memory address can be

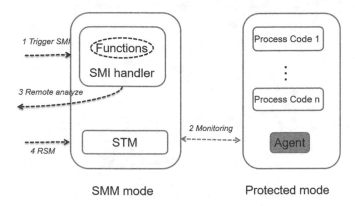

Fig. 1. Detection based on SMM

work out by an analyzing unit. After the SA get the process virtual address, the next step is to find the process code segment, which should be working in System Management Mode, cooperating with cleanroom management module in SS to provide the safety services. If the user applies for security proof, the server records the software identity and return the monitoring trigger command. When the client receives the trigger command, it creates a trigger instruction for detecting. Meanwhile, the client inputs the identify token, then the client system jumps to the SMM mode.

As the Fig. 1 shown, the functions running in SMM handler is security because the SMM provides an isolated execution environment. But the SMRAM is a small memory space, we need to design a smaller but very efficient program for process information extracting, analyzing, matching and other operations.

2.4   Process of Software Detecting

After the system is initialized, the user attempt to run some software in or out of cleanroom protocol. Once the SA hooks a system call triggered by any other software, the program information and process identity could be caught from system information table like System Services Descriptor Table (SSDT). Those program information is use to compute a virtual address *addr* about the first field of the process which runs in system memory. Then, the SA trigger the System management interrupt (SMI).

As the Fig. 2 shown, once the real-time system switch into SMM mode, the SMM handler will runs some functions to extract process code segment. Then it computes the hash value of code segment, the value and the process information are send to the SS for next hash matching. If the SS gets the matching result, it returns to client for prompting and process stopping. More details will be described in next section.

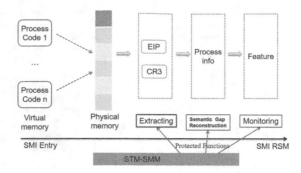

Fig. 2. The process of memory detection

3   Design and Evaluation

This section is intend to describe the processes of software detection based on SMM. Firstly, we get the virtual address of the process handler, and set a SMI for SMM check which send a process handler address to SMRAM at the same time. Secondly, we design the extracting function to read the process code segment with the physical memory dump and CR3 register value. Lastly, the function compute the process code segment to get a hash value and match it with original value in SS. The key factor for this mechanism is to protect it from attacks, the next section we depict the key technologies. Finally, we simulate the process of software detection, and develop a kernel-level agent for testing.

3.1   Secure Agent with Protected Mechanism

In Sect. 3, we already designed a model about secure agent in the OS kernel. In the current implementation, we directly create a system call intercepted module and place it into OS kernel. The main function for this module is to hook the process events, and the monitor runs as a daemon in the background when the OS started. Then, the agent is designed to be a module with the functions for events hooking, process handler analyzing, virtual memory address acquiring.

Any modifications for kernel module in OS is easy to cause system crashes. In order to reduce the impact on system performance, we build the agent in a modular fashion, which creates little association with other system kernel module but only uses some specific kernel functions. The software running in OS cannot be bypassed with kernel-based agent. Based on kernel detecting, system call interposition is a powerful technique for reading program behaviors and obtaining process handler in run-time memory. The details for process detecting in Security agent are depicted in Algorithm 1. As the workflow in Algorithm 1, when the software runs in OS, it will continually trigger the system call interruption, those system events contain lots of process information. The functions can be easy to read the process identity, file path and the others. Some special system APIs could read the memory address with process identity. In Windows,

---

Algorithm 1. Process Information Collected by Security Agent(*event*, *paddr*)

Input: Event *event* for a new process hooking by the agent.
Output: The virtual address for process handler *paddr*.

1: **Add** Special identity code (*mark*);
2: **Insert** Hooking Function(Output: *pHandler*);
3: **if** *pHandler* $\notin \phi$ **then**
4:     **Analyze** Address(*pHandler*, *pAddr*);
5:     **Trigger** SMI(*pAddr*);
6: **else**
7:     Waiting for next event.
    return *true*;

Algorithm 2. Protection Mechanism for Agent based on SMM(*mark*, *pos*,*result*)

Input: Special code array *mark* from agent module.
        pos is a location array for *mark* from pre-set.
Output: The *result* show if the Agent is correct or not.

1: **get** first address *kaddr* of kernel code page;
2: **divide** physical memory into a sequence pages array *pagearr*;
3: **for** $p_i = 1; i \le len(pagearr); j + +$ **do**
4:     **while** not end of *pagearr*(p_i) **do**
5:         $index \leftarrow 0$;
6:         $offset \leftarrow 0$;
7:         **if** $Code(pagearr(p_i)) \leftarrow mark(index + offset)$ **then**
8:
9:             **Match** the next *mark*;
10:             $result \leftarrow ture$;
11:         **else**
12:             **Jump out** to *While*;
13:             $result \leftarrow false$;
14: **return** *result*;

GetModuleHandler is a function for program to read the process handler with process identity, then symbol & is used to get the process memory address. Above steps help the user to get the process position (in virtual memory) from the run-time system. Some steps like the "trigger" are re-defined with new context which different from original data structure. Interruption should be modified to transfer some messages to System Management RAM (SMRAM) for next computation. This message include *pddr* and the process identity *pHandler*.

While the security agent sets in OS kernel, the kernel-based rootkit can lead the agent in an unsafe state. Thus, it is important to design a protection mechanism for agent to keep security. As the agent is created by the secure server, the secure server provide the software for user to build a computing environment, the agent will remake again. Then, the user could develop the agent code by himself, this helps for the user set some special code in agent module, the Algorithm 2 shows the steps to create a protection scheme.

Through verifying the correctness of the security agent, we provide a trust base for the SA to catch the user space process in a safety way. But the SA can not transfer itself handler to SMM for security detecting, we need other methods to find the agent code in physical memory space. As a self-design module, the SA code could insect some function-useless code for external work, like the serial number. We define a unique string as a program mark at the first line in the main function.

We do not have the accuracy physical address of agent, but we can scan the low-level (896 M) physical memory space in 4 kb (one page) mode, to match the identifier strings in each physical pages. If we can not find the identifier strings, then the agent may be broken. We will analyze the reason deeply, and if the mark strings are found, we compute a segment code to be hash value, and match it with the origin code in servers. Thus, we get the result if the agent is correct or not. Because the agent is protected by functions on SMM, we consider that the information-gathering operation is also security.

Algorithm 3. Software detection based on SMM($vaddr$, $cr3$,$result$)

Input: Virtual address of Software $paddr$ from agent module.
       Page address $cr3$ from cpu register.
Output: The $result$ shows the correctness of Software code.
Initialization: get first address $vaddr$ of the new process; $addr \leftarrow paddr$; **divide** physical memory into a sequence pages array $pagearr$; $pde \leftarrow cr3$; $pte \leftarrow pde * 4$

1: **get** physical memory address about the process $paddr$;
2: **if** $pde \neq \phi \& cr3 \neq \phi$ **then**
3:     $paddr = addr * offset1 + pte * offset2 + addr * offset3$;
4: **else**
5:     $result \leftarrow false$;
6:     break;
7: **Locate** $paddr$ in physical memory space;
8: **Copy** these page memory $pagemeory$;
9: **if** $pagememory \neq \phi$ **then**
10:     **Compute** hash value v_code;
11:     **Remote attest** v_code;
12:     **Feedback** the $result$
13: **else**
14:     $result \leftarrow false$;
15:     break;
16: **return** $result$;

With the security agent and its protection mechanism, we can get the first virtual address $paddr$ of a process safety. Based on SMM, The CPU can access the register unlimited, we use a SMRAM space to receive the CR3 value like $Move\&cr3\&smem$, the $smem$ is a new space in SMRAM.

As the Algorithm 3 shown, the system fast traverse physical memory page, to find the special positions and match the value. This operation is to check if it is the monitor module code. While special positions that is used to mark the module, and the fast traverse algorithm should be simple and effective because of the small memory space in SMRAM. With the *paddr* and *smem*, the extracting function could find out the physical memory of this process. Then we get a segment code to check the correctness with a origin code. The traverse algorithm should be changed in a fast way, the function get the first page, each physical memory page is 4 K, then, it find out the first special code. If here, find the second, go on the same step, if not here, go to next page.

If the process code segment less than 4 k, the first code will be the main function handler of process, if we insect special code in next pos, we will mixed the code position. In this method, matching process is not doing locally. The critical problem for those two methods is how to promise the monitoring module in a trust environment. We assume that communication channel is safety enough, and add some remote attestation mechanisms to check the correctness of the computation about monitoring module.

3.2   Evaluation and Analysis

We propose a new mechanism for software detection in network computing mode. Now we use a simulation environment to test the effectiveness about this mechanism.

Firstly, we analyze the security level about our mechanism, through comparing with application level, kernel-level, hypervisor-level protected methods. The application and kernel anti-virus software are both running in the user space, it use to check whether the (user or kernel) file data is broken. If the anti-virus software is attacked by the same privilege program, it will be useless. The Hypervisor-level detecting methods run in a isolate position to monitor the virtual machines. However, it is controlled by the cloud servers that it can no be resists the risks from inner-attack. Our mechanism puts the key functions in SMM execution environment, which get firmware-level trusted base. The SA runs in OS kernel but it protects by the functions in SMM handler. Then, we get a higher level security promise in the network computing mode.

To pre-acquire the process information, we develop a security agent in kernel space, named cleanroom monitoring module. It can hooks almost all system call events, the events information then transfer to SMM after analyzing and simplifying. All experiments are performed in a lab environment. The server runs RedHat 6. The client includes two types, including virtual machine provided by the server and a lab-assembling PC which with special lab-made x86 mainboard. The OS running in clients is CentOS 6 with Linux core version 2.6.32. The testing case running in system shows that the SA works in a perfect performance.

As the software detection algorithm is finally comparing the hash value of binary code between real-time software code segment and original code segment. We design a simulation methods to validate the feasible of the algorithm. We use the *winhex* to transfer the self-defined execute file into binary file, and get the code segment. Then, we use *visstudio* tool to debug the execute code, then decompile the code to find out the memory data. Both the code segment are use to compute the hash value, and make a comparison to show that the original data base is the same as the physical memory data if the software isn't broken. Otherwise, it is not the same. The testing shows that it is a feasible way to check the software state.

We will continually work for a integral system experiment to guarantee the network computing services running in a safety environment. Finally, we intend to develop a prototype for further research on cleanroom security service.

4   Conclusion

In this paper, we propose a new software detecting mechanism based on SMM, it will perform a more secure result than the kernel-level detection approaches and VMM introspection technology. Because the System Management Mode can provide a higher-level privilege (ring -2) for the user to access the physical memory and register value, while the kernel-level or hypervisor-level attack can not touch this isolate execution environment.

As the necessity for detecting the correctness of software in SMM, we design a security agent (SA) in OS kernel and a memory forensics approach to solve the semantic gap problem between process and physical memory data. The SA hooks the system call events and transfer the address of the process handler to SMM handler. Meanwhile, it trigger the SMI and the system switch to SMM for further analysis. The memory forensics approach traverse the physical address space to protect the security agent from attack and get the real-time process memory dump for integrity verification. To conclude, the SMM execution environment provides a high-level trust base and security services.

Our future work will continually extends our framework to implement a cleanroom security system, focus on testing the complexity and efficiency about this approach.

Acknowledgments. This work is supported in part by the National Natural Science Foundation of China under Grant Numbers 61632009, 61472451 and 61272151, the High Level Talents Program of Higher Education in Guangdong Province under Funding Support Number 2016ZJ01.

References

1. Al-Saleh, M.I., Abuhjeela, F.M., Al-Sharif, Z.A.: Investigating the detection capabilities of antiviruses under concurrent attacks. Int. J. Inf. Secur. **14**(4), 387–396 (2014)
2. Abazari, F., Analoui, M., Takabi, H.: Effect of anti-malware software on infectious nodes in cloud environment. IEEE Comput. Secur. **58**, 139–148 (2016)
3. Kang, M.H., Park, J.S., Froscher, J.N.: Access control mechanisms for inter-organizational workflow. In: Proceedings of the Sixth ACM Symposium on Access Control Models & Technologies, pp. 66–74 (2015)
4. Tang, S., Li, X., Huang, X., et al.: Achieving simple, secure and efficient hierarchical access control in cloud computing. IEEE Trans. Comput. **61**(4), 2325–2331 (2016)

5. Saravanakumar, C., Arun, C.: Survey on interoperability, security, trust, privacy standardization of cloud computing. In: International Conference on Contemporary Computing and Informatics (IC3I) (2014)
6. Jain, P., Rane, D., Patidar, S.: A survey and analysis of cloud model-based security for computing secure cloud bursting and aggregation in renal environment. In: World Congress on IEEE Information and Communication Technologies (WICT), pp. 456–461 (2011)
7. Hofmann, O.S., Kim, S., Dunn, A.M., Lee, M.Z.: Inktag: secure applications on an untrusted operating system. In: ACM SIGARCH Computer Architecture News, vol. 41(1), pp. 265–278 (2013)
8. Zhang, F., Wang, H., Leach, K., Stavrou, A.: A framework to secure peripherals at runtime. In: Kutyłowski, M., Vaidya, J. (eds.) ESORICS 2014. LNCS, vol. 8712, pp. 219–238. Springer, Heidelberg (2014). doi:10.1007/978-3-319-11203-9_13
9. Kim, J., Kim, D., Park, J., Kim, J., Kim, H.: An efficient Kernel introspection system using a secure timer on TrustZone, 25(4), 863–872 (2015)
10. Bauman, E., Ayoade, G., Lin, Z.: A survey on hypervisor-based monitoring: approaches, applications, and evolutions. ACM Comput. Surv. (CSUR) 48(1), 10 (2015)
11. Xie, X., Wang, W.: Rootkit detection on virtual machines through deep information extraction at hypervisor-level. Commun. Netw. Secur. 411(6), 498–503 (2013)
12. Zhang, N., Sun, K., Lou, W., Hou, Y.T., Jajodia, S.: Now you see me: hide and seek in physical address space. In: ACM Symposium on Information, Computer and Communications Security, pp. 321–331 (2015)
13. Pfoh, J., Schneider, C., Eckert, C.: Nitro: hardware-based system call tracing for virtual machines. In: Iwata, T., Nishigaki, M. (eds.) IWSEC 2011. LNCS, vol. 7038, pp. 96–112. Springer, Heidelberg (2011). doi:10.1007/978-3-642-25141-2_7
14. Zhou, L., Liu, X., Liu, Q., Wang, G.: A cleanroom monitoring system for network computing service based on remote attestation. In: 2016 IEEE Trustcom (2016, accepted)
15. Embleton, S., Sparks, S., Zou, C.: SMM rootkit: a new breed of OS independent malware. Secur. Commun. Netw. 6(12), 1590–1605 (2013)
16. Xu, W., Zhang, X., Hu, H., Ahn, G., Seifert, J.: Remote attestation with domain-based integrity model and policy analysis. IEEE Trans. Dependable Secure Comput. 9(3), 429–442 (2012)
17. Reina, A., et al.: When hardware meets software: a bulletproof solution to forensic memory acquisition, pp. 79–88 (2012)
18. Korkin, I., Nesterov, I.: Applying memory forensics to rootkit detection. In: ADFSL Conference on Digital Forensics, Security and Law (2014)
19. Huang, Y., et al.: HMTT: a hybrid hardware/software tracing system for bridging the DRAM access trace's semantic gap. ACM Trans. Architect. Code Optim. (TACO) 11(1), 7 (2014)

4th International Workshop on Network Optimization and Performance Evaluation (NOPE 2016)

Optimizing Propagation Network of Certificate Revocation in VANET with Meet-Table

Baohua Huang[1,2(✉)], Jiawei Mo[1], Qi Lu[1], and Wei Cheng[2]

[1] School of Computer and Electronic Information, Guangxi University,
Nanning 530004, Guangxi, China
bhhuang66@gxu.edu.cn, 327998377@qq.com, 547566452@qq.com
[2] Department of Computer Science, Virginia Commonwealth University,
Richmond, VA 23220, USA
wcheng3@vcu.edu

Abstract. Certificate is widely used in VANET (Vehicle Ad hoc Network) to make it secure. But when a certificate is untrustworthy, it must be revoked. Propagation of certificate revocation information in VANET is not only essential but also challenging. In order to optimizing the propagation network of certificate revocation, Meet-Table is proposed. The Meet-Table of a vehicle records vehicles it met in the past. With the help of Meet-Table, a vehicle only needs to broadcast CRL (Certificate Revocation List) related to vehicles in its Meet-Table, so the network communication complexity and storage complexity of CRL in VANET can be optimized. Both of the two complexities are discussing formally. Comparing the schema proposed in this paper with CRL in classical PKI, road side unit broadcasting and epidemic fashion shows that the Meet-Table can significantly reduce the complexity of CRL propagation.

Keywords: PKI · CRL · OCSP · RSU broadcasting · Epidemic · VANET · Meet-Table based propagation

1 Introduction

VANET (Vehicle Ad hoc Network) is a mobile ad hoc network targets to improve road safety and travelling comfort. It consists of OBU (On Board Unit), AU (Application Unit) and RSU (Road Side Unit). In VANET, there are three communication domains: In-vehicle domain, ad hoc domain and infrastructure domain [1]. In this paper, we focus on the latter two domains, so we use vehicle to represent OBU and AU and the In-vehicle domain.

Mobility, wireless character and privacy requirement bring VANET huge security challenging. It requires ID authentication, message integrity, communication confidentiality, availability, and access control [2, 3]. In order to achieve the security goal of VANET, many solutions were proposed. In these solutions, public key cryptography is widely used. As a result, certificate must be used in VANET to make it secure. These certificates can be divided into two types: long life certificate and short life certificate. Short life certificate needs not to consider the problem of revocation. But long life

© Springer International Publishing AG 2016
G. Wang et al. (Eds.): SpaCCS 2016 Workshops, LNCS 10067, pp. 147–154, 2016.
DOI: 10.1007/978-3-319-49145-5_15

certificate revocation is a problem unavoidable. There are many conditions, such as compromise or loss of private key, severing of organizational affiliation, etc., can cause certificate to be untrustworthy and revoked [4].

CRL (Certificate Revocation List) is a main technology used by PKI (Public Key Infrastructure). It is issued by CA (Certificate Authority) in a periodical manner. The CRL is stored on LDAP (Lightweight Directory Access Protocol) server for retrieving [5]. Its problem is that application must retrieve the recent CRL and store it periodically. In addition, CRL is not suitable for real time certificate revocation. OCSP (Online Certificate Status Protocol) offers a possibility of gathering knowledge of the status of a particular certificate without the acquiring of CRL. A client can request OCSP responder to sign a response for a certificate [6]. Instead of directly accessing Internet, vehicle in VANET often access Internet through infrastructure domain. In some areas there are not RSUs, vehicle can't access LDAP server and OCSP responder. So CRL and OCSP are not very suitable in VANNET.

VII (The Vehicle Infrastructure Integration) tries to distribute CRL to vehicle through RSU broadcasting [7]. This method required very large number of RSU and high cost. Haas et al. try to propagate CRL in an epidemic fashion [8]. Epidemic method can distribute CRL to all vehicles with less number of RSU and less time, but it requires large storage and communication capacity in VANET.

In order to optimize the propagation network of CRL in VANET, we propose Meet-Table to record the vehicles a vehicle met in the past. Utilizing the Meet-Table, we can reduce the epidemic fashion's storage and communication complexity from $O(n^2)$ and $O(n^h)$ to $O((\gamma n)^2)$ and $O((\gamma n)^h)$. n is number of vehicles in VANET, h is hops of broadcasting, γ is the ratio of meeting of vehicles in the whole VANET.

2   Problem Modeling

For large scale and mobility of VANET, CRL in classical PKI and OCSP are not applicable in it. So broadcasting becomes the only choice. There are two typical broadcasting schema, RSU based broadcasting and epidemic fashion broadcasting. In order to discuss the problems confronting these schemas, we first evaluate the size of CRLs of VANET.

2.1   Size of CRLs in VANET

Let's use n_v to denote the number of vehicles in an area, n_c to denote number of certificate, and r_{issue} denote ratio of issuing of certificate to vehicle, then the number of certificate in VANET,

$$n_c = n_v \times r_{issue} \tag{1}$$

Let's use r_{revoke} denote ratio of revoking of certificates, then the number of certificate in CRLs,

$$n_{crs} = n_v \times r_{issue} \times r_{revoke} \tag{2}$$

In United States, number of vehicles in 2014 is 260,350,940 [9]. In VANET a vehicle needs one certificate at least. According to research, r_{revoke} is about 8 % [10]. So the number of certificate in CRLs of USA's VANET,

$$n_{crs\_USA} \approx 260,350,940 \times 1 \times 8\% = 20,828,075 \tag{3}$$

The size of a CRL varies from several KB to several hundred KB. Let's suppose a CRL contains ten certificates' revoking information and the size of a CRL is 100 KB, then the total size of CRLs in USA's VANET,

$$s_{CRLs\_USA} \approx 20,828,075 \times 1/10 \times 100KB = 208,280,750KB \approx 208GB \tag{4}$$

So from Eq. 4 we can see that the total size of CRLs in a nationwide VANET is huge.

2.2 Problems of RSU Based Broadcasting

RSU based broadcasting schema utilizing road side unit to push CRLs to vehicles passing it. There are two main problems this schema has to face.

(1) Vehicle is not able to store and process huge CRLs. The ultimate goal of this schema is to push all CRLs to all vehicle. As what shows in Eq. 4, the size of all CRLs is huge. In fact, a vehicle not only can't store and process all CRLs but also needn't to do so, because it couldn't meet and communicate with most of vehicles in all CRLs forever.
(2) It's hard for RSU to choose a subset of CRLs to broadcast. Broadcasting the whole CRLs is not possible, so RSU can only to broadcast the recent CRLs. How to define the recent CRLs isn't an easy question.

2.3 Problems of Epidemic Fashion

The epidemic fashion use vehicle to vehicle communication to broadcast CRLs. It's a flooding method, so it's communication cost is very high. The following shows two key problems of this method.

(1) Its ultimate goal is also targeted to make all vehicles have all CRLs. As described before, this goal is hard to achieve and not necessary.
(2) The communication cost is very high. The complexity of communication,

$$c_{epdemic} = O(n_v^h) \tag{5}$$

Where h is hops in broadcasting. According to the research result of Chuha et al., VANET is Small world [11, 12], so h may be limited to 6.

$$c_{epdemic} = O(n_v^6) \tag{6}$$

From Eq. 6 we can see that in a nationwide VANET, in which v_n is about hundreds of millions, the broadcasting can crash down all communication.

2.4   Our Contributions

For the purpose of limiting complexities of storage and communication, we propose Meet-Table to record vehicles a vehicle met in the past and let vehicle to broadcast CRLs only to vehicles in its Meet-Table. Our major contributions to the problem of propagation of certificate revocation information in VANET are following:

(1) We formally give the size of CRLs in VANET, and point out that both RSU based broadcasting and epidemic fashion ignored the huge size of CRLs in a nationwide VANNET.
(2) We propose Meet-Table to reduce the scale of a vehicle's related vehicles to decrease storage and communication complexity of CRLs propagation.
(3) We give algorithm of Meet-Table based CRL propagation and analyze its security and performance.

3   Meet-Table Based CRL Propagation

3.1   Meet-Table

Meet-Table exists in every vehicle. A vehicle's Meet-Table simply record vehicles it met. In order to maintain it dynamically, we can add some additional information. So the structure of Meet-Table can be as showing in Table 1. With the help of information recorded in Meet-Table, new met vehicle can be added into Meet-Table, or replace existed vehicle in Meet-Table with algorithms such as NRU (Not Recently Used), LRU (Least Recently Used), etc.

Table 1. Data structure of Meet-Table

Name	Type	Note
VID	String	Vehicle ID, is key
FMT	Date and time	First Meeting Time
LMT	Date and time	Last Meeting Time
MC	Number	Meeting Count

In addition to Meet-Table, we must record serial numbers of certificates of vehicles, because the revoked certificates are listed in CRL by their serial number. So we design Meet-Cert table to do this. The structure of Meet-Cert is shown in Table 2. In order to cache CRLs for future broadcasting, we design Meet-CRL to do it. The data structure of Meet-CRL is shown in Table 3.

Table 2. Data structure of Meet-Cert

Name	Type	Note
CSN	String	Certificate Serial Number, is key
VID	String	Vehicle ID
CRLS	String	Certificate Revocation List Signature

Table 3. Data structure of Meet-CRL

Name	Type	Note
CRLS	String	Certificate Revocation List Signature, is key
CRLC	String	CRL content

3.2 Propagation Algorithm

When a vehicle meets another vehicle, it executes Meeting algorithm showing in Fig. 1. VID is the ID assigned to the met vehicle. CSNs is serial numbers of certificates issued to the met vehicle.

```
Name: Alg-meeting
Input: VID, CSNs
If not VID   Meet-Table
  Add VID into Meet-Table
End if
For each csn   CSNs
  If not csn   Meet-Cert then
    Add csn into Meet-Cert
  End if
End for
```

Fig. 1. Meeting algorithm

When a vehicle receives a crl from RSU or other vehicle, it executes propagation algorithm showing in Fig. 2.

```
Name: Alg-propagation
Input: crl
For each
 If                then
   Put crl into Meet-CRL
   Broadcast crl
   Exit for
 End if
End for
```

Fig. 2. Propagation algorithm

3.3 Procedure of Certificate Revocation in VANET

VANET executes certificate revoking procedure showing in Fig. 3 to revoke certificates until the VANET stops as a whole.

```
Name: Alg-revoking
Input: void
Do
   CA issues crl and puts it into LDAP server
   RSU gets crl from LDAP server
   RSU broadcasts crl
   v receives crl
   v propagats crl by calling Alg-propagation
Until be asked to stop
```

Fig. 3. Certificate revoking procedure

In Alg-revoking, all steps may be executed in a parallel and asynchronous model. That means CAs, RSUs, and all vehicles are executing tasks of themselves respectively at the same time.

4   Security and Performance Analyzing

4.1   Attack Model and Security of CRL

CRL is a major method used to release certificate revocation information. So attackers usually block or delay the CRL distributing procedure. In other words, anti-DoS and timeliness are two key aspects can be used to measure the security of CRL schema.

Classical PKI issues CRL into LDAP server for clients to retrieve. For clients don't retrieve CLR in real time model and LDAP server is a single-failure point, classical PKI is bad at timeliness and anti-DoS. OCSP provides real time status check of certificate but also has the problem of single-failure point, so it is good at timeliness but bad at anti-DoS.

RSU based broadcasting is a positive and semi-distributed model, so it has an average score in timeliness and anti-DoS of security.

Epidemic fashion and Meet-Table based propagation(MTBP) that we proposed work not only in a positive model, but also in a completely distributed environment, so both of them are good at timeliness and anti-DoS.

4.2   Communication Complexity

In classical PKI, OCSP and RSU broadcasting, CRL is not send to vehicle by vehicle, so the communication complexity of them is respectively

$$c_{PKI} = c_{OCSP} = c_{RSU} = O(n_v) \tag{7}$$

In epidemic fashion, CRL is broadcast in VANET from vehicle to vehicle, so its communication complexity is shown in Eqs. 5 and 6.

In MTBP, CRL is only broadcast to a subset of vehicles, so its communication complexity,

$$c_{MTBP} = \mathrm{O}\big((\gamma n_v)^h\big) \qquad (8)$$

γ is the ratio of a vehicle's met vehicles in all vehicles of VANET. For the same reason of Eq. 6, h can be equal to 6. So

$$c_{MTBP} = \mathrm{O}\big((\gamma n_v)^6\big) \qquad (9)$$

4.3 Storage Complexity

In classical PKI, RSU broadcasting and epidemic fashion, all vehicles tends to store all other vehicles' CRL, so the whole storage complexity of VANET in these schemas is respectively

$$s_{PKI} = s_{RSU} = s_{epidemic} = \mathrm{O}\big(n_v^2\big) \qquad (10)$$

In OCSP model, CRL only stores in a central server, so its storage complexity,

$$s_{OCSP} = \mathrm{O}(n_v) \qquad (11)$$

In MTBP, all vehicles only store a subset of CRLs of met vehicles, so its storage complexity,

$$s_{MTBP} = \mathrm{O}\big((\gamma n_v)^2\big) \qquad (12)$$

4.4 Comparing of Certificate Revocation Schemas

Now we put all the things discussed above into Table 4. From Table 4, we can see that MTBP is secure and efficient than other CRL schemas.

Table 4. Comparing of certificate revocation methods

	Timeliness	Anti-DoS	Communication complexity	Storage complexity
Classical PKI	Bad	Bad	$\mathrm{O}(n_v)$	$\mathrm{O}\big(n_v^2\big)$
OCSP	Good	Bad	$\mathrm{O}(n_v)$	$\mathrm{O}(n_v)$
RSU broadcasting	Average	Average	$\mathrm{O}(n_v)$	$\mathrm{O}\big(n_v^2\big)$
Epidemic	Good	Good	$\mathrm{O}\big(n_v^6\big)$	$\mathrm{O}\big(n_v^2\big)$
MTBP	Good	Good	$\mathrm{O}\big((\gamma n_v)^6\big)$	$\mathrm{O}\big((\gamma n_v)^2\big)$

5   Conclusion

Through formal calculating of the size of CRLs and communication complexity of RSU based broadcasting and epidemic fashion of CRL propagation in nationwide VANET, we find both of them are not applicable in large nationwide VANET. By proposing Meet-Table, we give a Meet-Table based CRL propagation schema. Comparing to classical

PKI, OCSP, RSU based broadcasting and epidemic fashion, the proposed schema is secure and efficient. So Meet-Table based CRL propagation schema can be used in nationwide VANET.

In the next step, we will develop simulating system to evaluate our proposed schema on several real vehicle trace data sets to study its real effect. We are also considering to merge the advantages of CRL and OCSP in VANET utilizing DHT (Distributed Hash Table) and the schema proposed in this paper.

Acknowledgments. This work is supported by National Natural Science Foundation of China under Grant No.71262072.

References

1. Al-Sultan, S., Al-Doori, M.M., Al-Bayatti, A.H., et al.: A comprehensive survey on vehicular ad hoc network. J. Netw. Comput. Appl. **37**(2), 380–392 (2014)
2. Jindal, V., Bedi, P.: Vehicular ad-hoc networks: introduction, standards, routing protocols and challenges. Int. J. Comput. Sci. Issues **13**(2), 44–55 (2016)
3. Engoulou, R.G., Bellaïche, M., Pierre, S., et al.: VANET security surveys. Comput. Commun. **44**(2), 1–13 (2014)
4. Chokhani, S.: Toward a national public key infrastructure. IEEE Commun. Mag. **1994**(9), 70–74 (1994)
5. Yeh, Y.-S., Lai, W.-S., Cheng, C.-J.: Applying lightweight directory access protocol service on session certification authority. Comput. Netw. **38**(5), 675–692 (2002)
6. Hormann, T.P., Wrona, K., Holtmanns, S.: Evaluation of certificate validation mechanisms. Comput. Commun. **29**(3), 291–305 (2006)
7. Farradyne, P.: Vehicle Infrastructure Integration-VII Architecture and Functional Requirements, v1.1. http://ral.ucar.edu/projects/vii.old/vii/docs/VIIArchandFuncRequirements.pdf
8. Haas, J.J., Hu, Y.-C., Laberteaux, K.P.: Efficient certificate revocation list organization and distribution. IEEE J. Sel. Areas Commun. **29**(3), 595–604 (2011)
9. Statista: Number of cars in the U.S. 1990–2014. http://www.statista.com/statistics/183505/number-of-vehicles-in-the-united-states-since-1990/
10. Roger, G.: The sorry state of certificate revocation. http://search.proquest.com/docview/1729017452
11. Cunha, F.D., Vianna, A.C., Mini, R.A.F., et al.: Are vehicular networks small world? In: IEEE Conference on Computer Communications Workshops, ON, Canada, pp: 195–196 (2014)
12. Ding, J., Gao, J., Xiong, H.: Understanding and modelling information dissemination patterns in vehicle-to-vehicle networks. In: 23rd SIGSPATIAL International Conference on Advances in Geographic Information Systems, New York, NY, USA, pp: 1–10 (2015)

Game Theoretical Analysis on System Adoption and Acceptance: A Review

Xueqin Liang[1], Zheng Yan[1,2(✉)], and Peng Zhang[1]

[1] The State Key Laboratory on Integrated Services Networks, School of Cyber Engineering,
Xidian University, Xi'an 710071, China
Dearliangxq@126.com, zyan@xidian.edu.cn,
pengzhangzhang@gmail.com
[2] Department of Communications and Networking, Aalto University, 02150 Espoo, Finland

Abstract. Game theory is a methodology using mathematics models to analyze the strategic interactions between participants. It has been widely used to analyze the acceptance of system models under various conditions. In this paper, we review the basic knowledge of game theory. After extensive literature study, we propose a series of model requirements that should be paid attention in game theoretical analysis. Furthermore, we classify the existing work into two categories: games in information systems and games in network systems, which have been analyzed in accordance with the aforementioned requirements. The review shows that game theory is a good tool to analyze the adoption and acceptance of a system model and can be used for improving system design towards practical deployment. Moreover, we present the advantages and limitations of existing studies, and propose future research directions.

Keywords: Game theory · System acceptance · Network performance · Equilibrium · Strategy analysis

1 Introduction

Game theory has shown its power in economic markets [26], government strategy [27] and some other fields. It makes interactions formulistic by considering predicted behaviors and actual behaviors. It recommends an optimal strategy for each game participant. It has evolved a lot since formed in 1928 by von Neumann. Harsanyi is a famous economist who has a conspicuous achievement in applying game theory in economics. He states game theory to be strategic interaction [25], which means each rational player needs to choose his actions based on other player's countermoves that he supposes in social situations. So some researches come up with an idea to use game theory to analyze and improve some existing models or systems. This methodology turns out to be more effective than applying simulation-based research methods. This discovery encourages researchers in different fields to investigate system models with game-theoretical analysis.

Many studies have been performed based on game theory. Coucheney et al. used game theory to help content providers choose the level of advertisement [18]. Duan et al. used game theory to handle a multi-objective scheduling problem in hybrid clouds [20].

© Springer International Publishing AG 2016
G. Wang et al. (Eds.): SpaCCS 2016 Workshops, LNCS 10067, pp. 155–167, 2016.
DOI: 10.1007/978-3-319-49145-5_16

Zhang et al. constructed an indirect reciprocity game in a spectrum access network that can help reduce the selfish behaviors of secondary users in reality [22]. Dandekar et al. performed empirical analysis based on game theory in a credit network to help an agent to transact with distrusted agents [16]. In order to make selfish nodes in mobile ad hoc networks to cooperate, a game theoretic approach with reputation mechanism was proposed by Li et al. [23]. A Global Trust Management system for unwanted traffic control may be hindered by the selfish nature of its stakeholders. For solving this problem, Shen et al. modeled the interactions among all stakeholders as a public goods game [24]. With the implementation of trust-based punishment mechanism, their cooperation is easy to achieve, which proves that the Global Trust Management system for unwanted traffic control can be highly accepted by its stakeholders.

With the rapid development of networking technologies and many other emerging technologies, e.g., cloud computing. The infrastructure of network based services is changed, which brings great convenience for users. However, there are some new issues generated subsequently besides the merits. For example, in cloud storage services, a user may lose direct control on its assets when its assets are moved to the cloud, which could cause a big security threat. Facing emerging technologies and systems designed based on them, it is essential to study their adoption and acceptance. Game theory becomes a potentially useful tool for such an analysis. However, the literature still lacks an overview on this field. Is game theory useful for such a research? What are the criteria to perform such a study with game theory? How to evaluate the performance of such a study? The above serious questions have not been investigated in the literature.

In this paper, we propose the requirements that should be considered when forming game-theoretical analysis. Then we extensively review game-theoretical studies in information and network systems and compare them according to the proposed requirements. Specifically, the contributions of our survey can be summarized as follows:

- Different from designing a core model to describe a certain kind of games in [13], we propose relatively comprehensive requirements that can be used to evaluate the performance of game theoretic techniques.
- We overview and analyze the current literature in the area of information and network systems with the application of game theory based on the proposed requirements.
- We come up with many open research issues that have not been considered in the existing work and further point out future research directions.

The rest of our paper is organized as below. Section 2 provides definitions on a number of basic concepts, followed by the requirements of game modeling and analysis in Sect. 3. In Sects. 4 and 5, we review a number of existing studies that applied game theory to study information systems and network systems based on the proposed, respectively. The open issues and future research directions are discussed in Sect. 6. A conclusion is summarized in the last section.

2 Overview of Game Theory

2.1 Definition

Game theory is a new subfield of applied mathematics. It is a subject to study optimal solutions in some conflicts. Game refers to the procedures that some people, groups or organizations choose and carry out the strategies that they choose from their action sets synchronously or successively, once or repeatedly under certain environments and rules, and achieve corresponding payoffs. In order to describe a game, there should be at least 3 basic elements: (1) player that is the entity involved in a game and can be an individual, a company, a nation, and so on; (2) strategy that a player may choose under a historical perspective of actions; (3) payoff, also called utility that each player obtains when all of them have chosen their actions from their strategy spaces. Apparently, the payoff not only relies on the player's own action, but also the actions of other players.

2.2 Classification

Games can be classified in different ways in terms of different aspects. Based on the number of players, games can be classified as two-person games and N-person games. If a game has two sides to make their decisions alone, and their strategies and benefits have an interdependent relationship, this kind of games is called two-person game. If the number of players is three or even more, the game is called N-person game. Based on the order of games, they can be divided into static games and dynamic games. The former, namely, means all the players choose actions or strategies at the same time, or although their actions are chosen successively, the latter has no idea about the former's actions, so it can also be called "simultaneous-move game". On the contrary, the latter means each player chooses and acts in an order and the latter player can observe the former's choices and actions. If each player understands the payoffs under every situation completely, this game is with complete information, while game with incomplete information means that some players have inaccurate knowledge about other players' characteristics, strategy spaces and payoff functions during gaming. Moreover, there is a very common principle of classification, which is based on the purpose of game. If every player chooses its strategy independently from the view of maximizing individual payoff, the game is called non-cooperative game. In cooperative games, players negotiate a binding contract or form a coalition with others in order to gain favor for all players.

2.3 Economic Definitions

In this part, we give the definitions of some economic terminologies and game models that will be used later.

The Stackelberg model models a situation that there is a leader firm who takes the first action and other follower firms take sequential moves. Finding the subgame perfect Nash equilibrium (SPNE) is a way to find the solution to this model. SPNE means no matter what happened in the past, player always chooses Nash equilibrium in every subgame. The prisoner's dilemma is a typical game model of non-zero sum game. It describes a possibility that cooperation between two complete rational individuals may be difficult to achieve. Although cooperation is the choice to the players' best interest, the Nash equilibrium is that they both betray. This model shows that the individual optimal options may not be the group optimal options. It is noticeable that the outcome of prisoner's dilemma played once is different from that played repeatedly. Since the observation of previous actions, players are induced to choose to cooperate in case of punishment. The economic term, public good, is a good with the characteristic of non-excludable and non-rivalries. It can bring great benefits but we need to concern about its quality and quantity, otherwise, the over-use of public good may cause negative to the whole society.

3   Requirements of Game Modeling

The literature on game modeling is very diverse according to its applied situations, assumptions, and modeling approaches. Herein, we propose a number of criteria in order to measure the quality of game modeling.

Stability (ST): A game should eventually enter such a state that every player is satisfied with its payoff, which means once this state is achieved, no one has motivation to change its strategy. The game may not end up with a deterministic result without this require-ment.

Correctness (C): All possible final states of a game are supposed to satisfy the demand or the goal of the model. For example, in a distributed lifetime-maximized target coverage game [15], its final states should meet a coverage requirement.

Efficiency (E): With the application of the designed game, the cost is the lowest, the payoff is the highest and there is no unnecessary waste of resources etc. For instance, in a distributed lifetime-maximized target coverage game [15], if in any final state, there exists active yet redundant sensors, we would say it does not satisfy the requirement of efficiency because it causes unwanted energy squander.

Feasibility (F): A feasible model should at least satisfy the following requirements. First, any player's payoff function should be defined just according to the information obtain-able by the player. Second, if someone wants to turn the game into a feasible solution, it would be difficult because of the parameters in the utility function, which contains integral knowledge. Finally, the algorithm used should be as simple as possible to save computing resources and ensure performance.

Scalability (SC): The designed model or algorithm supports scalability, which means that it is also suitably efficient and practical when applied into a large scale scenario with a less restrictive condition in pre-set assumptions with regard to input volumes and storage demands, etc.

4   Game Modeling in Information Systems

In this section, we provide an overview on a number of game modeling applications in information systems. We classify the applications into three categories: cloud storage services, catch problems, and others. We comment each existing work based on the requirements presented in Sect. 3, which is summarized in Table 1.

Table 1. Comparison of games in information systems based on model requirements

Application scenarios		ST	C	E	F	SC
Cloud computing	Ref. [1]	Y	Y	N	Y	Y
	Ref. [8]	Y	Y	Y	Y	N
	Ref. [21]	U	Y	Y	Y	N
Cache problem	Ref. [9]	Y	Y	Y	N	U
	Ref. [17]	N	Y	N	Y	Y
	Ref. [19]	Y	Y	N	N	N
Others	Ref. [10]	Y	Y	U	U	U
	Ref. [11]	Y	Y	Y	Y	U
	Ref. [12]	Y	Y	Y	Y	N

Y: Yes with consideration; N: No without consideration; U: Unknown with no discussion.

4.1   Cloud Storage Services

In the era of information explosion, the requirement of users' storage grows exponentially, with 70 % growth annually. The emergence of cloud storage services has brought a new opportunity and facility to lease memory to store data so that users do not need to store it locally.

The action that cloud storage providers lease out storage spaces to users is a cost effective but challenging decision. Khazaee et al. presented a repeated game with a number of proposed new strategies [1] to show that these strategies are the most profitable for game players. If both players in the constructed game choose the most profitable strategies, they would be motivated to return to cooperate rapidly and their payoffs can be increased correspondingly. This model can also be used to make decisions in distributed situations where the players are independent. However, the quality of the proposed strategy was not considered and evaluated. Evaluating with the proposed requirements, we find that the effectiveness of the proposed strategies is not ensured, while the others are satisfied.

As the agents in a decentralized storage system are independent, the agents with high availability will shape a faction where they can duplicate information with each other. However, this would harm the newcomers with low availability. A stochastic replication model was proposed in [8], which can maximize data availability with a limited memory space. There exists a unique SPNE, and a semi centralized "adoption" mechanism was proposed with formulated rules to ensure its truth. Heuristics for both centralized and decentralized allocation was proposed. Trough simulations, cooperation can be easily achieved. Based on the above analysis, we find that ST, C, E and F are satisfied while the scalability is missed because it assumes that all agents have the same storage.

Cloud computing offers massive types of services that can cater for various requirements of customers. Choosing the best services that satisfy the customer's requirements on the quality and expense of a service is crucially important. Esposito et al. solved this service selection issue by applying fuzzy inference and a non-cooperative game with complete information [21]. The efficiency of the proposed solution is empirically evidenced through properly crafted simulation experiments. The simulation shows that the solution converges and the chosen service is the optimal one. Overall, ST is unknown because the authors did not discuss about the existence of equilibrium. SC is out of consideration because the model just considers one customer at a time and assigns only one service, while C, E and F are supported based on simulations.

4.2 Cache Problems

Cache is a memory that can be used for high-speed data exchange. The cache is normally considered to improve the performance of network dramatically.

A revenue-rewarding scheme was proposed by Ip et al. to award the cooperative proxies on the basis of their resources contributions [9]. At first, a non-cooperative game was proposed but it turned out to be undesirable since there was no guarantee that the equilibrium is socially optimal. Then two cooperative games, the profit maximizing game, which is a Stackelberg game, and the utility maximizing game, which is a resource allocation game, were proposed to support ST. The games perform well in Cooperative Proxy-And-Client Caching (COPACC) system based on incentive, then C and E are ensured. However, there still needs a cheat proof mechanism, which can detect the actions of participants, to make the scheme feasible. Unfortunately, there are not any measures taken to ensure SC.

In order to deal with the design of efficient algorithms to schedule workloads over available cores, Tsompanas et al. presented a parallel bio-inspired model [17] that was used to simulate the utilization of shared memory on multicore systems. It is a public goods problem. A Common Pool Resource (CPR) game was modeled. This model can capture the dynamic interactions of multiple players over the utilization of a public resource under the same rules sufficiently. At the same time, it can be used in many general cases. However, the equilibrium was not discussed in this paper. The considerations on cache memory levels were also limited. Incorporating other levels of CPR games should be considered in the future in order to emulate the contentions over other shared resources. According to the above introduction, ST and E should be concerned.

Hoiles et al. used a nonparametric learning algorithm to evaluate the request probability of YouTube videos based on the past behaviors of users [19], and formulated a non-cooperative repeated game to model an adaptive caching problem. Because the game was non-stationary, an adaptive popularity-based video caching algorithm was proposed. ST is ensured because a correlated equilibrium can be achieved. The result that video servers can assort their caching strategies in a distributed way proves C. However, the transport energy, routing energy and the information-centric network had not been considered. In reality, there is more than one Content Distribution Network

(CDN) and the types of caches are diverse. According to the analysis, E, F and SC of the scheme are limited.

4.3 Others

In [10], Biran et al. stated that companies should take the competitive intelligence seriously in order to understand the tactical and strategic plans of the adversaries. Otherwise, they may lose profitable opportunities. A non-symmetric mixed strategy game was used and an analytic architecture was proposed to evaluate the worth of carrying out a competitive intelligent information gathering system. It was showed that equilibrium can be achieved in this game, which satisfies the requirement of stability. It can help decision makers to make comprehensive decision in a competitive situation. It means the model satisfies the requirement of correctness, while the other requirements (namely, E, F and SC) are out of discussion.

Feedback implosion in wireless terrestrial networks makes such networks less scalable. Anastasopoulos et al. presented a large-scale multicast service with autonomy and high reliability, inspired by social psychology [11]. A contribution game was used to model the processes of the proposed autonomic framework. Equilibrium can be achieved. Simulations were carried out to show that this method can suppress feedback messages in a pretty effective way with a high data transfer productiveness. But it also has shortcomings, e.g., the evaluated delaying period is basically stable even if the difference between the numbers of users is diverse. The discussion about SC of the scheme was not provided, while the other requirements are satisfied based on aforementioned analysis.

Learning agents in multi-agent distributed resource allocation problem may be needed to allow adaptation if considering the dynamic requirements and constraints [12]. Observing previous outcomes, which can be used to improve future decisions, can contribute to accomplishing learning. Once the memories or observation capabilities of agents are assumed to be limited, one must decide the size of the observation window. The impacts to the game players' performance of the allocation can be evaluated by dispersion games. There exists equilibrium. In addition, a new evolutionary-based learning algorithm was designed and applied to improve a traditional learning algorithm, which makes the model more efficient and feasible than other existing work. But it only deals with such a situation that the agents just face with information that is created by their own, with the assumption that the agents are essentially bias-free, which is not realistic. Only SC is not considered in this work.

5 Game Modeling in Network Systems

We review game modeling in network systems based on three application categories: network selection, risk assessment and lifetime maximization in wireless sensor networks. We comment each existing work based on the aforementioned requirements, which is summarized in Table 2.

Table 2. Comparison of games in network systems based on model requirements

Application scenarios		ST	C	E	F	SC
Network selection	Ref. [2]	Y	Y	Y	Y	N
	Ref. [3]	Y	Y	Y	U	U
Risk assessment	Ref. [4]	Y	Y	Y	Y	N
	Ref. [5]	Y	Y	Y	N	N
	Ref. [6]	Y	Y	Y	Y	N
	Ref. [7]	Y	Y	Y	N	N
Maximize lifetime	Ref. [14]	Y	Y	Y	U	Y
	Ref. [15]	Y	Y	Y	Y	Y

5.1 Network Selection

Network selection becomes a serious issue with the emergence of various access networks that provide multiple access chances in the next generation wireless access networks because customers may have many choices with regard to network selection. Antoniou et al. studied cooperative user–network interactions and captured their interactions by utilizing game-theoretic tools [2]. Based on this study, the involved entities can achieve cooperation, which satisfies all of them through repeated interactions. The equilibrium was discussed. Theoretical results provide a proof that cooperation between users and networks would be incented by the developed method, and both players can obtain relative higher payoffs through cooperation than applying a non-cooperation strategy. However, the interactions between players who do not have perfect knowledge with each other or uncertain players should be considered in order to show the scalability of the proposed model.

Network Selection and Resource Allocation (NSRA) are strictly related. Traditional methods handled them separately, while Cesana, Malanchini, and Capone formed a non-cooperative game to dealing with them in an integrated way [3]. Nash equilibrium was characterized and mathematical programming was proposed to obtain the equilibrium. Simulation showed that even if the players take actions selfishly, they will not harm other players' interests. The end users can get the best quality of service and the access network can obtain the maximum number of users. This method satisfies the first three requirements (ST, C, E), while there is no discussion about the others (F and SC).

5.2 Risk Assessment

As the high utilization ratio of computer networks, it is crucial and essential to assess the risks of usage for the sake of the security of network. In [6], a non-cooperative non-zero-sum static game with complete information was introduced to compute the chance of threat, named Game Theoretical Attack-Defense Model (GTADM). The equilibrium can be reached, which shows that the game is stable and applicable. The model considers the payoffs of defenders and attackers, and the results are the optimal solutions. What's more, this risk assessment model can also be used for assessing other risks, for instance the ones designated by Attack Tree. In order to make the model more comprehensive, the weight of each node and the possibility of attacks should also be involved in the model. Only SC is not satisfied.

There is another method presented by Wang et al. to predict an attacker's behavioral decision [7]. The authors emphatically introduced GTADM and Hierarchical Risk Computing Model (HRCM) in the system, based on the model in [6]. This model can help researchers analyze game players' interaction. However, this scheme was only simulated. In order to make it applicable in practice, the parameters used in the players' payoff, the chance of attacks and the success rate of defense should be seriously set up or modelled. ST, C and E are supported while F and SC are out of consideration.

The foregoing models are too tactless to transform their conditions optionally and fleetly in the applications of cloud computing system. Furuncu et al. proposed an imperfect information non-cooperative non-zero static game model [5] to make it compatible in a scalable security risk assessment model. In principle, there was either a pure Nash equilibrium or a mixed Nash equilibrium. This game method uses the payoffs of a defender and an attacker, which makes the risk assessment process faster than any other traditional methods. And the defender's ideal strategy and the risks of the asset can be calculated by this method. But only one kind of risk has been involved in the assessment and the parameters used in the payoffs should also be refined. Only F and SC were not considered.

When considering the risk from the perspective of users, attackers may find the weakness of user device or cloud when moving asserts to the cloud [4] in order to attack user asserts easily. According to such attacks, the cost and benefit functions of players were formulated. The players in this model are the users while those are the network governors and cloud providers in GTADM. Based on this game model, a user can decide whether move assert to cloud or not. The novelty of this method is using user's trust value to calculate the payoffs. It was proved that there is exactly a pure Nash equilibrium under some given trust value. However, the assets, actions and players considered should be extended to make it more realistic. According to the analysis, only SC was not taken into considerations.

5.3 Lifetime Maximization in Wireless Sensor Networks

Wireless Sensor Network (WSN), whose peripheral is a sensor that can perceive and check the external world, is a distributed network. It communicates wirelessly, so its network settings are flexible that the position of equipment can be changed easily. A large number of sensor nodes have been disposed in a monitoring area to capture accurate information. However, it is impossible to deploy the exact number of nodes. In order to prolong the network lifetime, actions should be taken to save the energy of redundant sensors.

Voulkidis, Anastasopoulos and Cottis proposed a coalitional game theoretic scheme whose aim is to maximize the lifetime of wireless sensor network under prescribed QoS [14]. The authors exploited the spatial correlation of sensed phenomenon measurements to form nodes coalitions to drastically reduce the transmissions of representative nodes. The above research result showed that the scheme can prolong WSN lifetime noticeably and satisfy QoS specifications for proper WSN operations at the same time. What's more, the efficiency and stability of this scheme were studied through simulations. This scheme addresses implementation issues, which implies that the game design is practical. F was beyond discussion, while the others (ST, C, E, SC) were under consideration.

In [15], Yen et al. proposed a target coverage game, which is a non-cooperative dynamic game, to tackle a coverage problem. This research aims to find out a series of sensors that satisfy specific coverage requirements. This model satisfies the requirements of stability, correctness and efficiency according to rigorous proofs. Meanwhile, it was demonstrated that game theory is feasible even if there are different coverage requirements and different sensor capacity standards. An approach that can shorten convergence time and energy consumption was proposed and its efficiency was proved through simulations. This game can be implemented in hardware-constrained sensor devices because it only needs simple calculation. The requirements we proposed are all satisfied.

6   Open Issues and Future Research Directions

According to the above review based on the model requirements, we notify that game theory indeed provides great help on many strategic related analyses to solve a number system and network problems or puzzles. Cooperation is more likely to be achieved between participants in repeated games. Equilibriums in static game can be improved to some degree when the players take actions sequentially, namely, changing the game into a dynamic game. In addition, improved mechanisms can be proposed or innovated through game theoretical analysis. Thus, game theory is a good tool to evaluate a system model and further optimize it.

However, we also find some problems in using game theory to analyze systems. First, in some existing work, the selected or applied game models are not so accurate for simulating the interactions between players. Second, the assumptions proposed are too rigorous to apply into a real world. The game modeling is normally designed by simplifying the real system, which is hard to reflect the real complicated world. Third, due to lack of knowledge and experimental limitations, the problem taken into account may not be so comprehensive. We should do our endeavor to overcome. Fourth, lots of the models can handle a specific problem perfectly, but it cannot be migrated to other situations appropriately, thus lack generality.

The shortcomings presented above will motivate future studies. In what follows, further propose some promising research direction with regard to game-theoretical analysis by considering the game modeling requirements and the weaknesses of existing work.

First, it is crucial to make sure which equilibrium is the most practical one. As presented in [15], the stability requirement in some games corresponds to Nash equilibrium. But there may be multiple equilibriums in practice. In the mainstream game theory, people are keen on using a pure mathematical logic to analyze rational actions and determine the determinacy and feasibility of Nash equilibrium. But it is crucial to justify which equilibrium is the best one that fits into real practice.

Second, historical experiences should be used in the game modeling and analysis in order to reduce the loss caused by lack of comprehensive information. In practice, strategic decision is impacted by many factors, e.g., information communications, social habits, common background, regulation of legal rules, existence of external options, and so on. Some of them are hard to obtain. Therefore, historical experience analysis should be used when the players lack understanding of each other's values or strategic choices.

Third, semi-rational players who would take rational actions in a certain condition should be considered. In the existing work, the players in game theory are generally supposed to be rational, which is not realistic and may hinder the scalability of the game. Any entity in society may follow the fashion if they have preference or the distinction between each choice is insignificant, which would induce social cooperation. When humanity is considered, a designed model would be wide-range. Irrational players following some reasonable patterns could be concerned in the game modeling and analysis. Since a system could act in a ubiquitous environment with various participants playing therein, it is difficult or even impossible to design a universal model. But what we can do is to improve it on the basis of the present.

7   Conclusion

Game theory, as a promising approach, has shown its effectiveness in analyzing the adoption and acceptance of an information or network system. In this paper, we proposed a research model that contains the basic requirements on game modeling: stability, correctness, efficiency, feasibility and scalability. We used this research model to review and evaluate the performance of existing game-theoretical methods used to analyze and improve the information and network systems. We found that the game-theoretical analysis is effective to some degree but there still exist a number of limitations that restrain its performance. A number of open issues, e.g., the inappropriate model selection, the rigorous assumptions, the lack of comprehensive knowledge and the absence of scalability, motivate further investigation. Based on our review, we further propose several future research directions, which we believe are very interesting research topics.

Acknowledgments. This work is sponsored by the National Key Foundational Research and Development on Network and Space Security, China (grant 2016YFB0800704), the NSFC (grants 61672410 and U1536202), the 111 project (grants B08038 and B16037), the PhD grant of the Chinese Educational Ministry (grant JY0300130104), the Project Supported by Natural Science Basic Research Plan in Shaanxi Province of China (Program No. 2016ZDJC-06), and Aalto University.

References

1. Khazaee, P.R., Mirzadi, K., Yousefi, S.: Cooperative user and storage service providers interaction in cloud computing. In: 7th Conference on Information and Knowledge Technology (IKT), pp. 1–5. IEEE (2015)
2. Antoniou, J., Papadopoulou, V., Vassiliou, V., Pitsillides, A.: Cooperative user–network interactions in next generation communication networks. Comput. Netw. **54**, 2239–2255 (2010). ACM

3. Cesana, M., Malanchini, I., Capone, A.: Modelling network selection and resource allocation in wireless access networks with non-cooperative games. In: 5th IEEE International Conference on Mobile Ad Hoc and Sensor Systems, pp. 404–409. IEEE (2008)

4. Maghrabi, L., Pfluegel, E.: Moving assets to the cloud: a game theoretic approach based on trust Cyber Situational Awareness. In: International Conference on Data Analytics and Assessment (CyberSA), pp. 1–5. IEEE (2015)

5. Furuncu, E., Sogukpinar, I.: Scalable risk assessment method for cloud computing using game theory (CCRAM). Comput. Stan. Interfaces **38**, 44–50 (2015). Elsevier

6. He, W., Xia, C., Wang, H., Zhang, C., Ji, Y.: A game theoretical attack-defense model oriented to network security risk assessment. In: International Conference on Computer Science and Software Engineering, vol. 6, pp. 498–504. IEEE (2008)

7. Wang, B., Cai, J., Zhang, S., Li, J.: A network security assessment model based on attack-defense game theory. In: 2010 International Conference on Computer Application and System Modeling (ICCASM), vol. 3, pp. 639–643. IEEE (2010)

8. Rzadca, K., Datta, A., Kreitz, G., Buchegger, S.: Game-theoretic mechanisms to increase data availability in decentralized storage systems. ACM Trans. Auton. Adapt. Syst. (TAAS) **10**, 14:1–14:32 (2015). ACM

9. Ip, A.T.S., Lui, J.C.S., Liu, J.: A revenue-rewarding scheme of providing incentive for cooperative proxy caching for media streaming systems. ACM Trans. Multimedia Comput. Commun. Appl. (TOMM) **4**, 5:1–5:32 (2008). ACM

10. Biran, D., Zack, M.H., Briotta, R.J.: Competitive intelligence and information quality: a game-theoretic perspective. J. Data Inf. Qual. (JDIQ) **4**, 12:1–12:20 (2013). ACM

11. Anastasopoulos, M.P., Vasilakos, A.V., Cottis, P.G.: An autonomic framework for reliable multicast: a game theoretical approach based on social psychology. ACM Trans. Auton. Adapt. Syst. (TAAS) **4**, 21:1–21:23 (2009). ACM

12. Araujo, R.M., Lamb, L.C.: On the use of memory and resources in minority games. ACM Trans. Auton. Adapt. Syst. (TAAS) **4**, 11:1–11:23 (2009). ACM

13. Laszka, A., Felegyhazi, M., Buttyan, L.: A survey of interdependent information security games. ACM Comput. Surv. (CSUR) **47**, 23:1–23:28 (2015). ACM

14. Voulkidis, A.C., Anastasopoulos, M.P., Cottis, P.G.: Energy efficiency in wireless sensor networks: a game-theoretic approach based on coalition formation. ACM Trans. Sens. Netw. (TOSN) **9**, 43:1–43:27 (2013). ACM

15. Yen, L.H., Lin, C.M., Leung, V.C.M.: Distributed lifetime-maximized target coverage game. ACM Trans. Sens. Netw. (TOSN) **9**, 46:1–46:23 (2013). ACM

16. Dandekar, P., Goel, A., Wellman, M.P., Wiedenbeck, B.: Strategic formation of credit networks. ACM Trans. Internet Technol. (TOIT) - Special Issue on Foundations of Social Computing **15**, 3:1–3:41 (2015). ACM

17. Tsompanas, M.A.I., Kachris, C., Sirakoulis, G.C.: Modeling cache memory utilization on multicore using common pool resource game on cellular automata. ACM Trans. Model. Comput. Simul. (TOMACS) - Special Issue on ACAM and Special Issue Papers **26**, 21:1–21:22 (2016). ACM

18. Coucheney, P., D'acquisto, G., Maillé, P., Naldi, M., Tuffin, B.: Influence of search neutrality on the economics of advertisement-financed content. ACM Trans. Internet Technol. (TOIT) - Special Issue on Pricing and Incentives in Networks and Systems and Regular Papers **14**, 10:1–10:21 (2014)

19. Hoiles, W., Gharehshiran, O.N., Krishnamurthy, V., Đào, N.D., Zhang, H.: Adaptive caching in the youtube content distribution network: a revealed preference game-theoretic learning approach. IEEE Trans. Cogn. Commun. Network. **1**, 71–85 (2015). IEEE

20. Duan, R., Prodan, R., Li, X.: Multi-objective game theoretic scheduling of bag-of-tasks workflows on hybrid clouds. IEEE Trans. Cloud Comput. **2**, 29–42 (2014). IEEE
21. Esposito, C., Ficco, M., Palmieri, F., Castiglione, A.: Smart cloud storage service selection based on fuzzy logic, theory of evidence and game theory. IEEE Trans. Comput. **pp**, 1–14 (2015). IEEE
22. Zhang, B., Chen, Y., Liu, K.J.R.: An indirect-reciprocity reputation game for cooperation in dynamic spectrum access networks. IEEE Trans. Wireless Commun. **11**, 4328–4341 (2012). IEEE
23. Li, Z., Shen, H.: Game-theoretic analysis of cooperation incentive strategies in mobile ad hoc networks. IEEE Trans. Mob. Comput. **11**, 1287–1303 (2012). IEEE
24. Shen, Y., Yan, Z., Kantola, R.: Analysis on the acceptance of global trust management for unwanted traffic control based on game theory. Comput. Secur. **47**, 3–25 (2014). Elsevier
25. Haesanyi, J.C.: Games with incomplete information. Nobel Prize Committee (1994)
26. Matsui, M.: A management game model: economic traffic, leadtime and pricing setting. J. Jpn. Ind. Manag. Assoc. **53**(1), 1–9 (2002). CiNii
27. Xu Y., Chen B., Deng Y.T., Deng G.: The government strategy research on college student's employment based on game theory. In: International Conference on Optics Photonics and Energy Engineering, vol. 2, pp. 24–27. IEEE (2010)

An Energy-Efficient Caching Strategy Based on Coordinated Caching for Green Content-Centric Network

Huiqing Xu[1(✉)], Hengjie Huang[2], and Gaocai Wang[1]

[1] School of Computer and Electronic Information, Guangxi University, Guangxi 530004, China
huazhekanzhai@163.com, gcwang@gxu.edu.cn
[2] Educational Technology Center, Yulin Normal University, Yulin 537000, China
hengjiejie@21cn.com

Abstract. CCN (content-centric networking), a new network architecture, use content as centric to communicate to each other. In-network caching is a major feature of this promising architecture and takes advantage of in-network caching to low the latency requested from users and network transport load reduction. Thus, due to the wide in-network caching, CCNs have to cache much more replicas, which increases the caching energy. From the perspective of energy consumption and cost, the green CCNs find key factors influencing energy consumption. Under the situation of latest research of green CCNs, a autonomous regional network is choose as object of study and the nodes in network only needs locally available, caching and transport energy from cooperative caching group, content popularity and other information to make caching decision. The corresponding network energy consumption model is proposed, and a nonlinear programming formulates the network energy consumption problem. Furthermore an advanced genetic algorithm (GA) is used for solving nonlinear programming optimal solution. The results test and verify that the cooperative caching group exists an optimal caching depth for minimizing network energy consumption.

Keywords: Energy consumption optimization · Coordinating caching · Genetic algorithm

1 Introduction

Now, the existing caching decision of CCN don't considerer the integrated request hot, network energy consumption, content popularity, synergy between the nodes and other various factors. From the perspective of a domain, we study CCN caching system. Coordinated caching can be better diversity of content in domain, limit the requests in the domain, thus reducing hops that users accessing contents and network energy consumption.

Recently, most researchers pay attention to these issues such as data naming, content routing, in-network caching, security, etc., mainly on how to improve the utilization of network resources [1]. In-network caching of green content network are also attracted

© Springer International Publishing AG 2016
G. Wang et al. (Eds.): SpaCCS 2016 Workshops, LNCS 10067, pp. 168–175, 2016.
DOI: 10.1007/978-3-319-49145-5_17

by the academic communities, divided into centralized caching [1–6] and distributed in-network caching solution. In [7], the author proposed a distributed in-network caching scheme that content routers only make caching designs from local cache and transport energy consumption information, formulated the distributed in-network caching energy consumption problem, and proved the existence of Nash equilibrium in this solution.

In this paper, according to the short of centralized and non-collaborative manners about energy efficient in CCN, we study the impact of coordinated caching way for CNN on energy consumption.

2 Analysis of Energy Optimization Strategy and Energy Consumption Model for CCN

2.1 Network Model of CCN

We assume that the administrative domain has n content router nodes denoted as $r_1,\ldots,$ r_n. In steady state, a total of M kinds of contents in the entire network, represented by a set M, with M are far larger than capacity c, and administrative domain select m kinds of contents to cache. Referring to the content popularity model, in steady state, contents in administrative domain obeys Zipf distribution. In M different kinds of contents, the probability of access to the top k content may be expressed as follows:

$$F(k; M, \alpha) = \frac{\sum_{i=1}^{k} (1/i^{\alpha})}{\sum_{i=1}^{M} (1/i^{\alpha})}, k = 1, \ldots, M \tag{1}$$

where $\alpha \in (0,1)$ is constant, called Zipf characteristic index, indicates the degree of concentration content access.

2.2 Energy Optimization Strategy for CCN

We introduce parameter $x \in [0, c]$ to indicate the quantity of each node using coordinated way to cache content. According to the features of this coordinated group [8], we propose an intra-domain coordinated caching group strategy based on content popularity to achieve energy consumption minimization. With this strategy, nodes cache content in two stages:

(1) All nodes in this domain according to the local users' request, calculated out the top k content. We assume all nodes cache the local most popular content are the same, namely, all routers place the top c-x content;

(2) The n nodes in this coordinated group use the capacity of x to cache content in coordinated way, so intra-domain has nx kinds of coordinated content. After the above two stages, intra-domain has c + (n − 1)x kinds of content, and still being M-c − (n − 1)x kinds of content accessed from content sources S.

2.3 Energy Consumption Model for CCN

We describe that the whole energy consumption for CNN, E_{wh}^{ccn}.

(1) Energy for nodes caching replicas, E_m^{ccn}: We use energy proportional model [9]. In the given observation time t, if the number of replicas O_k is n_k and the size of replicas O_k is s_k, the caching contents energy is:

$$E_m^{cnn}(n_k) = w_{ca} n_k s_k t, \tag{2}$$

(2) The transferring energy, E_{tr}^{ccn}: This article assumes that any node or any one user in CCN only access one content from a single node, and in order to facilitate discussion Table 1 gives some key parameters in CCN energy consumption model. Here we introduce the average accessing hop between peer routers in coordinating caching group H_r, and can be expressed as follow:

$$H_r = A(n/n_k)^\mu, \mu > 0 \tag{3}$$

Table 1. Symbolic, meanings and the corresponding value in energy consumption model

Symbols	Notations	Values
p_d^r	Power density of a core router	1.7 *10-8 J/bit
p_d^{roadm}	Power density of a ROADM	1.95 *10-11 J/bit
p_d^{wdm}	Power density of a WDM link	5 *10-9 J/bit
p_d^e	Power density of Ethernet switches	8.21 *10-9 J/bit
p_d^g	Power density of Gateway router	1.38 *10-7 J/bit
p_d^{pe}	Power density of Provider edge routers	2.63 *10-8 J/bit
λ_{ik}	Request rate for object O_k at node i	Multiple values

Where n_k represents the number of content O_k stored in the coordinated caching group. The energy for one router accessing content from other peer routers can be estimated as follow:

$$E_{ik}^{tr}(n) = \lambda_{ik} s[(1 + H_r)(p_d^r + p_d^{roadm}) + H_r p_d^{wdm}] \tag{4}$$

Transferring energy generated by users getting content O_k from local nodes is expressed as:

$$E_{ik}^{tr} = \lambda_{ik} s[3p_d^e + p_d^g + 2p_d^{pe}] \tag{5}$$

Users in administrative domain accessing contents O_k from content source S produce transferring energy and can be expressed as:

$$E_{isk}^{tr} = \lambda_{ik} s p_d^s d_s \tag{6}$$

(3) Coordinated energy E_c: The entire coordinated energy can be expressed as follows:

$$E_c = w * n * x \tag{7}$$

In the above Formula (8), w is expected communication energy for single node and one content.

2.4 The Optimization Energy Consumption Model for CCN

Caching energy for coordinated caching group is expressed as:

$$E_s^{cnn} = w_{ca} ncst \tag{8}$$

By the Formula (2), we can conclude that the average intra-domain content requesting energy consumption:

$$E(x) = [F(c - x + nx; M, \alpha) - F(c - x; M, \alpha]$$

$$* \sum_{k=c-x}^{c+(n-1)x} \sum_{i=1}^{n} E_{ik}^{tr}(1)$$

$$+ [1 - F(c - x + nx; M, \alpha)] * \sum_{k=c+nx}^{M} \sum_{i=1}^{n} E_{isk}^{tr} \tag{9}$$

$$+ \sum_{k=1}^{M} \sum_{i=1}^{n} E_{ik}^{tr} + E_s^{cnn}$$

In practice, intra-domain transferring and content caching energy may be inconsistent with coordinated energy consumption. We introduce a weight parameter $\beta \in [0,1]$, and the energy consumption overall coordinated cache group can be expressed as follows:

$$E_a(x; \beta, w) = \beta E(x) + (1 - \beta)E_c \tag{10}$$

The optimization problem of minimize energy consumption for coordinated cache group can be expressed as:

$$\min E_a(x; \beta, w)$$
$$s.t. 0 \leq x \leq c, c \in N \tag{11}$$

3 Solving Energy Consumption Model and Analysis of Experiments

3.1 GA Solve the Network Energy Optimization Consumption Problem

We use an improved genetic algorithm [10] to solve the problem (11). Firstly, fitness function is designed to:

$$F(x) = E_a(x; \beta, w) + \rho(x - c) \tag{12}$$

ρ is the penalty factor. According to Formula (11), the number of individuals in this population is c, setting the number of feasible point in this population is p_1, the number of infeasible point in this population is c-p_1, feasible region is τ, standard deviation function is std, and the penalty factor ρ is:

$$\rho = \begin{cases} \dfrac{\dfrac{1}{p_1} \sum\limits_{x \in \tau} E_a(x; \beta, w) - \dfrac{1}{c - p_1} \sum\limits_{x \in \tau} E_a(x; \beta, w)}{\dfrac{1}{c - p_1} \sum\limits_{x \notin \tau} x - c}, & p_1 > c * 0.1 \\[4mm] \dfrac{std\,(f(x))}{std\,(x - c)}, & x \notin \tau, p_1 \leq c * 0.1 \end{cases} \tag{13}$$

The optimal seed $\bar{x}$ of populations makes:

$$\bar{x} = \min F(x_i) \tag{14}$$

Depending on the distance to optimal seed $\bar{x}$, the remaining population divide into population 1 and population 2. Using threshold L_k to define populations, seeds whose distance to $\bar{x}$ are less than or equal to L_k enter population 1 and the remaining seeding enter population 2. Two fitness functions can be used to represent the seed selection. Fitness function F_1 select seeds to population $pop1$ and $pop2$, and fitness function F_2 sorts the seeds in population. Noting $norm$ is Euclidean distance function; ε is the accuracy; popsize, popsize1, popsize2 respectively represents total population size, population 1 size, population 2 size; and k is the evolution of algebra.

$$F_1: \begin{cases} pop\ 1 = \{x \mid norm(x, \bar{x}) \leq L_k\}; & L_k > \varepsilon \\ pop\ 2 = \{x \mid norm(x, \bar{x}) > L_k\}; & L_k > \varepsilon \\ pop\ 1 = \{x \mid norm(x, \bar{x}) > L_k\}; & L_k \leq \varepsilon \\ pop\ 2 = 0; & L_k \leq \varepsilon \end{cases} \tag{15}$$

$$L_k = \min(\max(norm(x, \bar{x})) * 0.5, \overrightarrow{norm(x, \bar{x})} * (popsize * 0.45)) \tag{16}$$

$\underset{norm(x,\bar{x})}{\longrightarrow}$ is ascending sequence array of $norm(x, \bar{x})$. After two populations are sorted by fitness function $F(x)$, these two populations separately enter into the mating pool according to the roulette method, and roulette selection probability formula is:

$$Q(i) = \frac{q(1-q)^{i-1}}{1-(1-q)^n} \tag{17}$$

n_1, n_2 represent the mating pool size of population 1, 2 respectively, and is calculated as follows:

$$\begin{cases} n_1 = popsize * 0.5; & n_2 = popsize * 0.5; & L_k > \varepsilon \\ n_1 = popsize * 0.5; & n_2 = 0; & L_k \leq \varepsilon \end{cases} \tag{18}$$

3.2 Analysis of Experiments

We use *matlab* to simulate that Poisson distribution case what requests arrival rate of each network node is three times per second under the network in stable state. The x-axis in Figs. 1 and 2 represents the node capacity ratio of each node to cache content in coordinated caching way; y-axis represents the network energy consumption in the period of observation.

In this paper, we adopt a holistic energy consumption model. When coordinated caching depth in the coordinated caching group is 0, the administrative domain uses a Cache Everything Everywhere (CE^2) policy to cache content. According to Figs. 1 and 2, we can seen that the largest energy consumption appears at x = 0, namely, the coordinated caching depth is 0, which is the administrative domain using CE^2 strategy. Obviously, from the perspective of energy saving, the coordinated caching strategy we propose is much better than CE^2.

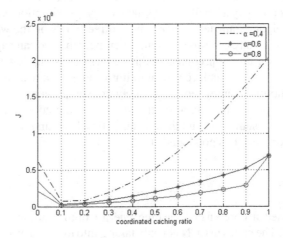

Fig. 1. Zipf index

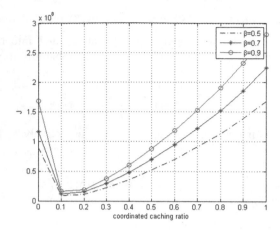

Fig. 2. Coordinated weight parameter

In Fig. 1, we focus on the impact of different Zipf index to the administrative domain energy consumption. We can observe smaller Zipf index, the greater the energy generated, which is due to a smaller Zipf index meaning that the content requested by the user is less not concentrated, and in the same observation period, there will be appeared relatively dispersion of requested content diversity, so that energy consumption increases. At the same time, the different Zipf index will lead to optimal caching depth, when $\alpha = 0.7$, 0.8 the optimal coordinated caching ratio is 0.2, indicating that the user requests content more concentrated, the intra-domain desired content diversity will be reduced, and the coordinated caching ratio for coordinated caching group will be reduced.

We observe Fig. 2 and find that the increasing coordinated energy consumption is with the increase of the weight parameter, but the trends of the three cases have no significant changes. By comparison of transport energy consumption, content caching energy consumption and coordinated energy consumption, we find that coordinated energy consumption is only a small part of total energy consumption, so no matter how the coordinated weight parameter changes, these three trends on the whole is approximately the same. This study gives us some enlightenment that we can pay more attention to transport energy consumption, content caching energy consumption, the intra-domain by using a better place, cache replacement algorithm and hardware technology to reduce the energy consumption, thereby reducing energy consumption of the whole network.

Above these situations, the administrative domain using coordinated caching way can reduce energy consumption, and there is an optimal caching depth to is minimize energy consumption, which is good guide to the deployment of CCN.

4   Conclusion

This paper proposed a coordinated caching energy optimization strategy based on content popularity. The nodes in CCN not only taking into the local most popular content and coordinated caching content among nodes account to improve content diversity of coordinated caching group, to reduce duplicate content transmission, enabling network energy consumption is minimized. According to the characteristics of this coordinated caching group, we establish relevant optimization energy consumption model, use an improved genetic algorithm to solve optimal solution for this coordinated caching group. Experimental results that compared with the existing cache policy, the proposed strategy can effectively reduce the energy consumption of CCN.

Acknowledgments. This research is supported in part by the National Natural Science Foundation of China under Grant Nos. 61562006, 61262003, in part by the Natural Science Foundation of Guangxi Province under Grant No. 2013GXNSFGA019006.

References

1. Lee, U., Rimac, I., Kilper, D., et al.: Toward energy-efficient content dissemination. Netw. IEEE **25**(2), 14–19 (2011)
2. Perino, D., Varvello, M.: A reality check for content centric networking. In: ACM SIGCOMM Workshop on Information-Centric Networking, pp. 44–49. ACM (2011)
3. Braun, T., Trinh, T.A.: Energy efficiency issues in information-centric networking. In: Energy Efficiency in Large Scale Distributed Systems, pp. 271–278 (2013)
4. Hancock, T.: On the energy efficiency of content delivery architectures. In: 2011 IEEE International Conference on Communications Workshops (ICC), pp. 1–6 (2011)
5. Choi, N., Guan, K., Kilper, D.C., et al.: In-network caching effect on optimal energy consumption in content-centric networking. In: IEEE International Conference on Communications, pp. 2889–2894. IEEE (2012)
6. Yonggong, W., Zhenyu, L., Qinghua, W., et al.: Performance analysis and optimization for in-network caching replacement in information centric networking. J. Comput. Res. Dev. **9**, 2046–2055 (2015)
7. Fang, C., Yu, F.R., Huang, T., et al.: An energy-efficient distributed in-network caching scheme for green content-centric networks. Comput. Netw. **7**(8), 91–96 (2014)
8. Fang, X., Chen, S., Ren, Z., et al.: Collaborative caching algorithm based on node similarity in content centric networking. Comput. Sci. **43**(4), 81–85, 96 (2016)
9. Barroso, L.A., Hölzle, U.: The case for energy-proportional computing. Computer **40**(12), 33–37 (2007)
10. Liang, X., Can, Z., Yan, D.: Novel genetic algorithm based on species selection for solving con strained non-linear programming pro problems. J. Central South Univ. (Sci. Technol.) **40**(1), 185–189 (2009)

Characterizing the Scalability and Performance of Analytic Database System

Yishui Li[1,2], Hui Li[1,2(✉)], Mei Chen[1,2], Zhenyu Dai[1,2], and Ming Zhu[3]

[1] Guizhou Engineering Lab of ACMIS, Guizhou University, Guiyang 550025, China
jackieleewater@gmail.com, {cse.HuiLi,gychm}@gzu.edu.cn
[2] College of Computer Science and Technology, Guizhou University, Guiyang 550025, China
[3] National Astronomical Observatories, Chinese Academy of Sciences, Beijing 100016, China
mz@nao.cas.cn

Abstract. Analytic database is designed for analytical applications which aim to explore the value of massive data. It has been widely used in many areas, from business analytics to scientific data discovery. In order to efficiently processing massive data, analytic database often can be scaled-out to achieve high perform-ance. In this paper, in order to understand the intrinsic performance characteristics of analytic database, we take the popular Greenplum database as the representa-tive analytic database system, and conduct a series of comprehensive performance evaluation over it to characterize its scalability and performance features. According to the experimental results and analysis, we obtained an series of initial insights of the factors which may significantly affect the performance paradigm of Greenplum, which will be helpful for analytic database system users to obtain better analytical performance.

Keywords: Analytic database · Scalability · Data loading · Parallel query processing · Performance evaluation

1 Introduction

In recent years, with the explosive growth of data, big data has become a hot topic in the academia and industry. And with the expanding quantity of data, data analysis becomes critical in many areas. With the emergence of this trend, the analytic database has been appeared to be a promising key technology for big data processing. Analytic database is an analytical application-oriented database which mainly designed for online analytical processing, data exploration, etc. It has been widely used in many areas, from business intelligence to scientific data discovery.

In this paper, we will take the popular Greenplum database as the representative analytic database system, and conduct a series of comprehensive performance evaluation over it to characterize the intrinsic features of analytic database system. Greenplum Database is a Share-Nothing database which is based on open source database system PostgreSQL [4–8]. It is an advanced, fully featured, open source analytical database system. It provides powerful and rapid analytics on petabyte scale data volumes. It can manage and handle a massive amount of data. By automatically partitioning data and

© Springer International Publishing AG 2016
G. Wang et al. (Eds.): SpaCCS 2016 Workshops, LNCS 10067, pp. 176–183, 2016.
DOI: 10.1007/978-3-319-49145-5_18

running parallel queries, it allows a cluster of servers to operate as a single database supercomputer performing tens or hundreds times faster than a traditional database.

In this paper, to study the extension ability of analytic database, and analyzes its performance, we design experiment which is based on the TPC Benchmark-H (TPC-H) to evaluate the analytic database, and the experimental study will provide the insights for the performance optimization of the analytic database.

2 Analytic Database

Analytic database is an important branch of database product which was built to store, manage and consume massive data. It is designed to be used specifically with business analytics, big data and business intelligence solutions. Unlike a typical database, which stores data per transaction or process, an analytic database stores business metrics data. An analytic database stores business, market or project data used in business analysis, projections and forecasting processes and also supports the compressed storage format, parallel processing and bulk data loading. Analytic databases also are massively parallel processing databases, which spread data across a cluster of servers, enabling the systems to share the query processing workload. There are many of the analytic databases on the market, like GBase 8a, SAP HANA, Greenplum Database and so on. In this section, we will introduce some of these analytic databases.

2.1 GBase 8a

The GBase 8a is a high-performance database product, which is developed by Nanda General Company [3]. It is for massive data analysis applications, and is based on a unique column storage, compression, intelligent indexing techniques. The GBase 8a aims to satisfy the need of the increasing data analysis of various data-intensive industries, data mining, data backup, bulk data processing and ad hoc queries and so on.

2.2 SAP HANA

The SAP HANA database is positioned as the core of the SAP HANA Appliance to support complex business analytical processes in combination with transactionally consistent operational workloads [1, 2]. The SAP HANA database consists of multiple data processing engines with a distributed query processing environment to provide the full spectrum of data processing – from classical relational data supporting both row and column-oriented physical representations in a hybrid engine, to graph and text processing for semi- and unstructured data management within the same system.

2.3 Greenplum Database

Greenplum Database is a representative analytic database system. It is a massively parallel processing database server that supports next generation data warehousing and large-scale analytics processing [4–8]. Greenplum Database is an array of individual databases working together to present a single database image. The master is the entry point to the Greenplum Database system. The master coordinates its work with the other database instances in the system, called segments, which store and process the data. And the Greenplum provides a choice of storage orientation models: row, column or a combination of both. And it also provides append-optimized tables which is optimized for bulk data loading and two types of in-database compression. With these reasons, we choose the Greenplum Database as an example to research and analysis the characteristics of the analytic database.

3 Experiment Design

3.1 Experiment Environment

In the experiment, our measurements were performed with the Greenplum Database (version 4.3.5.3) client application and the network bandwidth that connects the master and segments is 10G Ethernet and the environment of master and segments are shown in Table 1. We use the command that is provided by Greenplum to count the time. It support for millisecond timing statistics.

Table 1. The configuration of greenplum database

Node name	Master	Segment
Operating System	CentOS7 (Linux3.10.0-229.el7.x86_64)	
CPU	4 cores Inter(R)-Xeon-CPU-E5-2630@2.6 GHz	2 cores Inter(R)-Xeon-CPU-E5-2630@2.6 GHz
Memory	8 GB	4 GB
Disk	100 GB	

3.2 Experiment Design

In order to test the scalability and capability of the analytic database, we design the experiment which is based on the TPC-H benchmark to test the analytic database [9]. We use the TPC-H to generate test data (data size is 20 GB) and test the performance of bulk data loading, and then use the standard 22 queries to evaluating the system scalability, effectiveness of compression and the efficiency of parallel query processing of Greenplum.

4 Experiment Test

4.1 Scalability

In this experiment, we would like to take the Greenplum Database as an example to investigating the scalability of the analytic database. We mainly evaluate the impact of the different segments to the query performance. Greenplum Database enables dynamic extend node. The initial state of the Greenplum has one master and two segments, and then we extend node to one master, four segments and one mater eight segments. We test the query performance in these three situations by executing the queries which are provided by TPC-H. Figure 1 shows the query performance with various segments setup.

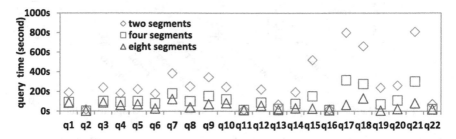

Fig. 1. Query performance with the segments varying

From Fig. 1 we can know that, different segments often lead to different query overheads. The query overheads of two segments is nearly twice the query time of four segments. The query overheads of eight segments is half the query time of four segments. This is mainly because each segment contains a distinct portion of data. The database server processes that serve segment data always running over the corresponding segment instances. When user issues a query, processes are created in each segment database to handle the work of that query. As the segments increases, the volume of data stored in each segment is less, this lead to the processes which are created in each segment to handle less data. So the query overheads are decreased.

This experiment shows that when the volume of data is determined, with the increasing the number of segments, the query overheads often to be reduced. And it also verify that the analytic database, Greenplum, has excellent scalability.

4.2 Efficiency of Bulk Data Loading

In this experiment, we evaluate the capability of the bulk data loading. Greenplum supports bulk data loading, and also provides append-optimized table storage. We use the COPY command copies data from a file or standard input into a table and appends the data to the table contents. We load data into the normal tables and the append-optimized tables and compare the capability of these two situations (The Greenplum has one master and four segments).

Figure 2 shows the data loading capability of append-optimized tables is faster than normal tables. This is because the storage model of append-optimized tables is optimized for bulk data loading. And in Fig. 2, the data loading capability of nation, region and supplier are not improved. This is because these tables have less data, unable to take advantage of append-optimized tables features.

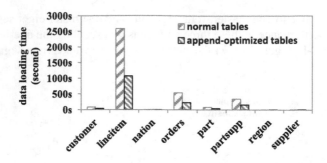

Fig. 2. Data loading capability of normal tables or append-optimized tables

This experiment shows the analytic database, Greenplum, supports bulk data loading and it also provides append-optimized tables which is optimized for bulk data loading. This experiment also shows that the append-optimized table storage works best with denormalized fact tables which are typically the largest tables in the system and are usually loaded in batches and accessed by read-only queries.

4.3 Effectiveness of Compression

In this experiment, we evaluate the effectiveness of data compressibility of the Greenplum. There are two types of in-database compression available in the Greenplum Database for append-optimized tables.

The following table summarizes the available compression algorithms (Table 2).

Table 2. Compression algorithms for append-optimized tables

Table orientation	Available compression types	Supported algorithms
Row	Table	ZLIB and QUICKLZ
Column	Column and Table	RLE_TYPE, ZLIB, and QUICKLZ

In this experiment, the tables which are stored in Greenplum are row-oriented. So we use ZLIB Algorithm to compress the data. ZLIB provides 9 compression levels and higher compression ratios at lower speeds. With the higher compression level can significantly increase the compression ratio, though with the lower compression speed. We compared three compression levels (1, 5, 9) in Greenplum which has one master and four segments.

Figure 3 illustrates the efficiency of data loading capability between append-optimized table and different compression levels. In Fig. 3, different compression level has different data loading capability, the higher compression level the lower data loading time. This is because the higher compression level needs more resources to compress the data and this consumes much time.

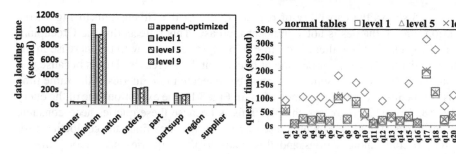

Fig. 3. Performance of data loading   **Fig. 4.** Performance of query execution

Figure 4 depicts the query performance between append-optimized table and different compression levels. In Fig. 4, the performance gap between the different compression levels is tiny and the query performance by using compression is better than using normal tables. This is because the higher compression level the lower speed, even though the data size is less than the lower compression level.

This experiment shows with the higher compression level can significantly increase the compression ratio, though with the lower compression speed. When choosing a compression type and level for append-optimized tables, consider CPU usage, compression ratio, speed of compression, data loading time and query time. Even though the higher compression level will save the storage space but it may affect the performance of data loading.

4.4 Parallel Query Effectiveness

In this experiment, we evaluate the performance of parallel query processing. We build Greenplum database cluster with one master and four segments and execute a number of queries concurrently. Table 3 shows the query combination.

Table 3. The query combination

Query combination	Type
Query1, Query2	The cost of query1 is high and the cost of query2 is low
Query11, Query16	Low query costs
Query3, Query4	High query costs
Query1, Query2, Query3	The cost of query2 is lower
Query1, Query10, Query15	High query cost
Query2, Query11, Query16	Low query cost
Query1, Query2, Query3, Query5, Query16	The cost of query1, 3 and 4 are high and the cost of query2 and 16 are low
Query12, Query17, Query18, Query19, Query20	High query cost

Figure 5 shows the capability of parallel query of the Greenplum. In Fig. 5, the execution time of queries is not significant increase. This reflects that the Greenplum has good capability of parallel query. In Fig. 5(a), (d) and (g), with the increase in the number of queries, the execution time of query 1 and 2 increases. This is because that execute the query need consume resources, but execute more queries at the same time means competition for resources intensifies. In Fig. 5(h), the execution time of the query 12, 17, 18, 19 and 20 increases sharply. This is because these queries need consume many resources and while execute these queries at the same time, the competition for resources become more serious and this leads to these queries need more time to complete the execution.

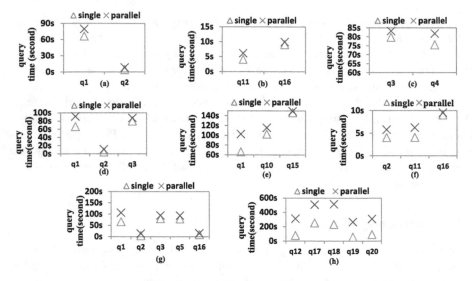

Fig. 5. Capability of parallel query

This experiment shows the Greenplum has good performance when concurrently parallel processing a number of queries. And the number of concurrency and the complexity of query will heavily impact the performance of the parallel query processing.

5   Conclusion

In this paper, we take the Greenplum database as the representative analytic database system, and conduct a series of performance study to investigate its scalability and performance features. According to the experimental results and analysis, we obtained an series of initial insights of the factors which may significantly affect the performance paradigm of Greenplum, which will be the initial insights for the performance optimization of the analytic database. For the analytic database, with the increasing number of segments and the correct compression algorithms and levels could improve the performance of query or data loading. And the number of concurrency and the complexity of query also can heavily impact the performance of the analytic database. We hope that this paper will provide some solutions to improve the performance of analytic databases for the users.

Acknowledgments. This work was supported by the China Ministry of Science and Technology under the State Key Development Program for Basic Research (2012CB821800), Fund of National Natural Science Foundation of China (No. 61462012, 61562010), the Joint Research Fund in Astronomy under cooperative agreement between the National Natural Science Foundation of China and Chinese Academy of Sciences (No. U1531246), the Strategic Priority Research Program "The Emergence of Cosmological Structures" of the Chinese Academy of Sciences (No. XDB09000000), High Tech. Project Fund of Guizhou Development and Reform Commission (No. [2013]2069), Industrial Research Projects of the Science and Technology Plan of Guizhou Province (No. GY[2014]3018), the Major Applied Basic Research Program of Guizhou Province (No. JZ20142001, JZ20142001-01, JZ20142001-05).

References

1. Färber, F., Cha, S.K., Primsch, J., Bornhövd, C.: SAP HANA database: data management for modern business applications. ACM SIGMOD Rec. **40**(4), 45–51 (2012). ACM, New York
2. Lee, J., Kwon, Y.S., Färber, F., Muehle, M., Lee, C.: SAP HANA distributed in-memory database system: transaction, session, and metadata management. In: 2013 IEEE 29th International Conference, pp. 1165–1173. IEEE (2013)
3. Huang, J.: Research on data storage of eID. In: 2012 2nd IEEE International Conference on Computer Science and Network Technology (ICCSNT), pp. 1843–1846. IEEE (2012)
4. Soliman, M.A., Antova, L., Raghavan, V., El-Helw, A.: Orca: a modular query optimizer architecture for big data. In: Proceedings of the 2014 ACM SIGMOD International Conference on Management of Data, pp. 337–348. ACM, New York (2014)
5. Rajput, E., Yadav, H., Singh, A.: Comparative study of EMC greenplum and oracle exadata. J. Eng. Comput. Appl. Sci. **2**, 50–54 (2013). BORJ
6. Jha, M., Jha, S.: Integrating big data solutions into enterprize architecture: constructing the entire information landscape. In: SDIWC, pp. 3–10 (2015)
7. Pivotal Greenplum Database Documentation. http://gpdb.docs.pivotal.io/4380/common/welcome.html
8. da Silva Fernandes, F.: Parallel relational databases for diameter calculation of large graphs. In: Proceedings of the International Conference on Parallel and Distributed Processing Techniques and Applications (PDPTA), pp. 213–220 (2016)
9. TPC-H benchmark specification. http://www.tcp.org/hspec.html

An Analysis of the Survivability in SEER Breast Cancer Data Using Association Rule Mining

Fangfang Li and Yu Duan[✉]

School of Information Science and Engineering,
Central South University, Changsha 410083, China
{lifangfang,yuduan}@csu.edu.cn

Abstract. Medical professionals need a reliable methodology to predict the survivability of patients with breast cancer. In this work, a classical association rule mining algorithm-Apriori was adopted for analyzing the related association relationship between medical attributes of records and the survivability of patients. The SEER Dataset was used in this research. After the dataset was preprocessed, 29606 records was obtained. Each record contains 17 breast cancer related attributes. Then apriori algorithm was applied in these preprocessed records, 326 association rules about 'survived' and 22 association rules about 'not survived' were obtained finally. These discovered association rules indicate that the attributes of EOD-Lymph Node Involv and SEER historic stage A play important roles in the survivability of patients after analyzed and compared.

Keywords: Breast cancer · SEER dataset · Apriori · Association rule · Survivability

1 Introduction

Breast cancer is one of the most common malignant tumors in the world. According to the statistics [1], in the USA, approximately one in eight women has a risk of developing breast cancer over their lifetime. Similarly, breast cancer is also a high concern among Asian women. Breast cancer account for 22.8 % in all malignant tumors among women and the mortality rate of breast cancer account for 14.1 % in all cancer [2]. In the recent 30 years, with the improving of people's living standards, the incidence of breast cancer has continued to grow in the world [3].

Data mining is the process of discovering new patterns from large data sets [4]. Association rule mining is a kind of data mining, which is extracting frequent item sets with high probability from data sets and extracting hidden association rule based on already extracted frequent item set [5]. Data mining has been successfully used in the medical field [6], like in lung cancer [7] and breast cancer [8]. Moreover, this trend continues to grow in the studies of Cios et al. [9] and Houston et al. [10].

© Springer International Publishing AG 2016
G. Wang et al. (Eds.): SpaCCS 2016 Workshops, LNCS 10067, pp. 184–194, 2016.
DOI: 10.1007/978-3-319-49145-5_19

The SEER Public-Use Data [11] has been used in many research like [12,13]. SEER dataset contains many attributes that are related with breast cancer like Primary Site, stage, tumor size, cause of death [14] and so on, therefore, SEER dataset is satisfied with our needs in research.

In this paper, firstly, the preprocessed data was classified into two categories which are 'survived' and 'not survived'. Then, apriori algorithm was applied in these two categories respectively. Finally, association rules about 'survived' and 'not survived' were obtained and these rules reflect that the attributes of EOD-Lymph Node Involv and SEER historic stage A play important roles in the survivability of patients after analyzed and compared.

2 Association Rule Mining

2.1 Related Concepts

Association rule mining is related to collection, database, transaction and other concepts. $E = \{e_1, e_2, ..., e_n\}$ is a collection of n different items. D is a transaction set of a pending database. Each transaction T contains several $e_i(e_i \in E, i = 1, 2, ..., n)$. Association rule is represented as the form of $X \rightarrow Y, X \in T, Y \in T$. The process of association rule mining involves two important attributes which are support and confidence. Support $(X \rightarrow Y) = P(X \cup Y)$, Confidence $(X \rightarrow Y) = P(Y|X) = P(X \cup Y)/P(X)$.

Next, a minimum threshold of support (minsupp) and a minimum threshold of confidence (minconf) are set. Finally, the extracted associated rule $X \rightarrow Y$ will satisfy $P(X \cup Y) \geq minsupp$ and $P(Y|X) \geq minconf$ at the same time.

2.2 Apriori Algorithm

Apriori [5] is a classical algorithm for association rule mining. Specific steps of Apriori is as follows:

① Firstly, scanning transaction set D and calculatting support of every item in D, if the support of an item is greater than or equal to the inputed minmum threshold of support, then this item is regarded as a frequent 1-item. Apriori will find out the set of all frequent 1-item L_1.

② If the set of $L_K - 1$ has already found, then the set of L_K is generated based on $L_K - 1$. Supposing L_1 belongs to $L_K - 1$, and L_2 belongs to $L_K - 1$, if the first $k - 2$ items of L_1 are respectively correspond to L_2's, then connecting L_1 and L_2 to form candidate k-item set. Repeating these operations to get the set C_k of all candidate k-item sets.

③ For each $c \in C_k$, if a $k-1$ items subset of c is not in L_K-1, then removing c from the set of C_k, otherwise, keeping c in C_k.

④ For each transaction d in D, if d contains candidate item set c in C_k, then plus 1 to the value (the initial value is zero) for support count. Traversing all candidate item set c in C_k, if finally the value of c for support count is greater than or equal to inputed threshold for support, then putting c into L_k which is a set of frequent k-items.

⑤ Repeating steps ② ~④ until L_k is empty.

⑥ Getting the final frequent items set L, $L = L_1 \cup L_2 \cup ... \cup L_k$.

3 Data Preprocessing

3.1 Attributes Acquisition

In this paper, 740506 records in SEER breast cancer data were adopted in research. Each record includes 146 attributes. Firstly, referring to the reference [14], records were classified into two categories-'survived' and 'not survived'. Cause of Death to SEER site recode (COD), Survival months (SM) and Vital Status recode (VSR) were included in the pre-classification process and these three attributes were used together to classify records together.

Pre-classification method is shown as follows:

① If $SM \geq 60$ and $VSR = alive$, then the record is pre-classified as 'survived'.

② If $SM < 60$ and $COD = 26000$ (which represents breast cancer), then the record is pre-classified as 'not survived'.

③ If the record is neither satisfied ① nor satisfied ②, then this record is ignored.

After pre-classification, 17 attributes were selected that are related to breast cancer after referring reference [15]. These 17 attributes are the cause of the outcome of survivability. The association relationships were obtained which are between some of 17 attributes and the survivability by apriori algorithm. The 17 attributes were included with 12 nominal variable attributes and 5 numeric variable attributes. Nominal variable attributes show in Table 1 and numeric variable attributes show in Table 2. These 17 attributes were numbered for the

Table 1. Nominal attributes

Nominal variable name	Number of distinct values
Marital Status at DX	6
Race/Ethnicity	29
Primary Site	9
Behavior Code ICD-O-3	2
Grade	5
EOD-Extension	32
EOD-Lymph Node Involv	9
RX Summ-Radiation	9
RX Summ -Surgery Type	24
Histology Recode-Broad Groupings	26
SEER historic stage A	5
First malignant primary indicator	2

Table 2. Numeric attributes

Numeric variable name	Mean	Range
Age at diagnosis	61.37	2–108
EOD-Tumor Size	20.16	0–985
Regional Nodes Positive	1.28	0–84
Regional Nodes Examined	7.54	0–88
Number of primaries	1.35	1–11

purpose of that data can be applied in Apriori algorithm. Table 3 shows the numbered attributes.

3.2 Data Conversion

Since numeric values are too much, these numeric values of selected attributes are segmented. The attribute of age is taken for example. 1–10 age group was classified as a class and it was marked as 01. Similarly, 11–20 age group was classified as another class and it was marked as 02. Table 4 shows the segmented numeric arguments.

Table 3. No. of attributes

Attribute name	No.
Marital status at DX	01
Race/Ethnicity	02
Age at diagnosis	03
Primary Site	04
Behavior Code ICD-O-3	05
Grade	06
EOD-Tumor size	07
EOD-Extension	08
EOD-Lymph node involv	09
Regional Nodes Positive	10
Regional Nodes Examined	11
RX Summ-Radiation	12
RX Summ-Surgery Type	13
Histology Recode-Broad Groupings	14
SEER historic stage A	15
Number of primaries	16
First malignant primary indicator	17

3.3   Records Filtering

Records were picked out from a total of 740506 records after attributes were confirmed to be adopted in this study. If some values are null or represent unknow of 17 argument attributes in a record, then the record was deleted. For example, Marital Status at DX = 9 or EOD-Tumor Size = 999 or RX Summ-Surgery Type = 09, these values represent unknown. Furthermore, records were deleted if they do not satisfy the conditions of pre-classification like above mentioned. Finally, 76655 records were obtained after the pre-processing. There are 61852 records belonging to 'survived' and 14803 records belonging to 'not survived'. Because the amount of 'survived' is more than the amount of 'not survived' too much, a random sample of 14803 records from 61825 records were taken for the purpose of data balancing.

Table 4. Segmentation of numeric attributes

Numeric variable name	Range	New value
Age at diagnosis	1–10	01
	11–20	02
	......	......
	101–110	11
EOD-Tumor Size	000	000
	001–010	001
	011–020	002
	......	......
	981–990	099
Number of primaries	01	01
	02	02
	......	......
	11	11
Regional Nodes Positive	00	00
	01–05	01
	06–10	02
	......	......
	86–90	18
Regional Nodes Examined	00	00
	01–05	01
	06–10	02
	......	......
	86–90	18

3.4 Transaction Sets Collection

After data pre-processing the 'survived' transaction set and the 'not survived' transaction set have been obtained which show in Table 5. Each transaction includes 17 values of breast cancer related attributes and a transaction set includes 14803 transactions. Taking the first transaction of Table 5 for example respectively and their corresponding interpretations are in Tables 6 and 7 which interpret the first five items from all 17 items.

Table 5. Transaction set of 'survived' and 'not survived'

No.	Transaction ('survived')	Transaction ('not survived')
1	012 0201 03007 04C504 053 062 07001 0810	015 0201 03008 04C508 053 069 07003 0810
	090 1000 1102 121 1320 1409 151 1601 170	096 1001 1102 120 1350 1409 152 1601 170
2	014 0201 03007 04C504 053 062 07002 0810	012 0201 03008 04C508 053 063 07004 0810
	090 1000 1102 120 1350 1409 151 1602 170	095 1097 1198 121 1320 1409 152 1601 170
......	......	......
14803	015 0201 03007 04C504 053 069 07001 0810	014 0202 03007 04C502 053 063 07003 0810
	090 1000 1103 120 1350 1409 151 1602 170	092 1002 1103 121 1350 1409 152 1601 171

Table 6. Interpretation of a partial 'survived' transaction

Item	Interpretation
012	Marital Status at DX = 2 (2 represents married.)
0201	Race/Ethnicity = 01 (01 represents white.)
03007	Age at diagnosis = 007 (007 represents 61–70.)
04C504	Primary Site = C504 (C504 represents upper outer quadrant of breast.)
053	Behavior Code ICD-O-3 = 3 (3 represents malignant, primary site (invasive))

Table 7. Interpretation of a partial 'not survived' transaction

Item	Interpretation
015	Marital Status at DX = 5 (5 represents widowed.)
0201	Race/Ethnicity = 01 (01 represents white.)
03008	Age at diagnosis = 008 (008 represents 71–80.)
04C508	Primary Site = C508 (C508 represents breast cross)
053	Behavior Code ICD-O-3 = 3 (3 represents malignant, primary site (invasive))

4   Specific Application

4.1   Frequent Itemsets Acquisition

In this work, the minimum support threshold was set to 20 %. Since the 'survived' transaction set and 'not survived' transaction set include 14803 transactions respectively, there are 29606 transactions in total. The threshold number of occurence of each frequent item set is 5922. Apriori algorithm was applied to the transaction set of 'survived' and the transaction set of 'not survived' respectively and 483 frequent item sets of 'survived' and 169 frequent item sets of 'not survived' were obtained.

For example, the second frequent item set listed in Table 8 is {1350, 1409}. In the 'survived' transaction set, the occurence number of {1350, 1409} is 5993. Since 5993 is more than 5922, {1350, 1409} is a frequent item set which represents RX Summ-Surgery Type = 50 (50 represents the surgery type is Modified radical/total mastectomy with dissection of axillary lymph nodes), Histology Recode-Broad Groupings = 09 (09 represents the histology is ductal and lobular

Table 8. Frequent itemsets of 'survived'

No.	Frequent itemset	Occurence number	Support
1	1601	10232	34.561 %
2	1350 1409	5993	20.243 %
3	0810 171	11069	37.388 %
4	120 1409 171	5943	20.074 %
5	012 053 1601	6173	20.851 %
6	053 090 151	9289	31.375 %
7	090 1409 1601 171	5987	20.222 %
8	0201 1000 151 171	6796	22.955 %
9	053 090 1409 1601 171	5987	20.222 %
10	0201 053 090 1000 1409 151	6848	23.130 %
......	......	......	......

neoplams). The second frequent item set listed in Table 9 is {063, 171}. In the 'not survived' transaction set, the occurence number of {063, 171} is 5948. Since 5948 is more than 5922, {063, 171} is a frequent item set which represents that Grade = 3 (3 represents the cancer grade is 3), First malignant primary indicator = 1 (1 represents the tumor of breast cancer is a first malignant primary indicator).

4.2   Association Rules Acquisition

Association rules were obtained based on frequent itemsets. The association rules finally obtained are like the forms of $A \rightarrow 1$ (1 represents 'survived') or $B \rightarrow 2$ (2 represents 'not survived'). In this work, the minimum confidence threshold was set as 70 %. The algorithm for obtaining association rules in the form of $A \rightarrow 1$ is as follows:

① Frequent item set A was obtained after Apriori algorithm was applied to the transaction set of 'survived'. The occurrence number of A in transaction set of 'survived' was marked as *count1*.

② After searching for the transaction set of 'not survived', the occurrence number of A in it was obtained and the number was marked as *count2*.

③ $confidence1 = count1/(count1 + count2)$.

④ If $confidence1 \geq 70\%$ then $A \rightarrow 1$ is a strong association rule.

The algorithm for obtaining association rules in the form of $B \rightarrow 2$ is as follows:

① Frequent itemset B was obtained after Apriori algorithm was applied to the transaction set of 'not survived'. The occurrence number of B in transaction set of 'not survived' was marked as *count1*.

② After searching for the transaction set of survived, the occurence number of B in it was obtained and the number was marked as *count2*.

③ $confidence2 = count1/(count1 + count2)$.

④ If $confidence2 \geq 70\%$ then $B \rightarrow 2$ is a strong association rule.

Finally, 326 association rules were obtained which are in the form of $A \rightarrow 1$ and 22 association rules were obtained which are in the form of $B \rightarrow 2$. We consulted with professional doctors in breast cancer and they said these association rules have a certain reference value. A few representative and comparable association rules are listed. Table 10 shows some association rules about 'survived'. Table 11 shows some association rules about 'not survived'.

In Table 10, The first association rule (Race/Ethnicity = 01 and EOD-Lymph Node Involv = 0 and SEER historic stage A = 1 → survivability = survived) represents if the race is white and no lymph node is involved, and the tumor is localized, then the patient is more likely to survive more than 5 years. The third association rule (SEER historic stage A = 1 → survivability = survived) represents if the tumor is localized, then the patient is more likely to survive more than 5 years. The seventh association rule (EOD-Lymph Node Involv = 0 → survivability = survived) represents if no lymph node is involved, then the patient is more likely to survive more than 5 years.

Table 9. Frequent itemsets of 'not survived'

No.	Frequent itemset	Occurence number	Support
1	152	7979	26.951 %
2	063 171	5948	20.091 %
3	1409 171	11578	39.107 %
4	0201 1350 1601	5935	20.047 %
5	120 1409 1601	6668	22.522 %
6	0201 053 1350 1601	5925	20.013 %
7	0201 0810 1601 171	6240	21.077 %
8	0201 053 1409 1601	8769	29.619 %
9	0201 053 1350 1409 171	5925	20.013 %
10	201 053 0810 1409 1601	6130	20.705 %
......	......	......	......

Table 10. Partial association rules about 'survived'

No.	Association rules	Support	Confidence
1	0201 090 151 → 1	26.680 %	70.811 %
2	0810 090 1000 151 171 → 1	26.988 %	75.520 %
3	151 → 1	31.375 %	70.617 %
4	053 1000 1409 171 → 1	25.397 %	74.152 %
5	012 090 → 1	28.504 %	77.500 %
6	053 0810 151 → 1	31.335 %	70.596 %
7	090 → 1	40.144 %	71.493 %
8	012 1000 → 1	23.087 %	77.901 %
9	1000 151 171 → 1	27.011 %	75.536 %
10	012 0810 090 171 → 1	20.293 %	78.341 %
......	......	......	......

In Table 11, the first association rule (SEER historic stage A = 2 → survivability = not survived) represents that if the tumor is regional, then the patient survives less than 5 years. The third association rule (EOD-Lymph Node Involv = 6 → survivability = not survived) represents if the highest specific lymph node chain is 6 that is involved by the tumor, then the patient survives less than 5 years. The eighth association rule (Behavior Code ICD-O-3 = 3 and SEER historic stage A = 2 and First malignant primary indicator = 1 → survivability = not survived) represents that if tumor is malignant and the primary site is invasive, and the tumor is regional, and the tumor is the first malignant primary indicator, then the patient survives less than 5 years.

Table 11. Partial association rules about 'not survived'

No.	Association rules	Support	Confidence
1	152 → 2	26.951 %	72.451 %
2	053 096 → 2	20.263 %	74.698 %
3	096 → 2	20.263 %	74.698 %
4	1409 152 1601 → 2	21.229 %	75.018 %
5	053 1409 152 1601 → 2	21.229 %	75.018 %
6	1409 152 → 2	25.397 %	72.076 %
7	053 1409 152 171 → 2	22.553 %	70.768 %
8	053 152 171 → 2	23.874 %	71.114 %
9	0201 152 → 2	21.526 %	71.607 %
10	053 152 1601 → 2	22.479 %	75.342 %
......	......	......	......

Therefore, the two attributes of EOD-Lymph Node Involv and SEER historic stage A play important roles in the survivability of patients. If no lymph node is involved, then the patient is more likely to survive more than 5 years. However, if the highest specific lymph node chain is 6 that is involved by the tumor, then the patient is more likely to survive less than 5 years. Furthermore, if the tumor is localized, then the patient is more likely to survive more than 5 years. However, if the tumor is regional, then the patient is more likely to survive less than 5 years.

5   Conclusion and Future Works

In this paper, association rule mining algorithm was applied to SEER breast cancer data and 326 association rules about 'survived' and 22 association rules about 'not survived' have been obtained. These rules reflect that the attributes of EOD-Lymph Node Involv and SEER historic stage A play important roles in the survivability of patients after analyzed and compared. Doctors can take advantage of these association rules in treatments of patients and can encourage treatments which are beneficial to the survivability. At the same time, these association rules can help doctors and patients identify the symptoms of survival.

In the future, we will invite medical experts to be involved in the selection of these association rules for the purpose of finding something more valuable. Moreover, Apriori algorithm needs to scan database every time when searching for a frequent item set, therefore it is in a low efficiency. We will improve Apriori algorithm to improve the efficiency of data mining.

Acknowledgments. This study is supported by the China Postdoctoral Science Foundation (2016M592450), and the Hunan Provincial Natural Science Foundation of China (2016JJ4119). Sincerely thanks to the National Cancer Institute, USA for providing the SEER cancer database in public.

References

1. American Cancer Society. Breast Cancer Facts & Figures 2005–2006. Atalanta: American Cancer Society, Inc. (http://www.cancer.org/)
2. Parkin, D.M., Bray, M.F., Ferlay, M.J., et al.: Global cancer statistics. CA Cancer J. Clin. **55**(2), 74–108 (2005)
3. Ferlay, J., Bray, F., Pisani, P., et al.: GLOBOCAN 2002: cancer incidence, mortality and prevalence worldwide. IARC CancerBase No. 5. version 2.0. Lyon: IARCPress (2004)
4. Chakrabarti, S., Cox, E., Frank, E., et al.: Data Mining: Know It All. Morgan Kaufmann, San Francisco (2008). pp. 32–33
5. Agrawal, R., Srikant, R.: Fast algorithms for mining association rules in large databases. In: International Conference on Very Large Data Bases. Morgan Kaufmann, San Francisco, pp. 487–499 (1994)
6. Richards, G., Rayward-Smith, V.J., Sönksen, P.H., et al.: Data mining for indicators of early mortality in a database of clinical records. Artif. Intell. Med. **22**(3), 215–231 (2001)
7. Agrawal, A., Choudhary, A.: Identifying hotspots in lung cancer data using association rule mining. In: 2011 IEEE 11th International Conference on Data Mining Workshops, Vancouver, BC, pp. 995–1002. IEEE (2011)
8. Fan, Q., Zhu, C.J., Xiao, J.Y., et al.: An application of apriori algorithm in SEER breast cancer data. In: International Conference on Artificial Intelligence & Computational Intelligence, Sanya, China, pp. 114–116. IEEE (2010)
9. Cios, K.J., Moore, G.W.: Uniqueness of medical data mining. Artif. Intell. Med. **26**(1–2), 1–24 (2002)
10. Houston, A.L., Chen, H., Hubbard, S.M., et al.: Medical data mining on the internet: research on a cancer information system. Nucl. Eng. Des. **223**(3), 255–262 (1999)
11. Surveillance, Epidemiology, and End Results (SEER) Program (www.seer.cancer.gov) Public-Use Data (1973–2012), National Cancer Institute, DCCPS, Surveillance Research Program, Cancer Statistics Branch, based on the submission, November 2014
12. Rajesh, K., Anand, S.: Analysis of SEER dataset for breast cancer diagnosis using C4. 5 classification algorithm. Int. J. Adv. Res. Comput. Commun. Eng. **1**(2), 1021–2278 (2012)
13. Rosenberg, J., Chia, Y.L., Plevritis, S.: The effect of age, race, tumor size, tumor grade, and disease stage on invasive ductal breast cancer survival in the US SEER database. Breast Cancer Res. Treat. **89**(1), 47–54 (2005)
14. Bellaachia, A., Guven, E.: Predicting breast cancer survivability using data mining techniques. Age **58**(13), 10–110 (2006)
15. Liu, Yaqin: Study on The Prognosis Model for Breast Cancer. Shanghai Jiao Tong University, Shanghai (2008). (in Chinese)

Second International Symposium on Dependability in Sensor, Cloud, and Big Data Systems and Applications (DependSys 2016)

Improving the Localization Probability and Decreasing Communication Cost for Mobile Users

Wenhua Wang[1], Tian Wang[1(✉)], Md. Zakirul Alam Bhuiyan[2], Yiqiao Cai[1], Hui Tian[1], and Yonghong Chen[1]

[1] College of Computer Science and Technology,
Huaqiao University, Xiamen 361021, Fujian, China
wangtian@hqu.edu.cn
[2] Department of Computer and Information Sciences,
Fordham University, New York, USA

Abstract. This paper studies the problem of localization for mobile users with low communication cost. Due to the sparse deployment of anchors, the localization probabilities achieved by the traditional fixed anchors-based methods are not acceptable. To solve this problem, we propose to exploit the localized users as the mobile anchors for localizing the non-localized users. In this way, the localization probability can be improved. Moreover, an algorithm for electing mobile anchors is designed to decrease the communication cost, with several provable properties. This electing algorithm is a distributed method, without negotiation among mobile users. Extensive experimental results demonstrate that in terms of localization probability, our method outperforms the traditional fixed anchors-based methods by approximately 30 % ~ 60 % with a small increment of communication cost.

Keywords: Localization for mobile users · Localization probability · Communication cost · Mobile anchors electing · Hashing

1 Introduction

In recent years, wireless localization has attracted considerable research interest for the increasing demands on location-based services such as mobile electronic commerce, emergency rescue, industry, military, and Wireless Sensor Networks (WSNs) [1, 2]. Among these, localizing the mobile user is the most significant. For example, when disasters occur, the uncertainty of the victims' positions brings great inconvenience to the rescue work. Global Positioning System (GPS) [3] has been widely used for the localization in the outdoor environment. However, two factors limit its applications: first, installing every node with a GPS receiver is expensive in cost; second, and more important, it performs poor in the indoor environment such as mine, market, airport and warehouse etc.

Recently, localization mechanisms with wireless signal have been proposed. The typical methods include Time of Arrival (TOA), Time Difference of Arrival (TDOA), Angle of Arrival (AOA) and Received Signal Strength Indication (RSSI) [4]. However,

© Springer International Publishing AG 2016
G. Wang et al. (Eds.): SpaCCS 2016 Workshops, LNCS 10067, pp. 197–207, 2016.
DOI: 10.1007/978-3-319-49145-5_20

the proposed solutions based on these technologies are acceptable only when there is sufficient distance information from anchors. For example, in some scenarios, due to sparse anchor deployments, short radio communication ranges, and physical obstacles, a sufficient number of ranging information usually cannot be well received, so that the localization probability declines sharply [5]. Hence, developing a reliable and effective algorithm to solve this problem is important and requires more investigations [6].

To solve the above problem, mobility-aided localization methods, in which mobile anchors are exploited to aid in localization, have been investigated recently in studies such as [7, 8] etc. However, it is well known that a moving anchor can cover only a small area within a reasonable time [9]. Therefore, adding more mobile anchors in the network area leads to better performance, but the movement of the anchor increases the energy consumption and introduces greater hardware support requirements, such as GPS and mobile elements. Consequently, having too many mobile anchors raises the cost prohibitively.

In this paper, we propose an approach for improving the localization probability of mobile users, in which the mobile users who have already been localized can be utilized as the mobile anchors for other users who have not. Moreover, to decrease the communication cost, an algorithm for electing mobile anchors is proposed.

The rest of this paper is organized as follows. Sect. 2 reviews the related work. The localization problem of mobile users based on mobile anchors is presented in Sect. 3. The details of the proposed algorithm and the analyses are elaborated upon in Sect. 4. Section 5 introduces the experiments and presents the experimental results. At last we conclude the paper in Sect. 6.

2   Related Work

With the development of the wireless communication and mobile computing technologies, applications based on location are becoming common, which has resulted in extensive research interest in it. According to whether distance information between anchors and users are required, wireless localization schemes can be broadly divided into two categories: range-based localization and range-free localization [10]. A common range-based localization approach is to utilize the ranging information between the user and a-priori known positions, called anchors. To ensure the localization performance, some studies propose to combine two or more of the methods [11]. However, combining methods increase the algorithm complexity. Besides, when the anchors are sparsely deployed, real-time position of the user still cannot be achieved.

In addition to the use of stationary anchors, several other studies introduce the mobile anchor to help with the localization process. In [12], a single mobile anchor is introduced to enable the sensor nodes to construct two chords of a communication circle of which they form the center point. The intersection of the perpendicular bisectors of these two chords is the sensors' positions. However, it introduces only one mobile anchor because of hardware costs, and it is possible that some of the sensor nodes still remain non-localized. To solve this problem, path planning schemes are proposed in [13, 14] that not only improve the localization accuracy but also maximize the number of sensor nodes that can be localized.

Another research interest is to localize the users cooperatively, namely the nodes cooperate with each other to improve the localization accuracy. In [15], the authors propose a cooperative approach in which the node whose position has been estimated is added to the reference node database for localizing other unknown nodes. The reference nodes locate their one hop neighbors first, and then newly added reference nodes further locate another one hop neighbors, but this process propagates and furthers the error in the network. A cooperative indoor localization method based on the smartphone is proposed in [16]. It proposes to consider the estimated positions as virtual APs, which can be used to estimate the next time positions combined with the IMU data, but its accuracy may be low if the users move very fast. However, all these studies need extra hardware supports, such as IMU, accelerometer and electronic compass etc. Besides, they cause very large communication cost.

In this paper, we propose to utilize the localized users as the mobile anchors for others who have not yet. Moreover, an algorithm for electing mobile anchors is proposed to decrease the communication cost. The electing technique used in this paper is different from the Pruning techniques used in Ad-Hoc Wireless Networks. The idea of Pruning technique is that when the nodes who are useless, then they will leave the forwarding tree automatically. While in our proposed technique, all the localized users are useful for the localization of others who have not yet more or less, and only some of them are elected as the mobile anchors for the consideration of communication cost. What's more, the election of the localized users is based on a random way. Therefore, the two techniques are different in essence.

3   Problem Formulation

In this section, we first introduce the traditional fixed anchors-based localization method using RSSI measurement, and then present our proposed mobile anchors-based localization method.

Suppose there are m fixed anchors located at points $Q = [(x_1, y_1), (x_2, y_2), ..., (x_m, y_m)]$, and n mobile users with their positions $P = [(X_1, Y_1), (X_2, Y_2), ..., (X_n, Y_n)]$. In RSSI-based localization, the signal propagation distance d_{ij} between user i and anchor j can be measured by: $d_{ij} = 10^{(rssi-A)/(10*\gamma)}$, where $rssi$ is the signal strength of anchor j received by user i, γ is the path loss exponent, and A is the signal strength received by the user who is 1 m away from the anchor. Then (X_i, Y_i), which is the location of user i can be estimated by using nonlinear equations of the following form:

$$d_{ij}^2 = (x_j - X_i)^2 + (y_j - Y_i)^2 \tag{1}$$

It represents a circle in a 2-D plane, with center (x_j, y_j), which is the location of anchor j observed beforehand, and radius d_{ij} measured with $rssi$. A signal circle represents a set of possible locations for user i. It can be uniquely localized when three or more signal circles represented by equations in the form of (1) have the common intersection point (X_i, Y_i).

In the proposed localization method, the users who have been localized can act as mobile anchors for others. Figure 1 gives a simple example, in which A_i ($i = 1, 2, 3, 4$) are the fixed anchors and U_i ($i = 1, 2, 3$) are the non-localized mobile users. U_2 can communicate with more than three anchors (A_1, A_2, A_3 and A_4). Consequently, its position can be estimated using the localization method introduced above. However, some users may not be able to receive signals from enough anchors successfully. For example, the user U_1 and U_3 may only communicate with the anchors A_1, A_2 and A_3, A_4, respectively. Therefore, these users cannot be localized based on the method mentioned above. However, they can receive signals from U_2, whose position can be estimated, which motivates us to consider U_2 as a mobile anchor to help calculate the locations of U_1 and U_3. Obviously, the use of such mobile anchors can help to localize users who cannot be localized by traditional fixed anchors-based methods, thus the localization probability can be greatly improved.

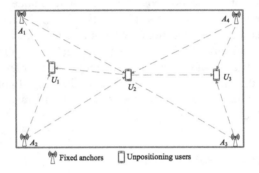

Fig. 1. A simple illustration of mobile localization (U_1 and U_3 cannot be localized based on traditional method with fixed anchors)

4   Localization Based on Elected Mobile Anchors

This section presents our proposed localization method. The innovation of the proposed method is that the users who have been localized can act as the mobile anchors for others who have not. Moreover, we design an algorithm for electing mobile anchors to decrease the communication cost. Four stages are included in the proposed method-LEMA (Localization based on Elected Mobile Anchors) which is shown as Algorithm 1, and the details are shown as follows:

Firstly, each user calculates the number of fixed anchors that it can communicate with, and the users who can communicate with more than three anchors localize themselves. The localized users become the candidates as mobile anchors. In the second stage, each localized user is allotted with a mini timeslot. Assume there are k users that have been localized, and we take T as the timeslot during which some of the localized users can be elected as the mobile anchors, which is divided into q (20 in our experiments) mini timeslots, sign as $T_1, T_2, T_3, \ldots, T_q$ ($q >= k$). Then we assign a unique mini slot to every localized user through a hash function, which is shown in Fig. 2.

Algorithm 1 LEMA: Localization based on elected mobile anchors

---

Input: the positions of the anchors;
Output: the locations of the users;
 1: Users calculate the numbers of anchors that they can communicate with;
 2: **if** one user can communicate with more than three anchors
 3: the user localizes itself;
 4: **end if**
 5: /* Assume k users have been localized; T is the timeslot which is divided into q
 6: slots, sign as T_1 to T_q ($q >= k$) */
 7: **for** the k localized users /* Candidates as mobile anchors*/
 8: Assign each user with one different mini slot in T by a hash function;
 9: **end for**
10: **for** i =1: q
11: The candidate user whose corresponding mini slot is T_i sends a signal
12: containing its location information; /*become the mobile anchors*/
13: **for** $j = i+1$: q
14:   **if** $d_{ij} < d$ /*d is the threshold.*/
15:    Remove T_j from T and it won't send signal in this round; /*no longer
16:    candidates*/
17:   **end if**
18: **end for**
19: **end for**
20: Other users compute their locations at the end of T according to the distance
21: information from both fixed anchors and elected mobile anchors;

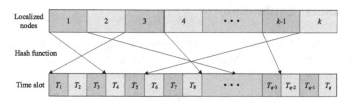

Fig. 2. The scenario of allotting mini slots

In the third stage, some of the localized users are elected as mobile anchors. The localized user who has been allotted to T_1 sends a signal with its location and other users estimate the distances from them to the first user according to the received signal strength. If the distances are less than the threshold d, the relevant localized users are removed away from T, and they are not the mobile anchors in this round again. Then the other users in T repeat the above steps in turn until the timeslot ends. The users who remain in T are the elected mobile anchors in this round. As shown in Fig. 3, assume the sequence of the localized users in T is: M_2, M_4, M_5, M_9, M_1, M_6, M_3, M_7, and M_8. M_2 sends a signal first as it is at the beginning of T and M_5, M_1 and M_3 can be removed from T as their distances to M_2 are less than d. Then M_4 sends a signal and M_7 is removed from T. Then M_8 is removed from T according to M_9. M_6 is also elected as a mobile anchor. Consequently, the elected mobile anchors are M_2, M_4, M_9 and M_6. At last, these users send signals to the users around. Then the other users estimate their locations according to the distances from both the fixed anchors and the elected mobile anchors.

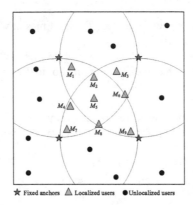

★ Fixed anchors △ Localized users ● Unlocalized users

Fig. 3. The scenario of mobile anchors electing

For the next time instant, the preceding processes can be conducted again to determine the new positions of the users.

5 Performance Evaluation

To demonstrate the effectiveness of our proposed algorithm, extensive simulation experiments are conducted in Matlab 2012b. The experiments and the results are introduced in this section.

5.1 Simulation Methodology

Nodes who act as the non-localized users walk randomly in a 200 × 200-m region. Four fixed anchors are deployed, and their positions are (50, 50), (50, 150), (150, 150), (50, 150), respectively. The number of users is 30 unless otherwise indicated. The communication cost of localization is the total information that should be exchanged among the users in the process of locating. We choose the regular model, which is widely used in many research work, as the signal attenuation model in our simulation. The communication radius of the anchors is 120 m and the communication radius of the users ranges from 80 m to 120 m, and the threshold d is half of the users' communication radius unless otherwise indicated.

5.2 Experimental Results

This section demonstrates the experimental results of our proposed algorithm. To evaluate the effectiveness of our proposed algorithm, we also conducted two different algorithms, LFA and LLMA. LFA (Localization based on Fixed Anchors) is the traditional method which is based on fixed anchors. LLMA (Localization based on Localized Mobile Anchors) is the method which chooses all the localized users as the mobile anchors.

Figures 4 and 5 show the snapshot of localization results, in which the four red stars are the fixed anchors, the blue "*" are the localized users achieved by LFA and the black circles are the users localized by our proposed method. Figure 4 is the localization results when the users' communication radius is 80 m, and Fig. 5 is the localization results when the users' communication radius increases to 100 m. It is obviously that LEMA can localize more users compared to LFA, and more users can be localized by both LFA and LEMA with the increment of the users' communication radius.

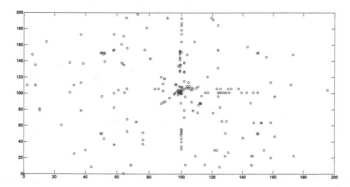

Fig. 4. The localization results when the user's communication radius is 80 m (Color figure online)

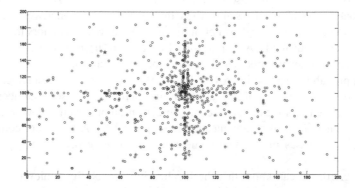

Fig. 5. The localization results when the user's communication radius is 100 m (Color figure online)

In more detail, Fig. 6 describes the localization probability change when the communication radius of the user increases from 80 m to 120 m. As it shows, the localization probabilities achieved by LFA are 11.59 %, 16.67 %, 24.01 %, 38.70 % and 48.59 % respectively, while that achieved by our proposed method are 42.92 %, 56.84 %, 71.77 %, 79.28 % and 85.13 % respectively. The increased ratios are 31.33 %, 40.17 %, 47.76 %, 40.58 % and 36.57 % respectively. The change of the communication cost as the users' communication radius increasing is shown in Fig. 7. It can be seen that the communication cost of our proposed method is a little larger than LFA, and it decreases sharply compared to LLMA. These results show that, our proposed method can achieve higher localization probability with a small increment of communication cost.

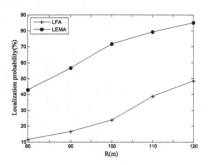

Fig. 6. Localization probability vs. users' communication radius

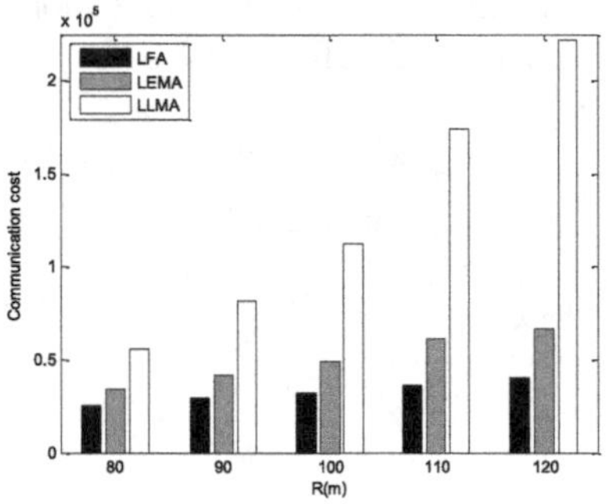

Fig. 7. Communication cost vs. users' communication radius

The change of the localization probability and the communication cost when the number of users increases is presented in Figs. 8 and 9. It can be seen from Fig. 8 that the localization probability achieved by LFA is about the same when the number of users increases. While the localization probability achieved by LEMA increases from 57.08 % to 69.31 % when the users' number increases from 10 to 40, and the localization probability is about the same when the users' number increases again. It is because that the users' number does not influence the number of anchors that the users can communicate with for LFA. While for LEMA, more users may be localized and elected as the mobile anchors with the increment of the users' number, thus the localization probability can be improved. Figure 9 shows that the communication cost of all methods have the trend of increase with the increment of users' number. This is because that more users means more communication among them. However, we can know that the increment of communication cost under LEMA is smaller compared to LFA, while it decreases much more compared to LLMA, especially when there are more users.

From Fig. 10, we can know that the localization probability achieved by LFA is about the same when the threshold d increases. This is because that d does not influence the number of fixed anchors that the users can communicate with, thus it does not

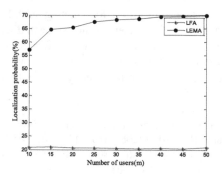

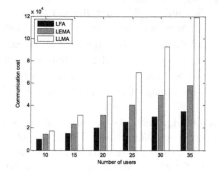

Fig. 8. Localization probability vs. users' number

Fig. 9. Communication cost vs. users' number

change the localization probability of LFA. While for the proposed method, the localization probability is about the same when d increases from $R/10$ to $R/4$, and it decreases when d increases from $R/4$ to R. It is obviously that less localized users can be elected as the mobile anchors when d increases, and then less users can be localized for some of them cannot receive signals from enough anchors. Figure 11 describes the communication cost when threshold d increases. We can see that the communication cost under LEMA decreases with the increment of d, especially when it is larger than $R/6$. It is because that less localized users can be elected as the mobile anchors with the increment of d, thus the communication cost decrease.

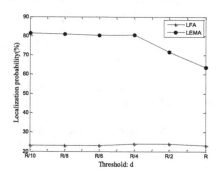

Fig. 10. Localization probability vs. threshold

Fig. 11. Communication cost vs. threshold

6 Conclusion

Focusing on the situation that the users may not be able to get enough range information from fixed anchors and the instability of wireless signals in the environment, we introduced a scheme for localizing mobile users in this paper. First, we proposed to exploit the users who have been localized to act as mobile anchors for others who have not. Second, to decrease the communication cost, an algorithm for electing mobile anchors was designed, by which only some of the localized users could be elected as the mobile anchors for other non-localized users. Finally, we validated the performance of the proposed method by extensive simulation experiments, and the results showed that our proposed method can improve the localization probability greatly with only a small increment of communication cost.

Acknowledgments. Above work was supported in part by grants from the National Natural Science Foundation (NSF) of China under Grant Nos. 61572206, 61672441, 61276151, 61370007, 61305085 and U1536115 and the project supported by the research and innovation ability of graduate students of Huaqiao University under Grant No. 1400214019.

References

1. Wang, T., Cai, Y., Jia, W., Wen, S., Wang, G., Tian, H., Chen, Y., Zhong, B.: Maximizing real-time streaming services based on a multi-servers networking framework. Comput. Netw. **93**, 199–212 (2015)
2. Wang, T., Jia, W., Zhong, B., Tian, H., Zhang, G.: BlueCat: an infrastructure-free system for relative mobile localization. Adhoc Sensor Wirel. Netw. **29**, 133–152 (2015)
3. Jurdak, R., Corke, P., Cotillon, A., Dharman, D., Crossman, C.: Energy-efficient localization: GPS duty cycling with radio ranging. ACM Trans. Sensor Netw. (TOSN) **9**(2), 1–33 (2013)
4. Han, G., Xu, H., Duong, T.Q., Jiang, J., Hara, T.: Localization algorithm of wireless sensor networks: a survey. Telecommun. Syst. **52**(4), 2419–2436 (2013)
5. Salari, S., Shahbazpanahi, S., Ozdemir, K.: Mobility-aided wireless sensor network localization via semidefinite programming. IEEE Trans. Wirel. Commun. **12**(12), 5966–5978 (2013)
6. Biswas, P., Liang, T.C., Toh, K.C., Wang, T.C., Ye, Y.: Semidefinite programming approaches for sensor network localization with noisy distance measurements. IEEE Trans. Autom. Sci. Eng. **3**(4), 360–371 (2006)
7. Chang, C.Y., Wang, T.L., Tung, C.Y: A mobile anchor assisted localization mechanism for Wireless Sensor Networks. In: IEEE Wireless Communications and Networking Conference (WCNC), pp. 2793–2798. IEEE (2014)
8. Bao, H., Zhang, B., Li, C., Yao, Z.: Mobile anchor assisted particle swarm optimization (PSO) based localization algorithms for wireless sensor networks. Wirel. Commun. Mob. Comput. **12**(15), 1313–1325 (2012)
9. Halder, S., Ghosal, A.: A survey on mobile anchor assisted localization techniques in wireless sensor networks. Wireless Netw. **22**, 1–20 (2015)
10. Wu, G., Wang, S., Wang, B., Dong, Y., Yan, S.: A novel range-free localization based on regulated neighborhood distance for wireless ad hoc and sensor networks. Comput. Netw. **56**(16), 3581–3593 (2012)
11. Sharma, Y., Gulhane, V.: Hybrid mechanism for multiple user indoor localization using smart antenna. In: 2015 Fifth International Conference on Advanced Computing & Communication Technologies (ACCT), pp. 602–607. IEEE (2015)
12. Ssu, K.F., Ou, C.H., Jiau, H.C.: Localization with mobile anchor points in wireless sensor networks. IEEE Trans. Veh. Technol. (TVT) **54**(3), 1187–1197 (2005)

13. Ou, C.H., He, W.L.: Path planning algorithm for mobile anchor-based localization in wireless sensor networks. IEEE Sens. J. **13**(2), 466–475 (2013)
14. Chen, H., Shi, Q., Tan, R., Poor, H.V., Sezaki, K.: Mobile element assisted cooperative localization for wireless sensor networks with obstacles. IEEE Trans. Wirel. Commun. **9**(3), 956–963 (2010)
15. Pandey, S., Varma, S.: A range based localization system in multihop wireless sensor networks: a distributed cooperative approach. Wireless Pers. Commun. **86**(2), 615–634 (2016)
16. Wang, X., Zhou, H., Mao, S., Pandey, S., Agrawal, P., Bevly, D.M.: Mobility improves LMI-based cooperative indoor localization. In: 2015 IEEE Wireless Communications and Networking Conference (WCNC), pp. 2215–2220. IEEE (2015)

Greedy Probability-Based Routing Protocol for Incompletely Predictable Vehicular Ad-hoc Network

Jian Shen[1,2,3]([✉]), Chen Wang[3], Aniello Castiglione[4], Dengzhi Liu[3],
and Christian Esposito[4]

[1] Jiangsu Engineering Center of Network Monitoring,
Nanjing University of Information Science and Technology,
Nanjing 210044, China
s_shenjian@126.com
[2] Jiangsu Collaborative Innovation Center on Atmospheric Environment
and Equipment Technology, Nanjing University of Information Science
and Technology, Nanjing 210044, China
[3] School of Computer and Software, Nanjing University of Information Science
and Technology, Nanjing 210044, China
wangchennuist@126.com, liudzdh@qq.com
[4] Department of Computer Science, University of Salerno, 84084 Fisciano (SA), Italy
castiglione@ieee.org, christian.esposito@dia.unisa.it

Abstract. Currently, VANETs are becoming more and more popular
and have been applied in many different applications. However, because
the feature of VANETs' topologies is relatively stable, the routing protocol designed for VANET can be more efficient from a macro perspective.
Specifically, the concept of incompletely predictable networks (IPNs),
where nodes travel around the basic positions, can be used to model
stable VANETs, as the ones related to taxis during our daily lives. In
this paper, we propose a new protocol, named Greedy Probability-based
Routing Protocol, for rather stable VANETs. A new concept named
"anti-pheromone" is put forward to achieve high energy efficiency. Simulation results illustrate that GPRP has proper utilization ratio of nodes
to achieve energy efficiency and has a stable performance when network
size changes.

Keywords: Greedy probability · Routing protocol · Ad-Hoc Network ·
VANET

1 Introduction

Mobile Ad-Hoc Networks (MANET) are becoming more and more common
in today ICT world. In MANETs, all the nodes are mobile in nature and
hence they can interact dynamically in a arbitrary fashion. A special subclass
of MANETs is represented by Vehicular Ad-Hoc Networks (VANET), which

© Springer International Publishing AG 2016
G. Wang et al. (Eds.): SpaCCS 2016 Workshops, LNCS 10067, pp. 208–217, 2016.
DOI: 10.1007/978-3-319-49145-5_21

share several similarities with MANETs but cannot use the same routing protocols [19,20] since they are not able to deliver required throughput since MANETs has fast node mobility. VANETs are a self-configuring, decentralized type of wireless network applied to Intelligent Transportation System (ITS) [9,25,30]. With every node participating in the routing, the main characteristic of VANETs is the complete lack of pre-existing infrastructure, such as the routers in wired networks. There are a lot of papers talking about time-evolving and predictable networks [10,11,14,15], where the node positions and link status are predictable in a long period of time. However, the predictable network has certain limitations due to the preset network infrastructure.

Node movements in VANETs are limited in a certain range or have known trajectories. The networks with these characteristics are named as the Incompletely Predictable vehicular ad-hoc Networks (IPN). In addition, repairing link failure is not so complex in IPNs. So in this case, carrying on the data transmission through complex calculation and path selection mechanism is not reasonable. Hence, for IPNs, lightweight routing algorithms are required. The contribution of this paper is to present the Greedy Probability-based Routing Protocol (GPRP), which uses the concept of "anti-pheromone" [2,24] and greedy algorithm [13,18] for optimizing throughput and energy consumption in VANETs.

2   Related Works

A large number of researches investigated the routing problem related to VANETs. Wang et al. [31] present a new routing algorithm with the help of vehicle mobility. They make full use of the relationship between the charging stations and the vehicles to find the breakthrough of communication. Bitam et al. [4] combine VANET with cloud to explore the possibility of new technology development. Akhtar et al. [1] propose a novel matching mechanism which consider the individual density and link state to tune the parameters of the lognormal model. Patel et al. [23] overview many important and novel protocols proposed for VANETs. They compare and analyze these protocols through its own judgment criterion. Their research results are of great significance for the further research and development in this field. Baiocchi et al. [3] focus on message dissemination problem in VANETs and they propose a solution by using simulation experiments. Shaheen et al. [26] compares the performance of AODV and DSR utilized in VANETs.

3   The Model of Incompletely Predictable Networks

Delay Tolerant Networks (DTNs) and Wireless Sensor Networks (WSNs) [5–7,27] widely mention the so-called time-evolving and predictable network, whose example is given in Fig. 1. In those networks, the node mobility can be predicted with a potential accuracy of about 93 percent [21]. Moreover, there is a specific situation where the node positions and the link status are fixed. IPNs are a suitable tool to model VANETs and we have used them as basis for our protocol.

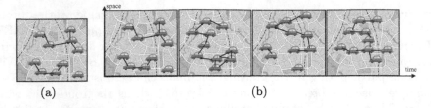

Fig. 1. A time-evolving network: (a) a snapshot of the network, (b) time-evolving topologies of the network.

Algorithm 1. Upon receiving RREQ$< S, D >$
---
  if $n_i == D$ **then**
    return RREP
  else
    return ACK<Confirmation message, APh>
    //APh: the value of Anti-pheromone of the certain node
  end if

Definition 1 (The Model of IPNs): We define IPNs as an undirected graph G. G is a two-tuple constructed with a finite nonempty set $V(G)$ and an unordered pair set $E(G)$. In other words, $G = (V(G), E(G))$. In detail, $V(G) = \{v_1, v_2, ..., v_n\}$ is called the BP set and each element $v_i(i = 1, 2, ..., n)$ in $V(G)$ represents the BP of each node. $E(G) = \{e_1, e_2, ..., e_m\}$ is the link set of graph G. Every element e_k in $E(G)$ is an unordered pair of two specific elements v_i and v_j, reported as $e_k = (v_i, v_j)$ or $e_k = v_i v_j = v_j v_i (k = 1, 2, ..., m)$.

Definition 2 (Moving Range): R_{mov} defines the radius of the movement range of each node. The movement range of a node in which it can travel through is described as a circle with BP as its center and with the radius of R_{mov}. The moving range or active range of node i is defined as a circle taking BP v_i as its center and R_{mov} as its radius.

Definition 3 (Transmission Range): The radius of transmission range is defined as R_{trans}. This definition indicates that nodes, in the circular area with the corresponding node of each BP as its center and with the radius of R_{trans}, can receive massage from the node.

4 Greedy Probability-Based Routing Protocol (GPRP)

4.1 Anti-Pheromone

In Ant Colony Optimization (ACO) algorithms, people define the concept of "pheromone" from natural phenomenon. The so-called "pheromone" gradually evaporates as time goes by. The value of pheromone indicates the characterization of path. In our model, there is a series of routes which have the same length. What's more, it is much easier for the network to figure out which routes are

Algorithm 2. Upon receiving Msg< S, D, data, Msg.x, Msg.y > from the other nodes.

---

if $n_i == D$ then
  The transport of this package is over.
else
  Locate(S)
  Locate(D)
  //obtain the coordinates of S and D
  Msg.$x = n_i.x$
  Msg.$y = n_i.y$
  //evaluate the coordinate of Msg with the one of this node
  if Msg.x ! $= D.x$ || Msg.y ! $= D.y$ then
    Multicast RREQ to those nodes who might on the shortest routes from S to D;

    Wait(T)
    Receive ACK from the nodes who are ready to transport the Msg;
    if $n_j ==$ Min(ACK.APh) then
      NextHop $== n_j$
      //find the next hop which has the minimal value of APh
    end if
    Unicast Msg to n_j
  end if
end if

---

the shortest ones. Under these circumstances, "anti-pheromone" is designed to create a more energy efficient network, to achieve energy-balance through the entire network and to attract other ants along a successful search path [8].

To be specific, if the length of the route would not increase when the message is sent to different neighbors, the node will choose a less used neighbor to relay the massage. Anti-pheromones of every neighbors are stored in the node. The node which holds the message waiting to be transmitted compares the values of its neighbors' anti-pheromones and chooses the one with a lower value to be the next hop. As shown in Algorithm 1, when a node n_i receives a RREQ packet, it will firstly confirm whether the destination is the node itself. If it is not the destination, the reception of RREQ indicates that node n_i is on one of the shortest routes from S to D. When the node replies to the sender of the RREQ with the ACK message, an information called APh is added to the ACK packet. APh denotes the value of anti-pheromone of the certain node. In other words, APh represents how many times the node has been used to transmit messages through the entire transport period. The sender of the RREQ will pick up one node with the lowest value of APh and send the message Msg to it. When a node receives a message packet, it will perform the steps shown in Algorithm 2. The node checks the coordinate of the message and constructs RREQ according to it. Secondly, the node multicasts RREQ to those nodes who might be on the shortest routes from S to D. After waiting for a proper period of time, it should have received ACKs from the nodes who are ready to transport the Msg.

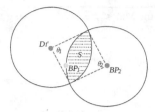

Fig. 2. The communication situation of two nodes.

The node will choose the optimal next hop and unicast the message to it. By using anti-pheromone, the consumption of energy can be kept in balance through the whole network.

4.2 Greedy Route Selection

In practice, some of VANET structures may have fixed borderlines to limit the activities of each node, for which the network can be regarded as fixed from a macro point of view. But individuals in the network, sending information to communicate with each other, may produce regular or irregular movement in the neighborhood of some fixed positions. For example, taxis with different IDs run different road sections every day. The moving ranges of taxis are limited. Furthermore, the field of medical and health care [22,28] and the information transmission between interstellar satellites [17,29] can also utilize our newly proposed protocol. To further simplify the model, we firstly set the activity radius R_{act} equal to the transmission radius of the node as well as the distance between two adjacent nodes. Our analysis begins with the communication situation of two nodes. As is shown in Fig. 2, node D_1 is not at BP but a position with a distance from BP, marked D'_1.

We marked the BP of D_2 as BP_2. The distance of these two nodes is $|D_1 D_2|$. If and only if $|D_1 D_2|$ is less than or equal to R_{trans}, D'_1 and D_2 can communicate with each other. It is easy to be proved that if and only if the node D_2 would appear in the shadow area, communication can be implemented. We use Eqs. (1)–(3) to calculate the probability of the situation that D_2 appears in the shadow area happens. $P_{1 \rightarrow 2}$ also represents the possibility that D_2 can receive the message sent by D'_1.

$$\theta = 2 \arccos \frac{|D'_1 BP_2|}{2R} \tag{1}$$

$$S = 2 \times \left(\frac{1}{2} R^2 \theta - \frac{1}{2} R^2 \sin \theta \right) = R^2 (\theta - \sin \theta) \tag{2}$$

$$P_{1 \rightarrow 2} = \frac{S}{\pi R^2} = \frac{\theta - \sin \theta}{\pi} \tag{3}$$

If S knows the position of its own BP, all the BPs of the other nodes could be calculated by themselves, because of which S could figure out the optimal

Algorithm 3. The GPRP Algorithm

$X \leftarrow$ all nodes that might have the chance to become the next hop
$d \leftarrow 65535$
$V \leftarrow$ the node chosen to be the next hop by the process in TABLE 1
while X **do**
    $n \leftarrow$ one of the nodes in X
    $X \leftarrow X - n$
    if $|SV_i| \leqslant R_{trans}$ **then**
        if $|DV_i| \leqslant R_{trans}$ **then**
            if $|DV_i| < d$ **then**
                $d \leftarrow |DV_i|$
                $V \leftarrow i|$
            end if
        else
            return
        end if
    else
        return
    end if
end while

alternative forwarder node which is closest to D. We assume that every δ seconds, B appears in a new position. The probability S could be heard by B in a period of time τ can be expressed as P_τ. Equation (4) shows the calculation method of P_τ.

$$P_\tau = 1 - (1 - P_{A \to B})^{\lfloor \frac{\tau}{\delta} \rfloor} \tag{4}$$

As can be inferred from Eq. (4), with a fixed time δ, the longer time τ the node is waiting for, the bigger the probability will be. Once the node B is chosen to be the forwarder, the hop number will drop. However, due to the waiting time τ, the delay of this route might change. In order to use this feature and find out a proper optimization method [12, 16], we propose a new algorithm named GPRP, which can be seen in Algorithm 3. It is worth noting that, X in Algorithm 3, is a collection of all nodes that might have the chance to become the next hop to forward the message. By drawing horizontal lines and vertical lines through node S and D, we can get a rectangular area R. In this paper, we define the nodes that can hear from S, and what's more, of which the BPs are in the area R as the elements in the collection X. In the actual transmission process, we introduce the concept of *hello message* to greedily select the optimal node. Nodes receiving the hello message will obtain their current positions by GPS, calculate the current distance to the BP of D and feedback to S. After that, S will send the message to the node who is closest to the BP of D. By this means, the algorithm should have the ability to avoid link failure when some of the nodes on the way to the destination are dead or out of contact.

5   Performance Evaluation

Simulation and comparison among DSDV, DSR, AODV and our proposed protocol are implemented by utilizing NS-2 simulator. In our simulation we use the version NS-2.35 and run the protocols on the Ubuntu 12.04 operating system.

In addition, running with the following parameters, we set proper test environments to simulate our protocol to figure out its performance. We model 16, 49, 100 and 144 mobile nodes moving in IPNs. The moving speed of each node is uniformly distributed between 0–5 m/s. Standard two-ray ground propagation model is used in our simulation, both with the IEEE 802.11 MAC, and omni-directional antenna model in NS-2. Some of the significant parameters in our simulation are given in Table 1. The performance of the protocols is evaluated in terms of three metrics: *Packet Delivery Ratio* (PDR), *Normalized Routing Overhead* (NRO) and *Average End-to-End Delay* (A2ED).

Table 1. Parameters used in simulation

Parameter	Value
Number of nodes	16, 49, 100, 144
Mac	IEEE 802.11 DCP
Traffic source	CBR for UDP-based traffic
Node speed	0–5 m/s
Propagation model	Two-ray ground reflection
Simulation time	1000 s

5.1   Results and Discussion

At the experimental stage, we consider node density as the only variable. 16 nodes, 49 nodes, 100 nodes and 144 nodes are set in a fixed topology according to their moving ranges and transmission ranges. PDR, NRO and A2ED are taken as the parameters of Y axis. The line of the data of each parameter of DSDV, DSR, AODV and GPRP are put in to the same figure as follow. The line charts are shown in Fig. 3, which shows that AODV as well as the proposed protocol GPRP perform relatively good levels. They can achieve higher packet delivery ratio, lower routing overhead and shorter delay. It is not difficult to see that when the number of nodes is small, the performance of the proposed protocol is a little better than AODV. Meanwhile, in the case of a gradual increase in the number of nodes, the performance of GPRP is not poor. Thanks to the routing strategies of GPRP utilizing anti-pheromone and greedy transmission strategy based on probability, the overhead and delay of the whole network is controlled in a proper range. Overall, with acceptable routing overhead, the GPRP can perform well in terms of packet delivery ratio and end-to-end delay.

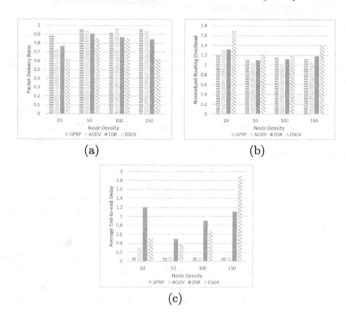

Fig. 3. Performance versus node density: (a) packet delivery ratio; (b) normalized routing overhead; (c) average end-to end delay.

6 Conclusion

In this paper, we presented GPRP, designed for incompletely predictable vehicular ad-hoc networks with a fixed, or relatively stable, structure. Firstly, we discussed the model of IPNs, in which nodes cannot move and are not settled down at all basic positions. IPNs can be regarded as the basis of our new protocol, we can make use of them in VANETs. Secondly, in the model of IPNs, the node can get rid of the basic position in a limited range. Combined with the "anti-pheromone", GPRP was put into practice. Through simulations, we found that our protocol performs well when the node density begins to change, especially in small scale networks. Moreover, we proposed a more efficient topology made up by equilateral triangles.

Acknowledgments. This work is supported by the National Science Foundation of China under Grant No. 61300237, No. U1536206, No. U1405254, No. 61232016 and No. 61402234, the National Basic Research Program 973 under Grant No. 2011CB311808, the Natural Science Foundation of Jiangsu province under Grant No. BK2012461, the research fund from Jiangsu Technology & Engineering Center of Meteorological Sensor Network in NUIST under Grant No. KDXG1301, the research fund from Jiangsu Engineering Center of Network Monitoring in NUIST under Grant No. KJR1302, the research fund from Nanjing University of Information Science and Technology under Grant No. S8113003001, the 2013 Nanjing Project of Science and Technology Activities for Returning from Overseas, the 2015 Project of six personnel in Jiangsu Province under Grant No. R2015L06, the CICAEET fund, and the PAPD fund.

References

1. Akhtar, N., Ergen, S.C., Ozkasap, O.: Vehicle mobility and communication channel models for realistic and efficient highway vanet simulation. IEEE Trans. Veh. Technol. **64**(1), 248–262 (2015)
2. Al-Ani, A.D., Seitz, J.: Qos-aware routing in multi-rate ad hoc networks based on ant colony optimization. Netw. Protoc. Algorithms **7**(4), 1–25 (2016)
3. Baiocchi, A., Salvo, P., Cuomo, F., Rubin, I.: Understanding spurious message forwarding in vanet beaconless dissemination protocols: An analytical approach. IEEE Trans. Veh. Technol. **65**(4), 2243–2258 (2016)
4. Bitam, S., Mellouk, A., Zeadally, S.: Vanet-cloud: a generic cloud computing model for vehicular ad hoc networks. IEEE Wireless Commun. **22**(1), 96–102 (2015)
5. Carrabs, F., Cerulli, R., Ambrosio, C.D., Gentili, M., Raiconi, A.: Maximizing lifetime in wireless sensor networks with multiple sensor families. Comput. Oper. Res. **54**, 121–137 (2015)
6. Carrabs, F., Cerulli, R., Ambrosio, C.D., Raiconi, A.: A hybrid exact approach for maximizing lifetime in sensor networks with complete and partial coverage constraints. J. Netw. Comput. Appl. **58**, 12–22 (2015)
7. Carrabs, F., Cerulli, R., DAmbrosio, C., Raiconi, A.: An exact algorithm to extend lifetime through roles allocation in sensor networks with connectivity constraints. Optimization Lett., 1–16 (2016)
8. Castiglione, A., Prisco, R.D., Santis, A.D., Fiore, U., Palmieri, F.: A botnet-based command and control approach relying on swarm intelligence. J. Netw. Comput. Appl. **38**(38), 22–33 (2014)
9. Cerrone, C., Cerulli, R., Gentili, M.: Vehicle-id sensor location for route flow recognition: Models and algorithms. Eur. J. Oper. Res. **247**(2), 618–629 (2015)
10. Cerrone, C., Cerulli, R., Raiconi, A.: Relations, models and a memetic approach for three degree-dependent spanning tree problems. Eur. J. Oper. Res. **232**(3), 442–453 (2014)
11. Chen, H., Shi, K., Wu, C.: Spanning tree based topology control for data collecting in predictable delay-tolerant networks. Ad Hoc Netw. **46**, 48–60 (2016)
12. Colella, A., Castiglione, A., De Santis, A., Esposito, C., Palmieri, F.: Privacy aware routing for sharing sensitive information across wide-area networks. In: 2016 IEEE 19th International Conference on Network-Based Information Systems, NBiS, pp. 70–75, September 2016
13. Coskun, C.C., Ayanoglu, E.: A greedy algorithm for energy-efficient base station deployment in heterogeneous networks. In: 2015 IEEE International Conference on Communications (ICC), pp. 7–12. IEEE (2015)
14. Huang, C.M., Lin, S.Y.: Timer-based greedy forwarding algorithm in vehicular ad hoc networks. IET Intel. Transport Syst. **8**(4), 333–344 (2013)
15. Li, F., Yin, Z., Tang, S., Cheng, Y., Wang, Y.: Optimization problems in throwbox-assisted delay tolerant networks: Which throwboxes to activate? how many active ones i need? IEEE Trans. Comput. **65**(5), 1663–1670 (2016)
16. Li, J., Li, X., Yang, B., Sun, X.: Segmentation-based image copy-move forgery detection scheme. IEEE Trans. Inf. Forensics Secur. **10**(3), 507–518 (2015)
17. Messerschmitt, D.G.: Interstellar communication: The case for spread spectrum. Acta Astronaut. **81**(1), 227–238 (2012)
18. de Oliveira, H.A., Boukerche, A., Guidoni, D.L., Nakamura, E.F., Mini, R.A., Loureiro, A.A.: An enhanced location-free greedy forward algorithm with hole bypass capability in wireless sensor networks. J. Parallel Distrib. Comput. **77**, 1–10 (2015)

19. Palmieri, F., Ricciardi, S., Fiore, U., Castiglione, A.: A multiobjective wavelength routing approach combining network and traffic engineering with energy awareness. IEEE Syst. J. **PP**(99), 1–12 (2015)
20. Palmieri, F., Castiglione, A.: Condensation-based routing in mobile ad-hoc networks. Mobile Inf. Syst. **8**(3), 199–211 (2012)
21. Pan, Z., Zhang, Y., Kwong, S.: Efficient motion and disparity estimation optimization for low complexity multiview video coding. IEEE Trans. Broadcast. **61**(2), 1 (2015)
22. Papazoglou, P.M., Laskari, T.I., Fourlas, G.K.: Towards a low cost open architecture wearable sensor network for health care applications. In: Proceedings of the 7th International Conference on PErvasive Technologies Related to Assistive Environments, pp. 1–8 (2014)
23. Patel, D., Faisal, M., Batavia, P., Makhija, S., Mani, M.: Overview of routing protocols in vanet. Int. J. Comput. Appl. **136**(9), 4–7 (2016)
24. Prabaharan, S.B., Ponnusamy, R.: Energy aware ant colony optimization based dynamic random routing strategy for MANET. Energy **5**(2), 1–5 (2016)
25. Qin, Y., Yuan, B., Pi, S.: Research on framework and key technologies of urban rail intelligent transportation system. In: Qin, Y., Jia, L., Feng, J., An, M., Diao, L. (eds.) Proceedings of the 2015 International Conference on Electrical and Information Technologies for Rail Transportation. LNEE, vol. 378, pp. 729–736. Springer, Heidelberg (2016). doi:10.1007/978-3-662-49370-0_76
26. Shaheen, A., Gaamel, A., Bahaj, A.: Comparison and analysis study between AODV and DSR routing protocols in vanet with IEEE 802.11b. J. Ubiquit. Syst. Pervasive Netw. **7**(1), 07–12 (2016)
27. Shen, J., Moh, S., Chung, I.: Comment: "enhanced novel access control protocol over wireless sensor networks". IEEE Trans. Consum. Electron. **56**(3), 2019–2021 (2010)
28. Shen, J., Tan, H., Moh, S., Chung, I.: Enhanced secure sensor association and key management in wireless body area networks. J. Commun. Netw. **17**(5), 453–462 (2015)
29. Shen, J., Tan, H., Wang, J., Wang, J., Lee, S.: A novel routing protocol providing good transmission reliability in underwater sensor networks. J. Internet Technol. **16**(1), 171–178 (2015)
30. Shinde, R., Mulinti, M., Shinde, P., Kadam, S.: Intelligent transportation system (apps): GPS based tracking. Int. J. Res. Eng. **3**(1), 6–7 (2016)
31. Wang, M., Liang, H., Zhang, R., Deng, R.: Mobility-aware coordinated charging for electric vehicles in vanet-enhanced smart grid. IEEE J. Sel. Areas Commun. **32**(7), 1344–1360 (2014)

Flexible Schema for Prediction
of Collaborator's Credits

Li Weigang[(⊠)]

TransLab, Department of Computer Science, University of Brasilia, C.P. 4466,
Brasilia - DF 70910-900, Brazil
weigang@unb.br

Abstract. For predicting the contributions of the collaborators of a scientific activity, such as a paper or a project, the First and Others (F&O) approach has been developed with the consideration of both a flexible formula by changing tuning parameters and weight preference to individual collaborator. This paper extends and generalizes the F&O approach to develop a meta flexible schema of "First and Others" credit-assignment mechanism, which is then proposed to modify geometric counting for amplified applications. With this extension, it makes the traditional approach more robust with flexible profiles. Compared to a set of survey data from medicine, the performance of the proposed flexible schemas is improved significantly.

Keywords: Bibliometrics · Credit of coauthorship · Informetrics Scholar data

1   Introduction

As a result of the development of Internet technology, at least 114 million English-language scholarly documents are accessible on the Web and related network media [6]. Efficiently analyzing and utilizing this great quantity of scientific products is a challenge for scholars and researchers in informetrics. Based on the published documents, scientific papers, project reports and others, how to evaluate the contributions of the collaborators of these documents is one important topic, even many scientific schemas have been developed [18, 22].

In some fields, such as medicine, career promotion, fund application and even new job admission, an evaluation of the profile of candidates based on their scientific contribution is required. Statistical methods are usually applied to obtain the survey data of the credit distribution as the standard criteria [10, 17, 21]. This type of method is useful for a specified field, but probably not applicable in other fields. Specifically, for a great scientific publication database, such as Google Scholar, Microsoft Academic Search, Scopus, Web of Science and others, an efficient schema is needed to evaluate the scientific contribution of an individual author, an institution and even a country. This is the main reason to develop collaborator credit-assignment schemas.

Based on the state of the art in informetrics, basically, there are four kinds of credit-assignment schemas for a publication or project with N collaborators. (1) Each author receives a score of 1 as credit under the *equal contribution* (EC) norm [10]. This statistical method is referred to as the *N/N whole counting (WC)*. (2) Each author has

© Springer International Publishing AG 2016
G. Wang et al. (Eds.): SpaCCS 2016 Workshops, LNCS 10067, pp. 218–228, 2016.
DOI: 10.1007/978-3-319-49145-5_22

a score of *1/N* [11] using *fractional counting* (FC) [12], which is referred to as the *1/N* evaluation model. (3) The contribution of the authors is determined by *sequence-determines-credit* (SDC) approaches [15], which have been effectively utilized to improve *N/N* and *1/N* models for more sophisticated scenarios. Traditional SDC approaches include arithmetic [1, 16], geometric [3], harmonic counting [4, 5], and A-index [13]. SDC can be classified as the *S/N* evaluation model. (4) Considering the special contribution of the corresponding author, the *first-last-author-emphasis* (FLAE) method was investigated by Trueba and Guerrero [14], Wren et al. [21], and Tscharntke et al. [15]. FLAE and other corresponding author emphasis methods are classified as the *U/N* evaluation model.

As Waltman [18] mentioned, the scientific citation impact indicators have been intensively studied. Xu et al. [22] summarized more than 15 credit-assignment schemas to evaluate the performance and applicability. With the challenge of big data, there is still space for deep research on this topic, e.g., developing new concepts and schemas.

F&O counting [19, 20] has been developed with the consideration of the above four aspects. In this new schema, a tuning parameters α is introduced to change the formula to be more flexible. Another factor β_i is designed as a weight to assign the preference for any individual partner, i. Two main properties of this schema are as follows: (1) flexible assignment credits by modifying the formula (with the change of α) and applying the preference to an individual collaborator by adjusting the weight (with the change of β_i); (2) calculation of the credits by separating the formula for the first author from others. With this separation, the credit of the second author shows an inflection point according to the change of α. The flexible property of F&O enables this new schema to achieve better performance.

The objective of this research is to extend and generalize the F&O approach to develop a meta flexible schema of "First and Others" credit-assignment mechanism. This meta flexible schema is then proposed to modify geometric counting for amplified applications. With this extension, it is expected that the traditional approach is more robust by flexibility. Compared to a set of empirical survey data from medicine field, the performance of the proposed flexible schemas is improved significantly.

2 Meta Flexible Schema of First and Others Counting

2.1 Meta Flexible Schema

Usually a counting to obtain *sequence-determines-credit* (SDC) is defined as a unique formula, such as the approaches of arithmetic, geometric, harmonic counting and A-index. Weigang [20] proposed a new approach with two equations to separate the measure value of the first from others. To extend this mechanism, Definition 1 gives a meta scheme with two separate equations.

Definition 1. For a cooperative activity with *N* partners, a meta scheme to obtain the measurement of the impact or contribution credit of the *i th* individual for a sequence-determines-credit is defined as *F(i,N)*, *i* = 1, 2, ..., *N*. There is

$$F(i,N) = \begin{cases} 1 - \sum_{j=2}^{N} F(j,N) & \text{for } i = 1 \\ f(i,N,\alpha,\beta,\gamma) & \text{for } i = 2,\ldots,N \end{cases} \tag{1}$$

By Definition 1, the estimated contribution of the first partner, $F(1,N)$, is calculated by subtracting the sum of others from 1. The values of others from second are determined by $f(i,N,\alpha,\beta,\gamma)$ separately, which is a special counting or modified counting.

α is a tuning parameter to adjust the formula $f(i,N,\alpha,\beta,\gamma)$ to be more flexible. In some cases, α may be defined as a vector, ALFA = $[\alpha_2, \alpha_3, \ldots,\alpha_i]$, i = 2, 3, ..., $N \geq 2$.

β is a weight factor to address the preference of individual partner. In many cases, the weight can be a vector BETA = $[\beta_2, \beta_3, \ldots, \beta_N]$, in the formula $f(i,N,\alpha,\beta,\gamma)$ and is used to adjust the credit of the i th individual, i = 2,3,..., $N \geq 2$. In the rest of the paper, the condition β = 1 means implicitly that no individual from N partners declares a special contribution in $F(i,N)$.

γ is another tuning parameter which is used to adjust the formula $f(i,N,\alpha,\gamma)$ for more flexibility. The effectiveness of γ makes $f(i,N,\alpha,\beta,\gamma)$ with nonlinear distribution.

For better understanding and describing the difference between the first and others, two ratios are defined.

The ratio of the credits between i and j is defined as ρ_i, where

$$\rho_i = F(i,N)/F(j,N), \ i \text{ or } j = 1,2,\ldots,N; i \neq j; N \geq 2. \tag{2}$$

With Eq. (2), the ratio of the credits between the first and second partners is $\rho_1 = F(1,N)/F(2,N)$.

The ratio of the credits between the first and the sum of others is defined as λ

$$\lambda = F(1,N)/\sum_{2}^{N}(i,N), N \geq 2. \tag{3}$$

2.2   First and Others (F&O) Counting

First and Others (F&O) counting was proposed by Weigang [20]. Its idea initially comes from Weigang et al. [19] which is aimed to evaluate the influence of researchers by scientific contribution.

Definition 2. First and Others (F&O) counting, $F\&O(i,N)$, is defined as a credit that estimates the contributions of the i th partner in a cooperation event or project, i = 1, 2, ..., N. There is

$$F\&O(i,N) = \begin{cases} 1 - \sum_{j=2}^{N} F\&O(j,N) & \text{for } i = 1 \\ \frac{\beta}{i^{\gamma} + (N-\alpha)} & \text{for } i = 2,\ldots,N; \ \alpha \leq N \end{cases} \tag{4}$$

where, $F\&O(i, N)$ presents the contribution credit of the ith collaborator, $0 \leq F\&O(i, N) \leq 1$, $i = 1, 2, ..., N$. α and γ are tuning parameters and β is the preference weight for individual partner. Similar to harmonic counting and A-index, Eq. (4) presents a formula of the SDC approach, and is noted as F&O counting. Table 1 gives the credit distribution of F&O counting, $\alpha = 2$.

In any case of α, there is $F\&O(i, N) = F\&O(i-1, N + 1)$, for $i = 3, 4, ..., N$. This means that the contribution of a collaborator in the i th position for N collaborators equals the contribution of the $(i-1)$th collaborator for $N + 1$ collaborators. In a special condition $\alpha = 2$, the credit of the second individual is $F\&O(2, N) = 1/N$, for any N.

Theorem 1 *(Balance theorem)*. *With F&O counting, for $\alpha = 2$, $\beta = \gamma = 1$, $N > 2$, there is:*

$$F\&O(1,N) - F\&O(2,N) = \sum_{2}^{N} (F\&O(2,N) - F\&O(i,N)) \qquad (5)$$

Theorem 1 means that the difference between the credits of first and second collaborators equals the sum of the differences between the credits of the second and others [20].

For understand better the profiles, the ratio between Δ_1 and $\sum_{i=2}^{N} \Delta i$ is defined as

$$\tau = \Delta_1 / \sum_{i=2}^{N} \Delta i, \text{ for } i = 2, 3, ..., N \qquad (6)$$

In F&O counting, for $\alpha = 2$ and $\beta = \gamma = 1$, τ is always 1, for any N. Also see Table 1 with the difference credits between any one and F&O(2,N) for up to 8 authors ($\alpha = 2$). The results of Table 1 support Theory 1 and related proof. Abbas [1] studied the difference of credits between the first and last authors. He concluded that the amount of increase in the positional credits of some of the authors is equal to the amount of decrease in the positional credits of the remaining authors. This property is an important topic to study.

Table 1. Difference credits between any one and F&O(2,N) for up to 8 authors ($\alpha = 2$)

Author number	Δ_1	Δ_2	Δ_3	Δ_4	Δ_5	Δ_6	Δ_7	Δ_8
3	0.083	0.000	0.083					
4	0.133	0.000	0.050	0.083				
5	0.165	0.000	0.033	0.057	0.075			
6	0.188	0.000	0.024	0.042	0.056	0.067		
7	0.204	0.000	0.018	0.032	0.043	0.052	0.060	
8	0.216	0.000	0.014	0.025	0.034	0.042	0.048	0.054

2.3   More Comprehensive Properties of F&O Counting

To determine the distribution credits of the collaborator in a scientific publication, Stalling et al. [13] proposed three axioms for collaboration indexes.

With the manner of separating the calculation of the credit of the first from others by F&O counting, some new important properties for this counting can be observed. When the number of partners, N, increases, the ratio between the first and second collaborators, ρ_1, increases, but the ratio between the first and the sum of the others, λ, decreases. When α decreases (from 1 to -100, for example), the ratio of credit of the first author over the sum of others, λ, increases. For $\alpha = 2$ and $I = N \geq 2$, Eq. (4) results in the credit distribution from the second author to be: $1/i$, $1/(i + 1)$, ..., $1/(2i -2)$. These patterns are important for understanding the distribution of credits in the cooperative event or project.

Theorem 2 *(Inflection theorem)*. *By F&O counting, the credit of the second collaborator, F&O(2,N), is an inflection point.*

Studying an inflection point in credit distribution is an interesting topic. Before this point, the schema follows a formula (credit distribution) and after and including this point, the schema follows another formula (credit distribution). The proof of Theorem 2 is provided by Weigang [20].

2.4   Extending Flexible Schemas to Traditional Counting as F&O

Geometric counting is a schema widely applied in the scientific community. Compared to F&O, it has a fixed formula and produces credits by a unique sequence for N collaborators. Using this meta flexible scheme by Definition 1, this subsection presents the flexible version of Geometric counting and discusses the new properties by the modifications.

Geometric counting was proposed by Egghe et al. [3] and defined as

$$\text{Geometric}\ (i, N) = \frac{2^{N-i}}{2^N - 1} \tag{7}$$

There are some important properties of geometric counting:

1) The credits of the individual are. *Geometric (1,N)* = $\frac{2^{N-1}}{2^N-1}$, *Geometric (2,N)* = $\frac{2^{N-2}}{2^N-1}$, *Geometric (3,N)* = $\frac{2^{N-3}}{2^N-1}$, ...
2) There is ρ_1 = *Geometric (1,N)/ Geometric (2,N)* = 2. Actually, for any i $\leq$ N, *Geometric (i,N)/ Geometric (i + 1,N)* = 2. This ratio is always 2.

According to the meta scheme of Eq. (1), Flexible Geometric counting $FG(i,N)$ is defined as Eq. (8).

$$FG(i,N) = \begin{cases} 1 - \sum_{j=2}^{N} FG(j,N) & \text{for } i = 1 \\ \frac{\beta_i 2^{N-i}}{2^{N-\gamma}-\alpha} & \text{for } i = 2,\ldots,N; \alpha \leq 2^{N-\gamma} \end{cases} \qquad (8)$$

where, $FG(i, N)$ represents the measuring credit for the ith individual from N partners, $0 \leq FG(i, N) \leq 1$, $i = 1, 2, \ldots, N$. α and γ are tuning parameters and β_i is the weight preference for the ith individual partner.

Some properties of Flexible Geometric counting should be mentioned: (1) When $\alpha = 1$, $\beta_i = 1$ and $\gamma = 0$, Eq. (8) gives the original Geometric counting. (2) For any $2 \leq i \leq N$, the Flexible Geometric counting keeps the original property, i.e., $FG(i,N)/FG(i+1,N) = 2$. However, the ratio between the first and second $\rho_1 = FG(1,N)/FG(2,N)$ depends on the values of α and γ. For example, $\alpha = 1$ and $\gamma = -1$, $\rho_1 = FG(1,N)/FG(2,N) = 6$. This ratio will increase very quickly according to the decrease of γ. As another example, $\alpha = 1$ and $\gamma = -10$, $\rho_1 = FG(1,N)/FG(2,N) = 4094$, see Fig. 1.

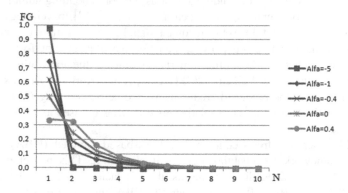

Fig. 1. Credits of Flexible Geometric with the change of α for $N = 10$.

Theorem 3 (Half and Half theorem). By Flexible Geometric counting $FG(i,N)$, when $\alpha = 2$, $\gamma = 0$ and $\beta_i = 1$, the credit of the first author equals the sum of others, i.e. $\lambda = 1$, for any N.

Proof: *For* $\alpha = 2$, $\gamma = 0$ and $\beta_i = 1$, there are
$FG(2,N) = \frac{2^{N-2}}{2^N-2}$, $FG(3,N) = \frac{2^{N-3}}{2^N-2}$, ..., $FG(N,N) = \frac{2^{N-N}}{2^N-2}$;
$N = 2$,
$FG(2,2) = \frac{2^{2-2}}{2^2-2} = \frac{1}{2}$; $FG(1,2) = 1 - FG(2,2) = \frac{1}{2}$; $N = 3$,
$FG(2,3) = \frac{2^{3-2}}{2^3-2} = 1/3$; $FG(3,3) = \frac{2^{3-3}}{2^3-2} = 1/6$; $\sum_2^3 FG(i,3) = \frac{1}{2}$; $FG(1,3) = 1 - \sum_2^3 FG(i,3) = 1/2$; ...
$N = N$,
$FG(2,N) = \frac{2^{N-2}}{2^N-2}$, $FG(3,N) = \frac{2^{N-3}}{2^N-2}$,   ..., $FG(N,N) = \frac{2^{N-N}}{2^N-2}$; $\sum_2^N FG(i,N) = \frac{2^{N-1}-1}{2^N-2} = 1/2$;
There is

$$FG(1,N) = 1 - \sum_2^N FG(i,N) = 1/2 \qquad (9)$$

Theorem 3 is proved. It is useful in the case of assigning the credit 50 % to the first partner, and the sum of others takes another 50 % for any N, $\alpha = 2$, $\gamma = 0$ and $\beta_i = 1$.

3   Application of Flexible Schema for Overfitting Problem

In some medical schools in USA and Canada, the promotion process of the medical doctorates considers their academic contributions [21]. Three types of authorship credit category are studied: initial conception (IC), work performance (WP), supervision (S) of the project. And the mean of these three items is calculated. Table 2 shows the perceived credit per author by their byline position on a hypothetical manuscript in these categories.

The byline position is classified into two situations: (1) last author as the corresponding author (LACA) and (2) middle author as the corresponding author (MACA). There are other sets of empirical data, such as chemistry [17], psychology [10] and Harvard survey data [2], but this set of medicine data [21] shows more divergence and is difficult to fit. That is why this paper uses the latter to evaluate the performance of the developed flexible schemas. For more comparison studies of the application of F&O in different empirical data, see Weigang [20], Hagen [4] and Kim and Kim [8].

Table 2 also gives the predicted credits using geometric counting for five authors ($N = 5$). The relative error and mean relative error (MRE) are used as the performance evaluation criteria.

Kim and Diesner [7] introduced a novel network-based approach (NBA) as a robust and flexible framework for coauthorship credit allocation. This model generates a different set of credits depending on the distribution factor d. For medicine data, in LACA, $d = 0.7$, the MRE is 0.1336 between the NBA and mean of survey data; the MRE is 0.3828 between the NBA and WP survey data. And in MACA, $d = 0.6$, the MRE is 0.0767 between the NBA and mean of survey data and the MRE is 0.3374 between the NBA and WP survey data, see Table 3.

Actually, Kim and Kim [8] proposed the flexible modification to arithmetic, harmonic and geometric counting. They used different tuning parameter d to obtain different credits from these approaches. As this mechanism still fixed the formulas without preference for individual partner, the effectiveness of improving the performance is limited. The example in Table 3 shows that there is no unique formula for satisfying WP survey data and the mean of IC, WP and S survey data. It is necessary to use more flexible approaches. In contrast, F&O counting can use the tuning parameters α and γ to change the formula and modify the weight β_i to give preference for individual partner. In case of medicine survey data, the predicted results by Flexible Geometric are listed in Table 4.

In LACA, for $N = 5$, $\alpha = 2$, $\beta = 1$, $\gamma = 0$, there is FG $(-,5) = [50, 26.67, 13.33, 6.67, 3.33]$. Let BETA $= [\beta_2, \beta_3, \beta_4, \beta_5] = [1, 1, 1.9, 1]$. The credits are modified as: NFG(2,5) $= \beta_2*FG(3,5)$, NFG(3,5) $= \beta_3*FG(4,5)$, NFG(4,5) $= \beta_4*FG(5,5)$, NFG(5,5) $= \beta_5*(FG(1,5) + FG(2,5)/2)$, and NFG(1,5) $= 100 - \sum NFG(i,5)$, $i = 2$,

Table 2. Medicine survey data and relative errors with geometric credits ($N = 5$)

Author Position	i	Geome. credit %	Initial conception		Work performance		Supervision		Mean	
			Survey data	Rel. error	Survey data	Rel. error	Survey data	Rel. error	Survey data	Rel. error
Last author as the corresponding author (LACA) MRE	1	38.71	29±16	0.3348	46±17	0.1585	29±20	0.3348	34±14	0.1385
	2	12.9	10 + 08	0.2900	16 + 07	0.1938	09±07	0.4333	12±10	0.0750
	3	6.45	06±06	0.0750	11±05	0.4136	07±06	0.0786	08±02	0.1938
	4	3.23	06±06	0.4617	10±05	0.6770	06±06	0.4617	07±02	0.5386
	5	38.71	48±25	0.1935	17±14	1.2771	49±28	0.2100	38±22	0.0187
				0.2710		0.5440		0.3037		0.1929
Middle author as the corresponding author (MACA) MRE	1	38.71	31±15	0.2487	44±17	0.1202	28±17	0.3825	34±09	0.1385
	2	6.45	10±07	0.3550	16±07	0.5969	12±13	0.4625	13±03	0.5038
	3	38.71	34±20	0.1385	20±10	0.9355	33±20	0.1730	29±08	0.3348
	4	3.23	07±09	0.5386	09±07	0.6411	08±07	0.5963	08±01	0.5963
	5	12.9	18±18	0.2833	11±09	0.1727	19±19	0.3211	16±04	0.1938
				0.3128		0.4933		0.3871		0.3534

Table 3. Medicine survey data and relative errors with NBA by different parameter (d)

Author position	i	NBA credit %	Initial conception		Work performance		Supervision		Mean	
			Survey data	Rel. error	Survey data	Rel. error	Survey data	Rel. error	Survey data	Rel. error
Last author as the corresponding author (LACA) MRE	1	35	29±16	0.2069	46±17	0.2391	29±20	0.2069	34±14	0.0294
	2	14	10 + 08	0.4000	16 + 07	0.1250	09±07	0.5556	12±10	0.1667
	3	10	06±06	0.6667	11±05	0.0909	07±06	0.4286	08±02	0.2500
	4	06	06±06	0.0000	10±05	0.4000	06±06	0.0000	07±02	0.1429
	5	35	48±25	0.2708	17±14	1.0588	49±28	0.2857	38±22	0.0789
		($d = 0.7$)		0.3089		0.3828		0.2953		0.1336
Middle author as the corresponding author (MACA) MRE	1	33	31±15	0.0645	44±17	0.2500	28±17	0.1786	34±09	0.0294
	2	11	10±07	0.1000	16±07	0.3125	12±13	0.0833	13±03	0.1538
	3	33	34±20	0.0294	20±10	0.6500	33±20	0.0000	29±08	0.1379
	4	08	07±09	0.1429	09±07	0.1111	08±07	0.0000	08±01	0.0000
	5	15	18±18	0.1667	11±09	0.3636	19±19	0.2105	16±04	0.0625
		($d = 0.6$)		0.1007		0.3374		0.0945		0.0767

..., 5. Then, there is NFG($-,5$) = [35.34,13.33,6.67,6.33,38.34]. With the flexible modification, the MRE in Table 4 is better than the results with Geometric counting in Table 2.

In MACA, for $N = 5$, $\alpha = 2$, $\beta = 1$, $\gamma = 0.3$, there is $FG\ (-,5) = $ [37.47, 33.34,16.67,8.34,4.17]. If applying BETA = $[\beta_2, \beta_3, \beta_4, \beta_5]$ = BETA = [1.7,1,1.7,1] to $FG(-,5)$. The credits are modified as: NFG(2,5) = β_2*FG(4,5), NFG(3,5) = β_3*(FG (1,5) + FG(2,5)/2), NFG(4,5) = β_4*FG(5,5), NFG(5,5) = β_5*FG(3,5), and NFG

Table 4. Medicine survey data and relative errors with Flexible Geometric credits

Author position	i	Geome. credit %	Initial conception		Work performance		Supervision		Mean	
			Survey data	Rel. error	Survey data	Rel. error	Survey data	Rel. error	Survey data	Rel. error
Last author as the corresponding author (LACA) MRE	1	35.34	29±16	0.2186	46±17	0.2318	29±20	0.2186	34±14	0.0394
	2	13.33	10 + 08	0.3330	16 + 07	0.1669	09±07	0.4811	12±10	0.1108
	3	06.67	06±06	0.1117	11±05	0.3936	07±06	0.0471	08±02	0.1663
	4	06.33	06±06	0.0545	10±05	0.3673	06±06	0.0471	07±02	0.0961
	5	38.34	48±25	0.2014	17±14	1.2550	49±28	0.2177	38±22	0.0088
	(γ = 0)			**0.1838**		**0.4829**		**0.2038**		**0.0843**
Middle author as the corresponding author (MACA) MRE	1	26.66	31±15	0.1401	44±17	0.3941	28±17	0.0479	34±09	0.2159
	2	14.18	10±07	0.4178	16±07	0.1139	12±13	0.1815	13±03	0.0906
	3	34.40	34±20	0.0413	20±10	0.7703	33±20	0.0729	29±08	0.2209
	4	07.09	07±09	0.0127	09±07	0.2123	08±07	0.1139	08±01	0.1139
	5	16.67	18±18	0.0739	11±09	0.5155	19±19	0.1226	16±04	0.0419
	(γ = 0.3)			**0.1372**		**0.4012**		**0.1078**		**0.1366**

$(1,5) = 100 - \sum NFG(i,5)$, $i = 2, \ldots, 5$. There is $NFG(-,5) = [26,66, 14.18, 35.40, 07.09, 16.67]$ and the RME achieved is 0.1366 between predicted credits and the mean of the survey data. It is much better than the results in Table 2.

It is important to mention that, using credit-assignment schemas is a simple manner to predict the credits of coauthors. To apply the weights to adjust the preference of individual coauthors should follow the axiomatic quantification principles [13].

4 Conclusion

The quickly developed Internet technology and applications present a challenge to effective evaluation of the contribution of scientific productions and scientists. The study of collaborator credit-assignment schemas is an important topic from this challenge. Based on the traditional schemas and F&O approach, this paper presented a meta flexible schema to separate the credit of the first collaborator from those of others and also considered two tuning parameters and weight preference for individual partner. This meta schema was then applied to geometric counting to obtain flexible schema for more robustness with new properties. The flexible schemas supplied alternative solutions to avoid overfitting problems compared to empirical survey data from medicine.

The proposal of a meta flexible schema and its application is an initial tentative and with the potential application in the large scale of scientific database. It is only a complementary mechanism to the traditional approaches. On the other hand, it is not applicable for a special paper and research group to divide the contribution to every individual coauthor. The further work will involve applying the developed flexible schemas to evaluate a great quantity of data from large databases of scientific productions. With the increase of the scale of data, the profile of the flexibility and simplification of the schema can be verified.

Acknowledgments. This research is partially supported by the Brazilian National Council for Scientific and Technological Development (CNPq Proc. 304903/2013-2). The author also thanks the review and suggestions from Mr. Zhai Ziyang and other colleagues.

References

1. Abbas, A.M.: Weighted indices for evaluating the quality of research with multiple authorship. Scientometrics **88**(1), 107–131 (2011)
2. Caruso, E., Epley, N., Bazerman, M.H.: The costs and benefits of undoing egocentric responsibility assessments in groups. J. Pers. Soc. Psychol. **91**(5), 857–871 (2006)
3. Egghe, L., Rousseau, R., Van Hooydonk, G.: Methods for accrediting publications to authors or countries: consequences for evaluation studies. J. Am. Soc. Inform. Sci. Technol. **51**(2), 145–157 (2000)
4. Hagen, N.T.: Harmonic publication and citation counting: sharing authorship credit equitably–not equally, geometrically or arithmetically. Scientometrics **84**(3), 785–793 (2010)
5. Hodge, S.E., Greenberg, D.A.: Publication credit. Science **213**(4511), 950 (1981)
6. Khabsa, M., Giles, C.L.: The number of scholarly documents on the public web. PLoS ONE **9**(5), e93949 (2014)
7. Kim, J., Diesner, J.: A network-based approach to coauthorship credit allocation. Scientometrics **101**(1), 587–602 (2014)
8. Kim, J., Kim, J.: Rethinking the comparison of coauthorship credit allocation schemes. J. Inf. **9**(3), 667–673 (2015)
9. Liu, X.Z., Fang, H.: Fairly sharing the credit of multi-authored papers and its application in the modification of h-index and g-index. Scientometrics **91**(1), 37–49 (2012)
10. Maciejovsky, B., Budescu, D.V., Ariely, D.: The researcher as a consumer of scientific publications: how do name-ordering conventions affect inferences about contribution credits? Mark. Sci. **28**(3), 589–598 (2009)
11. May, M., Brody, H.: Nature index 2015 global. Nature **522**(7556), S1 (2015)
12. Narin, F.: Evaluative bibliometrics: the use of publication and citation analysis in the evaluation of scientific activity. Computer Horizons, Washington, D. C, pp. 206–219 (1976)
13. Stallings, J., Vance, E., Yang, J., Vannier, M.W., Liang, J., Pang, L., Dai, L., Ye, I., Wang, G.: Determining scientific impact using a collaboration index. Proc. Nat. Acad. Sci. **110**(24), 9680–9685 (2013)
14. Trueba, F.J., Guerrero, H.: A robust formula to credit authors for their publications. Scientometrics **60**(2), 181–204 (2004)
15. Tscharntke, T., Hochberg, M.E., Rand, T.A., Resh, V.H., Krauss, J.: Author sequence and credit for contributions in multiauthored publications. PLoS Biol. **5**(1), e18 (2007)
16. Van Hooydonk, G.: Fractional counting of multiauthored publications: consequences for the impact of authors. J. Am. Soc. Inform. Sci. Technol. **48**(10), 944–945 (1997)
17. Vinkler, P.: Evaluation of the publication activity of research teams by means of scientometric indicators. Curr. Sci. **79**(5), 602–612 (2000)
18. Waltman, L.: A review of the literature on citation impact indicators. J. Inf. **10**(2), 365–391 (2016). arXiv:1507.02099
19. Weigang, L., Dantas, I.A., Saleh, A.A., Li, D.L.: Influential analysis in micro scholar social networks. In: Proceedings of SocInf@IJCAI 2015, Buenos Aires, vol. 1398, pp. 22–28 (2015)

20. Weigang, L.: First and others credit-assignment schema for evaluating academic contribution of coauthors. Front. Inf. Technol. Electron. Eng. (2016). Doi:10.1631/FITEE.1600991
21. Wren, J.D., Kozak, K.Z., Johnson, K.R., Deakyne, S.J., Schilling, L.M., Dellavalle, R.P.: The write position - a survey of perceived contributions to papers based on byline position and number of authors. EMBO Rep. **8**(11), 988–991 (2007)
22. Xu, J., Ding, Y., Song, M., Chambers, T.: Author credit-assignment schemas: a comparison and analysis. J. Assoc. Inf. Sci. Technol. (2015). Doi:10.1002/asi.23495

A Real-Time Processing System for Anonymization of Mobile Core Network Traffic

Mian Cheng[1](✉), Baokang Zhao[1], and Jinshu Su[1,2]

[1] College of Computer, National University of Defense Technology, Changsha, China
{cm,bkzhao,sjs}@nudt.edu.cn
[2] National Laboratory for Parallel and Distribution Processing,
National University of Defense Technology, Changsha, China

Abstract. With the advancement of mobile telecommunication technologies, the effective mining of user data is regard as an very important requirement. However, due to the original data may contain sensitive information about individuals, sharing user dataset can lead to serious privacy breaches, such as the notorious scandal, the privacy leakage of American on Line (AOL). Up to now, there are already existing several available tools or libraries for packet anonymization, like *PktAnon, Anonym, Pcaplib*. But little research has actually gone into supporting packets in high speed mobile core network which contains several packet encapsulation structure. In this paper, we propose a real-time processing system called ANTW for providing packet anonymization on mobile core network. It involves two mechanisms: First, real-time packet processing, such as decapsulation, decompression and PPP character unescape. Second, packet anonymization which protects the privacy in the sensitive fields of each packet while preserving the utility. We evaluated the performance and availability of ANTW over a wide-area real network. Evaluation results indicate that our system can achieve more than 10 Gbps.

Keywords: Anonymous system · Mobile core network · Real-time process · Hardware acceleration · High performance

1 Introduction

With the rapid development of Internet, we are observing a data explosion and the value of data is receiving more and more attention. People expect mining useful information and rules from large amounts of diverse data. However, due to the original data may contain sensitive information about individuals, sharing user dataset can lead to serious privacy breaches, such as the notorious scandal, the privacy leakage of American On Line (AOL).

In the past, the problem of anonymizing microdata has received significant attention. But most of recent researches focus on static or incremental environment of microdata, only a few studies have explored the link in network data. Network data can be studied in the same way as microdata, both of them contain n rows and m columns representing a single packet and the fields in the packet,

G. Wang et al. (Eds.): SpaCCS 2016 Workshops, LNCS 10067, pp. 229–237, 2016.
DOI: 10.1007/978-3-319-49145-5_23

respectively. But due to many fields often contain both public and private information, we also face a obvious challenge of the definition of information which is sensitive and should be protected. In other words, the main difficulty of network data lie in the correlation between each independent record.

Several research works have attempted to preserve the information of network data, Tanjila et al. [2] propose a MATLAB-based anonymization tool for network data which can anonymize MAC address, IP address, port number, packet length and timestamp field of *pacp* and *mrt* format packet file. Moreover, Lin et al. [4] designed PCAPLib system to automatically extract and classify application sessions from packet trace, and anonymize application field while preserving several semantic feature. McSherry et al. [5] has attempted to preserve network traces and let other analysts extract statistical information using differential privacy manner. Therefore, to fulfill global requirements for network security and privacy, anonymous systems have been extensively investigated and deployed over the world to provide anonymous communication services for users. However, to my knowledge, few researchers focus on real-time anonymization of network data and conventional anonymization methods are still limited to only a few common protocols.

With the continuous improvement speed of the mobile devices, numerous organizations attempt to maintain large collections of personal information for analysis and research. Mobile communication core network gather all the PS domain packets from base stations of several municipal areas and contains several packet encapsulation structure (e.g., GPRS Tunneling Protocol (GTP) and Generic Routing Encapsulation (GRE)) and point-to-point AHDLC frame structure. Special packet structure determines the complexity of the process, and advanced analysis of the message content (e.g., deep packet inspection and stream reassembly) will consume much capability of processing. Due to the complex structure, conventional method for recognizing and anonymizing user IP address may no longer be utilized in mobile core network.

In this paper, in spired by our previous work [7], we propose a real-time processing system called ANTW for providing packet anonymization on mobile core network. It contains two major components as Fig. 1 shows:

For the first part, we propose a FPGA-based hardware processing component to accomplish the anonymization of MAC address, International Mobile Subscriber Identity (IMSI) number, timestamp and user terminal IP address. While in WCDMA & TD_SCDMA core network, location field is anonymized as well. We employ block black marker, precision degradation, prefix-preserving pseudonymization and truncation algorithm for implementation. Then we rebuild a user-defined packet and forward to the software component for further processing.

For another part, we propose a muti-core NPU-based software component to deal with the packets from CDMA2000 network. We utilize our previous work: *TerIP* method [6] to discover the user terminal IP address, then anonyize it by prefix-preserving pseudonymize algorithm. In addition, software component also deal with the complicated calculation, such as fragment reassembly,

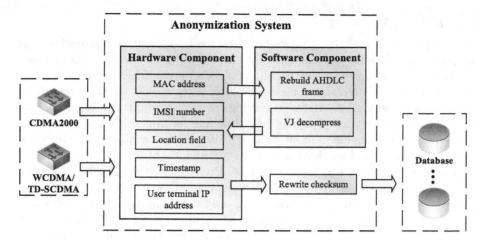

Fig. 1. Overview of anonymization system.

decompression of Van Jacobson compress packet and extract single packet from GRE encapsulation packet [7].

The rest of this paper is organized as follows: Sect. 2 we propose the background and related work of this paper. Section 3 we give a detailed introduction on hardware component and software component. Section 4 addresses the major system implementation and deployment issues. Section 5, the performance of ANTW system is evaluated on real dataset. Finally, Sect. 6 concludes our work.

2   Background

To build a strong, reliable and stable network, service providers and network researchers are attempt to work together through collaboration to discover and solve network problems. Collecting and analyzing network data help us to understand plenty of information as follows:

- *Discovering Internet Topologies:* Numerous researches design better application and routing strategy, develop more and more network protocol, provide shorter response time and maximum throughput with the aid of network topology.
- *Traffic Engineering:* Appropriate traffic collection, modeling and analyzing, can help to discover network user's behavior patterns form network data.
- *Network Security Analysis:* For detecting abnormal attacks, like *DDOS* attack, *www* attack and TCP session hijacking.

For example, a specific host port in combination with other domain information can be pointed out that the distribution of the host may be affected by a virus, and the analysis of the port also can be used for judging whether the user is visiting a illegal website. In addition, the port usage of hosts also can be pointed out that the services it provides.

2.1   Related Work

The problem of anonymizing microdata has received significant attention over the past three decades, and that attention has served to develop several methodologies for providing private and useful microdata to researchers. There are many existing anonymous technique includes block marker, enumeration, partitioning, precision degradation, prefix-preserving pseudonymize, truncation, time unit annihilation, permutation, random time shift and hash algorithm.

In network data, different field have different anonymization technology. Some fields like IP address, have a complex hierarchical ordering structure which require to be preserved after anonymization. Prefix-preserving pseudonymization [8] is the best way to anonymize while preserving privacy of users. Formally, A function A is one-to-one prefix-preserving only if for any two IP address i and j sharing the first m bits, the anonymized result also share the first m prefix. Moreover, for MAC address, we can use reverse truncation, permutation, block black marker and structured pseudonymization [2]. For timestamps, we can employ precision degradation, enumeration, block black marker and random time shift. Specifically, Block Black marker algorithm deletes or replaces with a fixed value. It reduces the usefulness of the anonymized dataset but entirely protects the dataset. Precision degradation [4] always use to anonymize timestamp field in specific case which requires no strict sequencing of flows (e.g., to perform statistical computation on total length of entire flow).

2.2   Characteristic of Mobile Core Network

A mobile telecommunication system consists of two layered networks, namely access and core networks. And core network is classified into circuit and packet core network which is deployed deployed for voice services (e.g., services in the public switched telephone network) and data services (e.g., services in the Internet).

CDMA2000 core network is mainly composed of Packet Control Function (PCF) and Packet Data Serving Node (PDSN). The interfaces between PCF and PDSN call A10 and A11. All data packets through A10 interface will be added generic routing encapsulation (GRE) header and according to the negotiated result of server node, there are Van Jacobson (VJ) compressed packets, Microsoft Point-to-Point Compressed packets and unavoidable fragmented packets. Therefore, it must be decompressed and reassembled each packet to restore the original user data. The logical link between PCF and PDSN is divided into uplink and downlink.

WCDMA&TD-SCDMA core network use the same architecture, mainly composed of Serving GPRS Support Node (SGSN) and Gateway GPRS Support Node (GGSN). Here GPRS technology indicates General Packet Radio Service and interface Gn indicates the transmission channel. The logical link between SGSN and GGSN also is divided into uplink and downlink. All data packets through Gn interface will be added GPRS tunnelling Protocol (GTP) header. Unlike the CDMA2000 standard, packet in WCDMA&TD-SCDMA core network only need to process decapsulation and fragmentation restructuring.

3   Anonymization Method

In this section, we describe our ANTW system which combine two components for processing and anonymizing packets from mobile core network. In hardware component, we operate most of the anonymization algorithm and pre-processing approach for packets. In software component, we take over the business of further packet in-depth treatment, like decompression and locating the user terminal IP address.

3.1   Hardware Component

Due to the high speed of data accumulation, real-time processing costs plenty of storage space if we adopt the way of post-processing. As a consequence, we propose a FPGA-based hardware component to accomplish the aim of real-time anonymization. For details, we employ five different algorithm to handle different packet fields as follows:

First, hardware component provides *permutation* method to anonymize MAC address. Source address sets as a self-define format to help transmitting information of packet content between two components. Destination address sets as the MAC address of back-end database for forwarding through switch equipments. The advantage of this method is that it hides the origin address for anonymization and helps to transmit information of packet between two components.

Second, for anonymizing the International Mobile Subscriber Identity (IMSI) number, *block black marker* is the best approach to completely remove any privacy information about individual users. It replaces with a fixed value which looks like below:

$$460013907601355 \quad \Rightarrow \quad 4600xxxxxxxxxxx \tag{1}$$

Third, we utilize *truncation* method to anonymize the location field. For the requirement of non-location statistic data, we only reserve the *country code* and *network code* field to indicate the country and the mobile service provider. Then for the data which need to be distinguished the areas, we further reserve the location area code (LAC) to indicate the code of the area where user appeared. And the service area code (SAC) will be set zero.

Forth, for anonymization of timestamp, *time precision degradation* algorithm removes the most precise content of a timestamp field. Due to the time unit at a coarser level of granularity, this anonymization approach can prevent network data flows from *insert* attack. However, the anonymized data may not be useful for applications that require strict sequencing of flows.

At last, as Fig. 2 shows, we utilize *Crypto-PAn* algorithm to anonymize user terminal IP address in prefix-preserving way. After receiving the result of user terminal IP address from software component, we run AES-128bit encryption algorithm and XOR encoding algorithm to achieve *Crypto-PAn* anonymization. It is a one-to-one mapping on a set of values generated from a block cipher. This algorithm preserves the structure by preserving the prefixes values.

Fig. 2. Example for perfix-preserving anonymization

3.2 Software Component

In CDMA2000 core network, Packet Control Function (PCF) decapsulates the CDMA air frame and rebuild an AHDLC frame into GRE tunnel. As the length of frame are unlimited, one encapsulated GRE packet may contain several incomplete AHDLC frame and each frame uses hexadecimal format 0x7e as a delimiter. In software component, after receiving the packet from hardware component, we first extract GRE-key to integrated AHDLC frame into a flow table, then determine the follow-up action. When the frame has a header, we decapsulate if it also has a tail. Otherwise we insert this frame into the flow table. After that, we lookup the flow table when the frame lack of header, so we integrated a complete frame. At this time, we begin to extract integral frame and decapsulate. Finally, if there is still remain incomplete AHDLC frame, we add it to the flow table for waiting next packet arrives.

For packet anonymization, we discover user terminal IP address which has already encapsulated in GRE and GTP header. For details, we utilize *TerIP* approach to obtain the IP address of server node (e.g., PDSN in CDMA2000 network) and the transmission direction of each packet, it helps to identify user terminal IP address in encapsulation packet. Then we decapsulate the raw packet to extract user data packet.

For *Van Jacobson* compress packet, software component handles three types of data packets: Type IP, uncompressed packet and compressed packet. The process of decompression is the following:

(a) Check connection number. If the bit which use to identify connection number is set, obtain the connection number directly and verify its existing in the corresponding cache; if not, the connection number is set to the last number received.
(b) We obtain TCP/IP header which store in corresponding cache based on the connection number. According to the parameters carry by compressed header, we modify the TCP/IP header within the current cache.
(c) To calculate a new total length of IP packet, we just add new TCP/IP header length to the original payload length, and then recalculate the checksum field.

4   Implementation

This section details the implementation of the ANTW, which is built on a board consist of FPGA and Muti-core processor.

The hardware pre-processor of ANTW system is implemented using FPGA produced by ALTERA. The Altera Stratix V GX FPGA circuit is used as target device configured with 12 bits LVTTL input ports and a configurable RAM buffer used as the output buffer which is employed to send the information from the circuit to the other components. Compare FPGA with ASIC, it allow a relatively inexpensive development costs, field-programmable which logic can be modified at any time.

The software pre-processor of NTW system is implemented using XLP432 produced by Broadcom company. The XLP432 processor is a third-generation architectural enhancement to NetLogic Microsystems's industry leading XLR multi-core MIPS Processor Family, providing single-chip solutions that scale from a single core to eight cores and every core has 4 threads. Moreover, multi-core NPUs have many hardware improvements on multi-threads operation, which decrease the thread switching overhead, hide the memory access latencies, and employ the memory access cycle efficiently [3].

4.1 Deployment

In this session, we describe our pre-processing system deployment both in 3G and LTE core network.

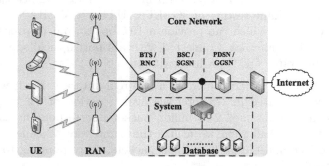

(a) 3G Mobile Network

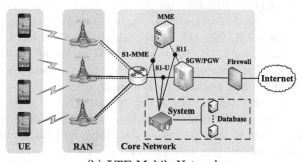

(b) LTE Mobile Network

Fig. 3. Deployment of NTW in 3G & LTE network

3G Mobile Network. In WCDMA&TD-SCDMA packet core network, we deploy our system to collect measurement data through all *Gn* links between SGSNs and GGSNs. From *Gn* interface, we can analyze a large amount of user business data and control signaling such as PDP activate signaling, route update information, location area update information and mobile management information, etc. In CDMA2000 packet core network, we do the same thing through all *A10/A11* links between PCFs and PDSNs. The key components of 3G network and the deployment of pre-processing system are illustrated in Fig. 3(a).

LTE Mobile Network. Compare LTE with 3G, there are many differences both in network architecture and in wireless technology. From network LTE access network flat structure led to the traditional signaling collection points disappeared. LTE network contain only the packet-switched domain and offer a large data transmission rate (over 100 Mbps). The key components of 3G network and the deployment of pre-processing system are illustrated in Fig. 3(b).

5   Experimental Result

Due to the low utilization of real core network, real link can not provide sufficiently large flow for testing. Therefore, in order to launch experiments on very large scale packet flow, we utilize tester to simulate the real mobile core network. *IPRO PowerHawk Analyzer* is a powerful multitechnology, multi-user solution that enables high-volume testing of 3G, LTE, UTRAN, GERAN, CS/PS core and IMS networks [1], which can provide a 10 Gbps output of prepared traffic in a standard SFP+ interface. Connected with a 4-port optical splitter, we can generate an input rate of 40 Gbps in maximum.

Data Collection. We experimented with two real datasets. First, we collected data from servers located in *Gn* interface over a period of 5 h from 11:00am through 4:00pm. We obtained 2.69 billion packets, corresponding to 1.5 TB of TD-SCDMA traffic. And then we utilize the same way to collect data from *A10/A11* interface and obtain 38 million packets, corresponding to 324 GB of CDMA2000 traffic.

For details on our dataset, we first calculate the proportion of each packet length of entire dataset. In Fig. 4(a), we observe that 0–63 byte length of packet accounted for 25.2 %, 64–127 bytes packet accounted for 20.8 %, 128–255 bytes packet accounted for 6.7 %, 256–511 bytes packet accounted for 7.4 %, 512–1023 bytes packet accounted for 3.7 %, 1024–1518 bytes packet accounted for 36.2 %. In general, we observe that almost 46 % of packet length lower than 128 byte. It indicates the distribution of packet length in real link.

Then we run our dataset on typical server and ANTW system to compare their performance. Figure 4(b) illustrates when incoming packet rate is increasing, typical server starts to drop packet at 450 Mbps, and packet loss rate get to 65 % when incoming packet rate reach to 1 Gbps. Then, due to a large amount of packets have been processing in hardware component, ANTW system has no packet leakage even the incoming packet rate reach to 10 Gbps. This means our NTW system has met the processing requirement of the mobile core network.

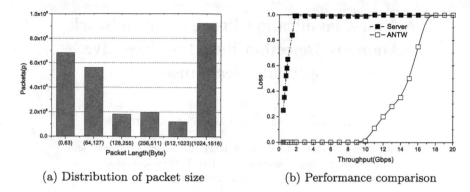

(a) Distribution of packet size   (b) Performance comparison

Fig. 4. Performance evaluation of ANTW

6 Conclusion

In this paper, we consider the problem of real-time processing of mobile core network while satisfying user privacy preserving. Then we have proposed a novel anonymization system called ANTW consisting of two components. Hardware component apply to anonymize packet fields and accelerate the packet processing. Software component use to deal with the complicated calculation. Evaluation results show that ANTW can achieve 10 Gbps.

References

1. Portable ipro. http://www.exfo.com
2. Farah, T., Trajković, L.: Anonym: a tool for anonymization of the internet traffic. In: 2013 IEEE International Conference on Cybernetics (CYBCONF), pp. 261–266. IEEE (2013)
3. Jacobson, V.: xlp400 series. http://www.broadcom.com/products/Processors
4. Lin, Y.D., Lin, P.C., Wang, S.H., Chen, I.W., Lai, Y.C.: Pcaplib: a system of extracting, classifying, and anonymizing real packet traces (2014)
5. McSherry, F., Mahajan, R.: Differentially-private network trace analysis. In: ACM SIGCOMM Computer Communication Review, vol. 40, pp. 123–134. ACM (2010)
6. Mian, C., Baokang, Z., Jinshu, S.: Terip: a data distribution approach for mobile core network intrusion detection. In: The Fifth CCF Internet Confernece of China (CCF ICOC) (2016)
7. Mian, C., Yipin, S., Jinshu, S.: A real-time pre-processing system for mobile core network measurement. In: The Sixth International Conference on Instrumentation, Measurement, Computer, Communication and Control (IMCCC) (2016)
8. Xu, J., Fan, J., Ammar, M.H., Moon, S.B.: Prefix-preserving ip address anonymization: measurement-based security evaluation and a new cryptography-based scheme. In: Proceedings of the 10th IEEE International Conference on Network Protocols, pp. 280–289. IEEE (2002)

A New Classification Process for Network Anomaly Detection Based on Negative Selection Mechanism

Naila Belhadj-Aissa[✉] and Mohamed Guerroumi

Faculty of Electronic and Computer Science, University of Science and
Technology Houari Boumediene, 16111 Algiers, Algeria
nbelhadj@usthb.dz, guerroumi@gmail.com

Abstract. Attacks on computer networks have become a major threat due to
the extensive use of internet in daily life. These attacks lead, mostly in huge
financial losses and massive sensitive data leaks. Intrusion Detection Systems
(IDS) are one of the security tools widely deployed in network architectures in
order to monitor, to detect and eventually respond to any suspicious activity in
the network. We propose in this paper a new approach for Network Anomaly
Detection based on Negative Selection process (NADNS). The Negative
Selection (NS) process in the biological point of view is the principle of dis-
criminating between self-cells and non-self-cells which is highly consistent with
the classification problem (normal/anomaly) in intrusion detection. Based on a
reduced dataset with a filter-based feature selection technique, NADNS generates a set of detectors (Antibodies) and uses them to classify events (instances)
as anomaly or normal. The accuracy of NADNS is tested with two intrusion
detection datasets: NSL-KDD and Kyoto2006+. The comparative results with
another Immune System-based algorithm namely CLONALG show that
NADNS outperform CLONALG regarding the detection rate, the False Positive
rate and f-measure.

Keywords: Network Intrusion Detection System · Feature selection · Artificial
immune system (AIS) · Negative selection · NSL-KD · Kyoto 2006+

1 Introduction

In recent years, intrusions, attacks or anomalies in network infrastructures have become
one of the major cause of great losses. A countless number of mechanisms are used to
minimize, to detect and counter these security issues. Anomaly detection is one of the
techniques proposed to ensure the integrity and the confidentiality of data. In general,
the problem of anomaly detection can be seen as a normal/anomaly classification
problem. Several modern techniques exist in the literature addressing this issue using
Neural Network, Bayesian Network, Support Vector Machine, Fuzzy Logic, Decision
Tree, Genetic Programming, Artificial Immune Systems (AIS) [1], ….

The Biological Immune System (BIS) has several properties such as robustness,
error tolerance, decentralization, recognition of foreigners, adaptive learning, memory,
and so on. These properties make the BIS a very complex and promising source of

© Springer International Publishing AG 2016
G. Wang et al. (Eds.): SpaCCS 2016 Workshops, LNCS 10067, pp. 238–248, 2016.
DOI: 10.1007/978-3-319-49145-5_24

inspiration for several domains. AIS, the field that tries to mimic the complex mechanisms of the BIS, has caught the interest of researchers since the early 1990's to solve complex engineering problems. Theories and algorithms were proposed and exploited for pattern recognition, data mining, optimization, machine learning, and anomaly detection. Indeed, anomaly detection approach [2] in network security relies on building normal models and discovering variation/deviation from this model in the observed data. This process is strongly similar to the main objective of the BIS, which is the protection of the human body from any harm including foreign invaders. For this purpose, models of immune cells network, clonal selection, and negative selection were proposed imitating the different mechanisms of BIS for classification and anomaly detection [3].

In this paper, we propose a new approach for Network Anomaly Detection based on Negative Selection process (NADNS). It is composed of three phases. In the first phase, the data space is reduced using feature selection algorithms. During the second phase, antibodies/detectors are randomly chosen from the training data, which contains self and non-self-instances. At this stage, we introduced a dispersion threshold regarding each feature in order to validate the detectors. The last phase corresponds to the classification process that relies on the detectors generated and their radius. If an observed data or an antigen activates a detector, it is classified as anomaly. However, if it fails to activate all the antibodies, the antigen is first matched to an Artificial HLA (human leukocyte antigen) before it is classified as normal. This last verification aims to detect new unknown attacks.

The remainder of this paper is organized as follows: in Sect. 2 we review some related work regarding AIS and IDS. Section 3 details our proposed approach. We present and discuss some results in Sect. 4 and we briefly conclude our work in Sect. 5.

2   AIS in Intrusion Detection

The ability of the human body to automatically distinguish between self-cells and non-self cells in order to protect himself from harmful pathogens is highly consistent with the concept of intrusion detection. Thus our interest in further investigate the application of such mechanisms in anomaly-based intrusion detection systems especially with more recent network patterns and up to date type of attacks.

One of the first application of AIS in intrusion detection was introduced by Forrest and her team in 1994 [4]. They proposed a self/non-self discrimination algorithm with two phases: (i) generation of a binary set of strings detectors (non-self). (ii) monitoring of the protected data by comparing them to the detectors. Later on, they designed an artificial immune system (ARTIS) framework [5], and applied it to network intrusion detection domain by implementing ARTIS into LISYS (Lightweight Intrusion detection SYStem). An Immune-Based Network Intrusion Detection System (AINIDS) was proposed in [6]. It is a set of multiple components, which the key component is an *antibody generation and antigen detection* component. This includes the generation of passive immune antibodies to detect known attacks and automatic immune antibodies that integrate statistic method with fuzzy reasoning system to detect novel attacks. L. Zhang et al. [7] proposed an integrated intrusion detection model based on artificial immunity (IIDAI) and a vaccination strategy. They also proposed a method to generate initial memory antibodies with Rough Set. IIDAI integrates misuse detection model as well as anomaly detection model. Authors in [8], presented a real-time anomaly detection system based on a probabilistic artificial immune algorithm. A first version named SPAI (Simple Probabilistic Artificial Immune method) used the probability density function as self-detectors. Then, they proposed a second version, namely CPAI (Clustered Probabilistic Artificial Immune algorithm) where normal profile was clustered into sub groups. These subgroups were given priority values in a third version of the proposed algorithm in order to reduce the response time. On the other hand, T. F. Ghanem et al. [9] presented a hybrid approach for anomaly detection using detectors generated based on multi-start metaheuristic method and genetic algorithms. Detectors were generated using normal and anomaly records from NSL-KDD training data. Authors in [10] applied Rough Set Theory to gure-Kddcup6percent dataset in order to eliminate irrelevant and redundant features. Then, they tested r-chunk and negative selection algorithm on the six resulted features. Most of the above-related work used a binary representation of data flow without fully explaining the conversion process from raw data connections or featured connections into binary strings and the computational cost of such operation. Besides, most of them tested their work using only kddcup99 dataset which was, for the past two decades, the benchmark for the evaluation of IDS and the only labeled dataset publicly available even though it is largely outdated.

In this paper, we detail the full process of our approach from the feature selection phase with a multi-type representation (real, nominal), through detectors generation to the decision rules and the classification phase. We also present the results of our evaluation on nsl-kdd dataset as well as Kyoto2006+ dataset.

3   Proposed Solution

We propose in this work a new approach for Network Anomaly Detection based on Negative Selection (NADNS). It has three main components shown in Fig. 1 and further detailed in this section.

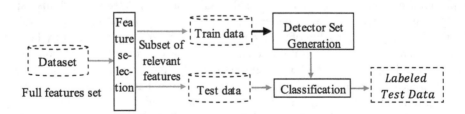

Fig. 1. Block diagram of NADNS

3.1   Feature Selection

Feature selection (FS) is an important data processing phase used to reduce the number of features and remove irrelevant, redundant and noisy data with respect to the description of the problem at hand. This reduction aims to enhance the data processing performance and reduce the computational complexity. FS methods can be globally divided into two classes, based on how they combine the selection algorithm and the learning method used to infer a model [11]. *(i) Filters* are a preprocessing step and are based on performance evaluation metric calculated from general characteristics of the training data. They are known for their low computational cost and their good generalization ability. *(ii) Wrappers* use the feedback of a classification algorithm to evaluate the quality of feature subsets that are created using some search strategy. They can detect the possible interactions between features but have a significant computation time, especially when the number of features is large. Techniques that fall in these approaches have been widely used in intrusion detection domain in order to fulfill the real time constraints and improve the IDS's response time, but almost all of the published results were using DARPA98 [12] or KddCup99 dataset [13, 14]. To the best of our knowledge, the work of M. Najafabadi et al. [15] is the only one that evaluates feature selection method for Network IDS with Kyoto dataset, However, the authors did not explicitly present their results of the best feature subset of Kyoto dataset.

In our work, filter-based FS algorithm is applied as provided by the Java-based open source data-mining software Weka (Waikato Environment for Knowledge Analysis) [16] on Kyoto2006+ dataset. The results are presented in Sect. 4.2 of this paper. A more detailed study is underway for an upcoming extension of this paper.

3.2 Detector Set Generation

In this phase, NADNS uses as input a training data containing normal instances, that represent the self set, and its output is a set of Antibodies that do not match any self data. Our matching function is based on the radius of normal data :

Let $T \in \mathcal{R}^p$ be the training data featured by p attributes. $S \subset T$ is a set of normal instances and r_{self} its radius. $D \in \mathcal{R}^p$ is a set of Non-Self detectors where $D \not\subset S$.

The Self radius $r_{self} = \{r_1, r_2, \ldots, r_p\}$ is the threshold beyond which an instance $X_{inst} = \{x_1, x_2, \ldots, x_p\}$ randomly picked from T is considered as a detector and $r_i = 2\sigma_{i_{self}}$ where $\sigma_{i_{self}}$ is the standard deviation of the attribute i in normal data.

An instance X_{inst} is added to the detector set D if the distance between this instance and all normal records is greater than r_{self} regarding each and all the attributes.

Moreover, we assigned to each detector $d = \{d_1, d_2, \ldots, d_p\}$ a radius $rd = \{rd_1, rd_2, \ldots, rd_p\}$ used to test its activation in the classification phase. Each element of rd is calculated as follow:

$$rd_i = \left(d_i - \mu_{self_i}\right) - \frac{\sigma_{i_{self}}}{2}, \ i = 1 \ldots p \tag{1}$$

Where μ_{self} and σ_{self} are a p dimensional vectors that represent, respectively, mean value and standard deviation of each attributes in normal data. The algorithm below details the process.

Algorithm . Detector set generation
Input: *Training_data*, **Output:** Set of non-self detectors D
Begin
$nbr\_detectors = 1\% \, Training\_data$ size; nbr_d = 0;
Compute self-radius $r_{self} = \left\{2\,\sigma_{1_{self}}, 2\,\sigma_{2_{self}}, ..., 2\,\sigma_{p_{self}}\right\}$
While (nbr_d < nbr_detectors)**do**{
  Randomly pick a candidate detector X from Training_data;
  For each *Inst* in self data **do** {
   $dist = \{x_1 - Inst_1, x_2 - Inst_2, ..., x_p - Inst_p\}$
   if $(dist_{\{i...p\}} < r_{self_{\{1...p\}}})$ **then** break; //X is a self}**endforeach**
    if(reached the last self data) **then** {
      Compute detector radius (Eq.1)
      add X to D;
      nbr_d ++;}**endif** }**endwhile**
End.

3.3 Classification

The classification phase is based on the antibodies (detectors) and their radius. For an antigen a (an instance from test data) to be detected by the detector d_i, the distance between d_i and a should be at most rd_i regarding each attribute.

In other words, for an instance a to be classified as anomaly, the inequality 2 should be satisfied for at least one detector in D.

$$(a_i - d_i) \leq rd_i, \; i = 1...p \tag{2}$$

If none of the detectors in D has been activated, the antigen a is compared to an Artificial HLA (A-HLA) analogously to the HLA (Human Leukocyte Antigen) complex of humans which are proteins in the outer part of all body cells that are unique to every person and which the human immune system uses to differentiate self cells from invaders. Indeed, we introduced the A-HLA verification in order to detect new attacks that could not activate the detectors. We identify the A-HLA as the tuple $\{\mu_{self}, r_{self}\}$ where : μ_{self} is the mean of self/normal instances and r_{self} is the radius.

In this case, for an antigen a to be classified as normal, it should: (i) not activate any detector in D and (ii) satisfy the inequality (3) regarding the A-HLA

$$(a_i - \mu_{self_i}) \leq r_{self_i}, \; i = 1...p \tag{3}$$

We present, in Sect. 4.2, the different results achieved with and without the A-HLA verification for nsl-kdd data as it contains attacks such R2L and U2R which are the most difficult to detect. The following algorithm details the classification process.

```
Algorithm . classification
Input: D, test_data, train_data, Output:labeled test_data
Begin
```
Compute $r_{self} = \{2\,\sigma_{1_{self}}, 2\,\sigma_{2_{self}}, ..., 2\,\sigma_{p_{self}}\}$

Compute $\mu_{self} = \{\mu_{self_1}, \mu_{self_2} ..., \mu_{self_p}\}$

```
for each Inst in test_data do{
   for each detector d in D do{
```
$dist = \{d_1 - Inst_1, d_2 - Inst_2, ..., d_p - Inst_p\}$

$\textbf{if}\,(dist_{\{i...p\}} < r_{d_{\{1...p\}}})\,\textbf{then}$ classify *Inst* as **anomaly**;
```
   break;}endforeachd
   // Inst is not in any detector's radius, check A-HLA
```
$\textbf{if}\,(\,(a_i - \mu_{self_i}) \le r_{self_i})\,\textbf{then}$ //for each attribute (1...p)
```
   Classify Inst as normal
   else classify Inst as anomaly}endforeachins
End.
```

4 Experimental Results

4.1 Dataset

Due to lack of labeled and publically available datasets to evaluate IDS, we used in this paper two well-known benchmarks: nsl-kdd, and a more recent dataset Kyoto+2006.

Nsl-kdd. It is the refined version of KDDcup99 dataset known for some deficiencies. It has some advantages over the original KDD data set such as the absence of redundant records and the availability of a sufficient number of records in the train and test data sets so the experiments are affordable on the complete set.

The dataset contains a large volume of network TCP connections, the results of 5 weeks of capture in the Air force network. Each connection consists of 41 attributes plus a label of either normal or a type of attack. Simulated attacks are grouped into four classes [17]: *(1) DOS (Denial Of Service)* are attacks that aim to making a service or a resource unavailable. *(2) U2R (User to Root)* where a simple user tries to exploit a vulnerability in order to obtain a root privileges. *(3) R2L (Remote to Local)* where attacker attempts to gain access (account) locally on a machine accessible via the network and *(4) PROBE,* which represents any attempt to collect information about the network, the users or the security policy in order to outsmart it.

NSL-KDD is actually available in the form of four datasets, *(1) NSL-KDD Train+* which is the complete train set. It contains up to 125973 records. *(2) NSL-KDD Train20%* is a compact training set usually used by researchers in order to reduce the computational cost. *(3) NSL-KDD Test+* is the labeled test set with the explicit type of attacks and a difficulty level. *(4) NSL-KDD Test-21* is a test set without records of difficulty level 21.

Kyoto 2006+. Dataset is a collection of over 2.5 years of real traffic data (Nov. 2006 ~ Aug. 2009). Gathered in Kyoto University for evaluating IDSs using a much recent dataset than kdd99, which was for a long time, the only publically available labeled dataset. Kyoto dataset was collected from/to 348 honeypots (Windows XP, Windows Server, Solaris...) deployed inside and outside of Kyoto University. All traffic was thoroughly inspected using three security software SNS7160 IDS, Clam AntiVirus, Ashula and since Apr. 2010, snort was added.

Connections are featured by 24 attributes; among which, the first 14's were extracted based on KDD dataset and the remaining 10 attributes were added to further analyze and evaluate network IDSs. A detailed analysis can be found in [18]. The dataset is available as text files[1] representing the daily traffic labeled as "normal" or "attack".

4.2   Evaluation and Discussion

Feature selection and normalization.

NSL-KDD. As stated before, a great number of feature selection techniques have been studied with nsl-kdd dataset. Based on the results presented in [13], the set of features we used in our experiments is : {1, 6, 12, 15, 16, 17, 18, 19, 31, 32, 37}. Furthermore, we noticed the huge difference in scale between attributes' values in the training data. This usually leads to biased results. To overcome this problem, we normalized the numeric attributes using Eq. 4.

$$x^p_{norm} = \left(\frac{x^p - min^p}{max^p - min^p} \right) \tag{4}$$

Where: x^p is the pth attribute's value in the instance x. max^p and min^p correspond, respectively, to maximum and minimum value of the Pth attribute in the dataset.

Kyoto2006+. Before applying feature selection techniques on Kyoto2006+ dataset, we excluded some features that, we believe, are irrelevant for the classification phase. We excluded the features related to security analysis so that our method can be generalized to other networks that might not have such software in their architecture. We also excluded the source and the destination IP addresses so that the method is independent from these particular addresses. We used the open source tool Weka to perform feature selection for Kyoto2006+ dataset. In Weka, two objects have to be set; an *attribute evaluator* and a *search method*. The first is used to assign a weight to each subset of features, while the latter determine the search method used to form features' subsets. In this work, Correlation-based Feature Subset Selection (CFS) was used as the attribute evaluator with *Rank Search* as the search method. The resulting set selected to perform our experiments is: {2, 3, 4, 5, 6, 8, 12, 13, 14, 16}.

---

[1] http://www.takakura.com/Kyoto_data/data/.

Input parameters.

Input parameters of NADNS are the number of detectors, which was set to 1 % of training-data size and the training data itself. We considered the 2009's Kyoto data for our work and took the first of each month, cumulatively, as the training set. It means that to test on January records, Jan. the 1st is set as the training input and to test on March records, 1st Jan., 1st Feb., and 1st March are set as input training data.

Moreover, we compared our approach against CLONALG algorithm presented by N. de Castro et al. and implemented in Weka[2]. It is a supervised, clonal selection based algorithm. Its input parameters are AntibodyPoolSize = 30, ClonalFactor = 0.1, numGeneration = 10 and SelectionPoolSize = 20. Details on the algorithm and its parameters can be found in [19]. All experiments were performed using Windows® 8– 64 bit platform with core i7 processor and 8 GB RAM. The distributions of test subsets of both nsl-kdd and Kyoto data are given in Tables 1 and 2 respectively.

Results.

The metrics usually used to evaluate the accuracy of intrusion detection techniques are True Positive Rate $(TPR = TP/TP + FN)$ and False Positive rate $(FPR = FP/FP + TN)$ where TP are anomalies successfully detected, TN are normal events successfully identified as such, FP are normal events wrongly identified as anomalies and FN are anomalies missed by the IDS and misclassified as normal. F-measure is another metric for test's accuracy. $F - measure = 2 * TP/(2 * TP) + FP + FN$. Due to the big difference in scale between NADNS results and those of CLONALG, we plotted them separately. Indeed the results of our approach applied on Nsl-kdd without and with A-HLA verification are given in Figs. 2 and 3 respectively. Figures 4 and 5 show a detailed detection results regarding each class of attack. Where Fig. 6 shows the results of CLONALG on the same dataset. As can be seen, both versions of NADNS

Table 1. NSL-KDD test subsets

Description	# normal	# attack	All
10 %F.nsl-kdd	7799	7052	14851
20 %F.nsl-kdd	15477	14226	29703
30 %F.nsl-kdd	23221	21334	44555
40 %F.nsl-kdd	30909	28497	59406
50 %F.nsl-kdd	38586	35672	74258
60 %F.nsl-kdd	46312	42798	89110
70 %F.nsl-kdd	54055	49906	103961
80 %F.nsl-kdd	61880	56933	118813
90 %F.nsl-kdd	69585	64080	133665
F.nsl-kdd[*]	77054	71463	148517

[*]Full NSL-KDD dataset.

Table 2. Kyoto test subsets

Description	#normal	#attack	All
20090103	65338	43815	109153
20090112	64255	37781	102036
20090206	78353	47841	126194
20090215	80082	45373	125455
20090302	77925	48014	125939
20090325	79296	46510	46510
20090403	81366	44338	125704
20090425	56375	68356	124731
20090508	74728	50160	124888
20090530	73341	51351	124692

---

[2] http://wekaclassalgos.sourceforge.net/.

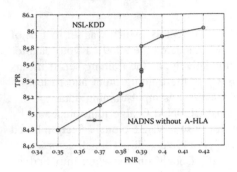

Fig. 2. NADNS without A-HLA on nsl-kdd

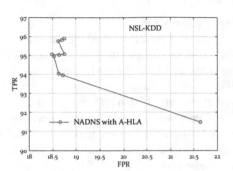

Fig. 3. NADNS with A-HLA on nsl-kdd

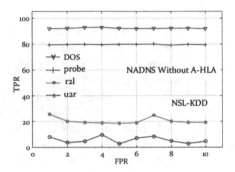

Fig. 4. Attacks detected without A-HLA

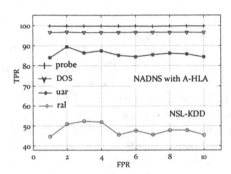

Fig. 5. Attacks detected with A-HLA

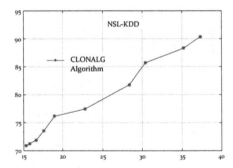

Fig. 6. CLONALG algorithm on nsl-kdd

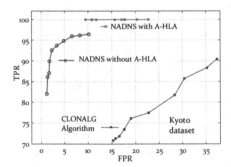

Fig. 7. NADNS and CLONALG on kyoto

outperform CLONALG algorithm in terms of TPR as well as FPR. Especially the version with A-HLA verification where the detection rate is up to 96 % with 18 % of false positives. Which means that new attacks were detected in the second stage. The results obtained on Kyoto dataset for both NADNS and CLONALG are shown in Fig. 7 NADNS still gives better results than CLONALG algorithm especially when

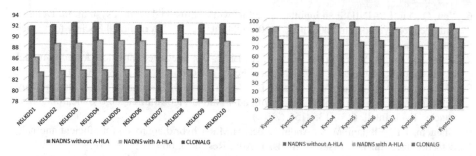

Fig. 8. F-measure with NSL-KDD dataset   **Fig. 9.** F-measure with Kyoto dataset

A-HLA verification is applied. Figures 8 and 9 show the f-measure of both algorithms applied on the considered datasets.

5   Conclusion and Future Work

In this paper, an AIS based approach was presented for data classification in Anomaly detection. The approach is inspired from the Negative Selection process which has for main purpose, the distinction between self cells and non-self cells. NADNS has three phases; a feature selection phase where the most relevant features are identified and selected. Detectors/antibodies generation phase in which instances from the non-self space are randomly picked and validated against normal data regarding a dispersion threshold of each attribute. The classification is achieved using the radius of the created detectors and an Artificial HLA which we defined as the tuple (mean normal data, radius self data). The accuracy of the approach was evaluated using both nsl-kdd and Kyoto2006+ datasets and compared to another AIS-based algorithm namely CLO-NALG. The experimental results showed a promising DR and relatively low FPR. However, we intend to further enhance this approach in the first phase using more challenging datasets as well as in the detection phase regarding the number of detectors.

References

1. Bhuyan, M., Bhattacharyya, D., Kalita, J.: Network anomaly detection: methods, systems and tools. IEEE Commun. Surv. Tutorials **16**(1), 1–34 (2014)
2. Liao, H.J., Lin, C.H.R., Lin, Y.C., Tung, K.Y.: Intrusion detection system: a comprehensive review. J. Netw. Comput. Appl. **36**(1), 16–24 (2013)
3. Al-Enezi, J., Abbod, M., Alsharhan, S.: Artificial Immune Systems-models, algorithms and applications (2010)
4. Forrest, S., Perelson, A.S., Allen, L., Cherukuri, R.: Self-nonself discrimination in a computer. In: IEEE Symposium on Security and Privacy, pp. 202–212 (1994)
5. Hofmeyr, S.A., Forrest, S.: Architecture for an artificial immune system. Evol. Comput. **8**(4), 443–473 (2000)

6. Yan, Q., Yu, J.: AINIDS: an immune-based network intrusion detection system. In: Defense and Security Symposium 2006, pp. 62410U-62410U-62419. International Society for Optics and Photonics (2006)

7. Zhang, L., Bai, Z.-Y., Lu, Y.-L., Zha, Y.-X., Li, Z.-W.: Integrated intrusion detection model based on artificial immune. J. China Univ. Posts Telecommun. 21(2), 83–90 (2014)

8. Mohammadi, M., Akbari, A., Raahemi, B., Nassersharif, B., Asgharian, H.: A fast anomaly detection system using probabilistic artificial immune algorithm capable of learning new attacks. Evol. Intell. 6(3), 135–156 (2014)

9. Ghanem, T.F., Elkilani, W.S., Abdul-Kader, H.M.: A hybrid approach for efficient anomaly detection using metaheuristic methods. J. Adv. Res. 6(4), 609–619 (2015)

10. Abas, E., Abdelkader, H., Keshk, A.: Artificial immune system based intrusion detection. In: 2015 IEEE Seventh International Conference on Intelligent Computing and Information Systems (ICICIS), pp. 542–546. IEEE (2015)

11. Boln-Canedo, V., Snchez-Maroo, N., Alonso-Betanzos, A.: Feature Selection for High-Dimensional Data. Springer, Switzerland (2016)

12. Hofmann, A., Horeis, T., Sick, B.: Feature selection for intrusion detection: an evolutionary wrapper approach. In: Proceedings of the 2004 IEEE International Joint Conference on Neural Networks, pp. 1563–1568. IEEE (2004)

13. Kayacik, H.G., Zincir-Heywood, A.N., Heywood, M.I.: Selecting features for intrusion detection: a feature relevance analysis on KDD 99 intrusion detection datasets. In: Proceedings of the Third Annual Conference on Privacy, Security and Trust (2005)

14. Olusola, A.A., Oladele, A.S., Abosede, D.O.: Analysis of KDD 1999 intrusion detection dataset for selection of relevance features. In: Proceedings of the World Congress on Engineering and Computer Science, pp. 20–22 (2010)

15. Najafabadi, M.M., Khoshgoftaar, T.M., Seliya, N.: Evaluating feature selection methods for network intrusion detection with kyoto data. Int. J. Reliab. Qual. Saf. Eng. 23(01), 1650001 (2016)

16. Hall, M., Frank, E., Holmes, G., Pfahringer, B., Reutemann, P., Witten, I.H.: The WEKA data mining software: an update. ACM SIGKDD Explor. Newsl. 11(1), 10–18 (2009)

17. Revathi, S., Malathi, A.: A detailed analysis on NSL-KDD dataset using various machine learning techniques for intrusion detection. Int. J. Eng. Res. Technol. 2(12), 1848–1853 (2013)

18. Song, J., Takakura, H., Okabe, Y., Eto, M., Inoue, D., Nakao, K.: Statistical analysis of honeypot data and building of Kyoto 2006+ dataset for NIDS evaluation. In: Proceedings of the First Workshop on Building Analysis Datasets and Gathering Experience Returns for Security, pp. 29–36. ACM (2011)

19. De Castro, L.N., Von Zuben, F.J.: Learning and optimization using the clonal selection principle. IEEE Trans. Evol. Comput. 6(3), 239–251 (2002)

Integrated Heterogeneous Infrastructure for Indoor Positioning

Yi-Wei Ma[1(✉)], Jiann-Liang Chen[2], Yao-Hong Tsai[3],
Pen-Chan Chou[2], Shyue-Kung Lu[2], and Sy-Yen Kuo[4]

[1] China Institute of FTZ Supply Chain,
Shanghai Maritime University, Shanghai 201306, China
yiweimaa@gmail.com
[2] Department of Electrical Engineering,
National Taiwan University of Science and Technology,
Taipei 106, Taiwan
[3] Department of Information Management,
Hsuan Chuang University, Hsinchu 300, Taiwan
[4] Department of Electrical Engineering,
National Taiwan University, Taipei 106, Taiwan

Abstract. This work proposes a novel Integrated Heterogeneous Infrastructure for Indoor Positioning (IHIIP) with a low-energy Bluetooth beacon to obtain positioning data. This study defines the fuzzy area of subspace selection to improve the indoor positioning accuracy. This study proposed a novel threshold mechanisms are used to select the signal transmitter for positioning and thus improve current positioning accuracy of indoor environment. The IHIIP outperforms both Wi-Fi Access Point (AP) and Beacon in that it provides greater positioning accuracy. Experimental results demonstrate that the mean error distance is 1.29 m only using Wi-Fi AP, 1.33 m only using Beacon and 1.21 m in the proposed IHIIP for indoor positioning.

Keywords: Indoor positioning · Bluetooth 4.0 low energy · Beacon · Received Signal Strength Indication (RSSI) · Multilateration · Fingerprinting · K-Nearest Neighbors (KNN)

1 Introduction

Most indoor positioning systems use only a signal transmitter (Wi-Fi) and a receiver to acquire reference point data. They then use the K-Nearest Neighbor (KNN) algorithm or a Multilateration algorithm for positioning. Therefore, positioning accuracy is limited by both the positioning algorithm and the use of a single source for the acquisition of reference point data [1–14].

The remainder of the paper is organized as follows. Section 2 introduces the proposed integrated heterogeneous infrastructure for indoor positioning. Its implementation and performance are analyzed in Sect. 3. Finally, conclusions are given in Sect. 4.

© Springer International Publishing AG 2016
G. Wang et al. (Eds.): SpaCCS 2016 Workshops, LNCS 10067, pp. 249–256, 2016.
DOI: 10.1007/978-3-319-49145-5_25

2   IHNIPS Architecture Overview

In this work, transmitters of two type of infrastructure are used for indoor positioning. This work proposes the IHIIP, which uses signals from the aforementioned two types of transmitter to improve indoor positioning accuracy. IHIIP is equipped with a target device, Access Point (AP), Beacon and a manager server, as shown in Fig. 1, which are described below.

- Target device: The target device is a handheld device such as a mobile phone or tablet on which is installed a receiving module and an association module. The receiving module receives the RSSI from AP or Beacon and then passes it to the manager server through association module.
- AP: On this device is installed a transmitter module, which can transmit an RSSI signal through Wi-Fi signal.
- Beacon: On this device is installed a transmitter module and an association module; the transmitting module transmits the RSSI through Bluetooth signal and the receiving module receives commands from the manager server.
- Manager Server: On this device is installed a database, a positioning module, a collection module and an association module. In the offline phase, the association module saves the RSSI to the database via the collection module. In the online phase, the positioning module reserves the RSSI. Then, the positioning module uses the reserved data and the positioning information in the database to calculate the location of the target, sending the result to the target device via the association module. The IHIIP has two phases of operation the offline phase and the online phase.

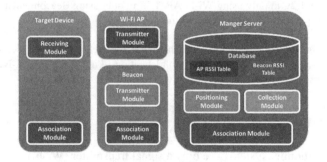

Fig. 1. IHNIPS architecture

2.1   Offline Phase

In the offline phase, target device collects three kinds of information. Firstly, the target device collects all reference points in the experimental environment, the $RSSI_{ARP}$ from each AP, and the $RSSI_{BRP}$ from each Bluetooth beacon at each reference point. Then, the collection module in the manager server saves a data to the database as positioning reference values. In the offline phase, the collection module calculates the threshold value of every single AP'. Then, the collection module in the manager server saves the data as a positioning reference value to the database.

2.1.1   AP's RSSI Threshold Mechanism

This work proposes a threshold selection mechanism for choosing a transmitter among Wi-Fi or Beacon device for indoor positioning. In the offline phase of the mechanism, the collection module in the manager server calculates the threshold value for use in the online phase.

2.2   Online Phase

In the online phase, two-tier positioning is used for indoor positioning. First, the target device receives the RSSI from AP. Next, the positioning module in the manager server compares the RSSI of the APs that were received by the target device with the threshold value in the database. If the received RSSIs of APs more than 75 % is greater than or equal to the threshold value, then AP is used for positioning. If not, then the mechanism proceeds to the second step in which Beacon is used for positioning. Before the RSSI is received from Beacon, the positioning module must know which subspace to use for positioning. It therefore uses the AP's positioning result to select the subspace. The positioning module awakes Beacon in the chosen subspace, and the target device then receives the Beacon's RSSI find the position of user location. Beacon is used for positioning.

2.2.1   Subspace Selection Method

Beacon was added to strengthen for positioning. However, the coverage of Beacon's signal is smaller than that of AP to a degree that depends on the transmission power. Therefore, more beacons than APs must be deployed in a given area, which is divided into subspaces. This integrated heterogeneous infrastructure scenario includes four subspaces and nine beacons. One subspace has four beacons. Each subspace has two overlapping beacons. The positioning module must identify the subspace in which Beacon must be awoken for positioning.

First, the subspace in which the target is located, so AP's positioning result is used as the location of the target device. AP's uses the Multilateration or Fingerprint position method. Next, AP's positioning result (X, Y) is used to select a subspace. However, since many points are at the edge of a subspace, positioning commonly misjudges location. To solve this problem, a subspace area that is often misidentified is defined as a Fuzzy Area. The Fuzzy Area is easy to find when only Beacon is used to position target location.

2.2.2   Fuzzy Area

The preceding section described the selection of a subspace for select positioning method. This section defines a Fuzzy Area in each edge in two subspaces is misidentified zone in only using Beacon's for positioning. The deep color zone in Fig. 2 represents a frequently misidentified subspace. Then integrate AP's signal coverage, the fuzzy area is eliminated, as shown in Fig. 3.

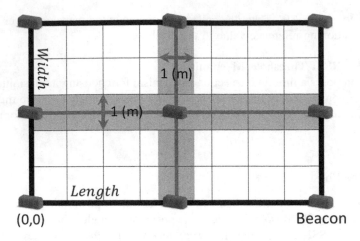

Fig. 2. Fuzzy area with beacon positioning

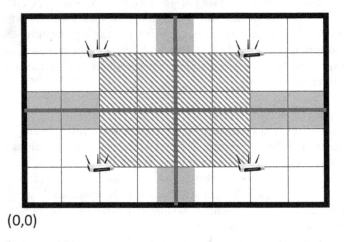

Fig. 3. Fuzzy area with AP's signal coverage

Subtracting the deep color zone from the AP's signal coverage yields the final fuzzy area, as shown in Fig. 4.

2.3 Positioning Mechanisms

This section introduces the positioning module in the IHNIPS, and describes how to find the location (X, Y) of the target. Two basic positioning methods, Fingerprint with KNN and Multilateration are used. The positioning efficiency is analyzed in seven cases. This section assumes four APs, nine beacons, 54 reference points and four subspaces.

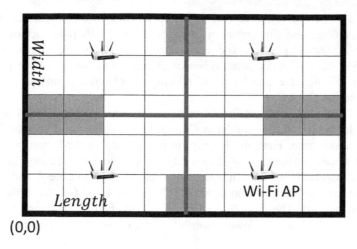

Fig. 4. Fuzzy area

- Case 1: Use APs to Position with Multilateration Method. In case 1, APs is used for positioning, and Multilateration is the positioning method. First, the weakest RSSI of the four APs is truncated. The three remaining APs are used for positioning. Finally, the Multilateration equation is used with the coordinates of three APs to find location (X, Y).
- Case 2: Use APs to Position with Fingerprint Method. In case 2, APs is used for positioning, and Fingerprint with KNN is the as positioning method. The received a_i is RSSI from target device to AP, b_i is RSSI from reference point to AP. Then, 54 values of d are obtained. Finally, the coordinates of all chosen reference points are averaged to yields the location (X, Y) of target device.
- Case 3: Combine Case 1 and Case 2. In case 3, combines positioning method of cases 1 and case 2 and adds a subspace selection method. First, as in case 1, the Triangulation method is used to obtain location (a, b). Then, the subspace that contains location (a, b) is the chosen subspace. Next, as in case 2, the Fingerprint with KNN method is used to choose k reference points. But the kth reference point must be in the chosen subspace. Otherwise, it is dropped and the $k + 1^{th}$ reference point is chosen. Finally, the coordinates of all chosen reference points are averaged to yield location (X, Y).
- Case 4: Use Beacon to position with Multilateration method. In case 4, Beacon is used for positioning, and Multilateration is the positioning method. Since beacons transmission power is poorer than AP, one beacon cannot cover most of positioning place. The RSSIs of four beacons in subspace are summed; then the subspace with the highest sum is the chosen subspace. Next, the weakest RSSI of the four beacons in the chosen subspace is eliminated. The three remaining beacons are used for positioning. Finally, the equation of Multilateration with the coordinates of their beacons is utilized to obtain location (X, Y).

- Case 5: Use Beacon to Position with Fingerprint Method. In case 5, Beacon is used for positioning, and Fingerprint with KNN is the positioning method. First, all beacons are used to position. The received a_i is RSSI from target device to beacon, b_i is RSSI from reference point to beacon. Then, 54 values d_i, i from 1 to 54, are obtained. Finally, the coordinates of all chosen reference points are averaged to yield location (X, Y).
- Case 6: Combine Case 4 and Case 5. In case 6, combines case 4 and 5. Only Beacon is used for positioning, so unlike in Case 5, the Multilateration method is used to select the subspace. First, the Fingerprint positioning method, used in Case 5, is used to obtain location (a, b). The subspace that contains location (a, b) is the chosen subspace. Next, the Multilateration method, used in Case 4, and the chosen subspace are used to obtain location (X, Y). Cases 4 and 6 differ in the subspace selection method. The case 6 use Fingerprint method is an improved subspace selection method with a lower probability than case 4 of selecting the wrong subspace.
- Case 7: Combine Case 3 and Case 6 with Threshold. In case 7, combines positioning method of case 3 and 6 and a threshold mechanism is added to choose the device for positioning. First, the target device receives the AP's RSSI, and compares it with the threshold value. If the received RSSIs of at least three APs are greater than or equal to the threshold value and the number, then the positioning in Case 3 is used for positioning. If the received RSSIs of at least three APs are not greater than or equal to the threshold value, then Case 6 is used for positioning.

3 Performance Analysis

This study uses seven kinds of case, as case 1, case 2, case 3, case 4, case 5, case 6 and case 7, to illustrate the performance analysis. In Case 1, Multilateration is the positioning method with APs infrastructure. In Case 2, Fingerprint is the positioning method with APs infrastructure. In Case 3, Multilateration positioning is used to select a subspace and then Fingerprint is used as the positioning method with APs infrastructure. In Case 4, Multilateration is the positioning method with beacons infrastructure. In Case 5, Fingerprint is the positioning method with beacons infrastructure. In Case 6, Fingerprint positioning is used to select the subspace and then Multilateration is used as the positioning method with beacons infrastructure. In Case 7, threshold is used to choose a positioning device, and the positioning results obtained in Case 3 and Case 6 are combined.

Based on the results above, the average error distance was smaller and the positioning accuracy was higher in Case 5 and Case 2 less than in the other cases. However, the main concern here is the use of two types of device for positioning. Case 7 is still better than Case 3 and Case 6. Figure 5 shows the overall positioning results.

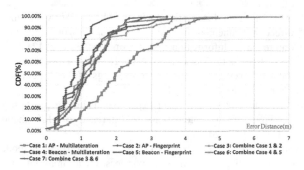

Fig. 5. Overall positioning performance result

4 Conclusion

This work proposes an IHIIP that includes a positioning device. Two types of device for receiving an RSSI are used to improve the accuracy of positioning. This work makes the following research contributions. AP and Beacon integrate the Multilateration and Fingerprint methods for indoor positioning, in which the RSSI is utilized to improve the accuracy of positioning. The results of a test experiment demonstrate that the mean error distance in the IHIIP is 1.21 m. This system outperforms both AP and Beacon in positioning, which yield mean error distances of 1.29 m and 1.33 m, respectively.

Acknowledgments. Authors thank for financial supports of the Ministry of Science and Technology, Tawan under contract MOST 105-2221-E-011 -078 -MY3 and 105-2221-E-011 -076-MY3.

References

1. Geng, Y., He, J., Deng, H., Pahlavan, K.: Modeling the effect of human body on TOA ranging for indoor human tracking with wrist mounted sensor. In: Proceedings of the International Symposium on Wireless Personal Multimedia Communications, pp. 1–6 (2013)
2. Wahab, A.A., Khattab, A., Fahmy, Y.A.: Two-way TOA with limited dead reckoning for GPS-free vehicle localization using single RSU. In: Proceedings of the International Conference on ITS Telecommunications, pp. 244–249 (2013)
3. Kaune, R.: Accuracy studies for TDOA and TOA localization. In: Proceedings of the International Conference on Information Fusion, pp. 408–415 (2012)
4. Yoon, J.Y., Kim, J.W., Lee, W.H., Eom, D.S.: A TDOA-based localization using precise time-synchronization. In: Proceedings of the International Conference on Advanced Communication Technology, pp. 1266–1271 (2012)
5. Uebayashi, S., Shimizu, M., Fujiwara, T.: A study of TDOA positioning using UWB reflected waves. In: Proceedings of the IEEE Vehicular Technology Conference, pp. 1–5 (2013)

6. Jiang, J.R., Lin, C.M., Lin, F.Y., Huang, S.T.: ALRD: AOA localization with RSSI differences of directional antennas for wireless sensor networks. In: Proceedings of the International Conference on Information Society, pp. 304–309 (2012)
7. Muswieck, B.D.S., Russi, J.L., Heckler, M.V.T.: Hybrid method uses RSS and AoA to establish a low-cost localization system. In: Proceedings of the Argentine Symposium and Conference on Embedded Systems, pp. 1–6 (2013)
8. Shuo, S., Hao, S., Yang, S.: Design of an experimental indoor position system based on RSSI. In: Proceedings of the International Conference on Information Science and Engineering, pp. 1989–1992 (2010)
9. Atia, M.M., Noureldin, A., Korenberg, M.J.: Dynamic propagation modeling for mobile users' position and heading estimation in wireless local area networks. IEEE Wirel. Commun. Lett. **1**, 101–104 (2012)
10. Alamri, S., Taniar, D., Safar, M.: Indexing moving objects in indoor cellular space. In: Proceedings of the International Conference on Network-Based Information Systems, pp. 38–44 (2012)
11. Li, G., Busch, C., Yang, B.: A novel approach used for measuring fingerprint orientation of arch fingerprint. In: Proceedings of the International Convention on Information and Communication Technology, Electronics and Microelectronics, pp. 1309–1314 (2014)
12. Zanganeh, O., Srinivasan, B., Bhattacharjee, N.: Partial fingerprint matching through region-based similarity. In: Proceedings of the International Conference on Digital Image Computing: Techniques and Applications, pp. 1–8 (2014)
13. Müller, C., Alves, D.I., Uchôa-Filho, B.F., Machado, R., Oliveira, L.L., Martins, J.B.S.: Improved solution for node location multilateration algorithms in wireless sensor networks. IET J. Mag. **52**(13), 1179–1181 (2016)
14. Gu, Y., Chen, M., Ren, F., Li. J.: HED: handling environmental dynamics in indoor WiFi fingerprint localization. In: Proceedings of the IEEE Wireless Communications and Networking Conference, pp. 1–6 (2016)

Optimal Data Replica Placement in Large-Scale Federated Architectures

Zhusong Liu[1], Jin Li[2]($\boxtimes$), Christian Esposito[3], Aniello Castiglione[3], and Francesco Palmieri[3]

[1] School of Computer Science and Technology, Guangdong University of Technology, Guangzhou 510006, China
liuzs@gdut.edu.cn
[2] School of Computer Science and Educational Software, Guangzhou University, Guangzhou 510006, China
lijin@gzhu.edu.cn
[3] Department of Computer Science, University of Salerno, 84084 Fisciano (SA), Italy
christian.esposito@dia.unisa.it, castiglione@ieee.org, fpalmieri@unisa.it

Abstract. Federated architectures are largely adopted for the design and implementation of large-scale ICT infrastructure by re-using existing legacy systems and integrating novel components and systems by means of proper middleware solutions. In these architectures, data needs to be replicated and deployed in multiple parts of the infrastructure so that it can be closer to the requesting entities, and available despite of crashes and network partitions. It is challenging to perfectly determine the required number and location of the data replicas within such infrastructures. This paper provides a solution to this issue by modeling it as a multi-objective problem and resolving it as a non cooperative game. A preliminary assessment of this solution is provided by means of simulations.

Keywords: Event-based communications · Forward error correction · Layered multicast · Loss tolerance

1 Introduction

The proliferation of Internet connections around the world and the increasing scale of the current ICT systems have paved the way to a radical rethinking of software systems from the "closed world" perspective to the "open word" one. In the first case, systems had a given mission with scarce (or no) possibilities of exchanging data and coordinating their decisions with the other neighboring systems. On the contrary, in this novel perspective, systems are designed according to federated architectures and interconnected by means of a proper middleware solution, such as the ones based on the publish/subscribe interaction model [1], so as to exchange data with the other systems and to take decisions in a collaborative manner by optimizing their efforts with the ones of the neighbors [2].

© Springer International Publishing AG 2016
G. Wang et al. (Eds.): SpaCCS 2016 Workshops, LNCS 10067, pp. 257–267, 2016.
DOI: 10.1007/978-3-319-49145-5_26

The advent of these "systems-of-systems" can be seen in several application domains, spanning from health information systems [3] to critical infrastructure [4] and crisis management [5].

The openness of these system-of-systems allows to have advanced and complex decision making process within each constituting systems and to retrieve a high volume of data on the environment, not only the ones produced within the system but also from other systems, so as to take better decisions. However, this also implies a set of novel challenges that the traditional systems, following the "closed world" perspective, did not have. We can have the following types of issues affecting the infrastructure:

- *big data problems*, since systems must deal with a high amount of information that may overwhelm some of their nodes, cause congestion phenomena, and increase the time to take a decision;
- *performance problems*, since system need data from other systems and it is needed to identify which system holds the datum of interest and retrieve it;
- *availability problems*, since nodes and links within a system and among systems may crash and be unavailable with the consequence impossibility of obtaining a certain datum of interest;
- *resiliency problems*, since data exchanged among systems may be lost due to network misbehaviors or may be delivered with an unpredictable delay.

The commonly recognized solution to deal with these problems is to make use of data replication [6], where a piece of information is not stored within the system that have generated it, but consistently replicated in several points of the overall infrastructure so as to reduce retrieval time, increase its availability and make the systems resilient to possible network failures. Despite the different possible replication schemes that can be adopted within an infrastructure, a key issue consists in deciding where to place a given datum in the infrastructure so as to optimize its benefits without increasing the relative costs (such as the waste of memory to hold the datum given its utility and/or the issue of keeping the several data copies consistent in case of changes). The contribution of this paper is to present a game theoretic approach for selecting the number (and location) of the copies of a critical data for an infrastructure.

2   Background and Related Work

A federated architecture underlying the deployment, and consequent realization of a system-of-systems, is depicted in Fig. 1, where we have a set of systems interconnected by means of a given network, such as the Internet or a cellular one. Each system is characterized by an internal architecture, made of several nodes that communicate among each others thanks to a given technology. Therefore, we can distinguish two levels of topologies: one within a system among its nodes, and one among the systems, as illustrated in [4]. Generally speaking, we can identify three kinds of networks in a system: (*i*) *gateways* (indicated with the capital letter 'G' in the figure), which are special nodes with the responsibility

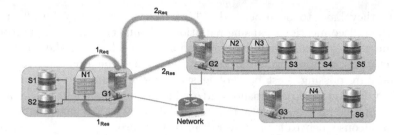

Fig. 1. Schematic representation of a federated architecture.

of managing the communications of a system with the other ones; (*ii*) *computing nodes* (indicated with the capital letter 'N' in the figure), which are commodities that host programs and/or computing tasks that produce novels information by analyzing certain data received as input; and (*iii*) *storage nodes* (indicated with the capital letter 'S' in the figure), which have the duty of storing data generated within the system and/or of interest for the computing nodes.

In order to successfully terminate its tasks, the computing nodes have the requirement of accessing the data on which the task has to work. If the data has been generated by previous elaborations within the system, it is reasonable that they are hosted on the storage nodes of the system. However, it is possible that such data have been produced in another system. In that case, the computing node has to issue a request in order to determine which system holds the data of interest. To this aim, we have that gateways typically have a list of the data stored in their system of reference, so that the computing nodes forwards a request message to its local gateway (i.e., interaction 1_{Req} in Fig. 1) looking for the location of the data of interest. If the data list in the contacted gateway does not contain any entry related to the requested data, the request is forwarded to all the connected gateways (interaction 2_{Req} in Fig. 1). If one or more of them contain an entry that satisfies the request, one or more responses are send back to the requesting gateway with the location of the data of interest (interaction 2_{Res} in Fig. 1). If the location of the correct storage node is within the system or in other system, the computing nodes receive one or even more responses (interaction 1_{Res} in Fig. 1). After receiving the responses the nodes decide which node to contact for obtain the data.

Such a behavior is vulnerable to several factors that may compromise the performance, availability and resiliency of the overall infrastructure, when each system keeps in its local data storage the data for which it is the producer. First, in case of network misbehaviors, the messages containing the requests and the responses may be lost in the network. This causes that the computing nodes may not receive a response to its request. Second, the identification within the infrastructure of the location of where the data of interest is stored takes a non-negligible time, which is proportional to the scale and complexity of the federation. Moreover, the data of interest may be located far from the requesting node, implying a certain time in order to transfer them from where they reside to where they have to be processed. Third, the network may be affected by intermittent disconnections, causing partitions within the federation. During the partitioning time, data hosted in a partition are unreachable to the nodes in the other partitions, compromising the correct execution of the processing tasks since input data are missing. Last but not least, nodes are subject to permanent or temporary failures, such as crashes and/or hangs, making them unavailable. If the compromised node holds data, the stored data may be lost, even permanently, with severe consequences for the overall infrastructure.

A well-known solution to tolerate this problem is to replicate the critical nodes within the infrastructure, such as the storage nodes, to make several copies of crucial data and to place such copies in several locations of the entire infrastructure, or to adopt resilient communication means so as to cope with network misbehaviors. Concerning resilient communications, in particular reliable publish/subscribe services, which are the widely-used for federated architectures, we remand interested readers to [7]. In this work, we are interested in the first two aspects of such a solution. Concerning node replication, literature is rich of solutions, which can be classified in two groups [6]. On the one hand, one option is to use a passive replication scheme, in which the failed entity is replaced by one of its backups. The case that both the entity and all of its replicas fail at the same time is extremely rare, so this solution improves the availability of the entity and the relative reliability of the overall system. However, timeliness is compromised since the entity would be down for a certain time window leading to the impossibility of satisfying some requests from its end-users. On the other hand, another option is to use an active scheme, in which the system exposes a virtual entity made up of a set of distinct replicated objects with equal responsibilities. In this case, a failing entity is instantaneously replaced without causing the unavailability of certain system functionalities, so that timeliness is achieved. However, there is still the possibility of a failure of all the coordinators due to common mode errors. In the literature, there are also hybrid schemes, such as semi-active replication [8], where the entity is actively p-redundant, i.e., there are p replicated objects active at the same time; moreover, there are k backups for each active object. The system designer is free to choose the robustness of the system by varying $< p, k >$. Such a replication scheme allows the system to tolerate entity crashes without having certain functionalities unavailable for a certain period of time. Thanks to backups, such a solution is not vulnerable to common mode errors as active replication. Hybrid schemes allow taking the best of the combined replication schemes without being affected by the same issues.

Despite how replication is implemented, the main problem is to determine how data should be replicated based on maximizing it benefits and reducing its costs. When data is replicated, the advantages achieved are (*i*) *lower time* to identify the location and retrieve the data of interest, since it can be placed closer to the requesting nodes; (*ii*) *higher data availability*, since if a node crashes and/or the infrastructure is partitioned, requests can be satisfied by one of the replicas with a higher probability; (*iii*) *optimized scalability*, since several copies of a certain piece of information are spread across the infrastructure and its requests are not concentrated towards a single node. These benefits come at the costs of consuming storage resources to hold all the copies, and considerable workload for keeping the copies consistent in case of eventual changes. In the second case, a proper middleware, typically based on the publish/subscribe model, is used to propagate the update details to all the nodes holding a copies of the data to be updated. All the copies have to be changed or none of them, so as to achieve a consistent view of the data within the infrastructure and avoid having different values depending of which replica is accessed. Based on this, it is evident that the naive solution of replicating all the critical data with a copy in all the system composing the federation is not viable. Therefore, only a subset of systems should be selected, where to place a copy of a given data. Within the literature, the problem of data replication has been investigated within the context of peer-to-peer systems [9], content delivery networks [10], data grids [11] and/or cloud computing [12], where the objective to be optimized is the data retrieval latency (by means of the so-called cashing mechanisms), or the data availability (targeted by the data replication). Issues raised by unpredictably delayed data access and asynchronous delivery are addressed in [13,14]. In this work we are interested in achieving both these features, by realizing a proper trade-off. The naive solution is to have a random placement of the data replica; however, despite being easy to realize, such a solution is not able to obtain optimal solutions. On the contrary, a typical approach is to formalize the overall task of data replica placement as an optimization problem and let a centralized node in the infrastructure to resolve it and to send commands to implement the determined placement strategy. This approach is able to return optimal, or sub-optimal, solutions, whose quality depends on the ability of the adopted optimization scheme to explore the space of admissible solutions and reach one or more global optima. However, for large-scale infrastructure assuming that a node is able to obtain global knowledge of the overall system and deal with the workload to resolve the above-mentioned optimization problem is not realistic. To this aim, our work follows a different approach by designing a distributed approach for data replica placement without requiring a centralized resolver. In fact, each node can take the decision to host the replica for a determined datum based on local decisions and knowledge.

3   The Proposed Approach

The contribution of our work is to design a solution to place data at certain systems within a federated architecture so as to achieve optimal data availability and retrieval latency, while keeping a lower storage resource consumption and consistency agreement workload. To this aim, the data available in the federation are classified according to a given criterion, such as determining a topic. Such a classification is indicated by associating to the data a special string. So that, the gateways, and their replicas, holds a map that associate each class of data to the address of the different nodes holding a replica of such data within the systems of the gateways. The main issue left to be solved is how to determine where to place replicas of each data class. Such a decision is taken without the intervention of any centralized managers, but the gateways collaborate among each other to find a solution to this problem in a distributed manner. Specifically, each gateway keeps a set of statistics for each class of data requested by any entity in its organization. We have envisioned two classes of statistics: data availability and retrieval time. In the first case, the gateways counts the number of successful write/read requests over the total number of requests; in the second case, they compute the average time to retrieve instances of the given class of data. Periodically, each gateway computes a satisfaction degree per each own system knowing the number of available replicas and their placement within the overall infrastructure:

$$\delta_i(n, \overline{P}) = \omega_A \left(\rho_A - \frac{\kappa_{Succ}}{\kappa_{Tot}} \right) + \omega_\Lambda (\rho_\Lambda - \kappa_\Lambda) \tag{1}$$

where ω_A and ω_Λ are weights chosen by the system administrator in the $[0, 1]$ interval to state the importance of availability over latency, κ_{Succ} is the total number of successful requests, κ_{Tot} is the number of requests, κ_Λ is the computed average retrieval latency, ρ_A and ρ_Λ are the required level of data availability and retrieval latency chosen for each class of data by the system administrator. If the satisfaction degree is positive, it means that the current setting of the platform satisfies the requirements of the users of the given organization and no further actions are needed. On the contrary, a negative value states that the current setting is not satisfactory and some changes are required. The costs for holding a replica for the given class of data can be formulated as follows:

$$cost_i = \omega_A \left(\frac{\theta_{data}}{\theta_{Tot}} \cdot 100 \right) + \omega_\Lambda \left(\frac{\iota_{data}}{\iota_{Tot}} \cdot 100 \right) \tag{2}$$

where the first contribution measure the fraction of the storage resources used to hold the replica (namely θ_{data}) over the total amount of available resources (namely θ_{Tot}), while the second one indicates the fraction of requests received for the hold replica (namely ι_{data}) over the total number of served requests (namely ι_{Tot}). The driving idea is to maximize the satisfaction degree at each organization and minimize the relative costs by determining the optimal number of replicas, and their relative placement of replicas for the class of data of interest:

$$\begin{aligned} \max_{i \in [0,N]} \delta_i(n, \overline{P}) \\ \min_{i \in [0,N]} cost_i \cdot P_i \end{aligned} \tag{3}$$

subject to:

$$\begin{aligned} n = \sum_{i=0}^{N} P_i \leq max \leq N \\ P_i = \begin{cases} 0 \text{ if no replica at the i-th organization} \\ 1 \text{ if replica at the i-th organization} \end{cases} \end{aligned} \tag{4}$$

where max indicates the maximum number of replicas to be placed in the infrastructure made of N systems integrated by the federation platform. This is an example of multi-objective optimization problem [15], since the two objective

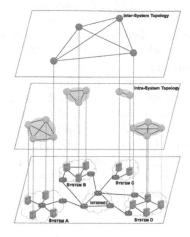

Fig. 2. Two-level topology interconnecting the nodes in a federated architecture.

functions to satisfy are opposing, i.e., a solution for the first maximization is not a solution for the second minimization, and a trade-off is needed. Such a trade-off is called Pareto solution, i.e., a configuration able to keep in balance the two objectives and a different solution is not able to improve such a situation. Classical solutions [16] are not viable in our case, since the federation platform has a large-scale nature and global knowledge in such systems is not achievable. A possible approach based on a mathematical formulation could be to consider the degree-dependent spanning tree problem, a NP-complete variant of the minimum spanning tree problem. In [17,18] some solution approaches and integer linear programming formulation are proposed to model such problems. But with this approach we can only cover instances of very small size. Therefore, we have considered a distributed approach to the resolution of this problem by means of a non-cooperative game [19]. More formally, let us consider the topology for the overlay interconnecting the gateways as an undirected graph (X, E), consisting in a set of nodes, namely X, and a set of edges connecting two nodes, namely E. Within the set of the available nodes, we define a subset of all the nodes, namely $Y \subset X$, containing the nodes where a player can be located. We consider a set of players $P := \{c1, c2, \cdots, cp\}$ of finite size $p \leq 2$. Formally, the strategy set for each player $c \in P$ is defined as $S^c = Y$, such that a strategy of a player is the selection of a node $s^c \in Y$. Combining the strategy sets of all the players, namely $S = S^{(c_1)} \times S^{(c_2)} \times \cdots \times S^{(c_p)}$, a strategy profile $s \in S$ implies a certain payoff to each player c, namely $\Phi^{c(s)}$, which are aggregated in the so-called profile of payoffs denoted as Φ^s. The payoff is the gain achievable by a player to host a given replica, considering the costs to store the replica and to manage the incoming requests to read/write it, as mentioned above (Fig. 2).

The scope of the game is to determine the best strategy profile that implies the maximum payoff for all the players. Despite the several possible formulations that came out within the literature, we have described such a game in terms of a non-cooperative game, where players are selfish, i.e., there is no direct communication between the players, and each one only cares to maximize its own profit or to minimize its own costs without considering the state of the other players (with the eventuality of damaging them, even if it is not intentional). Then, the normal form for the non-cooperative game for our replica placement problem is given by $\Gamma = (P, S, \pi)$, with the objective of maximizing the payoff for all the players, for which we are interested in finding Nash equilibria, i.e., given a certain strategy $s \in S$, it is not profitable for a player to select a different replica placement pattern than the one in the current strategy profile since adding or removing a replica will not change or even reduce the achievable payoff, so a player has no incentive to change strategy. The demonstration of the existence of such equilibria is a well-known NP-hard problem and is resolved by means of theorems. For a concrete example, the authors in [20] demonstrate the existence of at least a Nash equilibrium for games as ours and the conditions to induce such equilibrium are presented. We can model our replica placement problem as a non-cooperative game with N players, whose strategy is represented by a binary decision to hold a replica or not. Rather than formalizing the payoff of each player, we consider its costs, according to the previous formulation of $cost_i$, properly assigned to each player. Specifically, let us indicate with S_i the binary value representing the strategy chosen by the i-th player (which is 1 if the i-th player decides to hold a replica; otherwise, it is 0). The cost paid by the i-th player to follow its strategy can be formalized as follows:

$$C_i(S_i) = cost_i \cdot S_i + \delta_i \cdot (1 - S_i) \tag{5}$$

where $cost_i$ and δ_i are expressed in the previous equations. The game can start with a random strategy profile and evolve over the time where each player changes its strategy so as to minimize its costs formulated in the previous equation. Such an evolution will bring to a stable solution represented by the Nash equilibrium, where no player has an incentive to change its strategy. A strategy profile, namely s, represents a Nash equilibrium if and only if the two following conditions are guaranteed:

$$\exists i \in Y \, s.t. \ \delta_i \leq cost_i \tag{6}$$

and

$$\nexists i \in Y \, s.t. \ cost_i - \delta_i > 0 \tag{7}$$

The first condition indicates that the satisfaction generated by a replica placed at the i-th node is never greater than the cost of placing it; so, none of neighboring nodes has an incentive to act as a codec. While, the second condition states that, when the i-th node holds a replica, it is not convenient to stop holding it since the paid cost is already minimized. The condition in the first equation defines the control behavior of the super-peers to decide holding a replica or not.

4   Experimental Evaluation

To quantify the goodness of the proposed solution we have conducted a preliminary assessment by using a simulation approach, by implementing our solutions

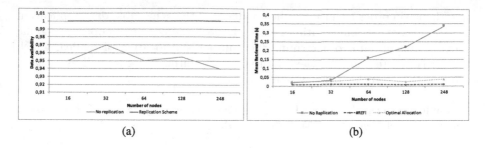

(a)   (b)

Fig. 3. Experimental results.

by using the OMNET++[1] simulator. In our first simulation, the exchanged messages have a size of 23 KB, the publication rate is one message per second and the total number of nodes is 40. The network behavior has 50 ms as link delay, and 0.02 as loss rate. We have assumed that the coding and decoding time are respectively equal to 5 ms and 10 ms. We have published 1000 events per each experiment, executed each experiment three times and reported the average. In the second simulation, we assumed that each organization (made of 4 nodes) periodically generates a datum of 23 KB, while others periodically make requests for a piece of data previously produced by one of the remaining organizations. We assume that nodes can crash with a probability of 0.05.

Our experiments investigate the data availability in our infrastructure, by determining the ratio between data request are successfully replied and the total number of made requests. Such an availability is quite low without any replication means in the infrastructure, as shown in Fig. 3(a), while our replication approach is able to tolerate node crashes without compromising the data availability. Figure 3(b) shows also the performance of our solution in terms of the needed time to retrieve a datum of interest. Our replication approach is able to achieve a speed up in the data retrieval operation than the case without any replication, as evident and expected. We have also compared such a performance to the one achievable when the data replication strategy has been performed with a centralized approach adopting a genetic algorithm to deal with the resolution of the multi-objective problem. Our solution achieve good performance but lower than the optimal case, as expected by a non-cooperative game.

5   Final Remarks and Future Work

In this work we have approached the problem of data replica placement in large-scale infrastructures adopting federated architectures, by analyzing the requirements for a successful data placement strategy and formalizing them as a multi-objective optimization. We have resolved it by means of non-cooperative game theory. We described a preliminary assessment campaign by means of simulations. As future work, we plan to investigate the application of cooperative

---

[1] www.omnetpp.org.

game theory in order to improve the goodness of the achievable data replication strategies. Moreover, our solution consists in performing a non-cooperative game for every unit of data to determine the number and location of replica, which may put the system into bottleneck problem. As future work we will investigate means to reduce such efficiency issue.

Acknowledgments. This work has been supported by Guangzhou scholars project for universities of Guangzhou (No. 1201561613).

References

1. Eugster, P., Felber, P., Guerraoui, R., Kermarrec, A.-M.: The many faces of publish/subscribe. ACM Comput. Surv. (CSUR) **35**(2), 114–131 (2003)
2. Palmieri, F., Fiore, U., Ricciardi, S., Castiglione, A.: GRASP-based resource re-optimization for effective big data access in federated clouds. Future Gener. Comput. Syst. **54**, 168–179 (2016)
3. Esposito, C., Ciampi, M., Pietro, G.D.: An event-based notification approach for the delivery of patient medical information. Inf. Syst. **39**, 22–44 (2014)
4. Cinque, M., Martino, C.D., Esposito, C.: On data dissemination for large-scale complex critical infrastructures. Comput. Netw. **56**(4), 1215–1235 (2012)
5. Cinque, M., Esposito, C., Fiorentino, M., Carrasco, F.P., Matarese, F.: A collaboration platform for data sharing among heterogeneous relief organizations for disaster management. In: Proceeding of the ISCRAM Conference (2015)
6. Wiesmann, M., Pedone, F., Schiper, A., Kemme, B., Alonso, G.: Understanding replication in databases and distributed systems. In: Proceedings of the 20th International Conference on Distributed Computing Systems, pp. 464–474 (2000)
7. Esposito, C., Cotroneo, D., Russo, S.: On reliability in publish/subscribe services. Comput. Netw. **57**(5), 1318–1343 (2013)
8. Defago, X., Schiper, A., Sergent, N.: Semi-passive replication. In: Proceedings of the Seventeenth IEEE Symposium on Reliable Distributed Systems, pp. 43–50 (1998)
9. Bhagwan, R., Moore, D., Savage, S., Voelker, G.M.: Replication strategies for highly available peer-to-peer storage. In: Schiper, A., Shvartsman, A.A., Weatherspoon, H., Zhao, B.Y. (eds.) Future Directions in Distributed Computing. LNCS, vol. 2584, pp. 153–158. Springer, Heidelberg (2003). doi:10.1007/3-540-37795-6_28
10. Wauters, T., Coppens, J., Turck, F.D., Dhoedt, B., Demeester, P.: Replica placement in ring based content delivery networks. Comput. Commun. **29**(16), 3313–3326 (2006)
11. Grace, R.K., Manimegalai, R.: Dynamic replica placement and selection strategies in data grids: comprehensive survey. J. Parallel Distrib. Comput. **74**(2), 2099–2108 (2014)
12. Lin, J.W., Chen, C.H., Chang, J.M.: QoS-aware data replication for data-intensive applications in cloud computing systems. IEEE Trans. Cloud Comput. **1**(1), 101–115 (2013)
13. Catuogno, L., Loehr, H., Winandy, M., Sadeghi, A.-R.: A trusted versioning file system for passive mobile storage devices. J. Netw. Comput. Appl. **38**(1), 65–75 (2014)
14. You, I., Catuogno, L., Castiglione, A., Cattaneo, G.: On asynchronous enforcement of security policies in "Nomadic" storage facilities. In: 2013 IEEE International Symposium on Industrial Electronics (ISIE), pp. 1–6, May 2013

15. Marler, R.T., Arora, J.S.: Survey of multi-objective optimization methods for engineering. Struct. Multi. Optim. **26**(6), 369–395 (2004)
16. Jones, D.F., Mirrazavi, S.K., Tamiz, M.: Multi-objective meta-heuristics: An overview of the current state-of-the-art. Eur. J. Oper. Res. **137**(1), 1–9 (2002)
17. Cerrone, C., Cerulli, R., Raiconi, A.: Relations, models and a memetic approach for three degree-dependent spanning tree problems. Eur. J. Oper. Res. **232**(3), 442–453 (2014)
18. Carrabs, F., Cerulli, R., Gaudioso, M., Gentili, M.: Lower and upper bounds for the spanning tree with minimum branch vertices. Comput. Optim. Appl. **56**(2), 405–438 (2013)
19. Cardinal, J., Hoefer, M.: Non-cooperative facility location and covering games. Theoret. Comput. Sci. **411**(16–18), 1855–1876 (2010)
20. Vetta, A.: Nash equilibria in competitive societies, with applications to facility location, traffic routing and auctions. In: Proceedings of the 43rd Annual IEEE Symposium on Foundations of Computer Science, pp. 416–425 (2002)

A Cost-Effective Criticality-Aware Virtual Machine Placement Approach in Clouds

Na Wu, Decheng Zuo$^{(\boxtimes)}$, Zhan Zhang, and Yan Zhao

School of Computer Science and Technology, Harbin Institute of Technology,
Harbin 150001, China
{wuna,zz}@ftcl.hit.edu.cn, {zuodc,yanzhao}@hit.edu.cn

Abstract. Virtual Machine (VM) placement is a key issue for addressing problems improving resources utilization, increasing customer satisfaction, reducing implementation cost, minimizing power consumption. Existing works on availability-aware VM placement deal with VM allocation task based on taking VM resource demand as constraints. In this paper, we present a novel Cost-Effective Criticality-Aware VM Placement (CECAVMP) approach based on criticality feature of VM, which has not been considered in previous works. A critical server free capacity controlling method is proposed to make a trade-off between availability and cost. We simulated VM placement using CECAVMP and other compared algorithms in different scale clouds. The experimental results show that CECAVMP keeps cloud application in higher availability range without loss of VM request satisfaction.

Keywords: Cost-effective · Criticality-aware · Availability · Free capacity controlling · VM Placement

1   Introduction

Cloud computing has become a highly demanded service or utility due to the advantages of high computing power, cheap cost of services, high performance, scalability, accessibility as well as availability. Resource management is critical in achieving high performance in cloud environments.

The process of mapping suitable Physical Machines for a set of Virtual Machines (VMs) is known as Virtual Machine Placement, an important topic in cloud resource management [1]. A well-designed VM placement algorithm can improve the efficiency and availability in infrastructure clouds.

VM placement is subject to many constraints originating from multiple domains, such as the resource requirement of the VMs, availability requirement, security requirement [3]. The VM placement problem under constraints poses interesting theoretical and practical challenges. Although it has been extensively studied over the last years, it lacks of comprehensive consideration on the constraints of VM placement.

Cloud applications usually consist of multiple components hosted in VMs. Since the role and usage of components are different, there is difference on the

© Springer International Publishing AG 2016
G. Wang et al. (Eds.): SpaCCS 2016 Workshops, LNCS 10067, pp. 268–277, 2016.
DOI: 10.1007/978-3-319-49145-5_27

criticality level of VMs hosting components. The availability of cloud application is affected differently by critical VM and non-critical VM. Therefore, there is necessary to also take the criticality feature of VM into considerations of VM placement.

In this paper, we study how to allocate VMs to servers considering criticality feature of VM. The proposed VM placement approach makes different priorities to allocate VMs. To improve the overall availability of cloud application, CECAVMP maintains the critical servers running stably by controlling resources utilization of servers.

2   Related Work

There is a wide-range of research work around resource provisioning proposed in infrastructure cloud. These approaches try to figure out optimal resource allocation with different goals [4].

Many schemes aim to improve performance of VMs. Jin et al. study efficient VM placement in data centers with multiple deterministic and stochastic resources [5]. Reference [2] provides a practical model of cloud placement management under a stream of request and present a technique to project the past demand behavior of a VM to a candidate target server. Jayasinghe et al. focus on improving performance and availability of services hosted on IaaS clouds [6].

Aiming to ensure availability, Liu et al. describe a novel resource management framework to ensure high-level QoS in cloud, which utilizes an aggressive resource provisioning strategy to substantially increase the resource allocation in each adaptation cycle when workload increases [7]. Wang et al. propose an availability-aware policy by performing both vertical and horizontal scaling to explore how and where to allocate computing resource [8].

Different from previos research works, our approach takes criticality feature into the constraints of VM placement which has not been studied in other research work. Besides of VM request satisfaction guarantee, maintaining cloud application availability in a high range has been investigated based on critical server free capacity controlling.

3   Problem Formulation

3.1   Motivation

Cloud applications usually consist of multiple components, each component hosted in a separate VM. Because the roles and usage of components are different, not all of the components are equally critical.

Fault tolerance is an effective way to improve availability by spreading components of cloud application across many fault domains, thus reducing the impact of single failure on cloud application, or equipping backup copies for critical components. If a primary component fails, the secondary component takes over. An example case of application components placement using fault tolerance is shown

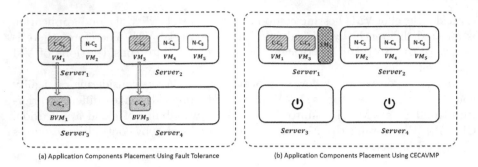

(a) Application Components Placement Using Fault Tolerance   (b) Application Components Placement Using CECAVMP

Fig. 1. Application components placement example case

as Fig. 1(a). However, the use of fault tolerant strategies introduces additional cost on designing and implement redundant components.

There is a conflict between improving the availability of cloud application and reducing the cost of renting cloud service. To relieve the conflict, we propose a novel approach to optimize the trade-off between the availability and the cost, named Cost-Effective Criticality-Aware Virtual Machine Placement (CECAVMP) Approach. Instead of equipping critical VM with redundant VM, The criticality feature of VMs is taken into account of VM placement. CECAVMP separates the allocation of the critical VMs and non-critical VMs, the critical VMs are entitled higher priority to be allocated on some centralized servers named critical servers. To provide a stable running environment for critical VMs, we proposed the critical server free capacity controlling method by assigning a safe margin to avoid critical servers being overloaded. Then the non-critical VMs are placed with the aim to maximize server resources utilization, minimize the number of servers used. An example case of the same application components placement using CECAVMP is shown as Fig. 1(b). Therefore, CECAVMP simultaneously enhances the availability of cloud application and controls the cost of renting cloud infrastructure.

3.2   VM Request Model

In typical commercial on-demand cloud, taking Amazon EC2 as an example, VMs requests from different customers are on discrete time.

In this paper, we focus on the improvement of VM placement based on criticality feature, instead of how to recognize critical VMs. We assume there are two criticality levels, critical and non-critical. We identify each VMs request of customer with a vector $VMR(t, cID, VMSET)$, where t is the time VM request is submitted to cloud, cID is the customer id used to identifying the affiliation of $VMSET$, and $VMSET$ is the set of VMs to be placed.

We study the placement problem in heterogeneous cloud which consist of distinct types of servers with different resources capacity, and provides multiple types of VM to customers. We consider an infrastructure cloud composed by

N servers. Each server is characterized by R types of resource, namely, CPU, memory, bandwidth, and power.

We assume that the scale of cloud is definite, that is the number of each type of servers is fixed. Placing VMs in the cloud with limited capacity may introduce the failure of VMs request. $S = \sum successVM / \sum VM \times 100\%$ is defined to indicate overall VM request satisfaction.

3.3   VM Placement Constraints

To improve resource utilization, most of existing research on VM placement usually tries to allocate VMs on the least amount of servers, and the VMs belonging to the same VM set are placed on a group of centralized servers. However, it also has disadvantage that VMs on the same server will affect mutually under the high workload.

A critical server crashes or runs under high workload will directly affect the availability of each critical VM deployed on the same critical server. To avoid this situation, the critical VMs belonging to the same VMs request will be placed on distinct servers, because it is less likely that the critical VMs belonging to the different customers run under high workload simultaneously. The probability of server overload even crash can be partly reduced.

Meanwhile, critical VMs of different customer can be placed on the same critical server. This is designed to enable cloud infrastructure providers to improve the overall utilization of critical servers and manage critical servers centrally. Based on such premises, the running environment for critical VMs can be kept stable while the cost for redundant cloud resource reduce.

Allocation Exclusion Constraint: The processes of placing critical VMs and non-critical VMs are separated, the server assigned to hold critical VMs is marked as critical server, and critical server is only used for holding critical VMs. Critical VMs of the same VMSET from the same customer must be placed on distinct servers, critical VMs of different VMs sets can be place on the same server, which can be formalized as:

$$max\{num(VM_i)|VM_i \in VMSET\} \leq 1 \tag{1}$$

Where $num(VM_i)$ is the number of VMs of the same VMSET placed on the server.

Server Capacity Constraint: The total amount of resources demand of VMs placed on a server cant exceed the server physical capacity, which can be represented as:

$$\sum_i^n r(VM_i) + T_c \cdot SM(S_i) \leq C(S_i) \tag{2}$$

Where n represents the number of VMs placed on $Server_i$. T_c is the class identifier of server. $T_c = 0$ means this is a non-critical server, which do not need controlling resources utilization. Otherwise, a dynamic Safe Margin (SM) is assigned for critical server with tag $T_c = 1$. The detail implication and computation of SM are explained in Sect. 3.4.

3.4   Critical Server Free Capacity Controlling

Server resource utilization is a key metric of VM placement. Low resource utilization denotes waste of server resource; extremely high resource utilization may reduce the overall server availability. For the above reasons, to maintain the stability of servers, keeping the resource utilization in a rational range is an effective and pratical way.

When CECAVMP allocates a VM, it needs to select a most suitable server from the partial occupied servers or start an unoccupied one. The selection depends on the free capacity of servers. In our approach, CECAVMP keeps the critical servers utilization in a rational rage by controlling dynamic Safe Margin. The critical server claim its present free capacity is the remainder after actual free capacity subtracting Safe Margin, so that a critical VM would not be placed on this server, if the resource utilization of this server after placement is going into the risky high utilization range.

The Criticality Degree of $Server_i$ depends on two factors: the number of critical VMs and the total resource demand of critical VMs placed on $Server_i$. We define the Criticality Degree of $Server_i$ $CD(S_i)$ as following:

$$CD(S_i) = \alpha \times [\phi_{num}(S_i) \times \phi_{ut}(S_i)] \tag{3}$$

Where $\phi_{num}(S_i)$ is the percentage of the number of critical VMs on $Server_i$, $\phi_{ut}(S_i)$ is the percentage of the occupied resources of $Server_i$, and α is a balance coefficient for $\phi_{num}(S_i)$ and $\phi_{ut}(S_i)$, which are computed using Min-max normalization.

We try to control the resource utilization of critical servers in a rational range, by assigning a Safe Margin $SM(S_i)$. The value of Safe Margin depends on the Criticality Degree of the server, and is proportional to the criticality degree.

$$SM(S_i) = \beta \times CD(S_i) \tag{4}$$

Where β is the free capacity controlling factor, it is a customized variable which ranges in value from 0 through 1.

The critical servers claim its current free capacity $FC(S_i)$ as shown in Eq. (5) to avoid overload.

$$FC(S_i) = C(S_i) - \sum_{i}^{n} r(VM_i) - SM(S_i) \tag{5}$$

The failure of each VM affects the availability of cloud application. When the VM request satisfaction rate is less than 100 %, it implies there are some VMs that are not assigned successfully to customer. The failure of this part of VMs will lead to lower availability of the application. We denote w_c as the impact weight of critical VM, and w_n as the impact weight of non-critical VM. From a practical point of view, the value of w_c is larger than w_n. Thus, the average impact on the availability of cloud application app_i introduced by the failed VMs can be calculated by the Eqs. (6) and (7) as following.

$$FA(app_i) = w_c \times fr_c + w_n \times fr_n \tag{6}$$

$$FA(app_i) = fr \times [w_c \times Cr + w_n \times (1 - Cr)] \tag{7}$$

Where fr_c and fr_n represent the probability of the failed VM is a critical VM or a non-critical VM, fr is the overall failure probability of the VM requirement, and Cr is the percentage of the critical VMs in VMSET.

4 Cost-Effective Criticality-Aware VM Placement Algorithm

4.1 Algorithm Description

The basic idea of CECAVMP is as follows. Each time new coming VMs requirement is received, CECAVMP divides the original VMSET into critical VMs subset and non-critical VMs subset according to the users criticality label of VM. Then the critical VMs and the non-critical VMs placement is handled sequentially.

CECAVMP algorithm contains 6 steps as following, and the pseudocode is shown in Algorithm 1.

1. **Divides** VMSET into critical VMs subset and non-critical VMs subset.
2. **Sorts** VMs subsets by descending resource requirements separately.
3. **Selects** the best fit occupied server capable of fulfilling the resource requirements, or start an unoccupied server as a candidate.
4. **Places** the present VM on the candidate.
5. **Updates** the free capacity of server.
6. **Adjusts** the location of the selected server in the servers list ordered by ascending free capacity.

4.2 Algorithms Implement and Simulation

To evaluate the performance of CECAVMP algorithm, we chose CloudSim as our simulation platform. CloudSim is a popular simulation tool modeling a cloud computing environment for evaluation of resource provisioning algorithms [4]. In this work, we modified CloudSim to support simulation of CECAVMP algorithm and the other compared algorithms. To this end, we extended the existing vmAllocationPolicy class to 3 classes: VmAllocationPolicyFCFS, VmAllocationPolicySortDynamic, and VmAllocationPolicyCECAVMP, which represent different allocation policy strategies. Based on these classes, we realized 3 VM placement algorithms, namely: Best-Fit Ascending (BFA), Best-Fit Descending (BFD), and CECAVMP.

The best-fit algorithm chooses a most suitable server whose free capacity is greater than or equal to the size requested, and there is no other server is smaller than the selected server. To this end, it usually arrange the servers in the ascending or descending order, called BFA or BFD algorithm.

The simulation mainly contains 3 steps. Firstly, we model a fixed scale heterogeneous infrastructure cloud and generated VMs requirement sequence in

---

Algorithm 1. Pseudocode for CECAVMP Algorithm

1: **Preprocessing:**
2: divide $VMSET$ into $CVMs$ and $NVMs$
3: $sortedCVMs \leftarrow$ sort $CVMs$ by descending order of requirement
4: $sortedNVMs \leftarrow$ sort $NVMs$ by descending order of requirement
5: **for** $iteration = 1$ **to** $numCVMs$ **do**
6:    **repeat**
7:       $candidate \leftarrow chooseBestFitServer(VMR, CServerList, unoccupiedServer)$
8:    **until** meetCriticalServerCondition
9:    allocate VM on $candidate$
10:    update free capacity of $candidate$
11:    adjust the location of candidate in $CServerList$
12: **end for**
13: **for** $iteration = 1$ **to** $numNVMs$ **do**
14:    **repeat**
15:       $candidate \leftarrow chooseBestFitServer(VMR, NServerList, unoccupiedServer)$
16:    **until** meetNon-criticalServerCondition
17:    allocate VM on $candidate$
18:    update free capacity of $candidate$
19:    adjust the location of candidate in $NServerList$
20: **end for**
21: **return** $MapVMSETServer, unsatisfiedVMPercentage;$

CloudSim. Then, the VMs are placed using 3 aforementioned algorithms separately. Lastly, the simulation results including mapping relations between VMs and servers, VMs request satisfaction and cloud application availability affection rates were showed and stored into the record files.

5 Evaluation

In this section, we present the performance evaluation results of the CECAVMP algorithm. Simulation configurations are described in Sect. 5.1 Experimental results and analysis are described in Sects. 5.2 and 5.3.

5.1 Simulation Configuration

In the simulations, we employ two types of servers in infrastructure cloud, Intel Xeon E5310 (4 cores * 1.6 GHz) and Intel Xeon E5506 (4 cores * 2.13 GHz). Converting into MIPS (Million Instruction Per Second), the two types of servers are with different MIPS: 6400 and 8250, as shown in Table 1(a).

To simulate VMs request, we configure multiple sets of VMs with different resource demand and critical VM percentage in sequence, 4 types of VMs were designed, as shown in Table 1(b). The proportion of 4 types of VMs and the critical VMs percentage Cr are specified in each experiment case.

Table 1. Simulation configurations

(a) Server configurations

Type	#1	#2
MIPS	6400	8520

(b) VM configurations

Type	small	medium	large	huge
MIPS	2000	4000	6000	8000

5.2 Performance Comparison

In our first set of experiments, We evaluate the performance of BFA, BFD and CECAVMP by first looking at the VM request satisfaction. This metric represents a cumulative level of satisfaction for the whole placement. Then we observed the VM request satisfaction of 3 algorithms as accumulation of VM request increases continually.

To test the scalability of CECAVMP, two evaluation scenarios involves different scale infrastructure clouds have been designed. A small-scale cloud consisting of 50 type #1 servers and 50 type #2 servers, and a large-scale cloud consisting of up to 500 type #1 servers and 500 type #2 servers. The experimental results are reported in Table 2.

Table 2. VM request satisfaction comparison of BFA, BFD and CECAVMP

Cloud Scale	Algorithms	Sum(VM)/Cloud							
		0~85 %	90 %	95 %	100 %	105 %	110 %	115 %	120 %
Small	BFA	100 %	95.80 %	93.10 %	88.89 %	85.96 %	82.04 %	79.16 %	77.56 %
#1:50	BFD	100 %	97.14 %	93.79 %	89.78 %	86.19 %	82.83 %	79.33 %	77.49 %
#2:50	CECAVMP	100 %	96.97 %	93.10 %	90.67 %	86.24 %	83.11 %	79.50 %	77.80 %
Large	BFA	100 %	97.54 %	93.03 %	89.97 %	86.37 %	82.67 %	79.87 %	78.39 %
#1:500	BFD	100 %	98.22 %	93.24 %	90.33 %	86.41 %	83.55 %	79.98 %	78.34 %
#2:500	CECAVMP	100 %	97.68 %	93.00 %	89.84 %	86.95 %	84.35 %	80.27 %	78.53 %

$Sum(VM)/Cloud$ represents the ratio of the accumulation of VM demand to the cloud capacity. Since the cloud capacity is fixed, $Sum(VM)/Cloud$ increases with increasing VM request submitted. Table 2 lists the average VM request satisfaction of BFA, BFD and CECAVMP at main increasing VM demand points. The experimental results show that,

(1) The VM request satisfaction trends of BFA, BFD and CECAVMP are similar. With the increase of cumulative VM request, VM request satisfaction decreases. The specific trend of demand satisfaction is: at the early stage, request satisfaction of BFA, BFD and CECAVMP are 100 %. When the accumulation of VM request increases to about 85 % of the overall cloud capacity, VM request satisfaction begins to decrease.

(2) From the point of average VM request satisfaction, BFD has the highest VM request satisfaction, and the performance of CECAVMP is worse than BFD, better than BFA. It indicates that compared to BFA and BFD, CECAVMP dose not introduce much loss of VM request satisfaction.

(3) Shown by the two groups of results simulated in large-scale and small-scale clouds, the performance of CECAVMP fluctuates more obviously in small-scale cloud, and has good stability in large-scale clouds.

5.3   Impact on Availability Comparison

To demonstrate the impact of CECAVMP on availability of cloud application set up on the requested VMs, we applied a set of simulation in CloudSim with the large-scale cloud configure same as Sect. 5.2. And we assumed $w_c = 0.6$, $w_n = 0.4$ and $\beta = 0.5$. The simulation results of impact on cloud application availability under different value of Cr (from 10 % to 30 %) is shown as Fig. 2.

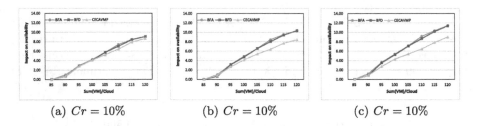

(a) $Cr = 10\%$ (b) $Cr = 10\%$ (c) $Cr = 10\%$

Fig. 2. Impact on availability under different value of Cr

Since BFA and BFD does not consider the importance feature of the VMs need to be placed, so we assume that the unplaced VMs are consisted of Cr critical VMs and $(1 - Cr)$ non-critical VMs. In contrast, CECAVMP makes it a priority to place critical VMs, so the unplaced VMs are non-critical VMs on the condition that the number of unplaced VMs is less than the number of non-critical VMs. Figure 2 illustrates that,

(1) As shown in Fig. 2. (a), (b) and (c), with the increase of $Sum(VM)/Cloud$, the impact of all 3 VMP algorithms on cloud application availability become larger.
(2) With the increase of Cr, the impact of BFA and BFD increase much faster than that of CECAVMP, indicating CECAVMP maintains stabler availability than BFA and BFD.

The above experimental results show, again, that CECAVMP maintains cloud application availability in higher range without loss of VM request satisfaction.

6   Conclusion

In this paper, We propose CECAVMP, a novel cost-effective criticality-aware VM placement approach considering criticality feature of VMs, which has not been discussed in other research work on VM placement. We propose a critical server free capacity controlling method to simultaneously maintain critical servers running stably and reduce the cost for renting infrastructure cloud service. To evaluate the performance of CECAVMP, we redesigned CloudSim to support simulation of CECAVMP algorithm and compared algorithms. The experimental results show that CECAVMP keeps the availability of cloud applications in higher range without loss of VM demand satisfaction.

Acknowledgments. This work was supported by the National High Technology Development 863 Program of China under Grant No. 2013AA01A215, the NSFC under Grant No. 61173020, and the Fundamental Research Funds for the Central Universities under Grant No. HIT.NSRIF.2014067.

References

1. Zheng, Q.H., Li, R., Li, X.Q., et al.: Virtual machine consolidated placement based on multi-objective biogeography-based optimization. Future Gener. Comput. Syst. **54**, 95–122 (2016)
2. Vasic, N., Novakovic, D., Miucin, S., et al.: DejaVu: accelerating resource allocation in virtualized environments. ACM SIGARCH Comput. Archit. News. **40**(1), 423–436 (2012)
3. Calcavecchia, N.M., Biran, O., Hadad, E., et al.: VM placement strategies for cloud scenarios. In: IEEE Conference on Cloud Computing, pp. 852–859 (2012)
4. Zhang, Q., Zhani, M.F., Boutaba, R., et al.: Dynamic heterogeneity-aware resource provisioning in the cloud. IEEE Trans. Cloud Comput. **2**(1), 14–28 (2014)
5. Jin, H., Pan, D., Xu, J., et al.: Efficient VM placement with multiple deterministic and stochastic resources in data centers. In: IEEE Conference on Global Communications Conference, pp. 2505–2510 (2012)
6. Jayasinghe, D., Pu, C., Eilam, T., et al.: Improving performance and availability of Services Hosted on IaaS clouds with structural constraint-aware virtual machine placement. In: IEEE Conference on Services Computing, pp. 72–79 (2011)
7. Liu, J.Z., Zhang, Y.X., Zhou, Y.Z., et al.: Aggressive resource provisioning for ensuring QoS in virtualized environments. IEEE Trans. Cloud Comput. **3**(2), 119–131 (2015)
8. Wang, W.T., Chen, H.P., Chen, X.: An availability-aware virtual machine placement approach for dynamic scaling of cloud applications. In: IEEE Conference on Ubiquitous Intelligence & Computing and Autonomic & Trusted Computing (UIC/ATC), pp. 509–516 (2012)

Accelerating Concurrent Analytic Tasks with Cost-Conscious Result Set Replacement Algorithm

Shengtian Min[1,2], Hui Li[1,2(✉)], Mei Chen[1,2], Zhenyu Dai[1,2], and Ming Zhu[3]

[1] Guizhou Engineering Lab of ACMIS, Guizhou University, Guiyang 550025, China
gzutian@gmail.com, {cse.HuiLi,gychm}@gzu.edu.cn
[2] College of Computer Science and Technology, Guizhou University, Guiyang 550025, China
[3] National Astronomical Observatories, Chinese Academy of Sciences, Beijing 100016, China
mz@nao.cas.cn

Abstract. High concurrent analytic applications such as SaaS based BI services face the problem of how to meet performance SLAs (Service Level Agreement) when the number of users and concurrency increased. In order to reduce the task processing overheads and services response time, analytic applications tend heavily rely on various main-memory data management and cache techniques. In this paper, we designed a cost-conscious cache replacement approach named CRSR (Cost-conscious Result Sets Replacement), which take task result sets as the essential data unit and replace the existing result set by a specialized cost estimation strategy. We conduct a series of evaluation to compare the proposed CRSR approach with representative cache management methods, the experiments show that in most cases, the proposed CRSR algorithm can efficiently reduce the response time of high concurrency analysis service and outperform its competitors.

Keywords: Cache replacement · Cost evaluation · Analytic workload · Result set cache · High concurrent

1 Introduction

With the rapid development of big data technology, the volume of data increased exponentially. Data analytic applications which target to transform data into big values have become critical in many areas. For instance, BI as a Services (SaaS based BI) has become a popular way to provide analytic capability to business users [1]. In SaaS model, users access the service remotely using web browser or Web Service clients [2, 3]. The SaaS based analytic services model not only has to process high concurrent requests but also needs to response quickly to meet the SLAs (Service Level Agreement). In analytic services, the task often consumes a considerable amount of CPU and I/O resources that result to long response time. In enterprise analytic services, many analytic tasks such as reports are inherently have the periodically feature, i.e., the task and the involved data may repeat in certain degree. Therefore, if we can reduce the duplicated processing overheads and maximum usage for the existing computation results that could be cached in the system, the average performance may achieve a significantly improvement.

© Springer International Publishing AG 2016
G. Wang et al. (Eds.): SpaCCS 2016 Workshops, LNCS 10067, pp. 278–287, 2016.
DOI: 10.1007/978-3-319-49145-5_28

Using cache to store the data of repeated request is an effective way to improve the average performance. The ultimate purpose of cache is to save the most important data that user may request subsequently, so that user can get the data at a low cost in subsequent request. In enterprise analytic services, it tends to have multiple user request data at the same time. Moreover, the data involved in different user's analytic tasks often to be not very relevant. According to above two reasons, conventional cache strategies which use data block as the basic cache element often tends to waste cache resources by single data block contains large number of other user's irrelevant data in multiple users' high concurrency scenario. In addition, the traditional cache algorithm such as LRU [4], ARC [14] and LIRS [5], which aims to improve hit ratio, but high hit ratio does not always mean high response speed.

In this paper, we propose a cost-conscious cache replacement approach named CRSR (Cost-conscious Result Sets Replacement), which takes task result sets as the essential data unit and replaces the existing result set by a specialized cost estimation strategy. CRSR can reduce the average response time by reduce the response time of complex request. The experimental results indicate the CRSR is able to reduce 10 %–50 % response time compared with LRU and LIRS, even though a little decrease in the cache hit ratio.

The rest of this paper is organized as follows. Section 2 introduces the related work of the cache algorithm and result set cache. Section 3 describes the main idea of CRSR. Section 4 evaluates the performance of CRSR. Section 5 draws the conclusion and summary of this paper.

2   Related Work

Analytic services provider often face the problem of how to meet performance SLAs when large number of concurrent users are issued analytic services request. Since during the processing, vast resources of CPU and I/O are consumed, reducing the response time of request means reducing the consumption of complex request. In order to reduce the task processing overheads and services response time, analytic applications tend heavily rely on various main-memory data management and cache techniques. The result set cache techniques is one type of techniques aim to solve this problem. This idea has been used in MySQL [6] and Oracle [7]. Oracle use result cache to store SQL query result and PL/SQL function result. When users execute queries and functions repeatedly, the Oracle database retrieves rows from the cache, and hence decreased response time. For MySQL, the cache stores the text of a SELECT statement together with the corresponding result that was sent to the client. If an identical statement is received later, the server retrieves the results from the query cache rather than parsing and executing the statement again.

Most of the existing cache replacement algorithms are focus on matching the pattern of requests, they are mainly designed to follow the characteristic of request sequence. We shortly characterize several representative cache methods as following:

LRU (least recently used) [4]: LRU evicts the cache element which is least and recently used. The algorithm is easy to implement and has less cost of calculating. Its disadvantage is the size and request cost of cache element are not considered.

SIZE [8, 12]: In SIZE, the biggest cache element would be evicted from the cache. Removing the biggest element makes the cache to store much smaller cache element. But the SIZE approach does not take the accessing frequency of cache element into account.

GDS (greedy dual-size) [9]: For each element stored in cache, GDS sets a weight-value H for it and the initial value H is set to 1/size (always positive). When replacement occurs, the cache element with lowest value will be replaced, the value of other cache element will minus a certain value (equal the value of replacement cache element) at the same time. If the cache element has been request again, restore its H as initial value. Therefore, the weight-value H of recently used cache element are bigger than long time unused cache element. The downside is not considering the cache utilization.

LIRS [5]: LIRS uses the Inter Reference Recency (IRR) to divide all the elements into two groups, one is the low IRR (LIR) and the other is high IRR (HIR). All the LIR element are stored in the cache, but few of HIR element are stored. During replacement, LIRS will remove the element in the HIR first. If the HIR element has been hit, the element will become LIR element. LIRS is much more effective than other algorithm due to it can match the request behavior and make replacement according to the past.

RDSLLC (Runtime-Driven Shared Last-Level Cache) [15]: It uses the input tags for subsequent tasks to instruct the hardware to prioritize data blocks with future reuse and evict blocks with no future reuse. It improves the cache performance effectively in hardware-only environment.

gFPca (Global Preemptive Fixed-Priority) [16]: In order to avoid the problem that tasks are running concurrently on different cores access the memories that are mapped to the same cache set may evict other's cache element from cache which resulting in cache misses and hard to predict, gFPca allocates cache to tasks dynamically at run time. It also considers the costs of mapping the memory accesses and reloading the memory content into the cache.

In this paper, the goal of our work is to reduce the average response time of cache system under high concurrent request scenario. Our core idea is to change the structure of basic cache element and design cache replacement algorithm based on the replace cost of cache element.

3   Description of CRSR

3.1   Overview of CRSR

An excellent cache replacement mechanism needs to replace the element which has low hit in low replacement cost, meanwhile, it stores the frequently used element. We incorporate request frequency and response time of request into CRSR through the use of a new utility value for the element stored in cache. The value c_i for an element i is defined as the excepted normalized cost removing from cache:

$$C_i = \frac{t_{ei} \cdot h_i}{t_i} \tag{1}$$

For each cache element i, h_i represents the total number of the cache element is hit. t_{ei} represents the time that response time of request, and t_i represents the last time the cache element is hit with the time interval of the previous one. Thus, C_i represents the cost remove the request result set as cache element from cache. With the C_i, cache system will choose to minimize the cost of the cache change, meanwhile, takes the request response time, request frequency, and other factors into consideration. Compare to other cost estimation methods, our strategy does not have any parameters, so it avoids the problem that parameter is not easy to be determined. But if the request frequency is not clear, for example, all of the cache element has not be request after they saved into cache. It is still not very clear to estimate the cost. To solve this problem, we proposed an initial value W_i for the cache element:

$$W_i = \frac{t_{ei}}{t_e} = \frac{t_{ei} \cdot n}{\sum\limits_{i=1}^{n} t_{ei}} \tag{2}$$

Where n represents the total number of user request. W_i represents the cost of the element which inserts into cache first time. Now to prove their effectiveness, assuming two request T_i, T_j, the response time of T_i is longer than T_j, that is,

$$t_{ei} > t_{ej} \tag{3}$$

When the cache elements are inserted into the cache,

$$h_{(i,j)} = 0 \tag{4}$$

By the formulae (2) (3) (4), we can get the cost of T_i, T_j,

$$W_i = \frac{t_{ei} \cdot 2}{t_{ei} + t_{ej}} > \frac{t_{ei} \cdot 2}{t_{ei} + t_{ei}} = 1 \tag{5}$$

$$W_j = \frac{t_{ej} \cdot 2}{t_{ei} + t_{ej}} < \frac{t_{ej} \cdot 2}{t_{ej} + t_{ej}} = 1 \tag{6}$$

By the formulae (5) and (6), we can simply get $W_i > W_j$, it shows that the cache element which has longer response time has higher cost than the one which has shorter response time.

In order to capture request frequency and avoid pollution by unclearly request, we designed a dynamic function $D(i)$:

$$D(i) = \begin{cases} W_i \cdots if(h_i = 0) \\ C_i \cdots if(h_i > 0) \end{cases} \tag{7}$$

This function can remove the cache element that least recently, minimum frequency of request and maximum response time out of cache. Since the function is used for cost comparison, functions do not need to set the parameter weight-value, just replace the cache which has minimum replacement cost that calculated based on cost function out of cache when the cache is full and need to replace.

3.2   Structures and Procedures of CRSR

In analytic services, high concurrent analytic requests often can be represent as complex SQL queries. Analytic request often does not involve data update, but it will take a lot of CPU and I/O overheads that greatly increase response time. When take user's queries result set as basic cache element, the result set and middle result set can be stored in cache directly. If user requests the data which have been store in cache as result set, server can obtain the data directly from cache that avoid access to large number of base table and time-consuming original computational operation, and hence effectively reduce the response time. Using result set cache can also avoid the data block as cache element that stored large number of irrelevant information to take up the cache space. Therefore, in order to reduce the response time and improve the cache utilization, we choose the result set of user's request as the basic element of cache. The key of cache element is the request SQL statement, and the value is SQL statement result set.

Figure 1 is the structure of CRSR algorithm. It uses two kinds of storage components. One is Key-Value Storage that uses double linked list to store all of the result set cache element and the definitions of request SQL queries. The other is cache metadata storage that use ordered set to keep the cache element metadata information, such as hits, response time and so on.

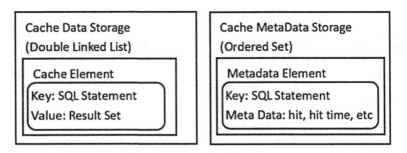

Fig. 1. The structure of CRSR

The procedures of CRSR are described in Fig. 2. When receiving request from client, server retrieves the request data from cache data storage at first. If the request data is already in the cache, server just returns the data to the client directly, and updates the relevant metadata of cache element in metadata storage. If the data is not in the cache, it would forward the request to the database. Then it checks whether the cache space is sufficient. If the space is not sufficient, the server directly accesses the metadata storage, retrieves the metadata element which has minimum replacement cost, frees the relevant space of it, and inserts the new cache element into the cache data storage and metadata storage. If the space is sufficient, just inserts the cache element into the cache data storage.

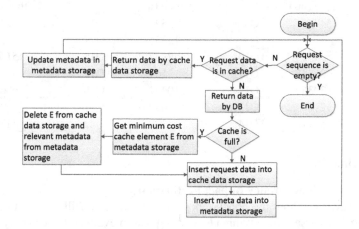

Fig. 2. The procedures of CRSR

4   Performance Evaluation

4.1   Experimental Method and Settings

In our experiment, we use Greenplum (GP) DB [10] to store the request data, and the data size is 5G that generate by TPC-H dbgen [13]. The DB version is 4.3.5.3 and runs on 5 nodes, one is master node, four is segment node. The settings are shown in Table 1.

Table 1. GP node setting

Name	OS	CPU	Memory	Disk
Master	CentOS7 Linux3.10.0-229.el7.x86_64	4x Inter(R)-Xeon-CPU-E5-2630@2.6 GHZ	8 GB DDR3	100 GB 7200 r/m
Segment	CentOS7 Linux3.10.0-229.el7.x86_64	2x Inter(R)-Xeon-CPU-E5-2630@2.6 GHZ	4 GB DDR3	100 GB 7200 r/m

We use Redis [11] as the cache data storage and cache metadata storage. Its version is 2.4.5 and we just use default settings without additionally tuning. We wrote Java Code to implement CRSR and the experimental framework. In our framework, we can adjust the total cache size which can be used and the number of request thread. We use 21 queries (except Q15) of TPC-H as the client requests. Each client thread has 100 requests. The TPC-H queries are divided into two request type, one is complex request whose response time is more than 5000 ms and they contain complex join and aggregate operation, the other is simple request whose response time is less than 5000 ms. The response time of TPC queries from GP by single thread request is shown in Table 2. Q1, Q7, Q9, Q10, Q12, Q13, Q17, Q18, Q20 and Q21 are complex request queries. The others are simple request queries.

Table 2. Response time of TPC-H queries

Query name	Response time (ms)	Query name	Response time (ms)	Query name	Response time (ms)
Q1	54723	Q8	3524	Q16	3922
Q2	3149	Q9	13335	Q17	28230
Q3	3486	Q10	42827	Q18	15120
Q4	2684	Q11	3164	Q19	3617
Q5	3936	Q12	10461	Q20	6068
Q6	2161	Q13	6699	Q21	13395
Q7	15197	Q14	4390	Q22	4173

4.2 Experiments

4.2.1 How the Concurrency Impact Performance

At first, we evaluate how the concurrency of analytic task will impact the average response time. We use different threads send request to evaluate the capacity of cache algorithm under high concurrent scenarios. Our requests are randomly generated, but satisfies proportions of simple request and complex request to 11:10. The utilized cache capacity is 50 %.

According to Fig. 3, we can see that CRSR is faster than original LRU and LIRS. Shorter response time means better capacity. We can find that the response time increases sharply when the concurrent thread become more than 5. With the development of thread number, the increase speed of CRSR response time is smaller than others. It shows that CRSR works well in high concurrent scenarios. Because we use ordered set to store metadata of cache element. Compare to List and Stack, set has better parallel capacity.

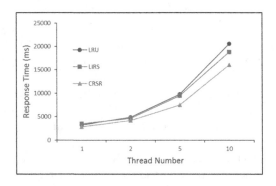

Fig. 3. The response time under different threads

4.2.2 How the Type of Analytic Task Impact Hit Ratio

In this experiment, we evaluate the cache hit ratio under different analytic task type. Firstly, three request loads are generated randomly and they contain different proportions of simple and complex request, such as 11:3, 11:10 and 3:10. Then we change the distribution of request sequences and the sequences satisfy Zipf distribution. The sequences have two types, one is simple type which means 80 % of requests are simple requests, and the other is complex type which means 80 % of requests are complex requests. We use these five types of task to evaluate the algorithms. The utilized cache capacity is 50 % and 5 threads run concurrently.

According to Fig. 4, CRSR drops to a certain extent. Because in CRSR, the replace cost of complex request is bigger than simple request. The complex request cache elements stay longer in the cache. If the number of simple request is more than complex request, for example, 11:3 and simple type, the hit ratio of simple request is decreased, which decrease the hit ratio of cache. Meanwhile, if the number of complex request is larger, such as 3:10 and complex type, the hit ratio of cache is increased.

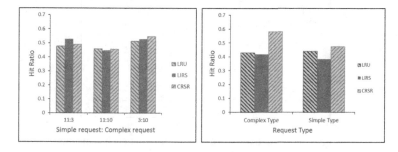

Fig. 4. The cache hit ratio under different request types

4.2.3   How the Type of Analytic Task Impact Performance

According to Fig. 5, we can see the response time of CRSR decreases clearly than other algorithms. Because compare to simple request, complex request take much time to compute result and load data. CRSR improves the replace cost of complex request cache element, the hit ratio of complex request is higher than simple request. It avoids the expensive CPU and I/O cost in complex request. In simple type, the simple request is the main request, reduce the response time of complex request does not work well. In briefly, CRSR reduces the average response time by reduce the response time of complex request.

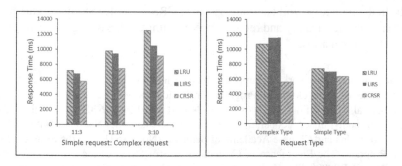

Fig. 5. The average response time under different request types

4.2.4   How the Cache Capacity Impact Performance

In this experiment, we use different cache capacity to evaluate how it impact average response time of different algorithms. The percentage of simple request is 50 % and the concurrency is 5.

According to Fig. 6, we can see the average response time of CRSR is less than LRU and LIRS before 70 % cache capacity. These mean that CRSR works well in the general case. After the cache size reach to 70 %, the response time of CRSR became larger than others, because in these case, almost all of request data can store in cache and calculate the cost of replace is meaningless.

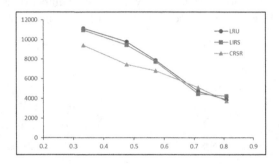

Fig. 6. The average response time in different cache capacity

5   Conclusions

In this paper, we proposed the CRSR algorithm to accelerate the performance of high concurrent analytic service. As the cache system plays a very important role in modern computation systems, many researchers devoted into this area and work to improve the cache hit ratio. In some applications, improve the cache hit ratio does not work well. In our work, we use a different strategy to improve the capability of cache system, which aims to reduce response time when processing the complex request. We use result set as the basic cache data element and calculate the replace cost of cache data element to choose the candidate elements to remove out of cache. Our evaluation verified that, CRSR can reduce 10 %–50 % response time than LRU, LIRS under high concurrent context. In the future, we will continue optimize CRSR and deeply investigate how the concurrency, cache capacity and request type will impact the average response time in more workload scenarios.

Acknowledgments. This work was supported by the China Ministry of Science and Technology under the State Key Development Program for Basic Research (2012CB821800), Fund of National Natural Science Foundation of China (No. 61462012, 61562010), the Joint Research Fund in Astronomy under cooperative agreement between the National Natural Science Foundation of China and Chinese Academy of Sciences (No. U1531246), the Strategic Priority Research Program "The Emergence of Cosmological Structures" of the Chinese Academy of Sciences (No. XDB09000000), High Tech. Project Fund of Guizhou Development and Reform Commission (No. [2013]2069), Industrial Research Projects of the Science and Technology Plan of Guizhou Province (No. GY[2014]3018), the Major Applied Basic Research Program of Guizhou Province (No. JZ20142001, JZ20142001-01, JZ20142001-05).

References

1. E. TenWolde: Worldwide Software on Demand 2007–2011 Forecast: A Preliminary Look at Delivery Model Performance, IDC No. 206240, IDC Report (2007)
2. What is Software as a Service (SaaS). https://www.salesforce.com/saas/
3. Aulbach, S., Grust, T., Jacobs, D., Kemper, A., Rittinger, J.: Multi-tenant databases for software as a service: schema-mapping techniques. In: SIGMOD, pp. 1195–1206 (2008)
4. Tanenbaum, A.S.: Modern Operating System. Prentice-Hall, Upper Saddle River (1992)
5. Jiang, S., Zhang, X.: LIRS: an efficient low interreference recency set replacement policy to improve buffer cache performance. In: 2002 ACM SIGMETRICS Conference on Measurement and Modeling of Computer Systems, 15–19 June (2002)
6. MySQL. http://www.mysql.com
7. ORACLE. http://www.oracle.com
8. Williams, S., et al.: Removal policies in network caches for world-wide-web objects. In: Proceedings of the 1996 ACM SIGCOMM Conference. ACM Press, New York, pp. 293–305 (1996)
9. Bestavros, A., Jin, S.: Popularity-aware greedy dual-size web proxy caching algorithms. In: ICDCS 2000, pp. 254–261 (2000)
10. GREENPLUM. http://greenplum.org
11. Redis. http://redis.io
12. Hyokyung, B., kern, K., Noh, S.H., et al.: Efficient replacement of nonuniform objects in Web caches. Computer 35(6), 65–73 (2002)
13. TPC-Current Specifications. http://www.tpc.org/tpch/default.asp
14. Megiddo, N., Modha, D.S.: ARC: a sef-tuning low overhead replacement cache. In: The 2nd USENIX Conference on File and Storage Technologies, pp. 115–130 (2003)
15. Pan, A., Pai, V.S.: Runtime-driven shared last-level cache management for task-parallel programs. In: The International Conference for High Performance Computing, Networking, Storage and Analysis. ACM (2015)
16. Xu, M., et al.: Analysis and implementation of global preemptive fixed-priority scheduling with dynamic cache allocation. In: 2016 IEEE Real-Time and Embedded Technology and Applications Symposium (RTAS). IEEE (2016)

An Asymmetric Signcryption Scheme for Cloud-Assisted Wireless Body Area Network

Changji Wang[1($\boxtimes$)], Jiayuan Wu[2], and Shengyi Jiang[1]

[1] Collaborative Innovation Center for 21st-Century Maritime Silk Road Studies, Cisco School of Informatics, Guangdong University of Foreign Studies, Guangzhou 510006, China
wchangji@gmail.com
[2] School of Data and Computer Science, Sun Yat-sen University, Guangzhou 510006, China

Abstract. Wireless body area network (WBAN) has emerged as one of the most promising technologies for e-healthcare. In recent years, cloud-assisted WBANs have attracted intensive attention from the academic and industrial communities. How to ensure data confidentiality, integrity, non-repudiation, and access control is an important and challenging issue for widespread deployment of cloud-assisted WBANs. In this paper, we introduce a new cryptographic primitive named key-policy attribute/identity-based signcryption (KP-AIBSC) scheme to address above challenge problem, which can fulfill the functionality of identity-based signature and key-policy attribute-based encryption in a logical step. We first give formal syntax and formulate security model of KP-AIBSC scheme. Next, we present a concrete KP-AIBSC construction from bilinear pairings. The proposed construction is proved to be indistinguishable against adaptive chosen plaintext attacks under the DBDH assumption and existentially unforgeable against adaptive chosen message and identity attacks under the CDH assumption in the random oracle model. Finally, we exhibit an efficient fine-grained cryptographic access framework for cloud-assisted WBANs by exploiting our proposed KP-AIBSC scheme.

Keywords: Identity-based signature · Key-policy attribute-based encryption · Signcryption · Wireless body area network · Cloud computing

1 Introduction

With the rapid development of wireless communication, low-power integrated circuits and physiological sensors, wireless body area network (WBAN) technology has attracted intensive attention from the academic and industrial research communities in recent years [1]. WBANs can be utilized in diverse applications such as physiological and medical monitoring, human computer interaction, education and entertainment [2].

© Springer International Publishing AG 2016
G. Wang et al. (Eds.): SpaCCS 2016 Workshops, LNCS 10067, pp. 288–296, 2016.
DOI: 10.1007/978-3-319-49145-5_29

The huge amount of data collected by WBAN nodes demands scalable, on-demand, powerful, and secure storage and processing infrastructure [3]. An alternative is to resort to the cloud computing, which possesses considerable storage and computational resource [4]. Figure 1 illustrates a cloud-assisted WBAN for prototypical healthcare scenario. A patient equipped with a number of wearable and implantable sensors that constantly measures various health-related parameters (e.g., saturation of oxygen, blood pressure, etc.). Sensors can interact with each other and with a controller (e.g., smart phone or monitoring device), and the controller will transmit all information to the health cloud server to be stored and processed, and these information will be shared by hospital staff and any other who needs to acquire the essential information for the patient's health. If an emergency is detected, the physicians will immediately inform the patient by sending appropriate messages or alarms.

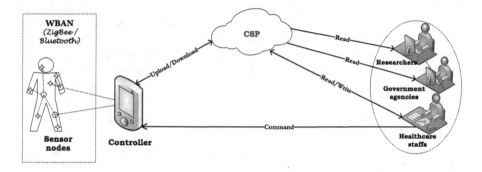

Fig. 1. Illustration of a typical cloud-assisted WBAN in healthcare domain.

Security and privacy issues have been described as two of the most challenging problems of cloud-assisted WBAN for healthcare scenarios [5]. As an example, it has been demonstrated that somebody equipped with a low cost device can eavesdrop on the data exchanged between a reader and a peacemaker and may even induce a cardiac arrest [6]. In recent years, extensive studies on security and privacy preservation for cloud-assisted WBAN have been carried out [7–10]. However, how to ensure data confidentiality, integrity, non-repudiation, and access control is still an important and challenging issue for widespread deployment of cloud-assisted WBAN.

To address the problem of secure and fine-grained data sharing and decentralized access control, Sahai and Waters [11] first introduced the concept of attribute-based encryption (ABE). Since then, ABE has attracted lots of attention from both academia and industry in recent years [12,13]. There are two main types of ABE schemes in the literatures, i.e., Key-Policy ABE (KP-ABE) and Ciphertext-Policy ABE (CP-ABE). In a KP-ABE system, ciphertexts are labeled by the sender with a set of descriptive attributes, and users' private keys are issued by the trusted attribute authority are associated with access structures that specify which type of ciphertexts the key can decrypt. In a CP-ABE system, when a sender encrypts a message, they specify a specific access policy in terms of access structure over attributes in the ciphertext, stating what kind of receivers will be able to decrypt the ciphertext. Users possess sets of attributes and obtain corresponding secret attribute keys from the attribute authority, such a user can decrypt a ciphertext if his/her attributes satisfy the access policy associated with the ciphertext.

Signcryption is a cryptographic primitive that simultaneously performs the functions of both digital signature and encryption in a single logical step, and the overheads of computation and communication is less than the traditional Sign-then-Encrypt approach. Since the concept of signcryption was introduced by Zheng [14], many signcryption schemes under certificate-based, identity-based and attribute-based settings have been proposed [15,16].

In this paper, we introduced a novel cryptographic primitive named key-policy attribute/identity-based signcryption (KP-AIBSC) scheme, which can fulfill the functionality of identity-based signature [17] and key-policy attribute-based encryption in a logical step. Then, we constructed a KP-AIBSC scheme from bilinear pairings, and proved the proposed scheme is indistinguishable against adaptive chosen plaintext attacks under the DBDH assumption and existentially unforgeable against adaptive chosen message and identity attacks under the CDH assumption in the random oracle model. Finally, we exhibited a fine-grained cryptographic access framework for cloud-assisted WBANs by exploiting our proposed KP-AIBSC scheme, which can provide data confidentiality, integrity, non-repudiation, and access control.

The rest of the paper is organized as follows. We give syntax and security model of KP-AIBSC scheme in Sect. 2. Then, we present a KP-AIBSC scheme and give security proofs of the proposed scheme in Sect. 3. Next, we exhibit a fine-grained cryptographic access framework for cloud-assisted WBANs by exploiting our proposed KP-AIBSC scheme in Sect. 4. Finally, we conclude our paper and discuss our future work in Sect. 5.

2   KP-AIBSC Scheme

Let **M**, **ID**, Ω be message space, identity space and attribute space, respectively. A KP-AIBSC scheme consists of the following five polynomial-time algorithms:

- **Setup**: The probabilistic setup algorithm is run by a trusted private key generator (PKG). It takes as input a security parameter κ. It outputs the public system parameters mpk, and the master key msk which is known only to the PKG.
- **IBKeyGen**: The probabilistic identity-based private key generation algorithm is run by the PKG. It takes as input mpk, msk, an identity id $\in$ **ID**. It outputs a private key sk_{id} corresponding to the identity id.
- **ABKeyGen**: The probabilistic attribute-based private key generation algorithm is run by the PKG. It takes as input mpk, msk, and an access structure $\mathbb{A}$ assigned to a user. It outputs a private key $dk_{\mathbb{A}}$ corresponding to the access structure $\mathbb{A}$.

- **Signcrypt**: The probabilistic signcrypt algorithm is run by a signcrypting party. It takes as input mpk, a message m, a signcryptor's identity-based private key sk_{id}, and a set ω of descriptive attributes. It outputs a signcrypted ciphertext σ.
- **UnSigncrypt**: The deterministic unsigncryption algorithm is run by a receiver. It takes as input mpk, a signcrypted ciphertext σ, identity id of a signcrypting party, a set ω of descriptive attributes, and a receiver's attribute-based private key dk_A. It outputs a message m if σ is a valid signcryption of m generated by the signcrypting party with identity id and $\mathbb{A}(\omega) = 1$. Otherwise it outputs a failure symbol $\bot$.

The set of algorithms must satisfy the following consistency requirement:

$$\textbf{Setup}(1^\kappa) \rightarrow (mpk, msk), m \xleftarrow{\$} \{0,1\}^*, \text{id} \xleftarrow{\$} \textbf{ID},$$
$$\textbf{IBKeyGen}(mpk, msk, \text{id}) \rightarrow sk_{id},$$
$$\textbf{ABKeyGen}(mpk, msk, \mathbb{A}) \rightarrow dk_A,$$
$$\textbf{SignCrypt}(mpk, sk_{id}, \omega, m) \rightarrow \sigma, \ \omega \in \Omega$$
$$\text{If } \mathbb{A}(\omega) = 1, \text{then } \textbf{UnSignCrypt}(mpk, dk_A, \text{id}, \omega, \sigma) = m$$

For the confidentiality, we consider the following indistinguishability against adaptive chosen plaintext attack (IND-CPA) game played between a challenger $\mathcal{C}$ and an adversary $\mathcal{A}$ in the selective-set model.

- **Init**: $\mathcal{A}$ declares a set of attributes, ω^*.
- **Setup**: $\mathcal{C}$ runs the Setup algorithm, gives mpk to $\mathcal{A}$, while keeps msk secret.
- **Phase 1**: $\mathcal{A}$ is allowed to issue the following queries adaptively.
  - Singing private key queries on identity id_i. $\mathcal{C}$ runs the IBKeyGen algorithm, and sends sk_{id_i} back to $\mathcal{A}$.
  - Decrypting private key queries on access structures $\mathbb{A}_j$. If $\mathbb{A}_j(\omega^*) \neq 1$, then $\mathcal{C}$ runs the ABKeyGen algorithm, and sends dk_{A_j} back to $\mathcal{A}$. Otherwise, $\mathcal{C}$ rejects the request.
- **Challenge**: $\mathcal{A}$ submits two equal length messages m_0 and m_1, and an identity id^* to $\mathcal{C}$. Then, $\mathcal{C}$ flips a random coin b, runs **IBKeyGen**$(mpk, msk, \text{id}^*) \rightarrow sk_{id^*}$ and **Signcrypt**$(mpk, sk_{id^*}, \omega^*, m_b) \rightarrow \sigma^*$ in sequence. Finally, $\mathcal{C}$ sends σ^* to $\mathcal{A}$.
- **Phase 2**: Phase 1 is repeated.
- **Guess**: $\mathcal{A}$ outputs a guess b' of b. $\mathcal{A}$ wins if $b' = b$.

The advantage of $\mathcal{A}$ in the above game is defined as

$$\text{Adv}_{\mathcal{A}}(\kappa) = |\Pr[b' = b] - \frac{1}{2}|.$$

Definition 1. *A KP-AIBSC scheme is said to be IND-CPA secure in the selective-set model if $Adv_{\mathcal{A}}(\kappa)$ is negligible in the security parameter κ.*

For the unforgeability, we consider the following existential unforgeability against adaptive chosen messages attack (UF-CMA) game played between a challenger $\mathcal{C}$ and a forger $\mathcal{F}$.

- **Setup:** Same as in the above IND-CPA game.
- **Find:** $\mathcal{F}$ is allowed to issue the following queries adaptively.
  - Singing private key queries. Same as in the above IND-CPA game.
  - Decrypting private key queries. Same as in the above IND-CPA game.
  - Signcrypt queries on $\langle m, \text{id}, \boldsymbol{\omega} \rangle$. $\mathcal{C}$ runs **IBKeyGen**$(mpk, msk, \text{id}) \rightarrow sk_{\text{id}}$ and **Signcrypt**$(mpk, sk_{\text{id}}, \boldsymbol{\omega}, m) \rightarrow \sigma$ successively. Finally, $\mathcal{C}$ sends σ back to $\mathcal{F}$.
- **Forgery:** $\mathcal{F}$ produces a new triple $\langle \sigma^*, \boldsymbol{\omega}^*, \text{id}^* \rangle$. $\mathcal{F}$ wins this game if the following conditions hold:
  - **UnSignCrypt**$(mpk, dk_{\mathbb{A}}, \text{id}^*, \boldsymbol{\omega}^*, \sigma^*) = m^*$ if $\mathbb{A}(\boldsymbol{\omega}^*) = 1$.
  - $\mathcal{F}$ has not issued a IBKeyGen query for id^*.
  - $\mathcal{F}$ has not issued a Signcrypt query on $(m^*, \text{id}^*, \boldsymbol{\omega}^*)$.

The advantage of $\mathcal{F}$ is defined as the probability that it wins.

Definition 2. *A KP-AIBSC scheme is said to be EUF-CMIA secure if no polynomially bounded adversary $\mathcal{F}$ has non-negligible advantage in the above game.*

3   Our KP-AIBSC Construction

Our KP-AIBSC construction from bilinear pairings is described as follows.

- **Setup:** The PKG performs as follows.
  1. Run $\mathcal{G}(1^\kappa) \rightarrow \langle q, \mathbf{G}_1, \mathbf{G}_T, \hat{e} \rangle$.
  2. Choose $P \xleftarrow{\$} \mathbf{G}_1$, $x, y \xleftarrow{\$} \mathbf{Z}_q^*$, $t_i \xleftarrow{\$} \mathbf{Z}_q^*$ for each attribute $\text{atr}_i \in \Omega$, three hash functions $H_1 : \{0,1\}^* \rightarrow \mathbf{G}_1$, $H_2 : \{0,1\}^* \rightarrow \mathbf{Z}_q^*$, and $H_2 : \mathbf{G}_2 \rightarrow \{0,1\}^\ell$ which are viewed as three random oracles.
  3. Compute $P_{pub} = [x]P$, $Y = \hat{e}(P, P)^y$ and $T_i = [t_i]P$ for $1 \leq i \leq |\Omega|$.
  4. Set $msk = \{t_1, \ldots, t_{|\Omega|}, x, y\}$.
  5. Publish $mpk = \{\Omega, T_1, \ldots, T_{|\Omega|}, P_{pub}, Y, H_1, H_2, H_3\}$.
- **IBKeyGen:** A user and the PKG perform as follows.
  1. The user sends identity-based private key request to the PKG with his/her identity id.
  2. The PKG sets the user's public key $Q_{\text{id}} = H_1(\text{id})$, and computes the corresponding identity-based private key $sk_{\text{id}} = [x]Q_{\text{id}}$.
  3. The PKG sends sk_{id} to the user via a secure channel.
- **ABKeyGen:** A user and the PKG perform as follows.
  1. Assign an LSSS access structure $\mathbb{A}$ described by $(M_{\ell \times n}, \rho)$ to the user.
  2. Choose a vector $\boldsymbol{u} = (u_1, u_2, \ldots, u_n)^\top \xleftarrow{\$} \mathbf{Z}_q^{*(n)}$ such that $\sum_{i=1}^n u_i = y$.
  3. Compute $\alpha_i = \langle \boldsymbol{M}_i, \boldsymbol{u} \rangle$ and $D_i = [\alpha_i / t_{\rho(i)}]P$ for each row vector $\mathbf{M}_i$ of $M_{\ell \times n}$.

4. Send the decryption key $dk_{\mathbb{A}} = \{D_1, D_2, \ldots, D_\ell\}$ associated with the access structure $\mathbb{A}$ to the user.

- **Signcrypt**: To signcrypt a message $m \in \{0,1\}^\ell$ along with a set ω of attributes, a signcryptor with identity id performs as follows.
    1. Choose $r \xleftarrow{\$} \mathbf{Z}_q^*$.
    2. Compute $R = [r]Q_{\mathsf{id}}$, $h = H_2(m\|R\|\mathsf{id}\|\omega)$ and $S = [r+h]sk_{\mathsf{id}}$. Here $\|$ is a concatenation symbol.
    3. Compute $c_0 = m \oplus H_3(Y^r)$ and $C_i = [r]T_i$ for all $\mathrm{atr}_i \in \omega$.
    4. Output $\sigma = \{\omega, \mathsf{id}, c_0, \{C_i\}_{\mathrm{atr}_i \in \omega}, R, S\}$

- **UnSigncrypt**: A receiver uses his decryption private key $dk_{\mathbb{A}}$ associated to the access structure $\mathbb{A}$ described by $(M_{\ell \times n}, \rho)$ to recover and verify the signcrypted ciphertext $\sigma = \{\omega, \mathsf{id}, c_0, \{C_i\}_{\mathrm{atr}_i \in \omega}, R, S\}$ as follows.
    1. Determine $\mathbb{A}(\omega) = 1$. If not, the receiver rejects σ and outputs $\perp$.
    2. Define $\mathbf{I} = \{i|\rho(i) \in \omega\} \subset \{1, 2, \ldots, \ell\}$. Let $\{\beta_i \in \mathbf{Z}_q\}$ be a set of constants such that if $\{\alpha_i\}$ are valid shares of y according to $(M_{\ell \times n}, \rho)$, then $\sum_{i \in \mathbf{I}} \alpha_i \beta_i = y$.
    3. Compute $V = \prod_{\rho(i) \in \omega} \hat{e}(C_i, D_i)^{\beta_i}$, $m = c_0 \oplus H_3(V)$ and $h = H_2(m\|R\|\mathsf{id}\|\omega)$.
    4. Check the equation

$$\hat{e}(P_{pub}, (R + [h]Q_{\mathsf{id}})) = \hat{e}(S, P).$$

If it holds, the receiver accepts and outputs the message m. Otherwise, rejects and outputs $\perp$.

Notice that if we scramble the sender's identity id with the message at the third step of the Signcrypt algorithm, i.e., computing $c_0 = (\mathsf{id}\|m) \oplus H_3(Y^r)$ instead of computing $c_0 = m \oplus H_3(Y^r)$, then our KP-AIBSC scheme realizes the sender anonymity. Furthermore, we can apply the idea of hybrid encryption if the message is large. That is, we compute $c_0 = \mathrm{Enc}(H_3(Y^r), m)$ instead of $c_0 = m \oplus H_3(Y^r)$. Here Enc is the encryption algorithm for a symmetric cipher (such as AES) and $H_3(Y^r)$ is the session key.

Theorem 1. *Our KP-AIBSC scheme satisfies consistency requirement.*

Proof. Consistency requirement can be verified as follows.

$$\hat{e}(P_{pub}, R + [h]Q_{\mathsf{id}}) = \hat{e}([x]P, [r+h]Q_{\mathsf{id}})$$
$$= \hat{e}([r+h]sk_{\mathsf{id}}, P) = \hat{e}(S, P)$$

$$V = \prod_{\rho(i) \in \omega} \hat{e}(D_i, C_{\rho(i)})^{\beta_i}$$
$$= \prod_{\rho(i) \in \omega} \hat{e}([\alpha_i/t_{\rho(i)}]P, [r \cdot t_{\rho(i)}]P)^{\beta_i}$$
$$= \hat{e}(P, P)^{ry} = Y^r$$

$$m' = c_0 \oplus H_3(V) = m \oplus H_3(Y^r) \oplus H_3(Y^r)$$
$$= m.$$

Theorem 2. *Our KP-AIBSC scheme is IND-CPA secure in the selective-set model under the DBDH assumption.*

Proof. Due to space limitation, we will provide detailed security proof in the extended version.

Theorem 3. *Our KP-AIBSC scheme is EUF-CMA secure in the adaptive model under the CDH assumption.*

Proof. Due to space limitation, we will provide detailed security proof in the extended version.

4   Application of KP-AIBSC in Cloud-Assisted WBANs

In this section, we exhibit a fine-grained cryptographic access framework for cloud-assisted WBANs by exploiting our proposed KP-AIBSC scheme. Figure 2 shows the proposed access framework, which involves four participants:

- One health authority (HA) who acts as the PKG. HA is responsible for generating system public parameters, issuing private keys for controllers based on their identities and private keys for hospital staff based on their assigned access structures.
- Patients with wearable or implanted sensors and smart phone (act as controller). Sensors can sense vital signs and transfer the relevant data to the corresponding controller. Controller can aggregate information from sensors and ultimately convey the information about health status across existing networks to the medical cloud service provider.
- One medical cloud service provider (CSP). CSP stores patient health information and provides various services to the users and medical staff.
- Multiple hospital staff (e.g., doctors, nurses etc.) who may access the patients' health information and provide medical services.

Sensors in and around the body collect the vital signals of the patient continuously and transmit the collected signals to the corresponding controller regularly. Each controller can be uniquely identified by the registered patient's identity who owns the controller. The controller aggregates the received signals and runs the Signcrypt algorithm with the controller's identity-based private key, the aggregated information and descriptive attributes. Then the controller uploads the signcrypted ciphertext to the CSP. Hospital staff can be identified by their own roles, and the HA issues private keys to hospital staff that associated with particular access structures by running the ABKeyGen algorithm. The private key would only open the signcrypted ciphertext whose attributes satisfied the access policy associate with the private key. Thus, data confidentiality, authenticity and unforgeability, anonymity for controller and hospital staff, and fine-grained access control are achieved in the proposed access framework.

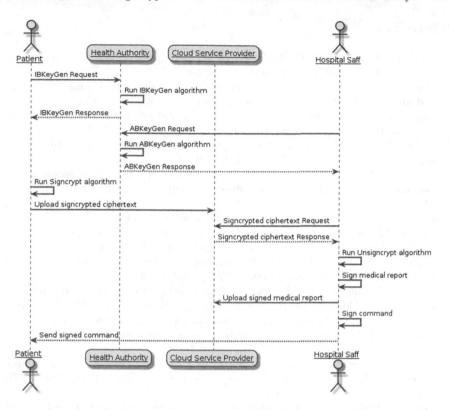

Fig. 2. Application of KP-AIBSC Scheme in cloud-assisted WBAN

5 Conclusions

In this paper, we proposed an asymmetric signcryption scheme from bilinear pairings by combining identity-based signature scheme with key-policy attribute-based encryption scheme, and proved the proposed scheme is indistinguishable against adaptive chosen plaintext attacks under the DBDH assumption and existentially unforgeable against adaptive chosen message and identity attacks under the CDH assumption in the random oracle model. We also exhibited a fine-grained cryptographic access framework for cloud-assisted WBANs by exploiting the proposed KP-AIBSC scheme. In future work we will consider efficient revocation mechanism in KP-AIBSC scheme.

Acknowledgments. This research is funded by National Natural Science Foundation of China (Grant No. 61173189).

References

1. Chen, M., Gonzalez, S., Vasilakos, A., et al.: Body area networks: a survey. Mob. Netw. Appl. **16**(2), 171–193 (2011)
2. Cordeiro, C., Fantacci, R., Gupta, S., et al.: Body area networking: Technology and applications. IEEE J. Sel. Areas Commun. **27**(1), 1–4 (2009)
3. Kupwade, P.H., Seshadri, R.: Big data security and privacy issues in health-care. In: IEEE International Congress on Big Data, pp. 762–765 (2014)
4. Sadiku, M.N.O., Musa, S.M., Momoh, O.D.: Cloud computing: opportunities and challenges. IEEE potentials **33**(1), 34–36 (2014)
5. Li, M., Yu, S.C., Guttman, J.D., et al.: Secure ad hoc trust initialization and key management in wireless body area networks. Acm Trans. Sensor Netw. **9**(2), 1–35 (2013)
6. Halperin, D., Heydt-Benjamin, T., Ransford, B., et al.: Pacemakers and implantable cardiac defibrillators: Software radio attacks and zero-power defenses. In: IEEE Symposium on Security and Privacy, pp. 129–142 (2008)
7. Malasri, K., Wang, L.: Design and implementation of a secure wireless mote-based medical sensor network. Sensors **9**(8), 6273–6297 (2009)
8. Hu, C.Q., Zhang, N., Li, H.J., et al.: Body area network security: a fuzzy attribute-based signcryption scheme. IEEE J. Sel. Areas Commun. **31**(9), 37–46 (2013)
9. Tan, Y.L., Goi, B.M., Komiya, R., Phan, R.: Design and implementation of key-policy attribute-based encryption in body sensor network. Int. J. Cryptol. Res. **4**(1), 84–101 (2013)
10. Liu, J.W., Zhang, Z.H., Chen, X.F., et al.: Certificateless remote anonymous authentication schemes for wirelessbody area networks. IEEE Trans. Parallel Distrib. Syst. **25**(2), 332–342 (2014)
11. Sahai, A., Waters, B.: Fuzzy identity-based encryption. In: Cramer, R. (ed.) EUROCRYPT 2005. LNCS, vol. 3494, pp. 457–473. Springer, Heidelberg (2005). doi:10.1007/11426639_27
12. Goyal, V., Pandey, O., Sahai, A., Waters, B.: Attribute based encryption for fine-grained access conrol of encrypted data. In: ACM conference on Computer and Communications Security, pp. 89–98 (2006)
13. Waters, B.: Ciphertext-policy attribute-based encryption: an expressive, efficient, and provably secure realization. In: Catalano, D., Fazio, N., Gennaro, R., Nicolosi, A. (eds.) PKC 2011. LNCS, vol. 6571, pp. 53–70. Springer, Heidelberg (2011). doi:10.1007/978-3-642-19379-8_4
14. Zheng, Y.: Digital signcryption or how to achieve cost(signature & encryption) ≪ cost(signature) + cost(encryption). In: Kaliski Jr., B.S. (ed.) Advances in Cryptology—CRYPTO 1997. LNCS, vol. 1294, pp. 165–179. Springer, Heidelberg (1997). doi:10.1007/BFb0052234
15. Barreto, P.S.L.M., Libert, B., McCullagh, N., Quisquater, J.-J.: Efficient and provably-secure identity-based signatures and signcryption from bilinear maps. In: Roy, B. (ed.) ASIACRYPT 2005. LNCS, vol. 3788, pp. 515–532. Springer, Heidelberg (2005). doi:10.1007/11593447_28
16. Wang, C.J., Huang, J.S.: Attribute-based signcryption with ciphertext-policy and claim-predicate mechanism. In: 2013 Ninth International Conference on Computational Intelligence and Security, pp. 905–909. IEEE Press (2011)
17. Choon, J.C., Hee Cheon, J.: An identity-based signature from gap diffie-hellman groups. In: Desmedt, Y.G. (ed.) PKC 2003. LNCS, vol. 2567, pp. 18–30. Springer, Heidelberg (2003). doi:10.1007/3-540-36288-6_2

Forecasting Availability of Virtual Machine Based on Grey-Exponential Curve Combination Model

Jionghao Jia, Ningjiang Chen[✉], and Shuo Zhang

School of Computer Science and Electronic Information, Guangxi University,
Nanning 530004, China
chnj@gxu.edu.cn

Abstract. The availability prediction of virtual machine can provide effective guidance for cloud task scheduling and resource allocation. The applicability of existing predictive models is analyzed in this paper, and then a high-precision prediction model is proposed based on grey-exponential curve combination model, which suits the changes in characteristics of availability for virtual machine in cloud. The model is used in the replacement of virtual machine. By predicting and analyzing the availability of virtual machine dynamically, certain virtual machines are replaced. The effectiveness of the prediction model is verified by experiments. The experimental results show that the accuracy of the prediction model given in the paper is better.

Keywords: Availability prediction · Prediction · Virtual machine · Availability distribution · Grey-exponential curve combination model

1 Introduction

Many factors including heterogeneity of infrastructure, dynamism or security could lead to cloud resources to be unavailable for cloud services. It brings great losses for cloud service providers, resulting in that the users couldn't use virtual machines properly. Therefore, availability prediction of virtual machine is meaningful to reduce the occurrence of unavailable event of virtual machine for guiding cloud scheduling and resource allocation.

There are a number of prediction models that have been applied to cloud applications, like choosing a certain prediction model to allocate resources. Generally, a resource allocation framework based on prediction is shown in Fig. 1. The designer applies the appropriate forecasting model according to their own needs.

In [1], the cloud resource adjustment is changed with the load of the system, and the two order auto-regressive model is used to predict the load change. But this prediction algorithm didn't remove noise for the sample data, there is a certain amount of interference data in the sample, and this may reduce the value of predictive accuracy.

G. Wang et al. (Eds.): SpaCCS 2016 Workshops, LNCS 10067, pp. 297–310, 2016.
DOI: 10.1007/978-3-319-49145-5_30

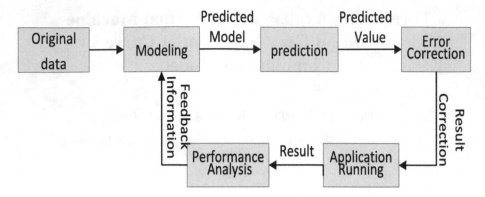

Fig. 1. The resource allocation framework based on prediction model

As shown in Fig. 1, the original data of the prediction model are collected through the monitoring tool, and then appropriate forecasting method is applied. The predicted value may be corrected by error correction, and then the performance analysis is made according to the practical application of the prediction model. In the end, the forecast model is adjusted through feedback information and gets the improvement of prediction accuracy.

In [2], the exponential smoothing method is used to predict the rate of access requesting among the users. In [3], a linear auto-regressive prediction model is proposed to predict the number of future time at a time of a physical machine. A sparse periodic auto-regressive prediction model is proposed in [4], which aims to predict the load of physical machine cyclically. In [5], it proposed a discrete Markov chain model to forecast the resource demand for short-term prediction. A dynamic trend prediction algorithm is proposed in [6], thus the trend of load rise or fall can be determined according to the last time and current load. In [7], the Holt-Winters exponential smoothing prediction model is designed to predict the demand of user based on seasonal trends and the changes in data. [8] proposes an elastic load balancing strategy based on prediction, which uses variable weights exponential smoothing method to suit for short-term load forecasting of virtual machine.

Usually, the prediction models, such as regression analysis, linear models, Markov chain, are mostly used to predict network traffic, host resource load and resource requirements, etc., and have their own shortcomings. For instance, the regression analysis model needs to have smooth and self-regressive requirements for historical data. When considering effective guidance for resource management of virtual machine, it needs short-term availability data of virtual machine to make more accurate predictions. In the face of the problem, a grey-exponential curve combination forecasting method is adopted in the paper.

2 The New Prediction Model

2.1 Evaluating Availability of Virtual Machine

First of all, we measure the availability of virtual machine, and then make use of let the

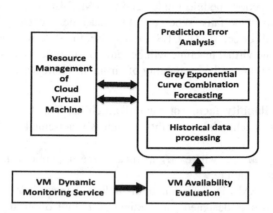

Fig. 2. Availability prediction of VM based on grey-exponential curve model

historical data for prediction, on the basis of dynamic monitoring. Secondly, the analysis of the actual value of the prediction error between the predicted values and the difference of the available virtual machine, on the basis of sample size in order to make the adjustment based on the guidance of the prediction. The availability prediction of virtual machine based on grey-exponential curve model is shown in Fig. 2. The error analysis is carried out according to the difference between the actual value and the predicted value. On this basis, the size of the prediction samples will be adjusted.

From the perspective of virtual machine failure, according to failure distribution characteristics of virtual machine, the degree of availability of virtual machine is defined as follows.

Definition 1. Availability of virtual machine: As the service provider, the probability of providing services by a virtual machine in a cycle is represented as:

$$VF_{vm_i} = f(t) \tag{1}$$

where VF_{vm_i} indicates the availability of virtual machine; f (t) is a function that changes when time t changes, and its value is a positive real number if the value is 1, then it means that there is no failure of virtual machine.

Heath et al. studied the failure logs of large-scale cloud computing systems [9]. According their work, by analyzing the failure logs of large-scale cloud computing systems, what is found out is that the failure of the system is subject to the Weibul (scale, shape) distribution with the parameter shape less than 1 [10]. There are the following two characteristics: 1) the node on which a virtual machine just failed is more likely to occur failure, after that becomes more and more stable during runtime [11]; 2) a virtual machine that repeatedly fails has higher failure probability. Based on the above two characteristics, we can find the number of failure in a certain time may greatly affect the availability of virtual machine. Thus, we design a VM availability measurement algorithm based on failure distribution, named VMAM-FD. A virtual machine failure detection module implementing VMAM-FD is plugged in to detect whether a virtual machine fails. When a virtual machine is detected successfully, the state (VMstatus) will be set to SUCCESS; otherwise, the state will be set to FAIL, and the availability of the virtual machine will be reduced. In order to describe the effect of virtual machine's failure on the availability of virtual machine accurately, the following definition is given.

Definition 2. Availability factor of virtual machine: The Increase or decrease in value of the virtual machine's availability, which is represented as RF:

$RF = 1/n$, $n \geq M_{Max}$, where M_{Max} means the maximum number of virtual machines' continuous failure.

In algorithm VMAM-FD, according to the failure characteristics of virtual machine, an elastic mechanism is designed for continuous failure of virtual machine, so the failure distribution of virtual machine can be directly reflected. The availability of virtual machine will be reduced if it occurs to failure, and the availability will be decreased when the virtual machine runs without failure. We give the formula of computing virtual machine's availability as follows.

$$f(t) \begin{cases} 1 & t = nT(n = 1) \\ f(t-1)(1+RF) & \{t = nT(n \geq 2) \wedge VMstatus = SUCCESS\} \\ f(t-1)(1 - M \times RF) & \{t = nT(n \geq 2) \wedge VMstatus = FAIL\} \end{cases} \quad (2)$$

In formula (2), T is the cycle of computing the virtual machine's availability, M is the number of virtual machine failure, RF is the availability factor. The maximum availability (*maxVF*) and the minimum availability (*minVF*) are the input datum of the algorithm VMAM-FD. At first, the values of availability of all virtual machines are initialized to 1. When a virtual machine is in continuous failure, the times of failure of virtual machine is indicated by M and availability factors *VF*, thus availability of virtual machines may be reduced flexibly and rapidly. The following gives the description of the algorithm VMAM-FD.

```
Input: RF, VMstatus , maxVF , minVF
Output: VF
BEGIN
(1) VF = 1, M = 1;// Initialization
(2) successCount = 0; /* successCount records the number of successful detection of virtual machine that
does not fail */
(3) IF VMStatus = SUCCESS THEN
(4)     VF ←VF + (VF * RF); /* Increase flexibly the availability of virtual machine */
(5) ENDIF
(6) IF M > 1 THEN /* When the virtual machine's failure time is greater than 1, the number of the virtual
machine's failure is reduced */
(7)     M ← M - 1;
(8) ENDIF
(9) success Count = success Count + 1
(10) ELSE IF VMStatus = FAIL THEN
(11) /* When the virtual machine becomes unavailable because of multiple failures, VF is reduced proportionally
*/
(12)    VF ←VF - (VF * RF * M);
(13)    M← M + 1;
(14) successCount = 0;
(15) ENDIF
(16) IF VF > maxVF THEN /* When the availability of virtual machine is larger than the maximum value,
it is set to the maximum value */
(17)    VF ←maxVF;
(18) ENDIF
(19) IF VF < minVF THEN /* When the availability of virtual machine is smaller than the maximum
value, it is set to the minimum value */
(20)    VF ←minVF;
(21) ENDIF
END
```

2.2   Predicting the Availability of Virtual Machine

Grey forecasting is a kind of method of predicting the system with uncertain factors, and it carries out the correlation analysis by identifying the different degrees of development trend of a system. The original data are processed and generated to find out the change rules, and the data sequence with strong regularity can be generated, then the corresponding differential equation model is established, so as to predict the development trend of system [12]. Considering the combination of the two methods, the grey forecasting model is to convert the exponential model into differential equation, and the exponential curve is to establish a linear regression model of the sample data [13]. The difference between the two methods is the parameter setting. Thus the arithmetic weighted average combination is used in the paper to connect the two models. In a word, the combination of the grey prediction and the exponential curve method is adopted to predict the availability of virtual machine, as described below.

Firstly, the historical data about availability of virtual machine are monitored and collected at runtime, and they are used as the sample data. The Grey forecasting GM (1, 1) model is established to generate prediction data sets $\hat{x}^{(0)}(k+1)$, and then the exponential curve $y = ae^{bx}$ is used to generate the prediction data sets $\hat{x}(k+1)_{(0)}$, and the final prediction data $\hat{x}(k+1)$ is generated by simple arithmetic weighted average combination. Suppose K cycle of virtual machine availability historical data are collected as sample data, there is:

$$VF = \{vf_1, vf_2, vf_3, \ldots vf_k\} = \{x^{(0)}(1), x^{(0)}(2), \ldots, x^{(0)}(k)\}$$
$$= \{x_{(0)}(1), x_{(0)}(2), \ldots, x_{(0)}(K)\}$$

Phase 1: the establishment of GM (1, 1) model.

(1) The original availability data of virtual machine are accumulated to get a data sequence:

$$x^1(j) = \sum_{i=1}^{j} x^{(0)}(i) j = 1, 2, \ldots, k \tag{3}$$

(2) The GM (1, 1) whitening differential equation of original sequence $x_{(0)}(k)$ is:

$$\frac{dx^{(1)}}{dt} + ax^{(1)} = b \tag{4}$$

where a is the development coefficient that reflects the development trend of actual value; b is the amount of grey representing the relationship between the availability of virtual machine.

Then formula (5) is obtained by discrimination:

$$\Delta^{(1)}(x^{(1)}(j+1)) + az^{(1)}(x(j+1)) = b \tag{5}$$

Where $\Delta^{(1)}(x^{(1)}(j+1))$ is a decreasing sequence of availability when $x^{(1)}$ occurs at time $j+1$, and $z^{(1)}(x^{(1)}(j+1))$ is the background value when $\frac{dx^{(1)}}{dt}$ occurs at time $j+1$. Since there are:

$$\Delta^{(1)}(x^{(1)}(j+1)) = x^{(1)}(j+1) - x^{(1)}(j) = x^{(0)}(j+1) \tag{6}$$

$$z^{(1)}(x(j+1)) = \frac{1}{2}(x^{(1)}(j+1) + x^{(1)}(j)) \tag{7}$$

Take (6) and (7) into formula (5), there is:

$$x^{(0)}(j+1) = a\left[-\frac{1}{2}(x^{(1)}(j+1) + x^{(1)}(j))\right] + b \tag{8}$$

By expanding formula (8), we get:

$$\begin{bmatrix} \{x^{(0)}(1)\} \\ x^{(0)}(2) \\ \vdots \\ x^{(0)}(k) \end{bmatrix} = \begin{bmatrix} -0.5(\{x^{(1)}(1)+x^{(2)}(2)) & 1 \\ -0.5(\{x^{(1)}(2)+x^{(2)}(3)) & 1 \\ \vdots & \vdots \\ -0.5(\{x^{(1)}(k-1)+x^{(2)}(k)) & 1 \end{bmatrix} \tag{9}$$

$$Y_n = \begin{bmatrix} \{x^{(0)}(1)\} \\ x^{(0)}(2) \\ \vdots \\ x^{(0)}(k) \end{bmatrix} \tag{10}$$

Let:

$$B = \begin{bmatrix} -0.5(\{x^{(1)}(1)+x^{(2)}(2)) & 1 \\ -0.5(\{x^{(1)}(2)+x^{(2)}(3)) & 1 \\ \vdots & \vdots \\ -0.5(\{x^{(1)}(k-1)+x^{(2)}(k)) & 1 \end{bmatrix} \tag{11}$$

The least square method is used to solve the parameters to be identified, $\hat{a}$ and $\hat{b}$:

$$[\hat{a}, \hat{b}]^T = (BB^T) B^T BY_n \tag{12}$$

Take $\hat{a}$ and $\hat{b}$ into formula (4), and the discrete solution is obtained:

$$\hat{x}^{(1)}(j+1) = \left(x^{(1)}(1) - \frac{\hat{a}}{\hat{b}}\right) e^{-j\hat{a}} + \frac{\hat{a}}{\hat{b}} j = 1, 2, \ldots, k \tag{13}$$

(3) The original data sequence of virtual machine's availability is restored:

$$\hat{x}^{(0)}(1) = \{x^{(0)}(1)\} \tag{14}$$

$$\hat{x}^{(0)}(j) = \hat{x}^{(1)}(j) - \hat{x}^{(1)}(j-1) = (1 - e^{\hat{a}})\left(x^{(0)}(1) - \frac{\hat{a}}{\hat{b}}\right) e^{-(j-1)\hat{a}} \tag{15}$$

Phase 2: Establishment of the index curve model ($y = ae^{bx}$).

(1) The sample data $x_{(0)} = \{x_{(0)}(i), i = 1, 2\ldots, k\}$ for virtual machines is used to generate the data series $x_{(1)} = \{x_{(1)}(i), i = 1, 2\ldots, k\}$, where:

$$x_{(1)}(i) = \ln x_{(0)}(i) \quad i = 1, 2, \ldots, k \tag{16}$$

(2) Make a linear regression prediction for $x_{(1)}(i)$:

$$b = \left[\sum_{i=1}^{k} ix_{(1)}(i) - \frac{k+1}{2} \sum_{i=1}^{k} ix_{(1)}(i) \right] \left[\frac{k(k+1)(k+2)}{6} - \frac{k(k+1)^2}{4} \right]^{-1} \tag{17}$$

$$a' = \frac{1}{n} \sum_{i=1}^{k} x_{(1)}(i) - \frac{b(k+1)}{2} \tag{18}$$

(3) Generate the prediction sequence of virtual machine's availability:

$$\hat{x}_{(0)}(i) = e^{-\hat{x}_{(1)}(i)} = e^{a' + bi} \tag{19}$$

Let $a = e^{a'}$, then there is:

$$\hat{x}_{(0)}(i) = ae^{bi} \quad i = 1, 2, \ldots, k \tag{20}$$

Phase 3: Establishment of the combination model.

(1) The predicted value of availability of virtual machine at k + 1 time period that are obtained by GM (1, 1) and exponential curve are $\hat{x}^{(0)}(k+1)$ and $\hat{x}_{(0)}(K+1)$ separately.
(2) The final availability of virtual machine is got by sum of arithmetic weighted average:

$$\hat{x}(k+1) = \omega_1 \hat{x}^{(0)}(k+1) + \omega_1 \hat{x}(k+1)_{(0)} \tag{21}$$

$\hat{x}_{(0)}(k+1)$ is the availability of the $k + 1$ time period, ω_1 and ω_2 are obtained by nonlinear programming method ($\omega_1^2 + \omega_2^2 = 1$, $\omega_1 > 0$, $\omega_2 > 0$):

$$\min \sum_{i=1}^{k} F(i) = \sum_{i=1}^{k} (\hat{x}(i) - x(i))^2 = \sum_{i=1}^{k} \left(\omega_1 \hat{x}^{(0)}(i) + \omega_2 \hat{x}_{(0)}(i) - x(i) \right)^2 \tag{22}$$

3   A Virtual Machine Placement Policy Based on Prediction

Nowadays a cloud data center has tens of thousands of virtual machines. Periodically conducting failure detection and calculating the availability of virtual machine may cost certain of computing resources. Also, the virtual machines with low availability may cause the risk of loss of service of applications deployed on them. We design a virtual machine placement policy (abbr. VMPAP) based on availability prediction of virtual

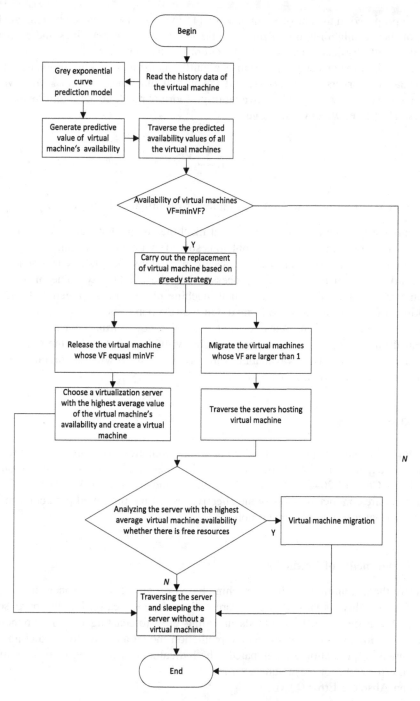

Fig. 3. The process of prediction-based virtual machine placement

machine proposed in the above Section, so that the virtual machines can be relocated in terms of their availability, optimizing the allocation of virtual machines and reducing the number of physical machines and the overall energy consumption.

We consider the placement problem as a multidimensional packing problem, where the virtualized servers are as boxes, and the virtual machines as items. Meanwhile, CPU, memory, bandwidth, and the availability of virtual machine are multidimensional vectors. Therefore, we have the target:

$$\min \sum_i y_i \wedge \frac{1}{n} \sum_{i=1}^{n} \widehat{VF}_{vm_i} \geq 1 \qquad (23)$$

where $\min \sum_i y_i$ represents the minimum number of virtualized servers, $\frac{1}{n} \sum_{i=1}^{n} \widehat{VF}_{vm_i} \geq 1$ represents the average availability of virtual machines is greater than or equal to 1.

The virtual machine placement problem is solved by greedy algorithm. The process of the prediction-based virtual machine placement strategy the strategy is given as the flow chart shown in Fig. 3. In the process, when the availability value of a virtual machine reaches the minimum, the virtual machine placement is triggered. There are two kinds of operations to be performed. On the one hand, the virtual machines with the lowest availability are released, and then the new virtual machines will be re-created on the nodes hosting higher available virtual machines. On the other hand, the virtual machines whose availability are greater than 1 will be migrated to the physical machines of high availability.

4 Experiments

We adopt cloudsim3.0 [14], a cloud computing simulation software, to conduct the simulation experiments. The experimental environment includes certain of computers with Intel Core i7-2640 CPU, 8 GB memory, and JDK1.6.0_43. Two kinds of experiment are conducted to verify the effectiveness of the presented prediction model and the virtual machine placement policy.

4.1 Experiments of Prediction

To verify the availability of virtual machine based on grey curve exponent model, the data of availability of virtual machine are collected periodically. For the purpose of comparative experiment, the methods including grey forecasting model, exponential curve prediction model and combination prediction model are used for predicting, and the accuracy of prediction are compared. The indicators of accuracy we use are mean absolute error and root mean square error.

Mean Absolute Error (MAE) is:

$$MAE = \frac{\sum_{i=1}^{k} |(x_i - \hat{x}_i)|}{k} \tag{24}$$

Root Mean Square Error (RMSE) is:

$$RMSE = \sqrt{\frac{\sum_{i=1}^{k} (x_i - \hat{x}_i)^2}{k}} \tag{25}$$

The comparisons of predicted availability value of three kinds of prediction model under various configuration of number of sampled virtual machine are shown in from Figs. 4, 5 and 6. From these figures, we can see the prediction values of combined grey-exponential curve forecasting model are more accurate than grey prediction model and exponential curve model. The reason is that using an arithmetic weighted average combination effectively improves the prediction accuracy.

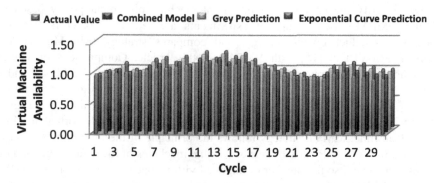

Fig. 4. Comparison of predicted availability value of three kinds of prediction model (the number of virtual machine is 30)

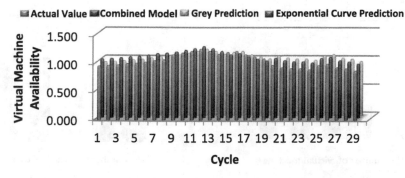

Fig. 5. Comparison of predicted availability value of three kinds of prediction model (the number of virtual machine is 40)

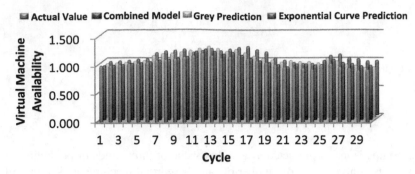

Fig. 6. Comparison of predicted availability value of three kinds of prediction model (the number of virtual machine is 50)

4.2   Experiments of Energy Consumption and the Number of VM Migration

In order to verify the effectiveness of virtual machine placement policy based on prediction(VMPAP), two groups of experiments are set. This experiment adopts Cloudsim to conduct DVFS strategy, and compares strategy (Min-Migrate VM Placement, MMVP) in [15] with VMPAP in this article. Comparisons on energy consumption and the number of migrated virtual machines are shown in Figs. 7 and 8. We can see VMPAP has good results in saving energy and the migration of virtual machines. Since DVFS strategy has no migration of virtual machine, it has great limitations in terms of energy saving, it is suitable for small-scale virtual machine cluster. Meanwhile, MMVP strategy follows the principle of the minimum number of migration, while VMPAP partially releases virtual machines of low availability and the recreates them again, so the number of migrated virtual machines is less. Both MMVP strategy and VMPAP strategy present better energy-saving effects in large-scale virtual machine cluster.

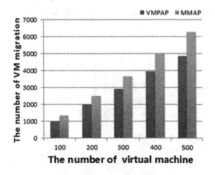

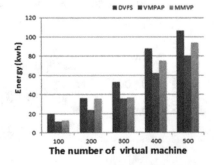

Fig. 7. Comparison of the number of migrated VM   **Fig. 8.** Comparison of energy

5   Conclusions

Availability prediction of virtual machine in cloud environment can provide effective guidance for task scheduling and resource allocation. Some comparisons of different forecasting models are given in Table 1. But the cost of the algorithm is still not to be neglected, and it needs to be further optimized in future work.

Table 1.   Comparative analysis and prediction model

Model	Core methods	Parameter estimation method	Prediction accuracy
Second order autoregressive model [2]	Auto regression	Custom parameters	General
Exponential smoothing model [2, 7, 8]	Exponential Smoothing	Smoothing factor	High specific environment
Linear Model [3]	Auto regression	least squares	General
Sparse periodic autoregressive model [4]	Auto regression	least squares	Cyclical trends higher
Discrete Markov chain model [5]	Fast Fourier Transforms Markov Chain	Chapman - Kolmogorov equation	Higher
Grey Forecasting Model [12]	GM(1, 1)	least squares	Higher
Exponential curve model [13]	Auto regression		General (exponential trend higher)
Grey exponential curve combined model	GM(1, 1) And autoregressive	least squares	High

Acknowledgments. This work is supported by the Natural Science Foundation of China (No. 61063012, 61363003), the National Key Technology R&D Program of China (No. 2015BAH55F02).

References

1. Roy, N., Dubey, A., Gokhale, A.: Efficient autoscaling in the cloud using predictive models for workload forecasting. In: IEEE International Conference on Cloud Computing (CLOUD), DC, pp. 500–507. IEEE Press, Washington (2011)
2. Ardagna, D., Casolari, S., Panicucci, B.: Flexible distributed capacity allocation and load redirect algorithms for cloud systems. In: IEEE International Conference on Cloud Computing (CLOUD), Washington DC, pp. 163–170 (2011)
3. Guenter, B., Jain, N., Williams, C.: Managing cost, performance, and reliability tradeoffs for energy-aware server provisioning. In: Proceedings of INFOCOM, pp. 1332–1340. IEEE Press, Shanghai (2011)
4. Chen, G., He, W., Liu, J., et al.: Energy-aware server provisioning and load dispatching for connection-intensive internet services. In: 5th USENIX Symposium on Networked Systems Design and Implementation, vol. 8, pp. 337–350. USENIX Association (2008)
5. Gong, Z., Gu, X., Wilkes, J.: Press: predictive elastic resource scaling for cloud systems. In: International Conference on Network and Service Management (CNSM), pp. 9–16. IEEE, Niagara Falls (2010)
6. Seddigh, M., Taheri, H., Sharifian, S.: Dynamic prediction scheduling for virtual machine placement via ant colony optimization. In: Signal Processing and Intelligent Systems Conference (SPIS), pp. 104–108. IEEE (2015)
7. Wu, Y.H., Cao, J., Li, M.L.: Research on energy saving allocation method based on demand forecasting in cloud computing environment. J. Chin. Mini-Micro Comput. Syst. **34**(4), 778–782 (2013)
8. Wu, H.S., Wang, C.J., Xie, J.Y.: TeraPELB: an elastic load balancing algorithm based on prediction in cloud computing. J. Syst. Simul. **25**(8), 1751–1759 (2013)
9. Heath, T., Martin, R. P., Nguyen, T, D.: Improving cluster availability using workstation validation. In: Proceedings of the ACM SIGMETRICS, pp. 217–227. Marina Del Rey, California (2002)
10. Schroeder, B., Gibson, G.A.: A large-scale study of failures in high-performance computing systems. IEEE Trans. Dependable Secure Comput. **7**(4), 337–351 (2009)
11. Tian, G.H., Meng, D., Zhan, J.F.: Reliable resource provision policy for cloud computing. Chin. J. Comput. **33**(10), 1859–1872 (2010)
12. Kayacan, E., Ulutas, B., Kaynak, O.: Grey system theory-based models in time series prediction. Expert Syst. Appl. **37**(2), 1784–1789 (2010)
13. Amol, C., Adamuthe, Rajendra, A., Gage, Gopakumaran, T.T.: Forecasting cloud computing using double exponential smoothing methods. In: International Conference on Advanced Computing and Communication Systems, pp. 1–5 (2015)
14. Cloudsim is a kind of cloud computing simulation software [EB/OL]. http://code.google.com/p/cloudsim/
15. Lu, Y., Li, Q., Guo, Y.: Improved prediction model of modified exponential curve. In: Third International Conference on Intelligent Control and Information Processing, pp. 513–516. IEEE (2012)

Scalable Iterative Implementation of Mondrian for Big Data Multidimensional Anonymisation

Xuyun Zhang[1]([⊠]), Lianyong Qi[2,3], Qiang He[4], and Wanchun Dou[2]

[1] Department of Electrical and Computer Engineering,
University of Auckland, Auckland 1023, New Zealand
xuyun.zhang@auckland.ac.nz
[2] State Key Laboratory for Novel Software Technology, Department of Computer
Science and Technology, Nanjing University, Nanjing 210023, China
lianyongqi@gmail.com, douwc@nju.edu.cn
[3] School of Information Science and Engineering, Qufu Normal University,
Qufu 276826, China
[4] School of Software and Electrical Engineering, Swinburne University of Technology,
Victoria 3122, Australia
qhe@swin.edu.au

Abstract. Scalable data processing platforms built on cloud computing are becoming increasingly attractive as infrastructure for supporting big data mining and analytics applications. But privacy concerns are one of the major obstacles to make use of public cloud platforms. Practically, data generalisation is a widely adopted anonymisation technique for data privacy preservation in data publishing or sharing scenarios. Multidimensional anonymisation, a global-recoding generalisation scheme, has been a recent focus due to its capability of balancing data obfuscation and data usability. Existing approaches handled the scalability problem of multidimensional anonymisation for data sets much larger than main memory by storing data on disk at runtime, which incurs an impractical serial I/O cost. In this paper, we propose a scalable iterative multidimensional anonymisation approach for big data sets based on MapReduce, a state-of-the-art large-scale data processing paradigm. Our basic and intuitive idea is to partition a large data set recursively into smaller data partitions using MapReduce until all partitions can fit in memory of each computing node. A tree indexing structure is proposed to achieve recursive computation on MapReduce for data partitioning in multi-dimensional anonymisation. Experimental results on real-life data sets demonstrate that the proposed approach can significantly improve the scalability and time-efficiency of multidimensional anonymisation over existing approaches, and therefore is applicable to big data applications.

Keywords: Big data · Cloud computing · MapReduce · Privacy preservation · Data anonymisation

© Springer International Publishing AG 2016
G. Wang et al. (Eds.): SpaCCS 2016 Workshops, LNCS 10067, pp. 311–320, 2016.
DOI: 10.1007/978-3-319-49145-5_31

1   Introduction

With the advent of big data era [14], an increasingly large volume of data from mobile devices, sensor networks, social media and the Internet of things has been generated and collected. Large-scale data mining and analytics are a key to deriving valuable insights from this deluge of data [3,14], motivating the necessity of big data analytics infrastructure [11]. Cloud platforms where most big data sets are stored, and the scalable data processing tools using cloud infrastructure have become increasingly attractive for supporting big data mining and analytics applications. Cloud infrastructure offers on demand the necessary amount of resources at massive scale parallel and distributed computing with large storage including both main memory and secondary storage for the application need. In particular, the public cloud platforms have many salient features including cost-effectiveness, easy-sharing, high scalability and elasticity. Despite of these benefits, privacy concerns are one of the major obstacles to the adoption of the public cloud resources in many privacy sensitive applications in sectors such as health, finance and defense [1,14]. Privacy risks in cloud environments are usually caused by the redundancy of information in big data sets from various data sources, as well as the ubiquitous access and multi-tenancy features of cloud computing.

In practice, data generalisation is a widely studied and adopted anonymisation technique for data privacy preservation in non-interactive data publishing or sharing scenarios [5]. It refers to hiding the identity and/or masking privacy-sensitive data by replacing detailed attribute values with more generalised ones, so that the privacy of an individual can be preserved while aggregate information of consistent syntax can still be exposed to data users for diverse analysis and mining tasks [10]. A variety of data generalisation methods has been recently proposed based on a series of privacy models. Interested readers could refer to [5] for a complete survey. Among those methods, we will investigate the multidimensional anonymisation scheme herein, which is a global-recoding scheme and strikes a balance between data distortion and data usability. As data sets are usually partitioned into groups in order to hide an individual data record, the anonymisation methods are classified into global-recoding and local-recoding schemes, where global recoding partitions data in terms of attributes, while local recoding in terms of instances. The local-recoding scheme [16] incurs the least data distortion for a certain privacy gain, but it has low usability due to its inconsistent anonymised data, and suffers from the data exploration problem [5]. Another well-studied global-recoding approach is the sub-tree scheme [6]. It partitions data in terms of one single attribute, and incurs much higher data distortion than the multidimensional scheme. Our previous work has examined the scalability problems for the sub-tree and local-recoding schemes and proposed solutions to improve their scalability [17,19]. However, the solutions fail to be applicable to the multidimensional scheme, because multidimensional anonymisation is characterised by recursive computation. Consequently, special considerations are required. A recursive partitioning algorithm named Mondrian [9] has been proposed to implement the scheme under k-anonymity [13].

The scalability problem of the multidimensional scheme has recently drawn the attention of researchers. Iwuchukwu and Naughton [8] proposed an R-tree index-based approach to achieve efficient index construction and bulk anonymisation. As pointed out in [10], the spatial indexing based approach fails to support workload-oriented splitting heuristics. Accordingly, Lefevre et al. [10] proposed two external adaptations of the Mondrian algorithmic framework based on RainForest scalable decision tree algorithms [7] and a sampling technique, respectively. The core of the two adaptations is how to split a data set into smaller data partitions that can be fit in memory. Our approach also relies on this basic method for scalability problems. However, the above approaches are serial in essence, although they are scalable to large data sets. They often scan the whole data set to obtain count statistics when choosing splitting attributes or domain values. The overheads for such heavy serial I/O will be overwhelmingly high for big data sets. For example [4], it takes more than 3 h to read 1 TB data for a single modern eSATA disk at 5 GB/min, let alone larger data sets like Twitter crawl (>12 TB) often stored on multiple disks. With respect to the recursive feature of multidimensional anonymisation algorithms, parallelisation seems to be an ideal solution to the scalability problem over big data. However, it is still a challenge to use state-of-the-art distributed and parallel paradigms directly for recursive computation, since these paradigms are originally designed for batch processing or stream oriented computing.

In this paper, we propose a scalable multidimensional anonymisation approach for big data sets using MapReduce [2], a state-of-the-art large-scale data processing paradigm. The approach is named as MRMondrian for reference by following the naming of Mondrian algorithms [9,10]. Our intuitive idea is to partition a large data set recursively into smaller data partitions using MapReduce until all partitions can fit in the memory of each computing node. Then, traditional Mondrian algorithms can be executed on each single node in a parallel fashion. To avoid launching multiple MapReduce jobs recursively for data partitioning, we propose to accomplish data partitioning in a single MapReduce job. We propose a Partition ID indexing tree structure (PID-tree) to support recursive computation on MapReduce. Both categorical and numerical attributes are allowed herein for the multidimensional scheme. Extensive experiments are performed on real-life data sets to demonstrate that our approach can significantly improve the scalability and efficiency of multidimensional anonymisation. The k-anonymity privacy model [13] is employed as a representative in our work.

The rest of this paper is organised as follows. The next section formulates our approach in detail. In Sect. 3, extensive experiments are conducted on real-world data sets to evaluate the proposed approach. We conclude this paper and discuss the future work in Sect. 4.

2   Iterative Mondrian with MapReduce (MRMondrian)

2.1   Overview

According to the recursive description of the Mondrian method [9], a straight-forward approach based on MapReduce is to invoke MapReduce jobs recursively. Specifically, we can run a MapReduce operation to compute the count statistics for the splitting heuristics for a given data set. Then, we run another MapReduce operation to divide the data according to the splitting attribute and domain values. These two MapReduce operations are executed on each partition recursively. As these two operations can be implemented in a highly scalable manner, this direct solution appears to be scalable. The details of recursive design have been presented in our previous work [18]. However, the number of data partitions can grow exponentially, meaning that the number of MapReduce jobs can become exponentially large but of course limited by the data size ($\leq (n/k)$). This consumes too many computing nodes and incurs high extra overheads for job initialisation and scheduling. To save computation cost, it is necessary to adjust the number of computing nodes for data sets at certain recursive levels.

To circumvent the problems, we propose to partition the data iteratively in a breadth-first fashion. Only one MapReduce job is executed within one round of iteration. Compared with the direct recursive implementation, the iterative one possesses several advantages. Only one MapReduce job is invoked in each round of iteration, avoiding extra initialisation and scheduling overheads incurred by multiple MapReduce jobs. Due to the breadth-first feature, the amount of computation in a round of iterative Mondrian is roughly equal to that of other rounds. Thus, we can use a constant number of computing nodes for all the rounds of the iteration. Most importantly, it is unnecessary to partition the original data set concretely in each round, which can avoid intensive data transmission among computing nodes. Concrete partitioning herein means that the data records belong to a partition are relocated into a single node, rather than distributed among multiple nodes. As such, only one MapReduce job is executed to compute certain splitting heuristics. The data set is only partitioned concretely once when some conditions are satisfied during the iteration, which will be elaborated later. Lastly, standard MapReduce supports iterative computation better than recursive computation.

To achieve iterative Mondrian using MapReduce, the pivot is to maintain the basic information of partitions, such as the partition ID, the quasi-identifier, splitting attributes and values, and count statistics. The partition information serves several main purposes including searching the partition ID for a data record and determining when to perform concrete data partitioning. Accordingly, we propose an indexing structure called a Partition ID tree (PID-tree) to manage the process of data partitioning by retaining the basic information of partitions. A PID-tree is constructed in a breadth-first manner with the count statistics calculated by the corresponding MapReduce job. The leaf nodes of the PID-tree together represent the current partitioning of the original data set. The PID-tree is delivered to the *Map* and *Reduce* functions, and is utilised to retrieve the partition ID of an original record to compute the count statistics for a partition. Details of PID-tree are described in Sect. 2.2.

The iteration process of the breadth-first Mondrian stops when certain conditions are satisfied. One effective condition is that all the data partitions are small enough to fit in the memory of a single computing node. Once this condition is satisfied, the original data set is partitioned concretely. The serial Mondrian algorithm can be run on each partition. The condition brings several benefits. A single node can make full use of its computing power to run the serial Mondrian algorithm. Usually, the serial version of an algorithm is more efficient than its parallel or distributed version over small-scale data sets that can fit in main memory, because the latter often incurs extra overheads for parallelisation. Another benefit can be that the scale of the PID-tree is limited, without suffering from the scalability problem. Since the leaf nodes of a PID-tree can proliferate exponentially with the growth of their depth, the size of a leaf data partition degrades exponentially as well. Even if an original data set is very large, tens of rounds of iteration will probably render each data partition small enough to fit in memory. Hence, the number of leaf nodes of the PID-tree will not be too huge. The scale of the PID-tree impacts the performance of the partitioning process as most operations are performed on the tree. Moreover, the PID-tree will be delivered to each *Mapper* and *Reducer* as a global variable by the distributed cache mechanism when running MapReduce jobs. The performance will be affected if the tree is too large.

2.2 Partition ID Indexing Tree

The Partition ID indexing tree (PID-tree) plays a core role in the iterative Mondrian algorithm with MapReduce. It is crucial for MapReduce jobs to identify which partition a data record belongs to during the process of computing splitting heuristics or dividing data sets. That is, given a record r, we try to find out its present partition $p \in P$. This enables simultaneously processing multiple data partitions having the same recursive depth in a batch manner with MapReduce. Initially, the tree is empty. Its nodes with the same depth are inserted simultaneously in one round of iteration after identifying the splitting attribute and value for each partition. The PID-tree is constructed iteratively in a breadth-first manner.

A node in the PID-tree mainly contains the following information for a data partition: the partition ID, the quasi-identifier of the partition, the splitting attribute, the splitting value, the partition size, the minimum child partition size and an available attribute set $\mathcal{A}^{Ava}$. The partition ID is generated automatically and monotonically increases from top to bottom and from left to right in the tree structure. The splitting attribute and value are retained to facilitate the search operation. The size of partition is used to determine whether it is the time to concretely partition data, while the minimum child partition size is also kept to check whether the partition is minimally k-anonymised. $\mathcal{A}^{Ava}$ refers to a set of attributes that can still be split further. This applies to categorical attributes. Once the quasi-identifier value of the attribute reaches to a leaf node in the

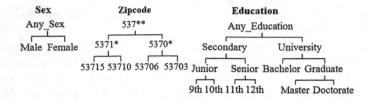

Fig. 1. Taxonomy trees for *Sex*, *Zipcode* and *Education*.

taxonomy tree, the domain value cannot be split any more. No matter whether a partition is already k-anonymised or not, it cannot be partitioned further if its $\mathcal{A}^{Ava} = \emptyset$. The amount of such meta data contained in a PID-tree node is minor compared to the amount of the data partition itself. Hence, the space cost of the tree is small even if the number of nodes is large.

Two basic operations are frequently performed on a PID tree, i.e., searching the partition ID for a record and inserting leaf nodes to update the tree after splitting attributes and values are identified. They are implemented as follows. The searching process starts from the root of the tree, and chooses a branch to descend by comparing the splitting value with the value of the record at the splitting attribute. When arriving at a leaf node, the process returns the partition ID. The *Map* and *Reduce* jobs will exploit the partition ID to distinguish records belonging to different partitions. To insert a new node, its parent will be found as the first step. Then, its basic information can be derived from its parent, the selected splitting attribute and value, and the resultant count statistics. For instance, its quasi-identifier can be constructed from its parent's quasi-identifier by replacing the quasi-identifier value of the splitting attribute with a corresponding child value. The partition size and the minimum child size can be obtained from the count statistics. The time complexity of both operations is $O(H)$, where H is the height of the PID-tree.

Example. Given the taxonomy trees in Fig. 1 and the hospital patient data in Table 1, Fig. 2 shows the PID-tree producing a 2-anonymous data partitioning via the multidimensional scheme. The immediate identifier attribute *Name*

Table 1. Hospital patient data.

No.	Name	Sex	Zip.	Edu.	Disease
1	Alice	Female	53715	Master	Flu
2	Bob	Male	53706	Doctorate	Hepatitis
3	Ellen	Female	53710	Doctorate	HIV
4	Beth	Male	53703	12th	Bronchitis
5	Jack	Male	53707	11th	Flu
6	Jim	Male	53711	Bachelor	HIV

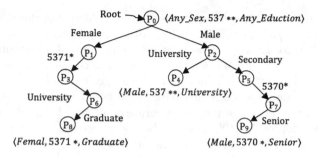

Fig. 2. An example of Partition ID indexing tree.

is removed. P_4, P_8 and P_9 are three leaf partitions of the tree, representing anonymised QI-groups in the anonymous data set.

It can be seen that a PID-tree itself is a centralised data structure, which is delivered to *Mapper* and *Reducer* as a global read-only variable. The PID-tree is stored and updated in the driver program which runs on the single master computing node. But note that the data intensive computation for calculating heuristics is accomplished on worker computing nodes in a parallel way. When the data set is extremely large, however, the master node may become a scalability bottleneck because the number of leaf partitions increase exponentially with the iteration proceeding. The amount of stored PID-tree meta data and the number of insertion operations within one round of iteration are proportional to the number of the number of leaf partitions. Thanks to the fact that we only target the final anonymous data set rather than the whole structure of the PID-tree, this scalability issue can be addressed through integrating the direct recursive implementation. Specifically, multiple MapReduce jobs are launched recursively in the early stages of data partitioning. Then, the iterative implementation can be applied on each partition at a certain stage. By this means, we can obtain multiple master computing nodes without suffering from the scalability bottleneck. Theoretically, this hybrid approach can handle data sets of any large size, where cloud resources are usually regarded as on-demand and "unlimited".

3 Experimental Evaluation

3.1 Experimental Settings

The experiments are conducted on a cloud platform. The Hadoop cluster consists of 20 virtual machines of type *m1.medium*, having 2 virtual CPUs and 4 GB Memory. The execution time is measured for scalability and time-efficiency. The data distortion is captured by *ILoss* [15]. The value of *ILoss* is normalised for comparison. Each round of experiments is repeated 10 times. The mean and standard errors of the measured results are reported for a comprehensive evaluation. We use the *Adult* dataset from UCI Machine Learning Repository[1], a

---

[1] http://archive.ics.uci.edu/ml/datasets/Adult.

publicly available dataset commonly used as a de facto benchmark for testing anonymisation algorithms [6,9,10,12,16]. After pre-processing, the dataset consists of 18,909 records. We utilise nine attributes out of 14 attributes in our experiments. The attribute *Work Class* is utilised as the sensitive attribute. The eight quasi-identifier attributes include both categorical and numerical ones like *Age*. Since we evaluate the scalability with respect to data volume, the size of the original *Adult* data set is blown up to generate a series of larger data sets, which is a technique adopted in [12]. The number of records in an enlarged data set can reach hundreds of millions, rendering most existing approaches incapable of handling such a data set. The enlarged data sets are big enough to evaluate our approach effectively, as big data usually means traditional tools fail to handle it within a tolerable elapsed time [14].

3.2 Experimental Process and Results

We compare our approach with the serial Mondrian method to show scalability problems of the serial algorithm while ours is still scalable. The k-anonymity parameter is set to 10 for all experiments except the third group of experiments.

Serial Mondrian vs. MRMondrian. We compare our approach with the serial Mondrian method in this group of experiments, to show the poor scalability of serial Mondrian for big data. To make a fair comparison, serial Mondrian is executed on a virtual machine of *m1.large* type that has 4 virtual CPUs and 8 GB memory. The number of records ranges from 500,000 to 5,000,000. In fact, serial Mondrian runs out of memory after the number of records beyond 5,000,000. θ ranges from 10 to 50 in terms of the number of records, which can keep partition sizes around 10,000 and strike a balance between the two phases of computation in terms of the experiments above. Figure 3 reports the results.

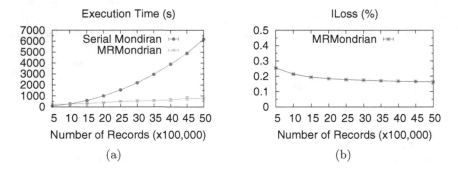

Fig. 3. Change of execution time and ILoss w.r.t. the number of records.

From Fig. 3(a), we can see that the execution time of serial Mondrian goes up dramatically when the number of records is increasing, while that of our approach MRMondrian grows slightly. Initially, the execution time of serial Mondrian is less than that of MRMondrian. When a data set is small (can fit in memory), serial Mondrian can be more efficient than MRMondrian because MRMondrian incurs certain extra overheads to make use of MapReduce. But after a point $(1,000,000$ here), MRMondrian becomes much more efficient, and the execution time difference becomes increasingly larger when the number of records increases. Moreover, serial Mondrian fails due to insufficient memory when the number of records is greater than $5,000,000$. Hence, it is incapable of scaling to big data sets, while MRMondrian manages to do this. We show later that MRMondrian is still effective and scalable over larger data sets.

The data distortions are the same, as shown in Fig. 3(b). This is because once the splitting heuristics are determined, different Mondrian algorithms will produce the same degree of data distortion. As illustrated in the figure, the data distortion degrades when data volume grows. This complies with the fact that more data produces less data distortion.

The experiments above demonstrate that our approach MRMondrian can significantly improve the scalability and time-efficiency of multidimensional anonymisation compared with state-of-the-art approaches.

4   Conclusions and Future Work

In this paper, we have proposed a highly scalable and efficient approach named MRMondrian for multidimensional anonymisation over big data based on the MapReduce paradigm. Following the basic idea of dividing data sets into small data partitions to make them fit into the main memory of a single node, we have proposed to conduct iterative data partitioning in a parallel manner. Concrete data partitioning is performed when all data partitions can fit into main memory. Then, each data partition is further divided recursively by the traditional serial Mondrian method on a single node. To support iterative data partitioning, a tree structure named PID-tree has been proposed to index data partitions for searching partition IDs. Experimental results from real-world data sets have shown that our approach can significantly improve the scalability and time-efficiency of the multidimensional scheme over existing approaches. In the future, we plan to integrate our approach with scalable data mining platforms to achieve scalable privacy-preserving big data mining.

Acknowledgments. This paper is partially supported by Open Project of State Key Laboratory for Novel Software Technology (No. KFKT2015A03), Natural Science Foundation of China (No. 61402258), China Postdoctoral Science Foundation (No. 2015M571739), Open Project of State Key Laboratory for Novel Software Technology (No. KFKT2016B22).

References

1. Chaudhuri, S.: What next?: a half-dozen data management research goals for big data and the cloud. In: Proceedings of the PODS 2012, pp. 1–4 (2012)
2. Dean, J., Ghemawat, S.: Mapreduce: a flexible data processing tool. Commun. ACM **53**(1), 72–77 (2010)
3. Fan, W., Bifet, A.: Mining big data: current status, and forecast to the future. ACM SIGKDD Explor. Newsl. **14**(2), 1–5 (2013)
4. Ferreira Cordeiro, R.L., Traina Jr., C., Machado Traina, A.J., López, J., Kang, U., Faloutsos, C.: Clustering very large multi-dimensional datasets with mapreduce. In: Proceedings of the SIGKDD 2011, pp. 690–698 (2011)
5. Fung, B., Wang, K., Chen, R., Yu, P.S.: Privacy-preserving data publishing: a survey of recent developments. ACM Comput. Surv. **42**(4), 14 (2010)
6. Fung, B.C., Wang, K., Yu, P.S.: Anonymizing classification data for privacy preservation. IEEE TKDE **19**(5), 711–725 (2007)
7. Gehrke, J., Ramakrishnan, R., Ganti, V.: Rainforest-a framework for fast decision tree construction of large datasets. In: Proceedings of the VLDB 1998, pp. 416–427 (1998)
8. Iwuchukwu, T., Naughton, J.F.: K-anonymization as spatial indexing: toward scalable and incremental anonymization. In: Proceedings of the VLDB 2007, pp. 746–757 (2007)
9. LeFevre, K., DeWitt, D.J., Ramakrishnan, R.: Mondrian multidimensional k-anonymity. In: Proceedings of the ICDE 2006, p. 25 (2006)
10. LeFevre, K., DeWitt, D.J., Ramakrishnan, R.: Workload-aware anonymization techniques for large-scale datasets. ACM TODS **33**(3), 17 (2008)
11. Lin, J., Ryaboy, D.: Scaling big data mining infrastructure: the twitter experience. ACM SIGKDD Explor. Newslett. **14**(2), 6–19 (2013)
12. Mohammed, N., Fung, B., Hung, P.C., Lee, C.K.: Centralized and distributed anonymization for high-dimensional healthcare data. ACM TKDD **4**(4), 18 (2010)
13. Sweeney, L.: *k*-anonymity: a model for protecting privacy. Int. J. Uncertainty Fuzziness **10**(05), 557–570 (2002)
14. Wu, X., Zhu, X., Wu, G.Q., Ding, W.: Data mining with big data. IEEE TKDE **26**(1), 97–107 (2014)
15. Xiao, X., Tao, Y.: Personalized privacy preservation. In: Proceedings of the SIGMOD 2006, pp. 229–240 (2006)
16. Xu, J., Wang, W., Pei, J., Wang, X., Shi, B., Fu, A.W.C.: Utility-based anonymization using local recoding. In: Proceedings of the SIGKDD 2006, pp. 785–790 (2006)
17. Zhang, X., Dou, W., Pei, J., Nepal, S., Yang, C., Liu, C., Chen, J.: Proximity-aware local-recoding anonymization with mapreduce for scalable big data privacy preservation in cloud. IEEE Trans. Comput. **PP**(99) (2014)
18. Zhang, X., Yang, C., Nepal, S., Liu, C., Dou, W., Chen, J.: A mapreduce based approach of scalable multidimensional anonymization for big data privacy preservation on cloud. In: Proceedings of the 3rd International Conference on Cloud and Green Computing (CGC2013), pp. 105–112 (2013)
19. Zhang, X., Yang, L.T., Liu, C., Chen, J.: A scalable two-phase top-down specialization approach for data anonymization using mapreduce on cloud. IEEE TPDS **25**(2), 363–373 (2014)

Annual Big Data Security, Privacy and Trust Workshop (BigDataSPT 2016)

Effective Task Scheduling for Large-Scale Video Processing

Jie Dai[✉] and Xin Wang

The Third Research Institute of the Ministry of Public Security,
Shanghai 201204, The People's Republic of China
olivierdai@163.com, xinwang.xjtu@gmail.com

Abstract. The rapid growth of video surveillance systems has brought the trend of analyzing video objects characteristics for subsequent semantic applications. However, the complexity of extracting object features from surveillance video is substantial due to resource consumption in video transmission and computation in a large-scale distributed environment. Video processing jobs should be adequately assigned to distributed processing servers, without violating the capacity requirement in processing video flows. To resolve this issue, we discuss fundamental design principles for the task scheduling in large-scale video processing systems. We present the architecture and methods of distributing jobs in a resource pool, with considerations on important factors such as the prediction of video flow traffic, the processing workload and the heuristic assignment decision. Proposed methods can be selectively implemented in practical systems with emphasis on satisfying different system requirements.

Keywords: Video surveillance · Video processing · Dynamic scheduling · Resource allocation · Server interaction

1   Introduction

The continuous development of video surveillance systems has brought the rapid growth of semantic object analysis in high-definition video. The behavior and characteristic of video objects can be extracted through effective content analysis. However, the deployment of large-scale surveillance cameras brought new challenges to the management of large-scale video processing, including the timely content analysis, the semantic association and the data management.

Due to the limitation of computing capacity, traditional video processing doesn't consider the requirement of parallel processing. On the contrary, current processing server can handle multiple video flows simultaneously. Moreover, certain front node can also extract basic characteristics of video content. Therefore, the proposed management mechanism should be able to smoothly work on large scale distributed systems with efficient operations. The large-scale video processing involves heavy computing workload, large amount of data transfer, and dynamic task variation. Thus, it demands the effective task coordination and workload balancing with great difficulty in this case.

© Springer International Publishing AG 2016
G. Wang et al. (Eds.): SpaCCS 2016 Workshops, LNCS 10067, pp. 323–331, 2016.
DOI: 10.1007/978-3-319-49145-5_32

In overall, the task scheduling is mainly constrained by the video flow variation, the computing capacity, the data traffic and other related issues. In this paper, we discuss the general task scheduling processes and policies for existing large-scale video analysis system based on aforementioned impacting factors. We explore and propose a variety of task scheduling mechanisms which can be employed in different dynamic video analysis systems. Compared with traditional stand-alone computing model and existing Hadoop system, the proposed mechanisms consider various factors including the prediction of incoming flows, the adaptive video segmentation and the interaction between front and back ends servers etc.

2 Related Works

Video processing indicates the extraction of object features from surveillance video streams [1, 2]. Due to the increasing amount of video surveillance systems deployed in the city, the scheduling of large-scale video processing tasks becomes a critical issue in practice. Similar scheduling systems appear in the MapReduce ecological system [3]. In existing MapReduce system, the master node first detects the slave location and the processing data location [4]. Then, it determines the scheduling strategy with a relatively small and fixed fragment of processing workloads being allocated to the nearby servers with sufficient computing power. The remaining jobs are dynamically scheduled online when certain servers finish previous jobs [5]. MapReduce jobs are always in a controllable environment since workload can be divided into small fragments with predictable computational requirement. In the contrary, the analysis of video files has large fluctuations in the amount of calculation which varies along the time [6]. Each online stream has heterogeneous processing time in different time slots that easily leads to the load imbalance of the cluster. Therefore, we need to investigate the flow characteristics, then employ different dynamic scheduling strategies in accordance with the variation of video processing requirement.

The resource allocation algorithm for video processing is proposed on a given infrastructure of service cloud in the background of video transcoding service [7]. The proposed algorithms provide mechanisms for allocation of virtual machines (VMs) to a cluster of video transcoding servers. A scheduling framework for adaptive video delivery over cellular networks is proposed in [8]. The optimal allocation of resources is computed for all users by determining and selecting an optimal bit rate for each user using the allocator. Our proposed methods mainly differ from above studies for the method employed in video processing. Consequently, the processing jobs also exhibit different requirements.

In many large-scale distributed systems such as cloud computing platforms, the virtualization technique [9] is utilized to schedule the system resource to meet the requirement of dynamic processing jobs. The virtual machine is started in case of highly dynamic scenario, which needs to be highly predictable to ensure that all dimensions of resources on a continuous period of time will not conflict [10]. Similarly, the scheduling decision of video processing jobs has to be adapted to the dynamic incoming flow, so that required server resources do not exceed the provisioned capacity. The proposed method can be implemented using virtual machines, in order to provide resource support to the dynamic system environment.

3   Design of Effective Task Scheduling for Large-Scale Video Processing

In large-scale video processing systems, task planning is divided into phases including the load analysis, the resource topology analysis and the optimization of overall allocation. In the real-time server collaboration, once the task scheduled to terminals exceeds the capacity of the node, the system efficiency will be greatly affected. Thus, the task needs to be deployed according to the long-term demand forecast based on statistical law. The accurate prediction of the workload is an important factor that ensures the timely complement of assigned tasks. After obtaining the load prediction result and the list of available resources, the control center needs to determine the optimal cooperation strategy based on the resource requirement and the network connection status etc. Both front nodes and back-end servers can process video flows nowadays. However, the transferred traffic can be evidently different while deploying jobs to different servers. Thus, we need to consider the interaction between front and back-end processing servers (Fig. 1).

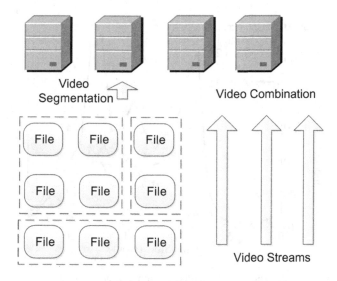

Fig. 1. Design of scheduling strategies

In the practical video analysis system, the task load is in a steady state in short running process. Therefore, the potential sub-optimal solution can be provided using heuristic algorithm. However, when the demand fluctuation occurs in different time slots, analysis tasks cannot be completed using the original resources related to tasks. In this case, the control system determines the reallocation of tasks by performing the strategy adjustment for the dynamic provision of resources. In overall, under the effect of dynamic characteristics and resource-intensive computing requirement in the video description, the problem of proposing an adequate scheduling decision is of high degree of complexity. The effective scheduling mechanisms should be based on the prediction of the workload, the consideration on the dynamically provisioned resources and other related factors. It selects the appropriate node on the basis of processing data flow in time to achieve an efficient distribution of tasks.

3.1 Prediction of Incoming Flows and Traffic

The effective task scheduling in large-scale video surveillance systems first relies on the accurate model of incoming traffic in each video flow. For example, the vehicle characteristic processing jobs are closely related to the amount of passing cars in different time slots, which can be possibly predicted according to statistical results.

The prediction problem is considered in two scenarios. First, the system is relatively stable in a short period of time, and each individual flow reflects different characteristics. In such stable large-scale systems, queuing theory is an effective operation for representing the system behavior [11]. For example, our previous study [12] utilizes the poisson process to characterize the incoming traffic of each flow with respective arrival rate. We denote the arrival request rate of flow i as λ_i, which indicates the incoming request processing rate for each camera in the scheduling optimization problem (Fig. 2).

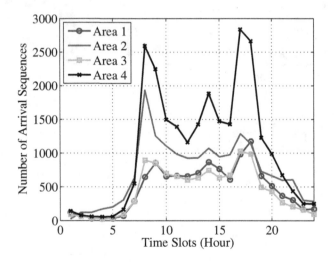

Fig. 2. The arrival rate distribution in practical systems

3.2 Interaction Between Front and Back End Servers

Some processing jobs have large file transfer size, thus it would be benefit to consider the timely interaction between front end and back end servers. With the development of intelligent front nodes, simple characteristics and behaviors of video objects can be detected and analyzed by the front end video processing equipment. Therefore, the interaction between front and back end servers is proposed in order to offload the heavy workload of network and back end servers (Fig. 3).

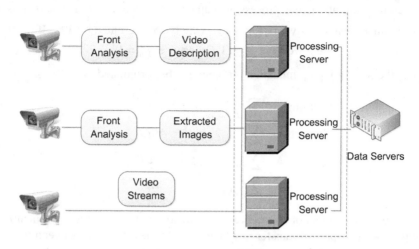

Fig. 3. The interaction between front and back ends

If videos are analyzed at the front node, only the description text and image will be transferred to the back end. This reduces the heavy network traffic in current video processing scenarios. In the optimization model, the transfer rate r between flow i and its associated front node j can be given as:

$$r_{ij} = 0 \tag{1}$$

On the contrary, if the video flow is transmitted to the back-end processing server j, the transfer rate is given as the following in which s_i represents the streaming rate of video flow:

$$r_{ij} = s_i \tag{2}$$

3.3 Flow Combination Strategy

Since the single server can usually process several streams simultaneously, different video flows can be combined to certain set of processing servers in the stable workload scenario of scheduling mechanism. This becomes an optimization problem that aims to maximize the amount of processing video flow requests.

If the arrival process is modeled as a poison process, the arrival rate of combined flows on a single server equals to the sum of their respective arrival rate. The optimization model is subject to following limitations:

1. Data transfer limitation, this is determined by the inter-bandwidth between video sources and processing servers, as well as the transmitting rate. We define the

parameter x_{ij}, in which $x_{ij} = 0$ if node j is the associated front-end server of flow i and $x_{ij} = 1$ otherwise. The downloading rate limitation of node j is r_j;

2. Processing limitation, the processing capacity in each individual server is the maximum allowable arrival rate at node j which is represented by λ_j^{max}. If the flow i is processed by node j, we have $p_{ij} = 1$. Otherwise, $p_{ij} = 0$.

Then, the scheduling optimization problem can be formulated as:

$$\text{Maximize} \quad \sum_{i \epsilon I} \sum_{j \epsilon J} p_{ij} \lambda_i$$

$$\text{Subject to:} \quad \sum_{i \epsilon I} p_{ij} \lambda_i \leq \lambda_j^{max} \quad \forall j \epsilon J$$

$$\sum_{i \epsilon I} x_{ij} p_{ij} s_i \leq r_j \quad \forall j \epsilon J \tag{3}$$

$$\sum_{j \epsilon J} p_{ij} \leq 1 \quad \forall i \epsilon I$$

Compared to conventional resource optimization problem, the aforementioned problem adds the impact of transfer rate factor due to the difference between front and back end servers. For front end servers in practice, the processing capacity is usually limited. On the contrary, the back-end server is mainly constrained by the transfer rate given the limitation and optimization target of the problem. Based on solutions of similar problems and aforementioned analysis, we propose a heuristic algorithm for the adequate allocation of video flows:

Algorithm 1. Scheduling Mechanism for Flow Combination Strategy

Input: r_j, λ_j^{max}, λ_i, s_i

Output: p_{ij}

1:     for each $j \epsilon J$ and j is a front node
2:       sort associated flows in ascending order of λ_i / s_i
3:       set $p_{ij} = 1$ until $\sum_1^i p_{ij} \lambda_i > \lambda_j^{max}$
4:     end for
5:     Sort I in descending order of λ_i / s_i
6:     for each $i \epsilon I$
7:       if $p_{ij} == 0$
8:         Sort J in descending order of $(\lambda_j^{max} - \sum_{i \epsilon I} p_{ij} \lambda_i) / (r_j - \sum_{i \epsilon I} x_{ij} p_{ij} s_i)$
9:         for each $j \epsilon J$
10:          if $\lambda_j^{max} - \sum_{i \epsilon I} p_{ij} \lambda_i \geq \lambda_i$ and $r_j - \sum_{i \epsilon I} x_{ij} p_{ij} s_i \geq s_i$
11:           Set $p_{ij} = 1$ and break
12:         end if
13:       end for
14:     end if
15:     end for

3.4 Video Segmentation Strategy

Compared to the flow combination strategy that achieves the service acceleration in a coarse adjustment manner, a more fine-tuned strategy is to split video streams of fixed amount of time into segments. Each segment i with different file size s_i contains relatively stable amount of λ arrival video objects. The video segmentation requires a precise prediction of task workload in certain amount of time for individual flows, which can be obtained by the prediction model.

Suppose node j can receive video segments with total size of r_j during this fixed amount of time, while it is able to process λ_j^{max} objects. The optimization problem is given as:

$$\text{Maximize} \quad \sum_{i \in I} p_{ij} \lambda \leq \lambda_j^{max}$$

$$\text{Subject to:} \quad \sum_{i \in I} p_{ij} \lambda \leq \lambda_j^{max} \quad \forall j \in J$$

$$\sum_{i \in I} x_{ij} p_{ij} s_i \leq r_j \quad \forall j \in J \tag{4}$$

$$\sum_{j \in J} p_{ij} \leq 1 \quad \forall i \in I$$

The corresponding heuristic algorithm is shown below.

Algorithm 2. Scheduling Mechanism for Video Segmentation Strategy

Input: r_j, λ_j^{max}, λ, s_i

Output: p_{ij}

```
1:   for each j∈J and j is a front node
2:       sort associated segments in descending order of s_i
3:       set p_ij = 1 until Σ_1^i p_ij λ > λ_j^max
4:   end for
5:   Sort I in ascending order of s_i
6:   for each i∈I
7:       if p_ij == 0
8:           Sort J in descending order of (λ_j^max − Σ_i∈I p_ij λ)/ (r_j − Σ_i∈I x_ij p_ij s_i)
9:           for each j∈J
10:              if λ_j^max − Σ_i∈I p_ij λ ≥ λ and r_j − Σ_i∈I x_ij p_ij s_i ≥ s_i
11:                  Set p_ij = 1 and break
12:              end if
13:          end for
14:      end if
15:  end for
```

In the video segmentation method, extra time is required for the video segmentation. However, the assignment of system requests to adequate server can be efficiently achieved by assigning fixed amount of video objects to them, based on their processing abilities. This also helps to achieve a better load balancing among a group of servers. In practice, the video is not divided into files in the operating system. Instead, the beginning frame and the end frame of assigned video streams are indicated to designated servers. The access to the video is based on the stream access or the efficient distributed file system such as HDFS, so that the access to video segments will be efficiently manipulated.

3.5 Task Reallocation Strategy

The task allocation strategies including flow combination and video segmentation can determine the near optimal distribution of video processing tasks in stable workloads. When the system fluctuation occurs in different time slots, the task reallocation strategy is applied to enable the redistribution of existing task flows.

Although the system is relatively stable in short periods of time, however, it greatly varies along the time according to our practical data trace analysis [12]. Therefore, the system will also use the statistical analysis to predict the future load of each video flow. The solution to the scheduling optimization problem is obtained with different system parameters to locate the appropriate resource supply in the next period of time. In practical scheduling, the optimal scheduling decision is made in each individual time slot based on the scheduling strategy.

Specific task migration can be divided into two collaborative approaches. The traditional way is to perform lightweight task migration which creates a new process on another processing server to complete the process. Another way is to achieve the dynamic migration of virtual machines in order to run analysis tasks on alternative available devices. As it involves the incremental transfer of virtual machine image file, higher consumption of resources is required in this method.

4 Conclusion

In this paper, we discuss fundamental design principles for the efficient task scheduling in large-scale video processing systems. The architecture and methods of distributing jobs with considerations on important factors such as the prediction of video flow traffic, the heuristic assignment decision and the online adjustment of the strategy are presented. Collaborative scheduling strategy ensures that the calculation is coupled with the data to improve the overall efficiency, while the assigned workload can be fulfilled by adequate server resources. Proposed mechanisms can be selectively implemented in practical systems concerning specific demand and system environment.

Acknowledgments. This work was supported in part by the National Science Foundation of China under Grants 61300028, in part by the Project of the Ministry of Public Security under Grant 2014JSYJB009.

References

1. Michalopoulos, P.G., Jacobson, R.D., Anderson, C.A., et al.: Automatic incident detection through video image processing. Ann. N. Y. Acad. Sci. **1078**(1), 15–25 (2015)
2. Wang, X.: Intelligent multi-camera video surveillance: a review. Pattern Recogn. Lett. **34**(1), 3–19 (2013)

3. Dean, J., Ghemawat, S.: MapReduce: simplified data processing on large clusters. Commun. ACM **51**(1), 107–113 (2008)
4. Verma, A., Cherkasova, L., Campbell, R.H.: ARIA: automatic resource inference and allocation for mapreduce environments. In: International Conference on Autonomic Computing, Icac 2011, Karlsruhe, Germany, pp. 249–256, June 2011
5. Cheng, D., Rao, J., Guo, Y., et al.: Improving MapReduce performance in heterogeneous environments with adaptive task tuning. In: The International MIDDLEWARE Conference, pp. 97–108 (2014)
6. Chen, T.P., Haussecker, H., Bovyrin, A., et al.: Computer vision workload analysis: case study of video surveillance systems. Intel Technol. J. **9**(2), 109–118 (2005)
7. Jokhio, F., Ashraf, A., Lafond, S., et al.: Prediction-based dynamic resource allocation for video transcoding in cloud computing. In: Euromicro International Conference on Parallel, Distributed, and Network-Based Processing, pp. 254–261 (2013)
8. Chen, J., Mahindra, R., Khojastepour, M.A., et al.: A scheduling framework for adaptive video delivery over cellular networks. In: International Conference on Mobile Computing & Networking, pp. 389–400 (2016)
9. Uhlig, R., Neiger, G., Rodgers, D., et al.: Intel virtualization technology. Computer **38**(5), 48–56 (2005)
10. Padala, P., Shin, K.G., Zhu, X., et al.: Adaptive control of virtualized resources in utility computing environments. ACM SIGOPS Operating Syst. Rev. **41**(3), 289–302 (2007)
11. Gross, D., Harris, C.M.: Fundamentals of Queueing Theory. Wiley, New York (2008)
12. Dai, J., Zhao, Y., Liu, Y., et al.: Cloud-assisted analysis for energy efficiency in intelligent video systems. J. Supercomputing **70**(3), 1345–1364 (2014)

Fuzzy and Semantic Search over Encrypted Data in the Cloud

Xiaoyu Zhu[1], Guojun Wang[2(✉)], and Dongqing Xie[2]

[1] School of Information Science and Engineering, Central South University,
Changsha 410083, China
zhuxiaoyu@csu.edu.cn
[2] School of Computer Science and Educational Software, Guangzhou University,
Guangzhou 510006, China
csgjwang@gmail.com

Abstract. Cloud computing is becoming more and more popular, many users choose to outsource their data to the cloud. The sensitive data need to be protected before outsourcing, and encryption is usually chosen to protect the data privacy, but it makes the data service such as search a very difficult work. Many searchable encryption schemes are proposed to allow users make effective search over encrypted data. But there is no tolerance of fuzzy and semantic keyword search in one scenario, which greatly affects the search usability. This weakness makes user's searching experiences very low. In this paper, we propose a privacy preserving fuzzy and semantic keyword search scheme over encrypted data in cloud computing. Fuzzy keyword search ability can allow users input search keyword with small typos, and semantic keyword search ability enable returns the matching documents when users' search keyword has the semantic relation with the keywords in the documents. In our scheme, we extract the fuzzy and semantic keyword set using the dictionary and WordNet technique. We also prove that our scheme is privacy preserving through security analysis.

Keywords: Cloud storage · Fuzzy search · Semantic search · Encrypted data · WordNet

1 Introduction

In recent years, cloud storage has becoming more popular than ever as it can allow data owners to store, access and share their data anytime anywhere. Many outsourced data are sensitive and need to be protected from the Cloud Service Provider, which has complete control of the uploaded data. However, for data privacy consideration, data owners usually encrypt the sensitive data before outsourced to the cloud, which makes the deployment of search on encrypted data a difficult task. The simplest way is to download all uploaded data from the cloud and decrypt the encrypted data locally, but the large amount of storage and bandwidth cost makes it an impractical way. Moreover, encryption significantly

© Springer International Publishing AG 2016
G. Wang et al. (Eds.): SpaCCS 2016 Workshops, LNCS 10067, pp. 332–341, 2016.
DOI: 10.1007/978-3-319-49145-5_33

complicates the search operation on the data. Thus, the cloud should explore effective search service on encrypted data while protecting the data privacy.

In order to solve the above problems, many schemes [1–5] have been proposed that provide the search service on encrypted data. Curtmola et al. [2] introduced a SE scheme based on inverted index, and its search process is extremely efficient. In [6–8], the authors proposed ranked keyword search schemes using order-preserving techniques, which can achieve efficient search and meanwhile maintain the accuracy. Boneh et al. [9] proposed the first generalization for symmetric searchable encryption, where data owners can outsource data to the cloud using public key and the data users can search over encrypted data using private key. Goh [10] proposed the first secure index scheme based on bloom filter, which may bring false positive into the result. Scheme [11] proposed a searchable encryption scheme which is not related to the public-key encryption algorithm, and the scheme supports incrementation efficiently. Kamara et al. [12] proposed a dynamic searchable encryption scheme, which supports data insertion and deletion on the encrypted data. Later in scheme [13], they improved their search process by parallelization.

The researchers studied verifiable search functionality extensively in the plaintext database scenario [14, 15]. Merkle hash tree is often adopted to verify the search results. But these works only focused on the verification functionality without considering the data privacy. Scheme [6] used hash chain to construct a single keyword search result verification scheme in encrypted data for the first time. Chai et al. [16] proposed a verifiable searchable encryption scheme under a semi-honest-but-curious model. Kurosawa et al. proposed a verifiable searchable encryption scheme against the malicious server in [17], then they extended it to a verifiable dynamic searchable encryption scheme [18], which supports dynamic update operation efficiently.

But almost all these schemes have been designed for exact keyword search. However, in real-life scenarios, the search keywords maybe input with spelling errors or format inconsistencies. The simplest method to implement keyword search over outsourced data is to encrypt all the keywords extracted from the documents. When the data user submits a trapdoor, the cloud server will search the index and return the encrypted document if the trapdoor is in the index list. The main weakness of this scheme is that it only supports exact keyword search.

However, if the users type the wrong keyword, the cloud server will fail to return the search results. Li et al. proposed the first fuzzy searchable encryption scheme using wild-card approach in [19]. This scheme builds the index based on the wildcard technique, which can tolerate the input typos under predefined edit distance. The index is built based on the keywords extracted from the files and the extended keywords generated based on the wildcard technique. But this scheme only supports the search that the input keyword may not exactly match the extended keywords set which includes the extracted keywords and the keywords that are very similar to the extracted keywords. Liu et al. [20] proposed a dictionary based fuzzy searchable encryption scheme with a small index, because the fuzzy keyword set based on wildcard technique contains many meaningless words, this scheme reduces the fuzzy set based on dictionary. In [21],

Kuzu et al. proposed a similarity search scheme over encrypted cloud data, the scheme utilized locality sensitive hashing to generate file index. Chuah et al. [22] built the index based on the bedtree technique and implemented the multi-keyword fuzzy search over encrypted cloud data.

However, all the fuzzy searchable encryption schemes mentioned above didn't consider the semantical keywords, for example, "holiday" and "vocation" are semantic related, but they don't have similar structure. Scheme [23] proposed a method which enables semantic keyword search over encrypted documents based on stemming algorithm. In order to support semantic keyword search, the basic way is to generate all the semantically close keywords based on the original keyword.

Scheme [24] proposed a semantic multi-keyword ranked search method, which supports synonym query. Scheme [25] proposed three synonym keyword search schemes and demonstrated the efficiency of their schemes. But these semantic schemes only consider the synonym search and ignore the fuzzy search. Scheme [26] proposed a fuzzy and synonym search scheme, this scheme generates the fuzzy set based on the gram technique and semantic set based on NARCT. However, the gram-based technique still contains many invalid words compared to the dictionary-based technique, and the semantic keyword set only considers the synonyms and ignores the other main semantic relationships. Due to the above drawbacks, the existing schemes signifies that it's important to develop a novel searchable encryption scheme which can support both fuzzy and semantic search, including main semantic relations, not just the synonyms.

We propose a fuzzy and semantic searchable encryption scheme based on dictionary and WordNet, which not only supports privacy preserving fuzzy keyword search, but also provides semantic search over encrypted cloud data, including three main kinds of relations. Fuzzy and semantic keyword search greatly increases the system usability. Our scheme returns all the matching documents when the searching input matches the fuzzy and semantic keyword set. The contributions are summarized as follows:

(1) We utilize the dictionary and WordNet to construct our fuzzy and semantic keyword sets, which reduces the size of the extracted keyword sets. Then we build our secure index using the privacy preserving techniques.
(2) The searching input is expanded based on dictionary and WordNet, the query expansion includes the fuzzy keywords and semantic keywords. The cloud server conducts the search operation and returns all the related files, which greatly improves the system flexibility.
(3) By combining the fuzzy keyword searchable encryption scheme with keyword-based semantic search scheme, we propose a fuzzy and semantic searchable encryption scheme supporting fuzzy and semantic search in one scenario. We prove our scheme is privacy preserving through rigorous analysis.

We organize the rest of this paper as follows. Section 2 introduces the problem formulation. Section 3 describes the details of our proposed fuzzy and semantic search scheme. In Sect. 4, we present the security analysis. The conclusion of our paper is in Sect. 5.

2   Problem Formulation

2.1   System Model

In our fuzzy and semantic keyword searchable encryption scheme, we consider a system comprising a data owner, a data user, and a remote cloud server. The data owner first encrypts a collection of n documents $D = \{d_1, d_2, \cdots, d_n\}$ into a set of ciphertexts $C = \{c_1, c_2, \cdots, c_n\}$, then the data owner outsources the ciphertexts and the index to the cloud. The authorized data user receives a trapdoor from data owner of her search interest via the search control mechanism and then send the trapdoor to the cloud server. Then the cloud server searches over the encrypted index and returns the search result. Figure 1 shows the overall architecture of our scheme.

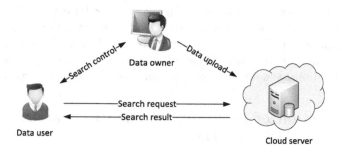

Fig. 1. Architecture of our scheme

2.2   Threat Model

The cloud server is assumed semi-honest-but-curious in this paper, which means that the cloud server may try to derive data privacy from the input trapdoors and search operation. In this work, we aim to propose a privacy-preserving search and protect the sensitive information from the server. While designing our privacy preserving fuzzy and semantic keyword searchable encryption scheme, we adopt the secure definition which are also used in the related work [2]. The cloud server can only access the encrypted files, the secure indexes and the submitted trapdoors. The cloud server can also know and record the search results. We require that the server should not be able to learn any more information.

2.3   Design Goals

In this paper, to enable secure fuzzy and semantic keyword search service over the ciphertexts, our scheme has the following design goals: (1) We propose a method to construct fuzzy and semantic keyword sets based on dictionary and WordNet; (2) We propose a scheme to allow users make fuzzy and semantic search over encrypted data; (3) We prove that our proposed scheme is secure and privacy-preserving.

2.4 Preliminaries

Edit Distance. There are many methods to calculate the string similarity, and we choose edit distance [27] in this paper. $d(w_1, w_2)$ is defined as the edit distance between two strings w_1 and w_2, which is the number of operations required to transform one string into another. There are three primary operations (1) Insertion: insert a character into a string; (2) Substitution: alter a character in a string; (3) Deletion: delete one character from a string.

Dictionary. Dictionary contains a set of legal words. The dictionary is used to reduce the size of the keyword set in this paper. The dictionary excludes all the meaningless English words, and removes all the stop words.

WordNet. WordNet [28] is a large English lexical database. The words are organized into a collection of synonym sets, which represents a lexicalized concept. Synonym sets are linked by different kinds of relations, including synonym, meronym, holonym, hypernym, hyponym and so on. In this paper, we consider three main relations: synonym, meronym/holonym, hypernym/hyponym.

3   Construction of Fuzzy and Semantic Search in Encrypted Cloud Data

3.1   Keyword Set Construction

Fuzzy Keyword Set. The fuzzy keyword search scheme [19] proposed the wildcard technique to generate fuzzy keyword set. The key idea of this scheme is to extract all possible fuzzy keywords under a predefined edit distance, and then build the encrypted index based on fuzzy keyword set. In the wildcard-based fuzzy keyword set construction, $*$ is used as a wildcard, set the edit distance as 1, the keyword set of use is $\{use, *use, *se, u*se, u*e, us*e, us*, use*\}$.

The main drawback of scheme [19] is that it pull in all the variations of the keyword, but most of them are invalid. Liu et al. [20] proposed a dictionary based fuzzy searchable encryption scheme with a small index. This scheme uses a dictionary which contains the valid keywords rather than all the variations. For example, considering the wildcard-based fuzzy keyword set of keyword use, the fuzzy keywords $*use$ are not valid words, and these meaningless keywords will be removed in this scheme based on dictionary. Thus, the index of [20] is much smaller than the index of [19]. In this paper, in order to reduce the index, we choose the dictionary-based technique to generate our fuzzy keyword set.

Semantic Keyword Set. But all the above fuzzy schemes didn't consider the users' real search intention. Although the two fuzzy schemes extract the keywords and their variations from the documents, but these schemes can only support search with minor typos. If the input keyword doesn't have a similar structure with the exact keyword, the search results will not contain these right documents.

However, there exists one situation, the input keyword may have a semantic relation with the keywords in the documents, so the search scheme should consider the semantic keywords of the original keyword. For example, when the input keyword is "corporation", the fuzzy keyword search scheme will return documents which contain keywords such as "corporation" or "corporations", but it will ignore the semantic keywords such as "firm", "enterprise" and "company". And for some verbs and its variation, such as "bring" and "brought", the fuzzy keyword search scheme didn't consider this scene and will not return the right results. In this paper, we consider three main semantic relations. For example, "firm" is a synonym of "corporation", "wheel" is a meronym of "bicycle" and "flower" is a hypernym of "rose".

In order to cover the ignored semantic keywords of the fuzzy keyword search schemes, the keyword set should consider the fuzzy keywords and the semantic keywords together in one scenario, including three kinds of semantic keyword sets mentioned above.

3.2   Construct Keyword Set

The data owner should first construct the keyword dictionary. The keyword dictionary contains two parts: the fuzzy keyword set and the semantic keyword set. The semantic keyword set contains three parts: synonym set, meronym/holonym set and hypernym/hyponym set.

Firstly, construct the fuzzy keyword set S_w using the dictionary-based method. Then retrieve all the synonyms of the original keyword w from the WordNet and add them into the semantic keyword set set1, then compared the fuzzy keyword set with the synonym set. If the synonym of the keyword is not contained in the fuzzy keyword set, then add it into the keyword set. If the synonym is duplicate, then remove it. The meronym/holonym set and hypernym/hyponym set can be processed in the same way as the synonym set. At Last, our keyword set contains the fuzzy keyword set and semantic keyword set. The keyword set construction is described in Algorithm 1, S_w is denoted as the fuzzy and semantic keyword set of keyword w.

3.3   Encryption

To construct the index for our fuzzy and semantic keyword search scheme, the data owner first generates secret keys (k, sk), where k is a secret key, sk is for algorithm Enc and Dec. Enc is used to encrypt the documents, and Dec is used to decrypt the documents. f is a pseudorandom function. FID_w denotes a set of document IDs whose corresponding documents contain the keyword w.

Our scheme constructs the secure index $Index$ by calling the algorithm SecIndex as follows:

(1) The document set D was encrypted into an encrypted form C by calling the algorithm Enc.

(2) For each keyword $w_i \in W$, construct the fuzzy and semantic keyword set S_{w_i} for the original keyword w_i by calling the algorithm FuzzySemanticSet;

(3) For each keyword $w_i' \in S_{w_i}$, compute the trapdoor set $T_{w_i'} = f(k, w_i')$;

(4) For each FID_{w_i}, compute the encrypted form $\text{Enc}(k, \text{FID}_{w_i}||w_i)$;

(5) The data owner finally generates the secure index $Index = \{\{T_{w_i'}\}_{w_i' \in S_{w_i}},$ $\text{Enc}(k, \text{FID}_{w_i}||w_i)\}_{w_i \in W}$;

Finally, the data owner sends the ciphertexts C and the index $Index$ to the server.

Algorithm 1. FuzzySemanticSet(w)

Input: Keyword w.
Output: Fuzzy and semantic keyword set S_w.

```
 1: fuzzy Sw= GetFuzzySet();
 2: synonym set1= GetSynonymSet();
 3: for w' in set1 do
 4:    if w' is not in Sw then
 5:        Add w' into Sw;
 6:    end if
 7: end for
 8: meronymholonym set2= GetMeronymHolonymSet();
 9: for w' in set2 do
10:    if w' is not in Sw then
11:        Add w' into Sw;
12:    end if
13: end for
14: hypernymhyponym set3= GetHypernymHyponymSet();
15: for w' in set3 do
16:    if w' is not in Sw then
17:        Add w' into Sw;
18:    end if
19: end for
20: return Sw
```

3.4 Search Process

When the data user inputs a search keyword w_a, he first generates the fuzzy and semantic keyword set S_{w_a} for the original keyword w_a by calling Algorithm 1, then computes the trapdoors $\{T_{w_a'}\}_{w_a' \in S_{w_a}}$ for $w_a' \in S_{w_a}$. After that, the data user sends the trapdoor set to the remote cloud. Then the server searches $Index$ and returns back all the possible encrypted FIDs as the search result. At last, the data user decrypt the search result using secret key k. If the data user intends to download the documents from the cloud. After receiving the download request from the data user, the server will return the corresponding encrypted documents. At last, the user can decrypt the encrypted documents using the secret key sk.

4 Security Analysis

In this section, we analyze privacy preserving issue for our fuzzy and semantic keyword search scheme.

Theorem 1. The proposed fuzzy and semantic keyword search scheme is privacy preserving.

Proof. In our dictionary based fuzzy and semantic keyword search scheme, we compute the secure index and the trapdoor using the same way. Suppose that there exists an simulator S, a challenger C, it does the followings:

(1) The challenger C sends $|d_1|, \cdots, |d_n|$ and $m = |W|$ to the simulator S.
(2) S keeps (k, sk) secret.
(3) S computes $c_j = \mathsf{Enc}(sk, 0^{|d_j|})$ for $j = 1, \cdots, n$.
(4) S chooses $\{T_{w_i'}\}_{w_i' \in S_{w_i}}$ as the trapdoor set and chooses the secure index $Index' = \{\{T_{w_i'}\}_{w_i' \in S_{w_i}}, \mathsf{Enc}(k, \mathrm{FID}_{w_i} \| w_i)\}_{w_i \in W}$ randomly for $i = 1, \cdots, m$.
(5) S sends $C' = (c_1, \cdots, c_n)$ and $Index'$ to C.
(6) S then computes $\{T_{w_a'}'\}_{w_a' \in S_{w_i}}$ as the trapdoor set to C.

In the search phase, C receives$(C', Index', \{T_{w_a'}'\}_{w_a' \in S_{w_i}})$ from S.

Because all the documents are encrypted with CPA-secure algorithms Enc in this scheme, we consider them as confidential to the cloud. Therefore C' and C, $(j, \mathsf{Enc}(sk, 0^{|d_j|}))$ and $(j, \mathsf{Enc}(sk, 0^{|d_j'|}))$ are indistinguishable. $Index'$ and $Index$ are indistinguishable as f is a pseudorandom function. The data privacy is preserved because C cannot learn more information.

5 Conclusion

We propose a fuzzy and semantic keyword searchable encryption scheme while maintaining privacy preserving. We combine the dictionary-based technique and WordNet to build our fuzzy and semantic keyword set. After constructing the keyword set, we further introduce the process of the constructing the secure index, then we propose the search process. Our scheme is an effective solution which enables users make fuzzy and semantic search over encrypted data. We prove that our scheme is privacy preserving through rigorous analysis.

Acknowledgments. This work is supported in part by the National Natural Science Foundation of China under Grant Numbers 61632009, 61472451 and 61272151, and the High Level Talents Program of Higher Education in Guangdong Province under Funding Support Number 2016ZJ01.

References

1. Song, D.X., Wagner, D., Perrig, A.: Practical techniques for searches on encrypted data. In: Proceedings of the 2000 IEEE Symposium on Security & Privacy (S&P), pp. 44–55. IEEE (2000)

2. Curtmola, R., Garay, J., Kamara, S., Ostrovsky, R.: Searchable symmetric encryption: improved definitions and efficient constructions. J. Comput. Secur. **19**(5), 895–934 (2011)
3. Cao, N., Wang, C., Li, M., Ren, K., Lou, W.: Privacy-preserving multi-keyword ranked search over encrypted cloud data. IEEE Trans. Parallel Distrib. Syst. **25**(1), 222–233 (2014)
4. Xia, Z., Wang, X., Sun, X., Wang, Q.: A secure and dynamic multi-keyword ranked search scheme over encrypted cloud data. IEEE Trans. Parallel Distrib. Syst. **27**(2), 340–352 (2016)
5. Fu, Z., Sun, X., Liu, Q., Zhou, L., Shu, J.: Achieving efficient cloud search services: multi-keyword ranked search over encrypted cloud data supporting parallel computing. IEICE Trans. Commun. **98**(1), 190–200 (2015)
6. Wang, C., Cao, N., Ren, K., Lou, W.: Enabling secure and efficient ranked keyword search over outsourced cloud data. IEEE Trans. Parallel Distrib. Syst. **23**(8), 1467–1479 (2012)
7. Swaminathan, A., Mao, Y., Su, G.-M., Gou, H., Varna, A.L., He, S., Wu, M., Oard, D.W.: Confidentiality-preserving rank-ordered search. In: Proceedings of the 2007 ACM Workshop on Storage Security and Survivability, pp. 7–12. ACM (2007)
8. Zerr, S., Olmedilla, D., Nejdl, W., Siberski, W.: Zerber+ r: top-k retrieval from a confidential index. In: Proceedings of the 12th International Conference on Extending Database Technology: Advances in Database Technology, pp. 439–449. ACM (2009)
9. Boneh, D., Di Crescenzo, G., Ostrovsky, R., Persiano, G.: Public key encryption with keyword search. In: Cachin, C., Camenisch, J.L. (eds.) EUROCRYPT 2004. LNCS, vol. 3027, pp. 506–522. Springer, Heidelberg (2004). doi:10.1007/978-3-540-24676-3_30
10. Goh, E.-J., et al.: Secure indexes. IACR Cryptology ePrint Archive 2003:216 (2003)
11. Chang, Y.-C., Mitzenmacher, M.: Privacy preserving keyword searches on remote encrypted data. In: Ioannidis, J., Keromytis, A., Yung, M. (eds.) ACNS 2005. LNCS, vol. 3531, pp. 442–455. Springer, Heidelberg (2005). doi:10.1007/11496137_30
12. Kamara, S., Papamanthou, C., Roeder, T.: Dynamic searchable symmetric encryption. In: Proceedings of the 2012 ACM Conference on Computer and Communications Security, pp. 965–976. ACM (2012)
13. Kamara, S., Papamanthou, C.: Parallel and dynamic searchable symmetric encryption. In: Sadeghi, A.-R. (ed.) FC 2013. LNCS, vol. 7859, pp. 258–274. Springer, Heidelberg (2013). doi:10.1007/978-3-642-39884-1_22
14. Li, F., Hadjieleftheriou, M., Kollios, G., Reyzin, L.: Dynamic authenticated index structures for outsourced databases. In: Proceedings of the 2006 ACM SIGMOD International Conference on Management of Data, pp. 121–132. ACM (2006)
15. Pang, H., Tan, K.-L.: Authenticating query results in edge computing. In: Proceedings of the 2004 20th International Conference on Data Engineering, pp. 560–571. IEEE (2004)
16. Chai, Q., Gong, G.: Verifiable symmetric searchable encryption for semi-honest-but-curious cloud servers. In: Proceedings of the 2012 IEEE International Conference on Communications (ICC), pp. 917–922. IEEE (2012)
17. Kurosawa, K., Ohtaki, Y.: UC-secure searchable symmetric encryption. In: Keromytis, A.D. (ed.) FC 2012. LNCS, vol. 7397, pp. 285–298. Springer, Heidelberg (2012). doi:10.1007/978-3-642-32946-3_21

18. Kurosawa, K., Ohtaki, Y.: How to update documents *verifiably* in searchable symmetric encryption. In: Abdalla, M., Nita-Rotaru, C., Dahab, R. (eds.) CANS 2013. LNCS, vol. 8257, pp. 309–328. Springer, Heidelberg (2013). doi:10.1007/978-3-319-02937-5_17

19. Li, J., Wang, Q., Wang, C., Cao, N., Ren, K., Lou, W.: Fuzzy keyword search over encrypted data in cloud computing. In: Proceedings of the 2010 IEEE International Conference on Computer Communications (INFOCOM), pp. 1–5. IEEE (2010)

20. Liu, C., Zhu, L., Li, L., Tan, Y.: Fuzzy keyword search on encrypted cloud storage data with small index. In: Proceedings of the 2011 IEEE International Conference on Cloud Computing and Intelligence Systems, pp. 269–273. IEEE (2011)

21. Kuzu, M., Islam, M.S., Kantarcioglu, M.: Efficient similarity search over encrypted data. In: Proceedings of the 2012 IEEE 28th International Conference on Data Engineering, pp. 1156–1167. IEEE (2012)

22. Chuah, M., Hu, W: Privacy-aware bedtree based solution for fuzzy multi-keyword search over encrypted data. In: Proceedings of the 2011 31st International Conference on Distributed Computing Systems Workshops, pp. 273–281. IEEE (2011)

23. Fu, Z., Shu, J., Sun, X., Zhang, D.: Semantic keyword search based on trie over encrypted cloud data. In: Proceedings of the 2nd International Workshop on Security in Cloud Computing, pp. 59–62 (2014)

24. Metkari, S.S., Sonkamble, S.B.: Multi-keyword ranked search over encrypted cloud data supporting synonym query. Int. J. Sci. Res. **5**(6), 2044–2048 (2016)

25. Moh, T.S., Ho, K.H.: Efficient semantic search over encrypted data in cloud computing. In: International Conference on High PERFORMANCE Computing & Simulation (2014)

26. Jayashri, N., Chakravarthy, T.: Ranked search enabled fuzzy and synonym query over encrypted document in cloud. Int. J. Sci. Eng. Appl. Sci. **1**(8), 215–222 (2015)

27. Levenshtein, V.: Binary codes capable of correcting spurious insertions and deletions of ones. Probl. Inf. Transm. **1**(1), 8–17 (1965)

28. Miller, G.A.: Wordnet: a lexical database for English. Commun. ACM **38**(11), 39–41 (1995)

A Closer Look at Syncany Windows and Ubuntu Clients' Residual Artefacts

Yee-Yang Teing[1,2(✉)], Ali Dehghantanha[2],
Kim-Kwang Raymond Choo[3,4], Zaiton Muda[1],
Mohd Taufik Abdullah[1], and Wee-Chiat Chai[1]

[1] Department of Computer Science, Faculty of Computer Science
and Information Technology, Universiti Putra Malaysia, UPM,
43400 Serdang, Selangor, Malaysia
teingyeeyang@gmail.com
[2] The School of Computing, Science and Engineering, University of Salford,
Newton Building, Salford, Greater Manchester M5 4WT, UK
[3] Information Assurance Research Group, University of South Australia,
Adelaide, SA 5001, Australia
[4] Department of Information Systems and Cyber Security,
University of Texas at San Antonio, San Antonio, TX 78249-0631, USA

Abstract. In this paper, we seek to determine the residual artefacts of forensic value on Windows and Ubuntu client machines of using Syncany private cloud storage service. We demonstrate the types and the locations of the artefacts that can be forensically recovered (e.g. artefacts associated with the installation, uninstallation, log-in, log-off, and file synchronisation actions). Findings from this research contribute to an in-depth understanding of cloud-enabled big data storage forensics related to the collection of big data artefacts from a private cloud storage service, which have real-world implications and impacts (e.g. in criminal investigations and civil litigations). Echoing the observations of Ab Rahman et al. (2006), we reiterated the importance of forensic-by-design in future cloud-enabled big data storage solutions.

Keywords: Cloud forensics · Cloud-enabled big data storage forensics · Syncany forensics · Client forensics · Memory forensics

1 Introduction

Cloud forensics is a research trend, which has real-world implications for both criminal investigations (including those involving national security matters) and civil litigations [1]. Due to the nature of cloud-enabled big data storage solutions (e.g. data physically stored in distributed servers), identification of the data may be a 'finding a needle in a haystack' exercise [2–6]. Even if the location of the data could be identified, traditional evidence collection tools, techniques and practices are unlikely to be adequate [7]. For example, existing digital forensic practices generally require the creation of a forensic copy of the storage media of interest. In cloud-enabled big data storage solutions such as Syncany, it is unrealistic, and perhaps computationally infeasible, to collect the data

© Springer International Publishing AG 2016
G. Wang et al. (Eds.): SpaCCS 2016 Workshops, LNCS 10067, pp. 342–357, 2016.
DOI: 10.1007/978-3-319-49145-5_34

of interest. These challenges are compounded in cross-jurisdictional investigations which could prohibit the transfer of evidential data due to the lack of cross-nation legislative agreements in place [8–11].

Syncany is a popular open source and cross-platform cloud storage written in Java. Syncany supports different backend platforms (e.g., FTP, Box.net, WebDAV and SFTP, Amazon S3, Google Storage, IMAP, Local, Picasa and Rackspace Cloud Files), and hence does not require a server-side software [12]. Syncany programmatically encrypts the sync files locally (using 128-bit AES/GCM encryption) before uploading the files to the central (offsite) storage by default; therefore, only the client in possession of the password can access the repositories. The data model consists of three main entities, namely: versioning, deduplication/chunking, and multichunking [12]:

- Versioning: Syncany captures different versions of a file and keeps track of the changes using metadata such as date, time, size and checksums as well as parts of the file (similar to the concept of 'commit' in a version control system). There are three primary versioning concepts, which are database versions, file histories, and file versions. A database version represents the point in time when the file tree is captured. Each database version contains a list of file histories, representing the identity of a file. Each file history contains a collection of file versions, representing the incarnations of a file.
- Deduplication/Chunking: Syncany uses data deduplication technique to break individual files into small chunks on the client. The chunks are represented in data blobs (each about 8-32 KB in size), which are identified by its checksum.
- Multichunking: Individual chunks are grouped into multichunks, compressed and encrypted before being uploaded to the offsite storage. The default size of a multichunk is 4 MB; however, it can be modified by the user.

Figure 1 shows an example of the logical data model of the Syncany repository. The entities are stored locally in the form of Java's plain-old-Java-object (POJOs) in the org.syncany.database package and tables in the local HSQLDB-based database,

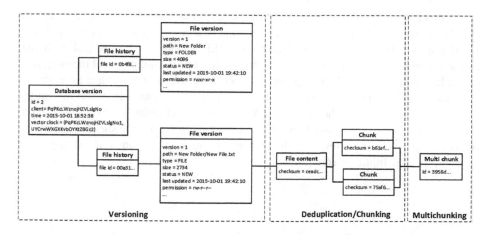

Fig. 1. Logical data model of the Syncany repository (Adapted from [12]).

while remotely (on the central repository) in .XML format [13]. Each entity creates a table in the database.

Syncany uses a command line interface by default, but the users can manually install the plugin for graphical user interface (GUI). The syntaxes of forensic interest are as follows [14]:

- *sy init*: To initialise the repository for a new sync directory. It creates a sync-directory-specific *%.syncany%/config.xml* and *%.syncany%/repo* file. The former holds the local configuration information while the latter contains the chunking/crypto details required to initialise the remote repository. This command also generates the sync link in two formats: a commonly used encrypted link structured as *syncany://storage/1/< master-salt >/<encrypted-config >*, where both < master-salt > and < encrypted-config > are base58 encoded; a plaintext link structured as *syncany://storage/1/not-encrypted/< plaintext-config >*, where the < plaintext-config > is a base58-encoded representation of the storage/connection config.
- *sy connect*: To connect to an existing repository using the sync link or manually using the repo URL. This command is similar to *sy init*, with the difference being that it downloads the repo files from the remote storage.
- *sy status*: Lists changes made to the local sync files by comparing the local file tree (e.g., last modified dates and file sizes) with the local database.
- *sy up*: Detects changes in the local sync directory (using the 'sy status' command), indexes new files and uploads changes to the remote repository (using the 'sy up' command). File changes are packaged into new multichunks and uploaded to the offsite storage, alongside the delta metadata database.
- *sy ls-remote*: Queries the remote storage and lists the client database versions that have not yet been downloaded/processed.
- *sy down*: Detects file changes made by other clients (as identified by the 'sy ls-remote' command). The command first downloads the metadata of relevance. Then, it evaluates which multichunks are changed or required. Finally, it downloads and arranges the multichunks according to the vector clocks, when necessary.

In this paper, we seek to identify residual client-side artefacts of using Syncany on Windows and Ubuntu devices. Similar to the approaches of Quick and Choo [15–17], we attempt to answer the following questions in this research: What residual evidential artefacts can be recovered from a client machine hard drive and physical memory after a user has used Syncany client applications, and the location of these data remnants on a Windows and Ubuntu client device? The structure of this paper is as follows. In the next section, we describe the related work. Section 3 highlights the experiment environment setup. In Sects. 4 and 5, we discuss the findings from the media storage and physical memory dumps (respectively). Finally, in Sect. 6, we conclude the paper and outline potential future research areas.

2 Literature Review

There have been numerous attempts at defining cloud computing, but the most widely accepted definition is that of the NIST, which defines cloud computing as *"[a] model for enabling ubiquitous, convenient, on-demand network access to a shared pool of configurable computing resources (e.g., networks, servers, storage, applications, and services) that can be rapidly provisioned and released with minimal management effort or service provider interaction"* [18]. The key aspects are to provide on-demand self-service, broad network access, resource pooling, rapid elascity, and measured services.

There are three cloud computing service models [18], which are Software as a Service (SaaS), Platform as a Service (PaaS), and Infrastructure as a Service (IaaS). NIST [18] also defined four deployment models as part of the cloud computing definition, which are public, private, community, and hybrid clouds. The public cloud is owned and operated by a provider organisation. Consumers can subscribe to the service for a fee, based on the storage or bandwidth usage. On the other hand, the private cloud is tailored to a single organisation's needs. In most cases, the organisation is the cloud service owner, but it can also be owned, managed, and operated by a third party; on or off premises. If the cloud infrastructure is administered by organisations sharing common concerns (e.g., mission, security requirements, policy, and compliance considerations), then there exists a community cloud. The hybrid cloud can be used to provide load balancing to two or more distinct cloud infrastructures aforementioned. For example, an organisation can deploy a private cloud system to store sensitive data, and host non-critical resources on a third party public cloud system.

Although cloud computing offers an unprecedented paradigm for storing and distribution of resources, use of cloud computing introduces new challenges in the digital forensics space. Challenges such as jurisdiction differences, loss of data control, physical inaccessibility of evidence, multi-tenancy, and lack of tools for large scale distributed and virtualized systems are often cited as the main causes of concern for cloud forensics [19–22]. However, Al Fahdi et al. [23] found that the perceived cloud forensic challenges may be vary between forensic practitioners and researchers. For example, the top three digital forensic challenges rated by the practitioner respondents in their survey are volume of data, legal aspect, and time, while the top three challenges according to researcher respondents are time, volume of data, and automation of forensic analysis. Other pinpointed challenges include diverse digital media types, anonymity of IP addresses, bring-your-own-device policy, decentralisation, and the application of anti-forensic and encryption techniques [21, 24, 25]. Delving deeper into the legal challenges, Hooper et al. [8] reviewed the 2011 Australian Federal Government's Cybercrime Bill admendment on mutual legal assistance requests and concluded that laws admendment on a jusrisdiction alone may not be adequate to address multi-jurisdiction investigation issues in the cloud computing environment. Martini and Choo [11], Taylor et at. [26], and Daryabar et al. [27] also agree on the need for harmonious laws across jurisdictions. Simou et al. [21] and Pichan et al. [22] added that the issues of CSP dependence could exacerbate the challenges in all stages of cloud forensics (e.g., identify, preserve, analyse, and report [28, 29]), but Farina et al. [30]

and Damshenas et al. [1, 31] suggested that such concern can be mitigated through clearly-defined Service Level Agreement between the provider and the consumers.

Martini and Choo [32] proposed the first cloud forensic investigation framework, which was derived based upon the frameworks of McKemmish [33] and NIST [29]. The framework was used to investigate ownCloud [34], Amazon EC2 [35], VMWare [36], XtreemFS [37], etc. Quick et al. [10] further extended and validated the four-stage framework using SkyDrive, Dropbox, Google Drive, and ownCloud. Chung et al. [38] proposed a methodology for cloud investigation on Windows, Mac OS, iOS, and Android devices. The methodology was then used to investigate Amazon S3, Google Docs, and Evernote. Scanlon et al. [39] outlined a methodology for remote acquisition of evidence from decentralised file synchronisation network and utilised it to investigate BitTorrent Sync [40]. In another study, Teing et al. [41] proposed a methodology for investigating the newer BitTorrent Sync application (version 2.0) or any third party or Original Equipment Manufacturer (OEM) application thereof. Unsurprisingly, the researchers determined that the newer BitTorrent Sync applications maintained a different data structure in comparison with the legacy versions. Do et al. [42] proposed an adversary model for digital forensics, and they demonstrated how such an adversary model can be used to investigate mobile devices (e.g. Android smartwatch – Do et al. [43] and apps). Ab Rahman et al. [44], on the other hand, proposed a conceptual forensic-by-design framework to integrate forensics tools and best practices in the development of cloud systems.

Marty [45] and Shields et al. [46] proposed a proactive application-level logging mechanism, designed to log information of forensics interest which can also be used in incident response. However, Zawoad and Hasan [47] argued that the proposed solutions have may not be viable in real world scenarios. Forensic researchers such as Dykstra and Sherman [48], Gebhardt and Reiser [49], Quick et al. [10], and Martini and Choo [36], on the other hand, presented methods and prototype implementations to support the (remote) collection of evidential materials using Application Programming Interfaces (API). Although data collection using APIs could potentially reduce interactions with the CSPs, it was argued that such evidence collection methods could be limited by the APIs' feature sets as well as resulting in additional event data in the organisation's logs [36]. Quick and Choo [50] and Teing et al. [51] studied the integrity of data downloaded from the web and desktop clients of Dropbox, Google Drive, Skydrive, and Symform and identified that the act of downloading files from client applications does not breach the evidence integrity (e.g., no change in the hash values), despite changes in file creation/modification times.

In addition to remote collection of evidence, scholars also studied the potential of on-device collection of cloud artefacts such as from Evernote [38], Amazon S3 [38], Dropbox [34, 58], Google Drive [17, 38], Microsoft Skydrive [16], Amazon Cloud Drive [52], BitTorrent Sync [53], SugarSync [54], Ubuntu One [55], huBic [56], Mega [57], as well as mobile cloud apps [58–60]. These forensics studies located artefacts of client applications from the user settings and application data reside on the media storage through keyword search. A number of studies also demonstrated that it is possible to recover parts of the cloud synchronizing history and synchronised files from unstructured datasets such as memory dumps, slack space, free space, and swap files in plain text. Quick and Choo [15–17] also identified that data erasing tools such as Eraser and CCleaner could not completely remove the data remnants from Dropbox, Google Drive, and Microsoft SkyDrive.

The majority of the existing literatures focused on forensic investigations of the public cloud deployment model. As noted by Martini and Choo [34, 37], using private StaaS cloud products as case studies provides a better chance to unveil the forensic artefacts that may exist on all StaaS systems (as most of the data artefacts may be concealed from investigators in the public cloud deployment model due to security and privacy concerns). Our research provides one of the few cloud forensic research that focuses on private cloud deployment model. We also provide the first insight into Syncany cloud service and one of the few studies that present a holistic approach for client forensics, which included volatile and log file datasets as part of the evidence – see Table 1.

Table 1. Cloud forensics solutions.

Related work	Areas covered			
	Public cloud	Private cloud	Volatile data analysis	Log file analysis
Ab Rahman et al. [44]	√			
Quick et al. [10]	√	√	√	√
Quick and Choo [15]	√		√	
Quick and Choo [16]	√		√	
Quick and Choo [17]	√		√	
Thethi and Keane [35]	√			
Martini and Choo [36]	√			
Martini and Choo [37]		√		
Chung et al. [38]	√			
Scanlon et al. [39]		√		
Scanlon et al. [40]		√		
Teing et al. [41]		√	√	√
Do et al. [42]	√			
Do et al. [43]	√			
Marty [45]	√			√
Shields et al. [46]	√			
Dykstra and Sherman [48]	√			
Gebhardt and Reiser [49]	√			
Martini and Choo [36]		√	√	
Quick and Choo [50]	√		√	
Teing et al. [51]	√		√	√

3   Experimental Setup

We adopted the research methodology of Quick and Choo [15–17] and Teing et al. [41, 51] in the design of our experiments. Our test environments consisted of three (3) VMware Workstations (VMs), one (1) for the server and two (2) for the desktop clients, involving the OS combinations as detailed in Table 2. The VMs were hosted using VMware Fusion Professional version 7.0.0 (2103067) on a Macbook Pro (Late 2012) running Mac OS X Mavericks 10.9.5, with a 2.6 GHz Intel Core i7 processor and 16 GB of RAM. As explained by Quick and Choo [15–17], using physical hardware to undertake setup, erasing, copying, and re-installing of the would have been an onerous exercise. Moreover, a virtual machine allows room for error by enabling the test environment to be reverted to a restore point should the results are unfavourable. It is noteworthy that the Syncany application does not require an account, and hence no user account was created in this research.

Table 2. System configurations for Syncany forensics.

Server configurations	Client configurations
Ubuntu Server:	**Windows Client:**
Operating system: Ubuntu 14.04 LTS	Operating system: Windows 8.1 Professional (Service Pack 2, 64-bit, build 9600)
Virtual memory size: 1 GB	Virtual memory size: 2 GB
Virtual storage size: 20 GB	Virtual storage size: 20 GB
Web application: Apache 2	Client application: Syncany 0.4.6-alpha
Storage type: WebDAV	Plugins installed: WebDAV and GUI
Database server: HSQL Database Engine 2.3.0	**Ubuntu Client:**
IP address/URL: http://172.16.38.180/webdav	Operating system: Ubuntu 14.04.1 LTS
	Virtual memory size: 1 GB
	Virtual storage size: 20 GB
	Client application: Syncany 0.4.6-alpha
	Plugins installed: WebDAV and GUI

In our experiments, we conducted a predefined set of activities including installation and uninstallation of the client applications, uploading, downloading, viewing, deleting, and unsyncing the sync files to simulate various real world scenarios using Syncany. After each experiment, a snapshot was taken of the VM workstations prior and after being shutdown, enabling acquisition of the volatile memory in the former. The 3111th email messages of the Berkeley Enron email dataset (downloaded from http://bailando.sims.berkeley.edu/enron_email.html) were used to create a set of sample files and saved in .RTF, .TXT, .DOCX, .JPG (print screen), .ZIP, and .PDF formats, providing a basis for replication of the experiments in future. The set of sample files were placed in a new directory on the clients' workstations, before being uploaded to the servers, and subsequently downloaded to the corresponding workstations concurrently.

For the purpose of this research, we used WebDAV as the carrying protocol to enable the study of the network's inner workings. Wireshark was deployed on the host

Table 3. Tools prepared for Syncany forensics.

Tool	Usage
FTK Imager Version 3.2.0.0	To create a forensic image of the .VMDK files
dd version 1.3.4-1	To produce a bit-for-bit image of the .VMEM files
Autopsy 3.1.1	To parse the file system, produce directory listings, as well as extracting/analysing the files, Windows registry, swap file/partition, and unallocated space of the forensic images
raw2vmdk	To create .VMDK files from raw dd image
HxD Version 1.7.7.0	To conduct keyword searches in the unstructured datasets
Volatility 2.4	To extract the running processes and network information from the physical memory dumps, dumping files from the memory space of the Syncany client applications, and detecting the memory space of a string (using the 'pslist', 'netstat'/'netscan', 'memdump' and 'yarascan' functions)
SQLite Browser Version 3.4.0	To view the contents of SQLite database files
Photorec 7.0	To data carve the unstructured datasets
File juicer 4.45	To extract files from files
BrowsingHistoryView v.1.60	To analyse the web browsing history
Thumbcacheviewer Version 1.0.2.7	To examine the Windows thumbnail cache
Windows Event Viewer Version 1.0	To view the Windows event logs
Console Version 10.10 (543)	To view log files
Windows File Analyser 2.6.0.0	To analyse the Windows prefetch and link files
NTFS Log Tracker	To parse and analyse the $LogFile, $MFT, and $UsnJrnl New Technology File System (NTFS) files
SQL Workbench/J Build 118	To view the contents of Hyper SQL Database (HSQLDB)

machine to capture the network traffic from the server for each scenario. The experiments were repeated thrice (at different dates) to ensure consistency of findings. Table 3 highlights the forensic tools we used for data analysis.

4 Directory Listings and Files of Forensic Interest

Artefacts of the Syncany client were predominantly located in the sync-folder-specific '.syncany' directory (note the dot prefixed the directory name) and the user–specific configuration directory at *%Users%\< User Profile >\AppData\Roaming\Syncany* and */home/< User Profile >/.config/syncany* on the Windows and Ubuntu clients (respectively). Within *%Syncany%/plugins/lib/*there maintained a list of plugins installed. The plugin information may enable a practitioner to estimate potential arte-facts based on the protocol in use e.g., if the WebDAV protocol is used, the web server logs can be a potential source of relevant information.

The files deleted (locally and remotely) could be recovered locally from the unallocated space. However, only the files deleted locally could be recovered from the Trash or Recycle Bin directory. Undertaking uninstallation of the client applications observed that both the '.syncany' and 'syncany' directories remained.

4.1   config.xml

Examination of the *%.syncany%/config.xml* revealed the 20-character machine and display names in the 'machineName' and 'displayName' properties, respectively. The second property of forensic interest with the*/%.syncany%/config.xml* file was the 'connection' property, which defined the type of backend storage in use in the 'type' entry. Additionally, we observed the URL, server's display name, and encrypted password for the repository in the 'url', 'username', and 'password' tags, respectively. The*/%.syncany%/config.xml* file also held the plain text masterkey and salt used to derive the encryption keys for the sync files, in the 'masterKey' property [14]. The machine name is the random local machine name used to technically identify a computer/user for a sync folder, while the display name is the human readable user name for the local machine [14]. These could be crucial identifying information when seeking to correlate cloud transaction records associated with a Syncany client from the server or any external data sources. Analysis of the */%syncany%/config.xml* file revealed the masterkey and salt used to encrypt the password and access token for the backend storage in the *%.syncany%/config.xml* file [14], in the 'configEncryptionKey' tag of the 'userConfig' property.

4.2   daemon.xml

The *%Syncany%/daemon.xml* held a list of sync folder metadata for the daemon in the 'folders' property. Each folder created a 'folder' tag housing the directory path and also property about whether the folder is enabled.

4.3   local.db

Analysis of the sync-folder-specific *%.syncany%/db/local.db* database revealed the repository directory paths, sizes, checksums, permission information in POSIX format, as well as last modified and updated times for the sync folders/files in the 'FILE-VERSION_MASTER', 'FILEVERSION', and 'FILEVERSION_MASTER_LAST' view tables. Specifically, the artefacts could be differentiated by the table columns 'PATH', 'SIZE', 'FILECONENT_CHECKSUM', 'POSIXPERMS', 'LASTMODI-FIED', AND 'UPDATED' respectively; each sync folder or file was identified by a unique file history ID (FILEHISTORY_ID). In all the mentioned view tables, the sync directories/files that were modified could be differentiated from the 'VERSION' table column given the value of more than 1. Additionally, the view tables also held the directory/file modification status in the 'STATUS' table column, indicating whether the sync directories/files were unmodified (new), modified (CHANGED), or deleted (deleted). Figure 2 shows portion of the 'FILEVERSION_MASTER' view table recovered in our research. In the 'FILEVERSION_FULL' view table, we located additional information such as the machine names for the clients that made changes to the repositories (e.g., adding and removing files and sub-directories), alongside the database local times associated with the changes in the 'DATABASEVERSION_-CLIENT' and 'DATABASEVERSION_LOCALTIME' table columns, respectively (see Fig. 3).

FILEHISTORY_ID	VERSION	DATABASEVERSION_ID	PATH	TYPE	STATUS	SIZE	LASTMODIFIED	LINKTARGET	FILECONTENT_CHECKSUM	UPDATED	POSIXPERMS	DOSATTRS
8509cfe7c5b1f82e305c0aaade57c8f0745de5c6	1		0 .syignore	FILE	NEW	279	2015-10-01 18:52:35		2148c99719c61f0ef455864bcd93f1316174259з	2015-10-01 18:52:38	rw-rw-r--	--a-
3a947cff54c9e3b748f9cb4f65752b16d4c637e8	1		1 Enron3111.zip	FILE	NEW	30967	2014-12-13 08:35:00		75a666ba87fef0f8425a71edcd621d0a4367aa47	2015-10-01 19:26:14	rw-r--r--	--a-
3d247e3ddc8f73c49c98a3a9abd89897dc0a8179	1		1 Enron3111.pdf	FILE	NEW	31747	2014-12-13 08:31:59		4f4e015d243cd652bb431342c48597fc26012db2	2015-10-01 19:26:13	rw-r--r--	--a-
9bec78b6de24d0df15e7469e72b77cdbf163bd55	1		1 Enron3111.txt	FILE	NEW	2734	2014-12-13 08:33:11		ceadc4b7d47af4125a68e03ec3141cb3fde407ff	2015-10-01 19:26:14	rw-r--r--	--a-
bab75c4cb7537d5a764186983491312 3eed4304c	1		1 Enron3111.rtf	FILE	NEW	43360	2014-12-13 08:32:19		c4760cf2251c498b4c1e0ec75e4a34d775f92bdc	2015-10-01 19:26:14	rw-r--r--	--a-
c3bd62f81eda2db41d6beb294ccfbb36f452f99c	1		1 Enron3111.jpg	FILE	NEW	287937	2014-12-13 08:34:02		11c49d1769adc7cbd82569a83949a3467477d4ea	2015-10-01 19:26:13	rw-r--r--	--a-
ee439cb563617c8a9d7de9c8c533bb015a946d1a	1		1 Enron3111.docx	FILE	NEW	78080	2014-12-13 08:31:43		b61ef5e5be6e6e7a6d408ad4c1978ea0c228156d	2015-10-01 19:26:13	rw-r--r--	--a-
00a31c436450b3a71e58ad12c28f9b4bebcc2c45	1		2 WindowsToUbuntu/Enron3111.txt	FILE	NEW	2734	2014-12-13 08:33:11		ceadc4b7d47af4125a68e03ec3141cb3fde407ff	2015-10-01 19:42:10	rw-r--r--	--a-
0b4f85e8b1435574e71332e7d023931219e37d4f	1		2 WindowsToUbuntu	FOLDER	NEW	4096	2015-09-28 21:40:44			2015-10-01 19:42:10	rwxr-xr-x	----
0fa188da9eb4c6aaa4d495d8ad9e20d972ff54fb	1		2 WindowsToUbuntu/Enron3111.docx	FILE	NEW	78080	2014-12-13 08:31:43		b61ef5e5be6e6e7a6d408ad4c1978ea0c228156d	2015-10-01 19:42:10	rw-r--r--	--a-
10f26510ae4b8f5c3a6fac86c499eca2266a914f	1		2 WindowsToUbuntu/Enron3111.zip	FILE	NEW	30967	2014-12-13 08:35:00		75a666ba87fef0f8425a71edcd621d0a4367aa47	2015-10-01 19:42:10	rw-r--r--	--a-
248eaab9dc360ee0a2ac601c1afad9fec6551842	1		2 WindowsToUbuntu/Enron3111.jpg	FILE	NEW	287937	2014-12-13 08:34:02		11c49d1769adc7cbd82569a83949a3467477d4ea	2015-10-01 19:42:10	rw-r--r--	--a-
2ab118932cfbf75a27f0657eefec8f1eb2b737b8	1		2 WindowsToUbuntu/Enron3111.pdf	FILE	NEW	31747	2014-12-13 08:31:59		4f4e015d243cd652bb431342c48597fc26012db2	2015-10-01 19:42:10	rw-r--r--	--a-
588275ee75c158cc3a1071207d17e82855281d7f	1		2 WindowsToUbuntu/Enron3111.rtf	FILE	NEW	43360	2014-12-13 08:32:19		c4760cf2251c498b4c1e0ec75e4a34d775f92bdc	2015-10-01 19:42:10	rw-r--r--	--a-
00a31c436450b3a71e58ad12c28f9b4bebcc2c45	2		3 WindowsToUbuntu/Enron3111.txt	FILE	DELETED	2734	2014-12-13 08:33:11		ceadc4b7d47af4125a68e03ec3141cb3fde407ff	2015-10-01 19:48:32	rw-r--r--	--a-
10f26510ae4b8f5c3a6fac86c499eca2266a914f	2		3 WindowsToUbuntu/Enron3111.zip	FILE	DELETED	30967	2014-12-13 08:35:00		75a666ba87fef0f8425a71edcd621d0a4367aa47	2015-10-01 19:48:32	rw-r--r--	--a-
588275ee75c158cc3a1071207d17e8285528 1d7f	2		3 WindowsToUbuntu/Enron3111.rtf	FILE	DELETED	43360	2014-12-13 08:32:19		c4760cf2251c498b4c1e0ec75e4a34d775f92bdc	2015-10-01 19:48:32	rw-r--r--	--a-

Fig. 2. Portion of the 'FILEVERSION_MASTER' table recovered in our research.

DATABASEVERSION_STATUS	DATABASEVERSION_LOCALTIME	DATABASEVERSION_CLIENT	DATABASEVERSION_VECTORCLOCK_SERIALIZED	FILEHISTORY_ID	VERSION	DATABASEVERSION_ID	PATH	TYPE	STATU
MASTER	2015-10-01 18:52:38	UYCrwWXGXKvbOYKtZBGc	(UYCrwWXGXKvbOYKtZBGc1)	8509cfe7c5b1f82e305c0aaade57c8f0745de5c6	1		0 .syignore	FILE	NEW
MASTER	2015-10-01 19:26:14	UYCrwWXGXKvbOYKtZBGc	(UYCrwWXGXKvbOYKtZBGc2)	3d247e3ddc8f73c49c98a3a9abd89897dc0a8179	1		1 Enron3111.pdf	FILE	NEW
MASTER	2015-10-01 19:26:14	UYCrwWXGXKvbOYKtZBGc	(UYCrwWXGXKvbOYKtZBGc2)	bab75c4cb7537d5a7641869834913123eed4304c	1		1 Enron3111.rtf	FILE	NEW
MASTER	2015-10-01 19:26:14	UYCrwWXGXKvbOYKtZBGc	(UYCrwWXGXKvbOYKtZBGc2)	9bec78b6de24d0df15e7469e72b77cdbf163bd55	1		1 Enron3111.txt	FILE	NEW
MASTER	2015-10-01 19:26:14	UYCrwWXGXKvbOYKtZBGc	(UYCrwWXGXKvbOYKtZBGc2)	c3bd62f81eda2db41d6beb294ccfbb36f452f99c	1		1 Enron3111.jpg	FILE	NEW
MASTER	2015-10-01 19:26:14	UYCrwWXGXKvbOYKtZBGc	(UYCrwWXGXKvbOYKtZBGc2)	ee439cb563617c8a9d7de9c8c533bb015a946d1a	1		1 Enron3111.docx	FILE	NEW
MASTER	2015-10-01 19:26:14	UYCrwWXGXKvbOYKtZBGc	(UYCrwWXGXKvbOYKtZBGc2)	3a947cff54c9e3b748f9cb4f65752b16d4c637e8	1		1 Enron3111.zip	FILE	NEW
MASTER	2015-10-01 19:42:10	PqPKd.WznojHZVLsigNo	(PqPKd.WznojHZVLsigNo1,UYCrwWXGXKvbOYKtZBGc2)	2ab118932cfbf75a27f0657eefec8f1eb2b737b8	1		2 WindowsToUbuntu/Enron3111.pdf	FILE	NEW
MASTER	2015-10-01 19:42:10	PqPKd.WznojHZVLsigNo	(PqPKd.WznojHZVLsigNo1,UYCrwWXGXKvbOYKtZBGc2)	00a31c436450b3a71e58ad12c28f9b4bebcc2c45	1		2 WindowsToUbuntu/Enron3111.txt	FILE	NEW
MASTER	2015-10-01 19:42:10	PqPKd.WznojHZVLsigNo	(PqPKd.WznojHZVLsigNo1,UYCrwWXGXKvbOYKtZBGc2)	10f26510ae4b8f5c3a6fac86c499eca2266a914f	1		2 WindowsToUbuntu/Enron3111.zip	FILE	NEW
MASTER	2015-10-01 19:42:10	PqPKd.WznojHZVLsigNo	(PqPKd.WznojHZVLsigNo1,UYCrwWXGXKvbOYKtZBGc2)	0fa188da9eb4c6aaa4d495d8ad9e20d972ff54fb	1		2 WindowsToUbuntu/Enron3111.docx	FILE	NEW
MASTER	2015-10-01 19:42:10	PqPKd.WznojHZVLsigNo	(PqPKd.WznojHZVLsigNo1,UYCrwWXGXKvbOYKtZBGc2)	588275ee75c158cc3a1071207d17e8285528 1d7f	1		2 WindowsToUbuntu/Enron3111.rtf	FILE	NEW
MASTER	2015-10-01 19:42:10	PqPKd.WznojHZVLsigNo	(PqPKd.WznojHZVLsigNo1,UYCrwWXGXKvbOYKtZBGc2)	248eaab9dc360ee0a2ac601c1afad9fec6551842	1		2 WindowsToUbuntu/Enron3111.jpg	FILE	NEW
MASTER	2015-10-01 19:42:10	PqPKd.WznojHZVLsigNo	(PqPKd.WznojHZVLsigNo1,UYCrwWXGXKvbOYKtZBGc2)	0b4f85e8b1435574e71332e7d023931219e37d4f	1		2 WindowsToUbuntu	FOLDER	NEW
MASTER	2015-10-01 19:48:32	UYCrwWXGXKvbOYKtZBGc	(PqPKd.WznojHZVLsigNo1,UYCrwWXGXKvbOYKtZBGc3)	10f26510ae4b8f5c3a6fac86c499eca2266a914f	2		3 WindowsToUbuntu/Enron3111.zip	FILE	DELETE
MASTER	2015-10-01 19:48:32	UYCrwWXGXKvbOYKtZBGc	(PqPKd.WznojHZVLsigNo1,UYCrwWXGXKvbOYKtZBGc3)	00a31c436450b3a71e58ad12c28f9b4bebcc2c45	2		3 WindowsToUbuntu/Enron3111.txt	FILE	DELETE
MASTER	2015-10-01 19:48:32	UYCrwWXGXKvbOYKtZBGc	(PqPKd.WznojHZVLsigNo1,UYCrwWXGXKvbOYKtZBGc3)	588275ee75c158cc3a1071207d17e8285528 1d7f	2		3 WindowsToUbuntu/Enron3111.rtf	FILE	DELETE

Fig. 3. Portion of the 'FILEVERSION_FULL' table recovered in our research.

4.4 syncany.log

Log files play an important role in the reconstruction of a criminal scene [61–65]. The Syncany log file could be located at *%syncany%/logs/syncany.log*. Examination of the log file revealed that the client application's access times as well as sync folder/file creation, modification, and deletion times could be recovered. The log entries also held the corresponding sync file metadata such as file sizes and IP addresses/URLs for the repositories, which replicated the records in the local.db database. Table 4 summarises the log entries of forensic interest.

Table 4. Log entries of forensic interest with syncany.log.

Relevance	Examples of log entries
Assists a practitioner in the identification of the server's display name	1-10-15 18:52:20.274 | PluginSettingsP | main | INFO : Setting field 'username' with value 'syncanyserver'
Assists a practitioner in identifying the repository initiation time for a sync folder (via the 'sy connect' command), alongside the directory path and repository URL	1-10-15 18:52:27.196 | ManagementReque | main | SEVE : Executing InitOperation for folder/home/suspectpc/SyncanyUbuntuClient ... 1-10-15 18:52:34.807 | WebdavTransferM | IntRq/SyncanyU | INFO : WebDAV: Uploading local file/home/suspectpc/SyncanyUbuntuClient/.syncany/master to http://172.16.38.180/webdav/UbuntuRepo/master ...
Assists a practitioner in identifying the time when a sync folder is connected to an existing repository, including the directory path	1-10-15 19:32:38.646 | ManagementReque | main | SEVE : Executing ConnectOperation for folder/home/suspectpc/SyncanyWindowsDownloadToUbuntu
Assists a practitioner in identifying the sync file addition time, including the property information such as the filename, file version, as well as last modified and updated times	1-10-15 19:26:14.015 | Indexer | Thread-68 | INFO : * Added file version: FileVersion [version = 1, path = Enron3111.zip, type = FILE, status = NEW, size = 30967, lastModified = Sat Dec 13 08:35:00 PST 2014, linkTarget = null, checksum = 75a666ba87fef0f8425a71edcd621d0a4367aa47, updated = Thu Oct 01 19:26:14 PDT 2015, posixPermissions = rw-r--r--, dosAttributes = --a-]
Assists a practitioner in identifying the sync folder addition time, including the property information such as the directory name, folder version, as well as last modified and updated times	1-10-15 19:42:18.751 | FileSystemActio | NotifyThread | INFO : with winning version : FileVersion [version = 1, path = WindowsToUbuntu, type = FOLDER, status = NEW, size = 4096, lastModified = Mon Sep 28 21:40:44 PDT 2015, linkTarget = null, checksum = null, updated = Thu Oct 01 19:42:10 PDT 2015, posixPermissions = rwxr-xr-x, dosAttributes = --]
Enables a practitioner in determining the deletion time of a sync folder.	1-10-15 20:14:17.091 | AppIndicatorTra | PySTDIN | INFO : Python Input Stream: Removing folder '/ home/UbuntuPc/SyncanyUbuntuClient' ...
By searching for the 'file' tag, a practitioner can identify the filenames associated with a sync folder	1-10-15 19:26:17.032 | AppIndicatorTra | Timer-0 | INFO : Sending message: < updateRecentChangesGuiInternalEvent> <recentChanges> <file >/home/suspectpc/SyncanyUbuntuClient/Enron3111. zip </file> <file >/home/suspectpc/SyncanyUbuntuClient/Enron3111. txt </file> <file >/home/suspectpc/SyncanyUbuntuClient/Enron3111. rtf </file> ... </recentChanges> </updateRecentChangesGuiInternalEvent>

5 Memory Analysis

Examinations of the running processes using the 'pslist' function of Volatility indicated the process names, process identifiers (PID), parent process identifiers (PPID), as well as process initiation and termination times. Although the process name was masqueraded with 'java.exe', we could differentiate the PID from the last used PID recorded in the *%Syncany%/daemon.pid* and Syncany.log files. Examinations of the memory dumps using the 'netscan' or 'netstat' function of Volatility recovered the network information associated with the processes such as the host and server's IP addresses, port numbers, socket states, and protocols, providing an alternative method for recovery of the network information.

Carving of memory space of the Syncany daemon process recovered the log and *config.xml* files and local.db database intact. The data remnants could also be recovered in plain text through manual keyword searching for the file entries of relevance (e.g., log file structures, tag names for the XML files, and database table column names as identified in our research). Further inspection of the memory dumps identified that the *%.syncany%/config.xml* file could be potentially carved from unstructured datasets, using the header and footer information of "3C 63 6F 6E 66 69 67 3E 0A...3C 2F 70 61 73 73 77 6F 72 64 3E 0A 20 20 20 3C 2F 63 6F 6E 6E 65 63 74 69 6F 6E 3E 0A 3C 2F 63 6F 6E 66 69 67 3E", but the finding may be subject to software updates.

6 Concluding Remarks

In this paper, we studied the data remnants from the use of Syncany private cloud storage service as a backbone for big data storage. Our research included setting up the cloud hosting environment, installing the client applications, as well as uploading, downloading, and deleting the sync directory/file. We determined that a forensic practitioner investigating the use of Syncany should pay attention to config.xml, local. db, and syncany.log files on the client devices. The creation of the sync-folder-specific '.syncany' sub-directory suggested that a practitioner can identify the sync directory and the associated timestamps from the directory listing as well as other OS-generated instances such as shortcuts, event logs, $LogFile, $MFT, $UsnJrnl, registry ('RecentDocs', 'UserAssist', 'Run', and 'ComDig32' etc.), Zeitgeist and recently-used. xbel logs, and thumbnail cache.

Our examinations of the physical memory captures indicated that the memory dumps can provide a potential alternative method for recovery of the application caches, logs, HTTP requests in plain text, but not for the encryption password. This suggested that a practitioner can only obtain the encryption password either via an offline brute-force attack or directly from the user. Nevertheless, a practitioner must keep in mind that memory changes frequently according to user activities and will be wiped as soon as the system is shut down. Hence, obtaining a memory snapshot of a compromised system as quickly as possible increases the likelihood of obtaining the encryption key before it is overwritten in memory. Taken together, we determined that the Syncany client artefacts could be broadly classified into five (5) categories, which

Table 5. Summary of findings from the Syncany private cloud storage service.

Artefact category	Sources of information
Sync and file management metadata	Sync-folder-specific *%.syncany%/config.xml* and *%.syncany%/db/local.db* files
	User–specific *%syncany%/logs/syncany.log*, *%Syncany%/daemon.xml*, and *%Syncany%/daemon.pid* files
Authentication and encryption metadata	Sync-folder-specific/*%.syncany%/config.xml* file
	User-specific/*%syncany%/config.xml* file
Cloud transaction history	Folder-specific *%.syncany%/db/local.db* database
	User–specific *%syncany%/logs/syncany.log*
Data storage	Directories containing the '.syncany' sub-directory
Memory analysis	The log files and local.db database in plain text
	Copies of the config.xml and local.db files

are sync and file management metadata, authentication and encryption metadata, cloud transaction history, data storage, and memory artefacts as outlined in Table 5.

Although a variety of incriminating artefacts could be recovered from Syncany use, our research pointed out challenges that could be faced by forensic investigations. While the use of deduplication/chunking and encryption technologies can benefit the users by providing an efficient and secure means for managing big data, evidence collection and analysis may necessitate the encryption password and vendor-specific application. This can be subject to potential abuse by cyber criminals seeking to hide their tracks. Without the cooperation of the user (suspect), forensics endeavours may end up an exercise in futility. Therefore, we suggest the vendor to implement a forensically friendly logging mechanism (e.g., providing information about who accesses the data, what data has been accessed, from where did the user access the data, and when did the user access the data) that supports the collection of the raw log data outside the encrypted datasets by default. In a recent work, for example, Ab Rahman et al. [44] highlighted the importance of forensic-by-design and presented a conceptual forensic-by-design framework.

Future work would include extending this study to other private cloud storage services (e.g., Seafile) to have an up-to-date understanding of the big data artefacts from the private cloud deployment model, which can lay the foundation for the development of data reduction techniques (e.g., data mining and intelligence analysis) for these technologies [4, 5].

References

1. Damshenas, M., Dehghantanha, A., Mahmoud, R., bin Shamsuddin, S.: Forensics investigation challenges in cloud computing environments. In: 2012 International Conference on Cyber Security, Cyber Warfare and Digital Forensic (CyberSec), pp. 190–194 (2012)
2. Cauthen, J.M.: Executing Search Warrants in the Cloud. https://leb.fbi.gov/2014/october/executing-search-warrants-in-the-cloud

3. Quick, D., Choo, K.-K.R.: Big forensic data reduction: digital forensic images and electronic evidence. Clust. Comput. **19**, 1–18 (2016)
4. Quick, D., Choo, K.-K.R.: Impacts of increasing volume of digital forensic data: A survey and future research challenges. Digit. Investig. **11**, 273–294 (2014)
5. Quick, D., Choo, K.-K.R.: Data reduction and data mining framework for digital forensic evidence: Storage, intelligence, review, and archive. Trends Issues Crime Crim. Justice. **480**, 1–11 (2014)
6. Watson, S., Dehghantanha, A.: Digital forensics: the missing piece of the Internet of Things promise. Comput. Fraud Secur. **2016**, 5–8 (2016)
7. Daryabar, F., Dehghantanha, A.: A review on impacts of cloud computing and digital forensics. Int. J. Cyber-Secur. Digit. Forensics IJCSDF. **3**, 183–199 (2014)
8. Hooper, C., Martini, B., Choo, K.-K.R.: Cloud computing and its implications for cybercrime investigations in Australia. Comput. Law Secur. Rev. **29**, 152–163 (2013)
9. National Institute of Standards and Technology (NIST): NIST Cloud Computing Forensic Science Challenges (2014). http://safegov.org/media/72648/nist_digital_forensics_draft_8006.pdf
10. Quick, D., Martini, B., Choo, R.: Cloud Storage Forensics. Syngress, Amsterdam (2013)
11. Martini, B., Choo, K.-K.R.: Cloud forensic technical challenges and solutions: a snapshot. IEEE Cloud Comput. **1**, 20–25 (2014)
12. Heckel, P.C.: Syncany explained: idea, progress, development and future (part 1). https://blog.heckel.xyz/2013/10/18/syncany-explained-idea-progress-development-future/
13. Heckel, P.C.: Deep into the code of Syncany - command line client, application flow and data model (part 2). https://blog.heckel.xyz/2014/02/14/deep-into-the-code-of-syncany-cli-application-flow-and-data-model/
14. Syncany: Syncany User Guide. https://syncany.readthedocs.io/en/latest/
15. Quick, D., Choo, K.-K.R.: Dropbox analysis: Data remnants on user machines. Digit. Investig. **10**, 3–18 (2013)
16. Quick, D., Choo, K.-K.R.: Digital droplets: microsoft SkyDrive forensic data remnants. Future Gener. Comput. Syst. **29**, 1378–1394 (2013)
17. Quick, D., Choo, K.-K.R.: Google drive: forensic analysis of data remnants. J. Netw. Comput. Appl. **40**, 179–193 (2014)
18. Mell, P., Grance, T.: The NIST definition of cloud computing (2011)
19. Ruan, K., Carthy, J., Kechadi, T., Baggili, I.: Cloud forensics definitions and critical criteria for cloud forensic capability: an overview of survey results. Digit. Investig. **10**, 34–43 (2013)
20. Ruan, K., Baggili, I., Carthy, J., Kechadi, T.: Survey on cloud forensics and critical criteria for cloud forensic capability: a preliminary analysis. Electr. Comput. Eng. Comput. Sci. Fac. Publ. (2011)
21. Simou, S., Kalloniatis, C., Kavakli, E., Gritzalis, S.: Cloud forensics: identifying the major issues and challenges. In: Jarke, M., Mylopoulos, J., Quix, C., Rolland, C., Manolopoulos, Y., Mouratidis, H., Horkoff, J. (eds.) CAiSE 2014. LNCS, vol. 8484, pp. 271–284. Springer, Heidelberg (2014). doi:10.1007/978-3-319-07881-6_19
22. Pichan, A., Lazarescu, M., Soh, S.T.: Cloud forensics: technical challenges, solutions and comparative analysis. Digit. Investig. **13**, 38–57 (2015)
23. Fahdi, M.A., Clarke, N.L., Furnell, S.M.: Challenges to digital forensics: a survey of researchers amp; practitioners attitudes and opinions. In: 2013 Information Security for South Africa, pp. 1–8 (2013)
24. Birk, D., Wegener, C.: Technical issues of forensic investigations in cloud computing environments. In: 2011 IEEE Sixth International Workshop on Systematic Approaches to Digital Forensic Engineering (SADFE), pp. 1–10 (2011)

25. Sibiya, G., Venter, H.S., Fogwill, T.: Digital forensics in the cloud: the state of the art. In: IST-Africa Conference, 2015, pp. 1–9 (2015)
26. Taylor, M., Haggerty, J., Gresty, D., Almond, P., Berry, T.: Forensic investigation of social networking applications. Netw. Secur. **2014**, 9–16 (2014)
27. Daryabar, F., Dehghantanha, A., Udzir, N.I., Sani, N.F., Binti, M., Shamsuddin, S.B.: A review on impacts of cloud computing on digital forensics. Int. J. Cyber-Secur. Digit. Forensics IJCSDF **2**, 77–94 (2013)
28. Wilkinson, S.: ACPO Good Practice Guide for Digital Evidence, http://www.cps.gov.uk/legal/assets/uploads/files/ACPO_guidelines_computer_evidence[1].pdf, (2012)
29. Kent, K., Chevalier, S., Grance, T.: Guide to Integrating Forensic Techniques into Incident (2006)
30. Farina, J., Scanlon, M., Le-Khac, N.A., Kechadi, M.T.: Overview of the forensic investigation of cloud services. In: 2015 10th International Conference on Availability, Reliability and Security (ARES), pp. 556–565 (2015)
31. Damshenas, M., Dehghantanha, A., Mahmoud, R.: A survey on digital forensics trends. Int. J. Cyber-Secur. Digit. Forensics. **3**, 209–235 (2014)
32. Martini, B., Choo, K.-K.R.: An integrated conceptual digital forensic framework for cloud computing. Digit. Investig. **9**, 71–80 (2012)
33. McKemmish, R.: What is Forensic Computing. Australian Institute of Criminology, Canberra (1999)
34. Martini, B., Choo, K.-K.R.: Cloud storage forensics: ownCloud as a case study. Digit. Investig. **10**, 287–299 (2013)
35. Thethi, N., Keane, A.: Digital forensics investigations in the cloud. Presented at the February (2014)
36. Martini, B., Choo, K.-K.R.: Remote programmatic vCloud forensics: a six-step collection process and a proof of concept. In: Proceedings of 13th IEEE International Conference on Trust, Security and Privacy in Computing and Communications (TrustCom 2014), pp. 935–942. IEEE (2014)
37. Martini, B., Choo, K.-K.R.: Distributed filesystem forensics: XtreemFS as a case study. Digit. Investig. **11**, 295–313 (2014)
38. Chung, H., Park, J., Lee, S., Kang, C.: Digital forensic investigation of cloud storage services. Digit. Investig. **9**, 81–95 (2012)
39. Scanlon, M., Farina, J., Kechadi, M.-T.: BitTorrent Sync: Network Investigation Methodology (2014)
40. Scanlon, M., Farina, J., Khac, N.A.L., Kechadi, T.: Leveraging Decentralization to Extend the Digital Evidence Acquisition Window: Case Study on BitTorrent Sync. ArXiv14098486 Cs (2014)
41. Teing, Y.-Y., Dehghantanha, A., Choo, K.-K.R., Yang, L.T.: Forensic investigation of P2P cloud storage services and backbone for IoT networks: BitTorrent Sync as a case study. Comput. Electr. Eng. 1–14 (2016)
42. Do, Q., Martini, B., Choo, K.-K.R.: A forensically sound adversary model for mobile devices. PLoS ONE **10**, e0138449 (2015)
43. Do, Q., Martini, B., Choo, K.-K.R.: Is the data on your wearable device secure? An Android Wear smartwatch case study. Softw. Pract. Exp. (2016)
44. Ab Rahman, N.H., Cahyani, N.D.W., Choo, K.-K.R.: Cloud incident handling and forensic-by-design: cloud storage as a case study. Concurr. Comput. Pract. Exp. (2016)
45. Marty, R.: Cloud application logging for forensics. In: Proceedings of the 2011 ACM Symposium on Applied Computing, pp. 178–184. ACM, New York (2011)
46. Shields, C., Frieder, O., Maloof, M.: A system for the proactive, continuous, and efficient collection of digital forensic evidence. Digit. Investig. **8**(Supplement), S3–S13 (2011)

47. Zawoad, S., Hasan, R.: Cloud Forensics: A Meta-Study of Challenges, Approaches, and Open Problems. ArXiv13026312 Cs (2013)
48. Dykstra, J., Sherman, A.T.: Design and implementation of FROST: digital forensic tools for the OpenStack cloud computing platform. Digit. Investig. **10**, S87–S95 (2013)
49. Gebhardt, T., Reiser, H.P.: Network forensics for cloud computing. In: Dowling, J., Taïani, F. (eds.) Distributed Applications and Interoperable Systems, pp. 29–42. Springer, Berlin Heidelberg (2013)
50. Quick, D., Choo, K.-K.R.: Forensic collection of cloud storage data: Does the act of collection result in changes to the data or its metadata? Digit. Investig. **10**, 266–277 (2013)
51. Teing, Y.-Y., Ali, D., Choo, K.-K.R., Conti, M., Dargahi, T.: Forensic investigation of cooperative storage cloud service: symform as a case study. J. Forensics Sci. 1–14 (in Press, 2016)
52. Hale, J.S.: Amazon Cloud Drive forensic analysis. Digit. Investig. **10**, 259–265 (2013)
53. Farina, J., Scanlon, M., Kechadi, M.-T.: BitTorrent Sync: First Impressions and Digital Forensic Implications. Digit. Investig. **11**(Supplement 1), S77–S86 (2014)
54. Shariati, M., Dehghantanha, A., Choo, K.-K.R.: SugarSync forensic analysis. Aust. J. Forensic Sci. **0**, 1–23 (2015)
55. Shariati, M., Dehghantanha, A., Martini, B., Choo, K.-K.R.: Ubuntu One investigation: Detecting evidences on client machines, Chap. 19. In: The Cloud Security Ecosystem. pp. 429–446. Syngress, Boston (2015)
56. Blakeley, B., Cooney, C., Dehghantanha, A., Aspin, R.: Cloud storage forensic: hubiC as a case-study. In: 2015 IEEE 7th International Conference on Cloud Computing Technology and Science (CloudCom), pp. 536–541 (2015)
57. Daryabar, F., Dehghantanha, A., Choo, K.-K.R.: Cloud storage forensics: MEGA as a case study. Aust. J. Forensic Sci. **0**, 1–14 (2016)
58. Martini, B., Do, Q., Choo, K.-K.R.: Mobile cloud forensics: an analysis of seven popular Android apps. In: The Cloud Security Ecosystem, pp. 309–345. Syngress, Boston, Chap. 15 (2015)
59. Daryabar, F., Dehghantanha, A., Eterovic-Soric, B., Choo, K.-K.R.: Forensic investigation of OneDrive, Box, GoogleDrive and Dropbox applications on Android and iOS devices. Aust. J. Forensic Sci. **0**, 1–28 (2016)
60. Norouzizadeh Dezfouli, F., Dehghantanha, A., Eterovic-Soric, B., Choo, K.-K.R.: Investigating Social Networking applications on smartphones detecting Facebook, Twitter, LinkedIn and Google + artefacts on Android and iOS platforms. Aust. J. Forensic Sci. 1–20 (2015)
61. Ibrahim, N.M., Al-Nemrat, A., Jahankhani, H., Bashroush, R.: Sufficiency of windows event log as evidence in digital forensics. In: Akan, O., Bellavista, P., Cao, J., Dressler, F., Ferrari, D., Gerla, M., Kobayashi, H., Palazzo, S., Sahni, S., Shen, X., Stan, M., Xiaohua, J., Zomaya, A., Coulson, G., Georgiadis, C.K., Jahankhani, H., Pimenidis, E., Bashroush, R., Al-Nemrat, A. (eds.) Global Security, Safety and Sustainability & e-Democracy, pp. 253–262. Springer, Heidelberg (2012)
62. Do, Q., Martini, B., Looi, J., Wang, Y., Choo, K.-K.: Windows event forensic process. In: Peterson, G., Shenoi, S. (eds.) Advances in Digital Forensics X, pp. 87–100. Springer, Heidelberg (2014)
63. Yang, T.Y., Dehghantanha, A., Choo, K.-K.R., Muda, Z.: Windows instant messaging app forensics: Facebook and Skype as case studies. PLoS ONE **11**, e0150300 (2016)
64. Yusoff, M.N., Ramlan, M., Dehghantanha, A., Abdullah, M.T.: Advances of Mobile Forensic Procedures in Firefox OS. Int. J. Cyber-Secur. Digit. Forensics. **3**, 183–199 (2014)
65. Yusoff, M.N., Mahmod, R., Abdullah, M.T., Dehghantanha, A.: Performance measurement for mobile forensic data acquisition in Firefox OS. Int. J. Cyber-Secur. Digit. Forensics. **3**, 130–140 (2014)

First International Workshop on Cloud Storage Service and Computing (WCSSC 2016)

A Weighted Frequency Based Cache Memory Replacement Policy for Named Data Networking

You Liao, Yupeng Hu[✉], Linjun Wu, and Zheng Qin

College of Computer Science and Electronic Engineering,
Hunan University, Changsha 410082, China
yphu@hnu.edu.cn

Abstract. This paper presents a weighted frequency based real-time data replacement policy (WFRRP) for named data networking (NDN) cache memory. Based on the temporal locality, WFRRP leverages the weighted request frequency within different time periods and the cost of data request to predictas well as evaluate the real-time popularity of data. Specifically, those real hot data and data further away from the source servers are able to obtain high real-time popularity so as to have the caching priorities over the cold data. Experimental results show that WFRRP has accurate prediction capability, and is able to gain considerable improvements of data hit rate so as to help the NDN reduce the average number of hops and transmission delay.

Keywords: Named data networking · Data replacement policy · Cache memory space · Data popularity

1 Introduction

Over the last forty years, the traditional TCP/IP based Internet architecture has brought great changes to our world. On the other hand, it is prone to a growing number of defects, such as security, scalability, mobility and so on [1]. A variety of network architectures have been proposed to overcome these defects so as to improve the performance of the Internet. The state-of-the-art network architecture could broadly be divided into two categories: "evolutionary" and "revolutionary" [2, 3]. The "evolutionary" advocates the improvements for the existing network main architecture in the form of the "patch", e.g., P2P (Peer to Peer) and CDN (Content Delivery Network) are representative methods [4, 5]. In contrary, the "revolutionary" is devoted to designing a new type of network architecture, such as the ICN (Information Centric Networking) [6].

As a typical architecture of ICN, NDN (Named Data Networking) has attracted a plethora of research efforts in recent years [7]. One key characteristic of NDN is that, every node has the CS (Content Store) to cache data it transits. However, the very limited cache space is unable to store all related information with regard to the huge amount of data. Therefore, the data replacement policy for cache plays a crucial role in the overall performance of NDN [8, 9].

© Springer International Publishing AG 2016
G. Wang et al. (Eds.): SpaCCS 2016 Workshops, LNCS 10067, pp. 361–370, 2016.
DOI: 10.1007/978-3-319-49145-5_35

There has been growing interest in the study of data replacement policy for NDN. The LRU (Least Recently Used) [10] strategy will store the latest requested data in the bottom of the cache so that the data in the top of cache will be firstly replaced if it is necessary, namely, LRU prefers to replace the least recently used data. In LFU (Least Frequently Used) [11] strategy, the data's request frequency will add one upon it has been requested, in this way, the data that has the minimum request frequency will be replaced. Therefore, the LRU strategy cannot reflect the popularity of data although it can reflect the real-time of data; on the contrary, the LFU strategy can only reflect the popularity of data but cannot reflect the real-time of data. In [12, 13], the proposed data replacement policies consider the cost of data request while fail to take the popularity and the real-time of data into account. As a result, most existing replacement policy can hardly reflect the popularity and real-time of data at the same time.

To address the problem aforementioned, this paper proposes a weighted frequency based real-time data replacement policy (WFRRP). The key idea of WFRRP is based on the temporal locality of request, that is, the data request frequency within different time period could make uneven contributions to the prediction of the popularity of data within the next time period which is called "real-time popularity" in this paper. Thus WFRRP gives the more recent time duration a bigger weight factor, which is used to calculate the real-time popularity of the requested data. Therefore the more requested real-time data (i.e., hot data) will have the priority to be stored in the limited cache. Moreover, WFRRP takes the cost of data acquisition/request procedure into account and thus saves the cache space for those hot data further from the source data server. Consequently, the WFRRP is able to store more hot data and thus increase the overall cache utilization of NDN nodes.

2   Background and Problem

2.1   The Mechanism of NDN

As an advanced instance of ICN, NDN is no longer host-centric but place an emphasis on the data request. There are two types of packets in NDN: interest/request packet and data packet. Instead of host address, the two kinds of packets take the name of data as the identifier. While the data packet is the response of the corresponding interest/request packet.

As shown in Fig. 1, the critical content store of a node in NDN is responsible for caching some data packets that the node transits and probably sends back later as a response to the corresponding request. In this way, the node can obtain network resources savings by avoiding forwarding the request packet to further source data server. Besides the content store mentioned above, each node of NDN includes a PIT (Pending Interest Table) and a FIB (Forwarding Information Base). The PIT is mainly used to store the interest/request packets that yet cannot find its corresponding data packets in content store in this node. Each PIT entry mainly consists of the name of a request packet and the interface it needs to enter the node. While the FIB works as a route table to forward the request packet. When a request packet arrives at a node, this node firstly finds out whether there is a corresponding data packet in content store:

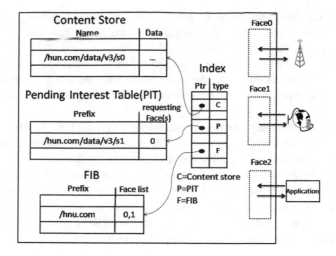

Fig. 1. The overview mechanism of NDN.

if there is and then it will return the packet; otherwise, it will redirect the request packet to the next hop according to the entries in the PIT and FIB.

2.2 The Data Replacement Problem

Figure 2 illustrates the data replacement problem of NDN. When a data packet arrives, the node has to decide if drop it or not by checking the PIT. If not, the node will judge whether replace some other tag in content store with the coming data packet and then forward it. Thus the data replacement policy of NDN determines which tag should be replaced.

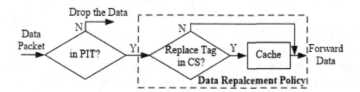

Fig. 2. The data replacement problem of NDN.

3 The Weighted Frequency Based Real-Time Data Replacement Policy (WFRRP)

3.1 Overview

This paper proposes WFRRP to reflect the real-time popularity of data in NDN. Unlike the static LFU [11] simply using the number of requests to measure the popularity, the WFRRP collects the real-time request frequencies of data of interest within different time periods and then uses them to predict the real-time popularity. As a result, WFRRP is able to avoid storing the cold data which has accumulated high request times so as to conserve limited cache for real hot data.

It is well known that the coming popularity of data is hard to predict. WFRRP is based on the temporal locality, i.e., the more recent time period is more important in predicting the real-time popularity. Specifically, the WFRRP has two major parameters as follows:

The weighted frequency. When a data packet arrives, the WFRRP collects its request frequencies within the closest 3 equal long time period, respectively. The more recent request frequency will be allocated a bigger weight factor.

The request frequency variance. In regard to the fluctuation of request frequency, the WFRRP gives the bigger weight to the more stable request frequency, and vice versa. That is, if the request frequency of data is more stable, it is more important in predict the real-time popularity. Specifically, the WFRRP exploits the mean square error to evaluate the stability of request frequency in the next section.

3.2   The Real-Time Popularity Model

This section shows the theory model of WFRRP. When a NDN node accepts a data packet, it has to put the data at the right position of the content store queue by assessing the real-time popularity. The overall model node n used to calculate the real-time popularity the data arriving at time t is as follows.

$$W_n = W * C^{\delta_{data}} + \beta L \tag{1}$$

Obviously, this model is composed of two parts: $W * C^{\delta_{data}}$ is used to evaluate the popularity within three recent time durations, i.e., $\gamma 1 = [t - \Delta t,\ t]$, $\gamma 2 = [t - 2\Delta t, t - \Delta t]$, $\gamma 3 = [t - 3\Delta t, t - 2\Delta t]$; while the is used to calculate the historical popularity within $[t^*,\ t - 3\Delta t]]$, where t^* denotes a distant past time.

In the first part, $W = \alpha_1 * f_1 + \alpha_2 * f_2 + \alpha_3 * f_3$, where $f1, f2$ and $f3$ denotes the request frequencies of the same data within the three different time periods $\gamma 1, \gamma 2$ and $\gamma 3$, respectively; $\alpha_1, \alpha_2, \alpha_3$ are corresponding weight factors given to $f1, f2$ and $f3$, and $\alpha_1 + \alpha_2 + \alpha_3 = 1$. Note that $\alpha_1 > \alpha_2 > \alpha_3$, according to the importance of theses tree time period. On the other hand, the WFRRP also takes the request frequency variance into account via the $C^{\delta_{data}}$, where C is a balance parameter and $C < 1$, and δ_{data} denotes the mean square error of request frequencies during $[t - 3\Delta t,\ t]$:

$$\delta_{data} = \sqrt{\frac{1}{3} \sum_{i=1}^{3} (f_i - E)^2} \tag{2}$$

Where E is the average frequency, $E = (f1 + f2 + f3)/3$. It is easy to find that the $C^{\delta_{data}}$ is a monotonically decreasing function of δ_{data}, in other words, the more stable popularity will obtain higher W_n. What's more, the C is defined as follows to take the cost of request procedure into consideration.

$$C = \frac{Hop_{data}}{Max\_hop} \tag{3}$$

Where Hopdata is the distance between the data accepting node n and the data source server; and Max_hop represents the maximum distance between the client and the data server in the network. The increase of C will enlarge the real-time popularity W_n. Therefore, WFRRP enables the node n give high priority to store the data further away from the source server.

In the second part, i.e., βL, L is the number of historical requests, and $0 < \beta < 1$, β is a adjustment parameter. By adjusting the β, the βL can reflect the influence of past time period. After substituting these above parameters into the Eq. (1), the real-time popularity is:

$$W_n = (\alpha_1 f_1 + \alpha_2 f_2 + \alpha_3 f_3) * \left[\left(\frac{Hop_{data}}{Max\_hop} \right)^{\sqrt{\frac{1}{3} \sum_{i}^{3} (f_i - E)^2}} \right] + \beta L \tag{4}$$

3.3   The Data Replacement Algorithm

Based on the W_n in Eq. (4), the specific data replacement algorithm of WFRRP is shown in Fig. 3. Eventually, some data with the smallest W_n in content store will be replaced by the received data packet. Thus the utilization of limited cache will be maximized.

---

1. **Initialize** ($W_n=0$, $f_1=0$, $f_2=0$, $f_3=0$)
2. **if** (data is first requested)
3.   caching the data;
4. **else**
5.   Get f_1, f_2, f_3 from γ_1, γ_2, γ_3;
6.   Calculate W and δ_{data} of data;
7.   Get Hop_data and Max_hop of data
8.   Calculate W_n of data
9.   Replacing data* in CS having smallest W_n with
                the received data.
10. **end if**

Fig. 3. The data replacement algorithm based on the real-time popularity

4 Simulation Results and Evaluations

This section performs extensive simulations to evaluate the performance of the WFRRP. WFRRP is implemented on the open-source ndnSIM [14] simulator which is based on NS-3. The experiments generate a random NDN topology with BRITE Topology Builder. The specific parameters of topology are shown in Table 1. Without loss of generality, the client's request of specific data in our simulations has a Zipf(α) distribution [15, 16], which issued to account for the relative popularity of a few data (i.e., hot data) and the relative obscurity of other data (i.e., cold data) of in specific NDN applications. Meanwhile the random request arriving at single NDN node has a Poisson distribution. For evaluation convenience, all nodes have the same cache size (denoting the maximum number of data packets can be stored) and each data packet in the experiments is set to 1 MB. Meanwhile the parameters in W_n are set according to the network size, i.e. α_1, α_2, α_3 and are set to 0.5, 0.3 and 0.2, respectively; and the β is equal to 0.1. To evaluate the performance, WFRRP is compared with existing traditional data replacement policies, such as LFU, FIFO and LRU.

Table 1. The parameters of network topology

Topology	Nodes number	Links number	Clients number	Servers number
Random	60	126	10	10

4.1 The Impact of Cache Size

The cache size of node is crucial to the performance and even the viability of the NDN. This subsection evaluates the performance of WFPPR with varying cache size.

As shown in Fig. 4, the average hit rate increases with the cache size since more data could be stored in the content store. The simple FIFO has the lowest hit rate. The performance of LFU is closest to WFRRP. While the proposed WFRRP still gains the highest hit rate that is about 7 % ~ 9 % higher than LFU and 90 % ~ 95 % higher than FIFO and LRU. The main reason is that WFRRP can more accurately predict the real-time popularity.

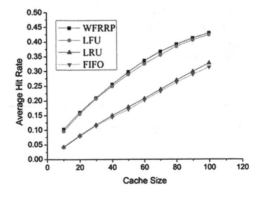

Fig. 4. The average hit rate with varying cache size.

This experiment performed in Fig. 5 evaluates the average number of hops needed to get the intended data from different clients. The increase of cache size results in the reduction of the number of hops as depicted in Fig. 6. Thus WFRRP needs the shortest route length to find the requested data. Specifically, when the cache size is set to 100, the average number of hops of WFRRP is only about 2.2.

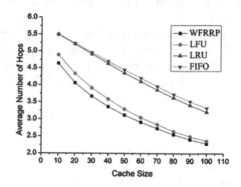

Fig. 5. The average number of hops with varying cache size.

As depicted in Fig. 6, the overall average transmission delay of request decreases sharply with the increase of cache size. Here the experiment results are consistent with the number of hops. Clearly, the performance of FIFO is the worst. While the WFRRP obtains the smallest delay due to the parameter C in Eq. (1) used to consider the cost of data request. Thus the data more further from the source server has the priority to be stored. When the node cache size is 30, the delay of RRPF is about 0.031 s, which is about 8 % less than the LFU.

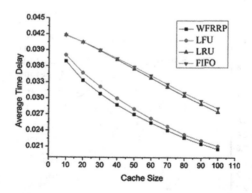

Fig. 6. The transmission delay with varying cache size.

4.2   The Impact of Zipf(α)

Generally, the request for specific data in NDN has a Zip f(α) distribution [15, 16]. The parameter α is the value of the exponent characterizing the distribution. It is worth noticing that the increase of α implies that more clients' requests focus on a few data, so that a greater number of other data get a moderate or even can hardly get requests. This subsection evaluates the impact of parameter α to the data replacement policies. Here the cache size is set to 100.

Since the increase α of leads to a promotion of popularity of a few hot data, it is high probability that the stored hot data will get hits. As shown in Fig. 7, the average hit rate of all policies increases with the α. Owing to the accurate prediction, the WFRRP still has the highest hit rate which is 7 %–8 % higher than LFU and 40 %–60 % higher than LRU.

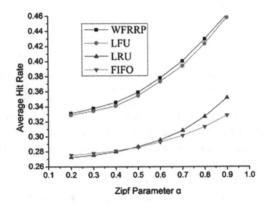

Fig. 7. The average hit rate with varying α.

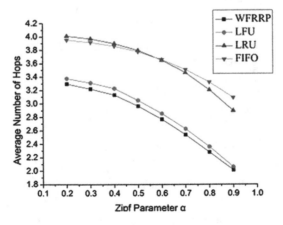

Fig. 8. The average number of hops with varying α.

Since the increase of hit rate will shorten the average route length needed to hit a requested data, as shown in Fig. 8, the increase of α leads to a significant reduction of the number of hops. The proposed WFRRP has an advantage over the other 3 policies. When the α is equal to 0.9, in WFRRP, the number of hops is merely 2 or so.

According to the decrease of number of hops, the increase of α also can obtain considerable savings of transmission delay as shown in Fig. 9. The WFRRP has the lowest transmission delay compared with other policies. When α is 0.9, the time delay of WFRRP is only about 0.018 s, which is almost half lower than LRU or FIFO. Thus the WFRRP can gain better users experience of data request.

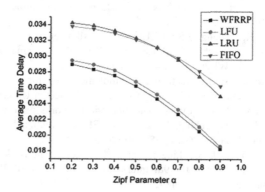

Fig. 9. The transmission delay with varying α.

5   Conclusion

In this paper, we have presented a WFRRP that exploits the weighted request frequency and the cost of data request to predict the real-time popularity of data, so as to give the cache priority to those real hot data. Experimental results show that WFRRP can gain considerable improvement of hit rate and thus help the NDN reduce the average number of hops and transmission delay.

Acknowledgments. This work is partially supported by the National Science Foundation of China under Grant Nos. 61572181, 61300218, 61472131 and 61272546; Research and Development Key Projects of Hunan Province (2016JC2013, 2016JC2012); Science and Technology Key Projects of Hunan Province (2015 TP1004).

References

1. Gaogang, X.: A survey on future internet architecture. Chin. J. Comput. **35**(6), 1109–1119 (2012)
2. Er Long, M.: Research progress of content center network. Netinfo Secur. 6–10 (2012)
3. Lin, X.: future internet architecture—content centric networks. Telecommun. Sci. **26**(4), 7–16 (2010)

4. Sprangle, E., Carmean, D., Kumar, R.: Distribution of tasks among asymmetric processing elements. US, US8930722 (2015)
5. Mu, R., Zhao, F.: CDN and P2P network model based on HCDN Technology. J. Softw. Eng. **9**(3), 469–486 (2015)
6. Ahlgren, B.: A survey of information-centric networking. IEEE Commun. Mag. **50**(7), 26–36 (2012)
7. Afanasyev, A.: SNAMP: secure namespace mapping to scale NDN forwarding. In: 2015 IEEE Conference on IEEE Computer Communications Workshops (INFOCOM WKSHPS) (2015)
8. Jacobson, V., Mosko, M., Smetters, D.: Content-centric networking. Whitepaper, Palo Alto Research Center, pp. 2–4 (2007)
9. Zhang, L., Estrin, D., Jacobson, V.: Named data networking project. Technical Report, NDN-0001 (2010)
10. Shin, S.W., Kim, K.Y., Jang, J.S.: LRU based small latency first replacement (SLFR) algorithm for the proxy cache. In: Proceedings. IEEE/WIC International Conference on IEEE Web Intelligence, WI 2003, pp. 499–502 (2003)
11. Karakostas, G., Serpanos, D.: Practical LFU implementation for web caching. Technical Report TR-622–00, Department of Computer Science, Princeton University (2000)
12. Wang, J.M., Bensaou, B.: Improving content-centric networks performance with progressive, diversity-load driven caching. In: 2012 1st IEEE International Conference on IEEE Communications in China (ICCC), pp. 85–90 (2012)
13. Chen, X., Fan, Q., Yin, H.: Caching in information-centric networking: from a content delivery path perspective. In: 2013 9th International Conference on IEEE Innovations in Information Technology (IIT), pp. 48–53 (2013)
14. Afanasyev, A., Moiseenko, I., Zhang, L.: ndnSIM: NDN simulator for NS-3. University of California, Los Angeles, Technical report (2012)
15. Carofiglio, G.: Modeling data transfer in content-centric networking. In: 2011 23rd International IEEE Teletraffic Congress (ITC), pp. 111–118 (2011)
16. Laoutaris, N., Syntila, S., Stavrakakis, I.: Meta algorithms for hierarchical web caches. In: 2004 IEEE International Conference on Performance, Computing, and Communications, pp. 445–452. IEEE (2004)

An Authentication Data Structure of Provable Data Possession with Dynamic Data Operation in Cloud Computing

Hongyun Xu, Jiesi Jiang, and Cheng Xu[(✉)]

School of Computer Science and Engineering,
South China University of Technology, Guangzhou 510006, China
xucrock@gmail.com

Abstract. In public cloud, storage devices are not within the control of the enterprises. Data stored in the cloud server may be tampered or deleted illegally. Remote data integrity checking protocol enables the client to verify the integrity of data which is not stored in local. Aiming at the dynamic update operation in remote data integrity checking protocol, we propose a new authentication data structure named CBT, by deploying the tags of all data blocks to the nodes of a binary tree in a given order. Both theoretical analysis and experimental data show that, the number of nodes updated in CBT is 50 %, 69 % and 67 % compared with that of MHT in batch modification, insertion and deletion operations respectively; the memory of CBT is only two-thirds of MHT.

Keywords: Dynamic data operation · Provable data possession · Authentication data structure · Certification binary tree · Merkle hash tree

1 Introduction

With the development of cloud computing, more and more enterprises have been willing to outsource storage to the cloud storage service providers. The public cloud brings great conveniences to the enterprises while it also poses some risks. The most significant risk is that the storage device is beyond the enterprise users' control, the data stored in the cloud server may be tampered or deleted illegally. Thus the integrity of data stored in the cloud server faces great threats. Remote data integrity checking aims to solve this problem, it enables the enterprises and the individuals to check the integrity of the data stored in the cloud server.

In 2004, Y. Deswarte et al. [1] first put forward the concept of integrity checking of remote data. In 2007, G. Ateniese et al. [2] proposed a complete remote data integrity checking protocol (Provable Data Possession, referred as PDP) which realized the integrity checking for static data. However, it did not support dynamic update operations. In 2008, G. Ateniese et al. [3] extended PDP through symmetric encryption, and proposed a new model named S-PDP which provided some dynamic update operations. C. Erway et al. [4] have introduced MHT (i.e. Merkle Hash Tree [5]) as the authentication data structure, and proposed dynamic PDP (referred as D-PDP) which is able to support both dynamic update operations and unlimited verifications.

© Springer International Publishing AG 2016
G. Wang et al. (Eds.): SpaCCS 2016 Workshops, LNCS 10067, pp. 371–381, 2016.
DOI: 10.1007/978-3-319-49145-5_36

Based on MHT, Q. Zheng et al. [6] have proposed 2–3 tree authentication data structure which sharply reduces both the computation and communication costs. J. Wang et al. [7] have proposed the concept of batch dynamic data operations (referred as batch-update) based on 2–3 tree. Batch-update has less computation, memory and communication costs than single dynamic data operation. However, both 2–3 tree and MHT deploy data block tags to the leaf nodes, so the updating and storage efficiency remains to be further improved. C. Li [8] and Y. Zhu [9] have used the SN-BN and index-hash tables as the authentication data structure, which reduces the computation complexity, whereas increases the space complexity.

Aiming at improving the updating and storage efficiency in remote data integrity checking protocol, this paper proposes a new authentication data structure, named as Certification Binary Tree (referred as CBT), by deploying the data block tags to the nodes of a binary tree in a given order, CBT can not only provide both single and batch dynamic data update operations, but also reduce the storage costs, thus promotes the efficiency of dynamic data operations.

The remainder of this paper is organized as follows: Sect. 2 is problem definition. In Sect. 3, we introduce CBT in detail. Section 4 is experiments and evaluations. We conclude this paper in Sect. 5.

2 Problem Definition

The data file in the cloud server is composed of n blocks, denoted as set F, $F = \{m_1, \ldots, m_n\}$, with their tags denoted as set T, $T = \{T(m_1), \ldots, T(m_n)\}$. In PDP [2], each data block corresponds to a data tag, and the ith ($1 \leq i \leq n$) data tag includes the index information i. If we want to insert a data block before the ith data block, the index of the original data tags from the ith to the nth should be updated to the $(i + 1)^{th}$ to the $(n + 1)^{th}$. Because the tag set is computed by the client that does not store data file F, the server should send data blocks from m_i to m_n to the client. Then, the client computes the tags of these data blocks, and obtains corresponding tags subset $\{T(m_{i+1})', \ldots, T(m_{n+1})'\}$, which will be sent back to the server later. However, this approach is infeasible because of the high time complexity and communication bandwidth consumption.

To solve the above problem, we separate the index of the data block from the data tag, i.e., transform tag $T(m_i)$ ($1 \leq i \leq n$) to $T(m_i)\|i$ (the symbol "$\|$" means connecting operation), thus it will not affect any other data tags when we insert a data block into the data file. Figure 1 shows the data file blocks and corresponding data tags before and after the insertion of data block m_j.

The server does not need to recompute the tags for data blocks m_4 and m_5 after data block m_j is inserted. Because both set F and set T are stored in the cloud server, if the client wants to check the integrity of data block m_1 and m_2, it can follow these steps:

(1) The client sends challenge [1] to the server to verify the integrity of m_1 and m_2;
(2) Receiving the challenge, the server sends m_1, m_2, $T(m_1)\|1$, $T(m_2)\|2$ to the client;
(3) The client checks whether $T(m_1)\|1$ and $T(m_2)\|2$ are the tags of index 1 and 2 respectively, then checks the data integrity by computing tags of m_1 and m_2.

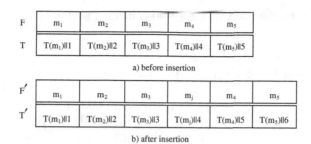

F	m_1	m_2	m_3	m_4	m_5	
T	$T(m_1)\|1$	$T(m_2)\|2$	$T(m_3)\|3$	$T(m_4)\|4$	$T(m_5)\|5$	

a) before insertion

F'	m_1	m_2	m_3	m_j	m_4	m_5
T'	$T(m_1)\|1$	$T(m_2)\|2$	$T(m_3)\|3$	$T(m_j)\|4$	$T(m_4)\|5$	$T(m_5)\|6$

b) after insertion

Fig. 1. Data blocks and corresponding data tags

In the second step, $T(m_i)$ does not include index information, so the server could send any other two data blocks to the client in the disguise of m_1 and m_2, e.g., $T(m_3)\|1$ and $T(m_4)\|2$, which is a typical spoofing attack.

In summary, to achieve the remote data integrity checking with dynamic data operation, the authentication data structure should meet the following two conditions:

(1) The tag of data block m_i should not include the index of the data block. (2) The client must have the ability to validate the index of m_i to prevent the spoofing attack.

3 Certification Binary Tree

3.1 Construct the Tree

MHT stores all the tags on the leaf nodes, so there needs extra memory to store the internal nodes, leading to a higher space complexity. To solve this problem, we propose CBT.

In CBT, the data file in the server is partitioned into n blocks, denoted as set F, $F = \{m_1,..., m_n\}$, with their tags denoted as set T, $T = \{T(m_1),..., T(m_n)\}$, then we could get set H, $H = \{h(T(m_1)),..., h(T(m_n))\}$, where h is a hash function. All elements of set H are deployed to a binary tree, element $h(T(m_i))$ locates on the node v_i $(1 \leq i \leq n)$.

Figure 2 is a CBT with 7 data blocks, $h(T(m_1))$ is on the node v_1, $h(T(m_2))$ is on the node v_2, and so on.

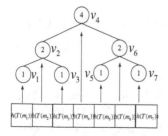

Fig. 2. CBT for 7 data blocks file

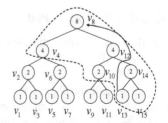

Fig. 3. CP for node v_{13}

In CBT, $x(v_i)$ for the node v_i $(1 \leq i \leq n)$ is defined by Eq. (1).

$$x(v_i) = \{h(T(m_i)), r(v_i), f(v_i)\} \tag{1}$$

where, $r(v_i)$ is defined by Eq. (2), called r value of v_i.

$$r(v_i) = \begin{cases} j - i & \text{if } v_i \text{ is the left child of } v_j \\ i - j & \text{if } v_i \text{ is the right child of } v_j \\ i & \text{if } v_i \text{ is the root} \end{cases} \tag{2}$$

where, i is the index of v_i, j is the index of v_j which is the parent of v_i.

In Fig. 2, the value in the circle is the r value of a node, e.g., v_2 is the left child of v_4, $r(v_2) = 4 - 2 = 2$, v_6 is the right child of v_4, $r(v_6) = 6 - 4 = 2$, v_4 is the root, r $(v_4) = 4$. The r value is designed to prevent spoofing attack.

$f(v_i)$ in Eq. (1) is defined by Eq. (3), and called f value of v_i. The f value is used to check the integrity of the data file.

$$f(v_i) = \begin{cases} h(h(T(m_i))||r(v_i)||f(v_{ilchild})||f(v_{irchild})) & \text{if } v_i \text{ is not a leaf} \\ h(h(T(m_i))||r(v_i)) & \text{if } v_i \text{ is a leaf} \end{cases} \tag{3}$$

where, h is a hash function which is collision resistant, $v_{ilchild}$ and $v_{irchild}$ are the left and the right children of v_i respectively.

In the following context, $x(v_i)$ and $h(T(m_i))$ are called x value and h value of v_i respectively.

3.2   Check the Data Integrity

The client can check the integrity of the data file by checking the index and the integrity of data block m_a $(1 \leq a \leq n)$.

Firstly, the client constructs CBT for data file F; then computes the x value of the root, i.e., $x(v_{root}) = \{h(T(m_{root})), r(v_{root}), f(v_{root})\}$ (where, m_{root} is the data block corresponding to v_{root}), and stores $x(v_{root})$; After that, the server stores both data file F and its CBT.

Definition 1. Verification Node (referred as VN) The corresponding node of the data block to be checked in CBT.

Definition 2. Update Path (referred as UP) The path from VN to the root in CBT.

Definition 3. Certification Path (referred as CP) The path used to check the integrity of the data file.

In Fig. 3, if the client checks m_{13}, then the VN is v_{13}. The UP for v_{13} is marked by a solid line connected with an arrow (i.e. $v_{13} \rightarrow v_{14} \rightarrow v_{12} \rightarrow v_8$). The CP for v_{13} is circled by a dotted line. For any VN v_a $(1 \leq a \leq n)$, the CP π_a is defined by Eq. (4).

$$\pi_a = \left\{ \pi_a^1, \pi_a^2, \cdots, \pi_a^k \right\} \tag{4}$$

where, k is the number of nodes on the UP of v_a. The nodes on the UP are denoted as set V, V = $\{V_i | 1 \leq i \leq k\}$, the data blocks corresponding to the elements of set V are denoted as set M, M = $\{M_i | 1 \leq i \leq k\}$.
where, π_a^i is defined by Eq. (5).

$$\pi_a^i = \{h(T(M_i)),\ r(V_i), r'(V_{ilchild}), f'(V_{ilchild}), r'(V_{irchild}), f'(V_{irchild})\} \tag{5}$$

where, $h(T(M_i))$ is the h value of V_i, $r(V_i)$ is the r value of V_i, $V_{ilchild}$ and $V_{irchild}$ are the left and the right children of V_i, respectively.

If $V_{ilchild}$ lays on the UP of V_i, then let $r'(V_{ilchild}) = f'(V_{ilchild}) = -1$; if $V_{irchild}$ lays on the UP of V_i, then let $r'(V_{irchild}) = f'(V_{irchild}) = -1$; if V_i is a leaf node, then let $r'(V_{ilchild}) = f'(V_{ilchild}) = r'(V_{irchild}) = f'(V_{irchild}) = 0$; otherwise, let $r'(V_{ilchild}) = r(V_{ilchild})$, $f'(V_{ilchild}) = f(V_{ilchild})$, $r'(V_{irchild}) = r(V_{irchild})$, $f'(V_{irchild}) = f(V_{irchild})$.

The client computes f and r values of root through the CP π_a received from the server, compares with those of values stored in local to check the integrity of the data file stored in the remote cloud server. The steps to check the data file integrity are illustrated by Algorithm 1.

Algorithm 1
input: the x value of root, the CP π_a;
output: true or false   // true means the data is integral, otherwise the data is not integral.

1: Initialize array F[1...k]={ 0 }; //array F stores f values of nodes located on the UP of v_a
2: position = $r(V_k)$;
3: F[1] = $h(T(M_1)\|r(V_1))$;
4: for i = 2 to k do //iterate to get f value of root through π_a
5:    { if r'$(V_{ilchild}) == -1$ and f'$(V_{ilchild}) == -1$ then
6:         F[i] = $h(h(T(M_i))\|r(V_i)\|f'(V_{irchild})\|F[i-1])$;
7:      if r'$(V_{irchild}) == -1$ and f'$(V_{irchild}) == -1$ then
8:         F[i] = $h(h(T(M_i))\|r(V_i)\|f'(V_{ilchild})\|F[i-1])$; }
9: for i = k to 2 do //iterate to get the index of m_a through π_a
10:   { if r$(V_{ilchild}) == -1$ and f$(V_{ilchild}) == -1$ then position = position - $r(V_{i-1})$;
11:      if r$(V_{irchild}) == -1$ and f$(V_{irchild}) == -1$ then position = position + $r(V_{i-1})$; }
12: if F[k] == f and position == a then return true; // check the integrity of the data file
13: else return false;

3.3 Modify Data Block

The protocol between the client and the server to modify a data block is as follows.

(1) The client sends a request to the server for modifying data block m_a;
(2) The server generates the CP π_a and sends it back to the client;
(3) The client checks the data integrity through Algorithm 1, if the output of Algorithm 1 is false, goto step (6);

(4) The client modifies data block m_a, gets updated data block m'_a, computes the tag $T(m'_a)$, updates the x value of root, sends data block m'_a and $T(m'_a)$ to the server;

(5) The server calls Algorithm 2 to update CBT, and generates the CP π_a of node v_a which corresponds to m'_a and sends it back to the client, the client calls Algorithm 1 to check the integrity of the data file;

(6) End

The steps to update CBT after modification are shown in Algorithm 2.

Algorithm 2

input: data block m'_a, the index a and $T(m'_a)$;

output: updated CBT

/* m'_a represents the modified data block m_a, v_a represents the node corresponding to m_a (before modification) or m'_a (after modification), $v_{alchild}$ and $v_{archild}$ are the left and the right children of v_a respectively. */

1: Initialize array F[1...k] = { 0 };

2: F[1] = h(h(T(m'_a))||r(v_a)||f($v_{alchild}$)||f($v_{archild}$));

3: for i = 2 to k do

4:    { if V_i only has a left child then   // V_i ($1 \leq i \leq k$) represents the ith node on the UP

5:        F[i] = h(h(T(M_i))||r(V_i)||f($V_{ilchild}$));   // M_i represents the data block corresponding to V_i

6:      else if V_i only has a right child then F[i] = h(h(T(M_i))||r(V_i)||f($V_{irchild}$));

7:      else F[i] = h(h(T(M_i))||r(V_i)||f($V_{irchild}$)||f($V_{ilchild}$)); }

8: for i = 1 to k do { f(V_i) = F[i]; }   // update the f values on the UP

9: x(v_a) = { h(T(m'_a)), r(v_a), f(v_a) }   // update the x value of node v_a

10: return

3.4   Insert Data Block

We assume that "insert the ath data block" means "insert data block m'_a before m_a", the protocol between the client and the server to insert data blocks is as follows.

(1) The client sends a request to the server for inserting the ath data block;

(2) The server searches the position to insert the data block node, issues a CP π_{a-1} (node v_{a-1} is the predecessor node of v_a) and sends it back to the client;

(3) The client checks the data integrity through Algorithm 1, if the output is false, go to step (6);

(4) The client computes $T(m'_a)$, updates the x value of root, sends m'_a and $T(m'_a)$ to the server;

(5) The server calls Algorithm 3 to update CBT and generates the CP π'_a of node v'_a which corresponds to m'_a and sends it back to the client, the client calls Algorithm 1 to check the integrity of the data file after insertion;

(6) End.

Algorithm 3 shows the steps to update CBT after insertion. The server searches the predecessor of the ath node and let the inserted node be its successor, then updates CBT.

Algorithm 3

input: data block m_a', the index for inserting the node and $T(m_a')$;

output: updated CBT

1: Initialize array F[1...k] = { 0 }, array R[1...k] = { 0 };

// array R stores r values of nodes located on the UP of node inserted

2: $x(v_a') = \{ h(T(m_a')), r(v_a'), f(v_a') \}$; // calculate the x value for v_a'

3: find the predecessor of the ath node in CBT, insert v_a', let v_a' be its successor;

4: $R[1] = r(v_a')$; // calculate the r values of nodes located on the UP of v_a'

5: for i = 2 to k do { R[i] = | parent node's index − current node's index |; } // $(2 \le i \le k)$

6: $F[1] = f(v_a')$; // calculate the f values of nodes located on the UP of v_a'

7: for i = 2 to k do

8:    { if V_i only has a left child then $F[i] = h(h(T(M_i))\|r(V_i)\|f(V_{ilchild}))$;

9:    else if V_i only has a right child then $F[i] = h(h(T(M_i))\|r(V_i)\|f(V_{irchild}))$;

10:    else $F[i] = h(h(T(M_i))\|r(V_i)\|f(V_{ilchild})\|f(V_{irchild}))$; }

11: for i = 1 to k do { $f(V_i) = F[i]$; } // update the f values of nodes located on the UP

12: for i = 1 to k do { $r(V_i) = R[i]$; } // update the r values of nodes located on the UP

13: return

3.5   Delete Data Block

After deleting the ath $(1 \le i \le n)$ data block m_a, the index of the ith $(a + 1 \le i \le n)$ data block changes to the $(i-1)^{th}$. The protocol to delete a data block is as follows.

(1) The client sends a request to the server for deleting the ath data block m_a;

(2) The server generates the CP π_a of v_a and sends it back to the client;

(3) The client checks the data integrity through Algorithm 1, if the output is false, go to step (6);

(4) The client updates the x value of root;

(5) The server deletes data block m_a, calls Algorithm 4 to update CBT and generates the CP $\pi_a'(\pi_a' = \pi_a - \{\pi_a^1\})$, then sends it back to the client, the client calls Algorithm 1 to check the integrity of the data file after deletion;

(6) End.

Algorithm 4 shows the steps to update CBT after deletion. The server searches for node v_a to be deleted, if v_a is a leaf node, we delete v_a and name v_a's predecessor as v_a'; if v_a has one child, name the child as v_a', delete v_a and replace it with v_a'; if v_a has two children, delete v_a and replace it with v_a's predecessor which is named as v_a', then update the f values and the r values on the UP of v_a'.

Algorithm 4

input: the index a of the data block to be deleted;

output: updated CBT.

1: Initialize array F[1...k] = { 0 }, array R[1...k] = { 0 };

2: if v_a has no child then // v_a is a leaf node

3:　{ if v_a has a Sibling node then

4:　　　{ let F[1], R[1] be its Sibling node's f value, r value respectively; }

5:　　else { let F[1], R[1] be its parent node's f value, r value respectively; }

6:　　delete v_a and let the predecessor node of v_a (say v'_a) replace it; }

7: else if v_a has only one child then // v_a has one child

8:　{ let F[1], R[1] be the only child node's f value, r value respectively ;

9:　　delete v_a and let the predecessor node of v_a (say v'_a) replace it; }

10: else if v_a has two children then // v_a has two children

11:　{ let F[1], R[1] be v_a's right child node's f value, r value respectively;

12:　　delete v_a and let the predecessor node of v_a (say v'_a) replace it; }

13: for i = 2 to k do // calculate the f values of nodes on the UP of v'_a

14:　{ if V_i only has a left child then F[i] = h(h(T(M_i))||r(V_i)||f($V_{ilchild}$));

15:　　else if V_i only has a right child then F[i] = h(h(T(M_i))||r(V_i)||f($V_{irchild}$));

16:　　else F[i] = h(h(T(M_i))||r(V_i)||f($V_{ilchild}$)||f($V_{irchild}$)); }

　　// calculate the r values of nodes on the UP of v'_a

17: for i = 2 to k do { R[i] = | parent node's index − current node's index | }

18: for i = 1 to k do { f(V_i) = F[i] } // update the f values of nodes on the UP of v'_a

19: for i = 1 to k do { r(V_i) = R[i] } // update the r values of nodes on the UP of v'_a

20: return

4 Evaluation

In this section, we will evaluate CBT in two aspects: memory consumption and performance for dynamic data update which can be reflected to time consumption, the less nodes needed to be updated, the less time needed to be consumed.

4.1 Memory Consumption

For any node v_i ($1 \leq i \leq n$) in CBT, there needs memory to store x(v_i) ($1 \leq i \leq n$); In MHT, there needs memory to store x(v_i) for leaf node v_i ($1 \leq i \leq n'$, n' means the number of leaf nodes) and x(v_j) for internal node v_j ($1 \leq j \leq n - n'$), where, x(v_i) = {h(T(m_i)), r(v_i), f(v_i)}, x(v_j) = {r(v_j), f(v_j)}. Assume that the hash function is SHA-1, both h(T(m_i)) and f(v_i) occupy 20 bytes. r(v_i) is an integer which occupies 4 bytes. For a data file with n data blocks, its corresponding CBT has n nodes, thus memory occupied by the CBT is: 44*n bytes; its corresponding MHT has 2*n−1 nodes, thus the memory occupied by the MHT is: 68*n−24 bytes.

In Fig. 4, we show the relation between memory costs and the size of data files for CBT and MHT. Memory consumption for CBT is less than that of MHT, which is

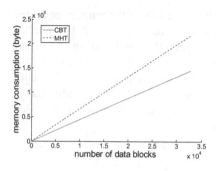
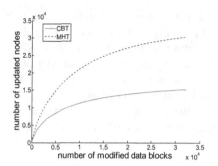

Fig. 4. Memory costs for CBT and MHT   **Fig. 5.** Modify a batch of data blocks

because data block tags are deployed on all nodes of CBT, whereas, only leaf nodes are employed to deploy data block tags in MHT.

4.2   Performance for Dynamic Data Update

As for the cost of an update operation mainly depends on the number of nodes updated. We designed an experiment to analyze the performance of dynamic data update for CBT and MHT. Programming language: JAVA, operating system: Windows XP, processor: Pentium(R) Dual-Core CPU T4300@2.10 GHz, memory: 3 GB.

In a single operation, we updated half nodes of CBT and MHT for files with size 128 MB, 256 MB and 512 MB respectively, averaged the number of nodes updated in 10 repeated experiments. We got the results shown in Table 1 from which we can identify the number of nodes updated in CBT is smaller than that of MHT in deletion and insertion.

Table 1. Number of nodes updated for CBT and MHT in a single dynamic update operation

Data file size	CBT			MHT		
	Modification	Insertion	Deletion	Modification	Insertion	Deletion
128 M	12.998	15.434	12.947	15	16.431	13.652
256 M	14.007	16.432	13.948	16	17.435	14.653
512 M	15.002	17.433	14.947	17	18.433	15.654

In a batch operation, we chose a 128 MB data file which was partitioned into 32768 data blocks with size 4 KB. We updated the data blocks ranging from 8 to 32768, and calculated the average number of nodes updated for CBT and MHT in 10 repeated experiments.

Figure 5 shows that when the number of modified data blocks is 8, the number of nodes updated in CBT is about 74 % of MHT's; when the number of updated data block is up to 32768, the number of nodes updated in CBT is about one half of MHT's, which is because the number of nodes in CBT is only one half of the number of nodes in MHT. Figure 6 shows that when the number of inserted data blocks is 8, the number of nodes updated in CBT is about 82 % of MHT's. When the number of inserted data blocks is up to 32768, the number of nodes updated in CBT is about 69 % of MHT's. In Fig. 7, when the number of data blocks deleted is about one-third of the file's data blocks, the number of nodes updated in CBT is about 67 % of MHT's. Additionally, with the number of data blocks deleted continuing increasing, the number of nodes updated in both CBT and MHT starts to decrease.

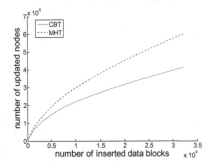

Fig. 6. Insert a batch of data blocks

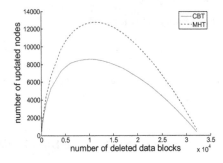

Fig. 7. Delete a batch of data blocks

5 Conclusion

We propose a certification binary tree for remote data integrity checking with dynamic data update operation. The tree is achieved by deploying data block tags to a binary tree in a given order. We design an algorithm to check the data integrity based on the tree. Additionally, we describe three feasible protocols for the client to modify, insert, delete data blocks and to check the data integrity after update operation. Theoretical analyses and experiments results show that, the memory consumption for CBT is lower than that of MHT and the number of nodes updated in CBT is smaller than that of MHT in both single dynamic data update operation and batch dynamic data update operation.

Acknowledgements. This work was partially supported by the Natural Science Foundation of China (No. 61272403), by the Fundamental Research Funds for the Central Universities (No. 10561201474).

References

1. Deswarte, Y., Quisquater, J.-J., Saïdane, A.: Remote integrity checking. In: 6th Working Conference on Integrity and Internal Control in Information Systems, pp. 1–11. Kluwer Academic Publishers (2004)
2. Ateniese, G., Burns, R., Curtmola, R., Herring, J., Kissner, L., Peterson, Z., Song, D.: Provable data possession at untrusted stores. In: Proceedings of the 14th ACM Conference on Computer and Communications Security, pp. 598–609. ACM (2007)

3. Ateniese, G., DiPietro, R., Mancini, L.V., Tsudik, G.: Scalable and efficient provable data possession. In: Proceedings of Secure Comm 2008, pp. 22–25. ACM (2008)
4. Erway, C., Kupcu, A., Papamanthou, C., Tamassia, R.: Dynamic provable data possession. In: Proceedings of the 16th ACM Conference on Computer and Communications Security, pp. 213–222. ACM (2009)
5. Wang, Q., Wang, C., Li, J., Ren, K., Lou, W.: Enabling public verifiability and data dynamics for storage security in cloud computing. In: Proceedings of the 14th European Conference on Research in Computer Security, pp. 355–370 (2009)
6. Zheng, Q., Xu, S.: Fair and dynamic proofs of retrievability. In: Proceedings of the 1st ACM Conference on Data and Application Security and Privacy, pp. 237–248. ACM (2011)
7. Wang, J., Liu, S.: Dynamic provable data possession with batch-update verifiability. In: 2012 IEEE International Conference on Intelligent Control, Automatic Detection and High-End Equipment (ICADE), pp. 108–113. IEEE Press, New York (2012)
8. Li, C., Chen, Y., Tan, P., Yang, G.: An efficient provable data possession scheme with data dynamics. In: 2012 International Conference on Computer Science & Service System (CSSS), pp. 706–710. IEEE Press, New York (2012)
9. Zhu, Y., Ahn, G.J., Hu, H., et al.: Dynamic audit services for outsourced storages in clouds. In: IEEE Transactions on Services Computing, vol. 6, no. 2, pp. 227–238. IEEE Press, New York (2013)

A Cost-Effective Cloud Storage Caching Strategy Utilizing Local Desktop-Based Storage

Li Zhang and Bing Tang[✉]

School of Computer Science and Engineering,
Hunan University of Science and Technology, Xiangtan 411201, China
btang@hnust.edu.cn

Abstract. This paper proposed a cost-effective cloud storage caching strategy by utilizing local desktop-based storage, called CloudCache. Nearly free desktop machines in local area network environment are utilized to build a local distributed file system, which is deployed as a data cache of remote cloud storage service. When the user reads a file, it first determines whether the file is in the cache. If it is in the cache, the file is read directly from the cache; otherwise, the file is read from remote cloud storage service. Least Recently Used (LRU) algorithm is used for cache replacement. Performance evaluation is accomplished, using Amazon Simple Storage Service (S3) and desktop PCs in laboratory to build the experimental environment. A case study of web cache has also been demonstrated. The results show that using the proposed caching strategy not only reduces cost, but also greatly improves file reading speed.

Keywords: Cloud storage · Data cache · Distributed file system · Cost-effective · P2P storage

1 Introduction

Data explosion is one of the biggest issues facing IT today. The amount of data that organizations store has grown exponentially in the last 10 years. How to store and manage these large-scale data is really a great problem. One solution to this problem is using cloud storage, an infrastructure that provides on-demand online storage services over the Internet. Cloud storage is now the new direction of storage technology, which uses virtualized and scalable storage resource pool to provide storage service for users. Cloud storage could deliver online services to individuals or companies, including online file hosting, storage and backup services. Cloud storage service providers, such as Google, Amazon, etc., usually provide different products with different quality of service (QoS). Generally, there are free and paid versions. It is allowed to use all kinds of method to consume cloud storage service through Internet, such as Web, client program and open interface, following the rule of pay-as-you-go [1].

Network conditions have great impact on the data I/O performance. Cloud storage access performance depends mainly on the network latency (such as

© Springer International Publishing AG 2016
G. Wang et al. (Eds.): SpaCCS 2016 Workshops, LNCS 10067, pp. 382–390, 2016.
DOI: 10.1007/978-3-319-49145-5_37

the delay of web servers, routers, gateways, proxy servers, and so on), as well as data transfer rate of point-to-point communication link over the Internet. Caching technology has been widely applied in the field of cloud computing [2–4]. Compared with traditional CPU cache and hard disk cache, the network cache is a new method to reduce Internet traffic and improve user's response time. By placing users frequently accessed data closer to users, it can reduce network traffic, and also decrease network delay. In order to achieve this object, the local memory and hard disk could be used to act like a "cache", while allowing users to cache content with size control policy.

Since the 1990s, P2P storage systems have shown their huge storage potential, most of them are implemented based on Distributed Hash Table (DHT) technology, such as the famous Pastry, Tapestry, Chord, etc. Through utilizing idle storage space contributed by peer nodes, combined with a variety of fault-tolerant strategies, reliable storage could be achieved. In [5], Wu et al. proposed a new cloud storage model based on Kademlia [6], using erasure coding redundancy and general redundant replicas for reliable storage. Another similar work includes AmazingStore [7], which also proposed a storage system based on P2P environment, considering node availability statistical model. A hybrid storage architecture called ThriftStore was proposed in [8], which combines clustered storage and desktop computer storage to achieve a high throughput data I/O. In [9], the authors proposed a dynamic, highly available and scalable cloud storage, called ppStore, which can integrate a lot of free storage services on the network, such as online file hosting, FTP, Email and other forms of storage together, and eventually form a unified distributed storage resource sharing community.

Different with conventional hardware enabled cloud storage cache, such as the cloud storage distributed cache implemented using solid-state hard disk in [10,11], this paper proposes a "virtual" and "soft" cache. Nearly free desktop machines in local area network environment are utilized to build a local distributed file system (DFS), which is deployed as a data cache of remote cloud storage service. When the user reads a file, it first determines whether the file is in the cache. If it is in the cache, the file is read directly from the cache; otherwise, the file is read from remote cloud storage service. This method reduces the cloud storage I/O request, while also reducing costs.

2   Cloud Storage Cache Architecture

The cloud storage cache architecture presented in this paper is shown in Fig. 1. Large number of local desktop PCs (e.g., PCs in university laboratory, the government department or enterprise), are utilized to build a local distributed file system, and each one contributes a certain of idle storage space. The local distributed file system is deployed as a data cache of remote cloud storage service. The rule of data read and data write are described as follows: when the user reads a file, it first determines whether the file is in the cache. If it is in the cache, the file is read directly from the cache; otherwise, the file is read from remote cloud storage service, and at the same time the file is copied to the cache, so that you

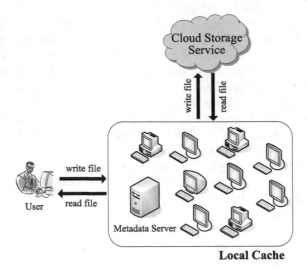

Fig. 1. Cloud storage cache architecture.

can read the file from the cache in subsequent read operations, without reading from remote cloud storage. The requested file can be found in the cache is called hit. Because the cache size is limited, non-popular and less accessed files are replaced. This mechanism allows a high hit rate. In general, since data traffic in LAN environment is usually faster than in WAN environment, the time of reading the required file from the local file system is much shorter than the time reading from remote cloud, which greatly reduces overhead of file reads.

2.1   Accessing Remote Cloud Storage Service

Current cloud storage services, such as Amazon Simple Storage Service (S3) and Google Drive, provide open platform and APIs to facilitate user's development, without having to log in directly to cloud storage sites. Most cloud storage service providers have released their own OAuth authentication service. The OAuth protocol provides a secure and simple resource authority, which also provides a set of OAuth-protected API, and all interface calls are required to pass the *access_token* as the authentication parameters. By calling the API functions, directly reading and writing files to the cloud storage system is feasible.

2.2   Local Desktop-Based Distributed File System

The architecture of local desktop-based distributed file system follows the general centralized Master/Slave mode. The communication between Master and Slaves is implemented by Remote Method Invocation (RMI). Slave performs as a storage node, and Master performs as a management node which is also responsible for responding to user requests. Large file is separated and stored with redundancy. File block size and number of copies are adjustable. The default file block size is 64 MB, while the number of copies defaults to 3. The system is designed to be scalable, and the maximal idle space for each Slave contributed could be configured. Metadata includes file ID, file name, file size, file type, file owner, file upload time, file modification time, and file block physical location, etc. Metadata server provides metadata queries.

The failure detection is achieved by the method of periodically heartbeating. Slave periodically sends "heartbeat" information to declare their online/offline status. The heartbeat interval is $T_{heartbeat}$, and another threshold called $T_{timeout}$ is also set to detect the failure. Once the Master cannot receive heartbeat from a Slave, the Slave is regarded to be unconnected, and have lost the communication. Then, the Master notifies other Slaves to reconstruct the missing files on the failed Slave to ensure that all file blocks in the system remain unchanged [12].

3   Caching Strategy

The core of cloud storage caching strategy is cache replacement algorithm. In this paper, it is based on the Least Recently Used (LRU) algorithm. The least recently

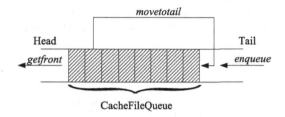

Fig. 2. The working principle of file identifier queue in cache (CacheFileQueue).

Table 1. Some symbols and their descriptions.

Symbol	Description
FileID	The file identifier returned by the system when file is written
genFileID	The function that generates file identifier when writing file
getFileSize	The function that retrieves the file size according to file identifier
CacheSize	Cache size defined in the system
CacheUsed	The size of space used in the cache
CacheFileQueue	File identifier queue in cache
deleteFileInDFS	The function that deletes the file in the cache (local DFS)
writeToDFS	The function that writes files to local DFS
writeToCloud	The function that writes files to remote cloud
readFromDFS	The function that downloads files directly from local DFS
readFromCloud	The function that downloads files directly from remote cloud

used data (cold data) are replaced, so as to make enough space to store additional data. In this paper, a simple queuing approach is used to implement caching and replacement policy. Before describing file writing and reading algorithm, we define some symbols as you see in Table 1.

The size of all files whose file identifiers are in the CacheFileQueue does not exceed CacheSize. CacheFileQueue provides three basic operations, as you see in Fig. 2.

(1) *enqueue* (file ID is inserted into the end of the queue, and the corresponding file is stored in cache);
(2) *getfront* (both the head of the queue and the corresponding file are deleted from the cache);
(3) *movetotail* (the file is hit in the cache, and move the file ID to the tail of the queue).

Algorithm 1. DATA WRITING ALGORITHM

Input: User's file File
Output: FileID

1. FileID ← genFileID(File)
2. **if** FileID in CacheFileQueue **then**
3.   //exist in the cache (cache hit), move FileID to the tail of CacheFileQueue
4.   movetotail(FileID)
5.   //no need to write the file, return directly
6.   return FileID
7. **end if**
8. **if** getFileSize(FileID)≤ (CacheSize − CacheUsed) **then**
9.   //cache is enough, enqueue directly
10.   CacheUsed ← CacheUsed + getFileSize(FileID)
11.   enqueue(FileID)
12.   writeToDFS(File)
13.   writeToCloud(File)
14. **else**
15.   //cache replacement, delete the head, until there is enough space
16.   **repeat**
17.   HeaderID ← getfront( )
18.   CacheUsed ← CacheUsed − getFileSize(HeaderID)
19.   //delete file from the distributed file system to make sufficient space
20.   deleteFileInDFS(HeaderID)
21.   **until** getFileSize(FileID) > (CacheSize − CacheUsed)
22.   //sufficient space, enqueue directly
23.   CacheUsed ← CacheUsed + getFileSize(FileID)
24.   enqueue(FileID)
25.   writeToDFS(File)
26.   writeToCloud(File)
27. **end if**
28. return FileID

Algorithm 2. DATA READING ALGORITHM

Input: FileID
Output: User's file File

1. **if** FileID in CacheFileQueue **then**
2.   //exist in the cache (cache hit), move FileID to the tail of CacheFileQueue
3.   movetotail(FileID)
4.   File ← readFromDFS(FileID)
5. **else**
6.   //not exist in the cache (cache miss)
7.   File ← readFromCloud(FileID)
8.   //store one copy in local at the same time
9.   **if** getFileSize(FileID) ≤ (CacheSize − CacheUsed) **then**
10.   //cache size is enough, enqueue directly
11.   CacheUsed ← CacheUsed + getFileSize(FileID)
12.   enqueue(FileID)
13.   writeToDFS(File)
14.   **else**
15.   //cache replacement, delete the head, until there is enough space
16.   **repeat**
17.   HeaderID ← getfront( )
18.   CacheUsed ← CacheUsed − getFileSize(HeaderID)
19.   //delete file from the distributed file system to make sufficient space
20.   deleteFileInDFS(HeaderID)
21.   **until** getFileSize(FileID) > (CacheSize − CacheUsed)
22.   //sufficient space, enqueue directly
23.   CacheUsed ← CacheUsed + getFileSize(FileID)
24.   enqueue(FileID)
25.   writeToDFS(File)
26.   **end if**
27. **end if**

The following Algorithms 1 and 2 describe the data writing and reading process in detail, respectively.

4   Performance Evaluation and Case Study

Prototype system is implemented using Java language, based on a data management middleware called BitDew [13]. In total, 11 desktop PCs in the laboratory are used to build a distributed file system. One PC is configured as the Master, and other 10 PCs are configured as Slaves. The "heartbeat" mechanism between the Master and Slaves is implemented using Java RMI. The value of $T_{heartbeat}$ is 10 s, and the value of $T_{timeout}$ is 40 s. Network bandwidth between the Master and Slaves is 100 Mbps. The number of file replicas is 3, and the data block size is set to 64 MB. MySQL server is used to store metadata information.

In the evaluation, Amazon S3 cloud storage service is used, and Java API interface is used to read and write files. In performance evaluation, we measured the time to read the file from local cache, as well as from the remote cloud.

4.1   File Reading/Writing Evaluation

In the evaluation of read and write speed, file access follows the traditional write-once-read-many model. In our evaluation, the CacheSize is set to 3 GB, 6 GB, 9 GB, 12 GB, 15 GB, respectively. In the above five scenarios, 100 files are sequentially written to Amazon S3 (total file size is around 25 GB), and file size is a random value (the minimum value is 1MB, and the maximum is 512 MB). Then, 400 file operations are performed (read 80 files by random, and each file is read 5 times). We recorded the hit rate and the average speed of 400 read operations. The results are shown in Fig. 3. Another evaluation has been shown that the average speed of reading directly from the local cache is about 10812 kbps, while the average speed of reading directly from Amazon S3 is about 157 kbps.

As you see from Fig. 3, as the increase of cache size, the hit rate is gradually increased, and the average reading speed is significantly increased, which proved the rationality of the proposed caching strategy, which can improve file read performance.

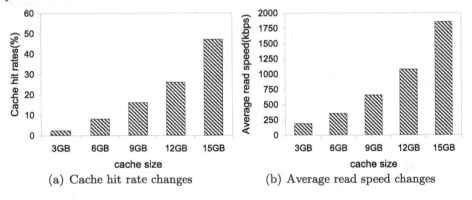

(a) Cache hit rate changes   (b) Average read speed changes

Fig. 3. The changes of performance as the increase of cache size.

4.2   Cost-Effectiveness Analysis

Cloud storage service follows the rule of pay-as-you-go, providing quality of service assurance. In this paper, we take Amazon S3 as an example (data store, data traffic from Amazon S3 to the Internet, and PUT/COPY/POST/LIST requests are charged). With the caching strategy in this paper, data traffic from Amazon S3 to the Internet is significantly reduced, which also means cost savings. In the above five scenarios, data traffic from Amazon S3 to the Internet were reduced 3.6 GB, 10.4 GB, 16.8 GB, 28.9 GB, 52.2 GB, respectively. If the price of data traffic from Amazon S3 to the Internet is $0.120 per GB, and if we read more files, the cost savings would be very impressive.

4.3 Case Study of Web Cache

In order to further demonstrate the effectiveness of proposed caching strategy, we studied the use case of web cache. We deployed a micro web site for experiment management for college students. Students can query experimental tasks, and download the required experimental development tools, as well as submit experimental reports and source codes. The store layer of the web site utilized the proposed caching strategy. The same as before, Amazon S3 is the remote cloud service. The cache size is set to 2 GB, which is build by 4 desktop PCs in the laboratory. We measure all data traffic from/to cloud, as well as from/to local distributed file system, and record the data traffic of every hour. Figure 4 has shown the data traffic evaluation in the scenario of web cache for two weeks. In the figure of total data traffic, it appeared twice crest. That is because, the teacher assigned an experimental task per week, students upload or download files at different times during these two weeks. As you see, more than 100 GB's data traffic from cloud has been saved, which means a conspicuous cost-saving. Using the cache can save some money for us, without compromising data I/O performance. Therefore, the proposed strategy by utilizing local desktop-based storage is a cost-effective caching strategy.

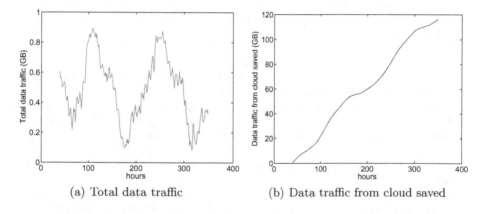

(a) Total data traffic   (b) Data traffic from cloud saved

Fig. 4. Data traffic evaluation in the scenario of web cache.

5 Conclusion

Network conditions have great impact on the data I/O performance for cloud storage. A cost optimization-oriented cloud storage caching strategy was proposed. Nearly free desktop machines in local area network environment are utilized to build a local distributed file system, which is deployed as a data cache of remote cloud storage service. This paper presented cache replacement and file reading/writing algorithm. Performance evaluation is accomplished, using Amazon S3 and 11 desktop PCs in the laboratory. A case study of web cache has also been demonstrated. The results show that using the proposed caching strategy not only reduces cost, but also greatly improves file reading speed. With our method, universities, government departments or enterprises can easily establish a low-cost local cache system.

Acknowledgments. This work is supported by the National Natural Science Foundation of China under grant no. 61602169, and the Natural Science Foundation of Hunan Province under grant no. 2015JJ3071, as well as the Scientific Research Fund of Hunan Provincial Education Department under grant no. 16C0643 and 12C0121.

References

1. Buyya, R., Yeo, C.S., Venugopal, S., Broberg, J., Brandic, I.: Cloud computing and emerging IT platforms: vision, hype, and reality for delivering computing as the 5th utility. Future Gener. Comp. Syst. **25**(6), 599–616 (2009)
2. Zhang, B., Ross, B., Kosar, T.: DLS: a cloud-hosted data caching and prefetching service for distributed metadata access. Int. J. Big Data Intell. **2**(3), 183–200 (2015)
3. Zhang, W., Mo, Z., Chen, C., Zheng, Q.: CBC: caching for cloud-based VOD systems. Multimedia Tools Appl. **73**(3), 1663–1686 (2014)
4. Hong, B., Choi, W.: Optimal storage allocation for wireless cloud caching systems with a limited sum storage capacity. IEEE Trans. Wirel. Commun. **15**(9), 6010–6021 (2016)
5. Wu, J., Fu, J., Ping, L., et al.: Study on the p2p cloud storage system. Acta Electronica Sin. **39**(5), 1100–1107 (2011)
6. Fedotova, N., Fanti, S., Veltri, L.: Kademlia for data storage and retrieval in enterprise networks. In: CollaborateCom 2007, pp. 382–386 (2007)
7. Yang, Z., Zhao, B.Y., Xing, Y., et al.: AmazingStore: available, low-cost online storage service using cloudlets. In: IPTPS10: Proceedings of the 9th International Workshop on Peer-to-Peer Systems. USENIX Association (2010)
8. Gharaibeh, A., Al-Kiswany, S., Ripeanu, M.: ThriftStore: finessing reliability tradeoffs in replicated storage systems. IEEE Trans. Parallel Distrib. Syst. **22**(6), 910–923 (2011)
9. Li, J., Yuan, P.: Study on cloud storage scheme based on distributed open source management service (ppStore). Comput. Appl. Softw. **28**(10), 208–210 (2011)
10. Li, D., Liu, P., Ding, K., et al.: Distributed cache strategy in cloud storage based on solid state disk. Comput. Eng. **39**(4), 32–35 (2013)
11. Lee, D., Min, C., Eom, Y.: Effective flash-based SSD caching for high performance home cloud server. IEEE Trans. Consum. Electron. **61**(2), 215–221 (2015)
12. Tang, B., Fedak, G.: Analysis of data reliability tradeoffs in hybrid distributed storage systems. In: IPDPS Workshops, pp. 1546–1555. IEEE Computer Society (2012)
13. Fedak, G., He, H., Cappello, F.: Bitdew: a data management and distribution service with multi-protocol file transfer and metadata abstraction. J. Netw. Comput. Appl. **32**(5), 961–975 (2009)

Author Index

Printed in the United States
By Bookmasters